A War of Ideas

For my parents and Murdo

A War of Ideas

British Attitudes to the Wars Against Revolutionary France 1792–1802

Emma Vincent Macleod

Ashgate
Aldershot • Brookfield USA • Singapore • Sydney

Published by
Ashgate Publishing Limited
Gower House, Croft Road
Aldershot, Hampshire GU11 3HR
Great Britain

Ashgate Publishing Company
Old Post Road
Brookfield, Vermont 05036—9704
USA

ISBN 1 84014 614 1

British Library Cataloguing in Publication Data
Macleod, Emma Vincent
A War of Ideas: British Attitudes to the Wars Against Revolutionary France, 1792–1802
1. Public opinion—Great Britain—History—18th century. 2. Great Britain—Foreign relations—France—1789–1820. 3. France—Foreign relations—Great Britain—1792–1815. 4. France—History—Revolution. 1789–1799. 5. Great Britain—History—George III, 1760–1820. I. Title.
941'.073

US Library of Congress Cataloging in Publication Data
Macleod, Emma Vincent
A War of Ideas: British Attitudes to the Wars Against Revolutionary France, 1792–1802 / Emma Vincent Macleod
p. cm. Originally presented as author's thesis. Includes bibliographical references (alk. paper)
1. France—History—Revolution, 1789–1799—Campaigns—Foreign public opinion, British. 2. Public opinion—Great Britain. I. Title.
DC158.8.M215 1998 98-19310
944.04–dc21 CIP

This volume is printed on acid free paper

Printed and bound in Great Britain by MPG Books Ltd, Bodmin, Cornwall

Contents

Preface

The responses of British people to the French Revolution have recently received considerable scholarly interest. Their views on the ensuing wars have been much less well covered, however, and this book seeks to provide a wide-ranging examination of these. Using government and parliamentary papers, pamphlet literature, printed ephemera, printed and manuscript letters, novels, poetry, newspapers, periodicals and graphic satires, the book considers the attitudes of various groups of people to the conflict. It highlights the debate in Britain provoked by the war, both as distinct from the polemic on the French Revolution and, more substantially, as the sequel to the Revolution debate and integrally linked to it; and it suggests that contemporaries saw this conflict as one which was significantly, if not crucially, shaped by ideological issues rather than by a struggle for power alone.

I am glad to acknowledge the help I have received from many people in researching and writing this book. I am grateful to the editors of the journal *Enlightenment and Dissent* for permission to reproduce in chapter 7 of this book a substantially similar version of my article 'Women at War: British Women and the Debate on the Wars against Revolutionary France in the 1790s' from no.15 (1996). I am indebted to the Scottish Education Department for funding my postgraduate research, and to the Universities of Edinburgh and Stirling for further support. I should also like to thank the staffs of Edinburgh University Library, the National Library of Scotland, the British Library, the Public Record Office, the Bodleian Library, Oxford, and Cambridge University Library, for their assistance. Dr Mary Hellier generously provided me with a very comfortable home for the months I spent researching in London. I also wish to thank Dr Andrew Mackillop for allowing me to read chapter 7 of his book, *'More Fruitful than the Soil': Army, Empire and the Scottish Highlands 1715–1815*, prior to publication.

I am grateful to the History Department at the University of Edinburgh for providing a stimulating and congenial environment in which to study as an undergraduate student and later, while I worked on the thesis from which this book has grown. My greatest academic debt is owed to Professor Harry Dickinson. I am deeply grateful for the fascination for the late eighteenth century he inspired in me during my undergraduate years, for his constantly kind and patient guidance, stimulation, interest and support while I was engaged in postgraduate study under his supervision, and for his continued encouragement and help since then. It is difficult to imagine a better academic mentor. Dr Frances Dow has also been a source of great encouragement, and she first helped me to recognize my interest in the history of ideas. She too read large sections of the book at various stages and offered perceptive and valuable advice. I should also like to thank Drs Nicholas Phillipson, John Brown, Jeremy Crang, Philip Cullis, Andrew Brown, Crispin Bates, Simon Coates, Richard Mackenney and Jill Stephenson for their general interest and support at various stages.

Colleagues in the History Department at the University of Stirling have also read and commented most helpfully on various parts of the manuscript—Dr Michael Rapport, Professor George Peden and Dr David Bebbington. I have also profited from conversations with Dr Colin Nicolson, and from the general friendship and support offered by the whole department. The book has benefited greatly from the kindness and advice of the examiners of my thesis, Professors John Cannon and Clive Emsley, and from the comments of an anonymous reader for Ashgate Publishing Limited.

My mother and father have lovingly supported and encouraged me in innumerable ways at every stage. Murdo has lived with the book since it was submitted as a thesis, and knew it well before then. It is dedicated to them with love and gratitude.

Emma Vincent Macleod
University of Stirling

Abbreviations

A-JR	*The Anti-Jacobin Review and Magazine*
BL Add. MSS	British Library Additional Manuscripts
BMC	British Museum, English Cartoons and Satirical Prints 1320–1832. Numbers refer to those set by F.G. Stephens and M.D. George, *Catalogue of Political and Personal Satires Preserved in the Department of Prints and Drawings in the British Museum*, 11 vol.s (1870–1954).
Burke Corr.	Thomas W. Copeland et al. (eds.), *The Correspondence of Edmund Burke*, 10 vol.s (Cambridge University Press, 1967–70)
Dropmore	Historical Manuscripts Commission, *Report on the Manuscripts of J.B. Fortescue, Esq., Preserved at Dropmore*, 10 vol.s (1892–1927)
HO	Home Office
LCGIII	A. Aspinall (ed.), *The Later Correspondence of George III*, 5 vol.s (Cambridge University Press, 1962–68)
Malmesbury Diaries and Correspondence	Third Earl of Malmesbury (ed.), *Diaries and Correspondence of James Harris, First Earl of Malmesbury*, 4 vol.s (London, 1844)
NMM	National Maritime Museum, Greenwich
PH	William Cobbett (ed.), *The Parliamentary History of England, From the Earliest Period to the Year 1803* (London, 1806–20)
PRO	Public Record Office

Year	Events in the war	Events in Britain	Important publications in the debate
1790			Edmund Burke, *Reflections on the Revolution in France*.
1792	20 April: France declares war on Austria; 24 July: Prussia joins the war; 20 September: Battle of Valmy; 6 November: Battle of Jemappes; 15 November: French decree of fraternity; 20 December: French decree on occupied territories.	May and December: royal proclamations against radicals; November: founding of the Loyal Associations.	Benjamin Vaughan, *Letters, on the Subject of the Concert of Princes* (to 1793); Helen Maria Williams, *Letters from France* (to 1801).
1793	1 February: France declares war on Great Britain and the United Provinces; First Coalition formed; British expeditions to Flanders and the West Indies; siege of Dunkirk.	August: sedition trials in Edinburgh; November–December: National Convention of radical society delegates in Edinburgh.	John Bowles, *The Real Grounds of the Present War with France*; Thomas Hardy, *The Patriot.*
1794	June: British naval victory in the Atlantic, the 'Glorious First';	January: sedition trials in Edinburgh;	Daniel Stuart, *Peace and Reform, against War and Corruption*;

(1794)	French defeat Austria at Fleurus; October: French overrun the United Provinces.	March: Volunteers raised; April: treason trials in London; July: Portland Whigs join Pitt.	Mary Wollstonecraft, *An Historical and Moral View of the Origin and Progress of the French Revolution.*
1795	February: France occupies the United Provinces; March: British army evacuated from Bremen; April: Prussia makes peace with France; May: United Provinces declares war on Britain; July: Spain makes peace with France; summer: French royalist rising in the Vendée fails; British invasion of Brittany fails; Britain captures Dutch bases in Ceylon and the Cape of Good Hope; December: Britain attempts to negotiate with France.	Mass meetings of the London Corresponding Society; many food riots; 'Two Acts' (Treasonable Practices Act and Seditious Meetings Act).	Hannah More, *Cheap Repository Tracts* (to 1798); Vicesimus Knox, *The Spirit of Despotism*; Charles Long, *The New Era of the French Revolution*; Lord Auckland, *Some Remarks on the Apparent Circumstances of the War in the Fourth Week of October 1795.*
1796	February, November: Second and third British expeditions to the West Indies;		Edmund Burke, *Letters on a Regicide Peace* (to 1797);

Year	Events in the war	Events in Britain	Important publications in the debate
(1796)	March, October: further attempts to negotiate with France; September: British fleet withdraws from the Mediterranean; October: Spain declares war on Britain; French victories in N. Italy; December: French invasion fleet driven from the Irish coast by storms.		Dennis O'Bryen, *Utrum Horum? The Government; or, the Country?* John Thelwall, *The Rights of Nature*.
1797	February: British naval victory at Cape St Vincent; April: Austrian armistice with France (formal peace in October); July: fourth attempt to negotiate with France; October: naval victory at Camperdown.	February: financial crisis; Bank of England stops cash payments; April, June: naval mutinies at Spithead and the Nore.	Thomas Erskine, *A View of the Causes and Consequences of the Present War with France*; John Robison, *Proofs of a Conspiracy against all the Religions and Governments of Europe*.
1798	French creation of Roman and Helvetian (Swiss) Republics;	December: income tax introduced;	John Gifford, *A Short Address, to the Members of the the Loyal Associations.*

(1798)	French capture of Malta and invasion of Egypt; August: Nelson's victory at the Nile (Aboukir Bay).	Foxite secession from Parliament; Irish Rebellion.	
1799	Creation of the Second Coalition; allied successes in Italy and Germany; August: British and Russian expedition to the Netherlands; capture of the Dutch fleet; September: Russians defeated at Zurich; November: evacuation of the Netherlands; British victories in India.	Bad harvest; food riots.	James Thomson, *The Rise, Progress, and Consequences of the new Opinions and Principles lately introduced into France.*
1800	January: Napoleon offers peace to Britain; Russian withdrawal from the war; September: Britain captures Malta; June, December: Austrians defeated at Marengo and Hohenlinden.	Further serious food rioting.	Herbert Marsh, *The History of the Politicks of Great Britain and France.*

Year	Events in the war	Events in Britain	Important publications in the debate
1801	February, March: Austria, Spain and Naples make peace with France. April: Nelson's victory at Copenhagen; collapse of the League of Armed Neutrality; August: French surrender in Egypt; October: preliminaries of British peace with France.	Fall of Pitt's ministry; Addington forms the new administration.	John Bowles, *Reflections at the Conclusion of the War*.
1802	March: Britain and France make peace with the Treaty of Amiens.		

Introduction

On 12 February 1793 the British Prime Minister, William Pitt, informed the House of Commons that the revolutionary government of France had declared war on Great Britain and its ally, the United Provinces. The news was not unexpected, for, although Britain had responded with strict neutrality to the French conflict against the Austrian Empire and Prussia which had begun in spring 1792, and had made strenuous efforts to preserve this stance, British alarm over the French abolition of the monarchy in August 1792 had developed into mutual suspicion and rising tension between the two countries by November. By January 1793 it was clear that patience on both sides was wearing thin and that attempts to reach an understanding were vain. Brissot and the revolutionary rulers of France claimed that the corrupt court of George III was leading Britain into the European war of tyrants and despots against the French Republic; this must be met with military force and the Republic itself must become an armed camp, dedicated to fighting tyranny on behalf of all the oppressed peoples in Europe, including those of Great Britain. The communications between the two governments over the past months had similarly failed to dispel the fears of the Pitt administration regarding a French threat to British security and European stability, fears which had arisen in the wake of French decrees of fraternity with the 'oppressed peoples' of Europe and of military intervention, annexations of territory to the Republic and the opening of the River Scheldt to international navigation. These appeared to be clear indications of the Republic's menace towards the Low Countries which, in the eyes of the British government, were tantamount to a direct challenge to Great Britain.

It has been shown that the French Revolution produced widespread and lasting effects in its impact upon Britain in many spheres.[1] The polarization of

---

1 See, for instance, the essays in H.T. Dickinson (ed.), *Britain and the French Revolution 1789–1815* (London, 1989). On the Revolution debate in Britain, see also idem, *British Radicalism and the French Revolution* (Oxford, 1985); Thomas Philip Schofield, 'English Conservative Thought and Opinion in Response to the French Revolution 1789–1796', unpublished Ph.D. thesis (University College, London, 1984); Yang Su Hsien, 'The British Debate on the French Revolution: Edmund Burke and His Critics', unpublished Ph.D. thesis (University of Edinburgh, 1989); Mark Philp (ed.), *The French Revolution and British Popular Politics* (Cambridge, 1991); Gregory Claeys, 'The French Revolution Debate and British Political Thought', *History of Political Thought*, xi (1990), 59–80.

British opinions on the Revolution and its consequences began slowly to crystallize after the publication of Richard Price's lecture, *A Discourse on the Love of Our Country*, in January 1790 and Edmund Burke's *Reflections on the Revolution in France* in November 1790. Over the next two years many replies were published to Burke's pamphlet,[2] which had argued that the French Revolution was an evil plot of massive dimensions directed against not only all the monarchies of Europe but the whole European moral and social order, and that it was a dire threat which must be combatted. Questions were raised of sovereignty and legitimacy, of the civil liberties and the natural rights of men and women, of absolute and relative truths and values, and of the adequacy of the British constitution itself. The passion of the polemics and the breadth of their application ensured that the debate was not purely literary and philosophical, but also political; and that it was not restricted to the traditional governing and literary classes of society. Popular societies and clubs had sprung up nationwide on both sides of the ideological divide before war was declared even between France and Austria in April 1792, such as the radical Constitutional Societies and the resurgent conservative Church and King clubs.[3]

But the outbreak of war between Britain and France in February 1793, in its more direct impact upon the British population, heralded the debate of problems of still greater political complexity. The war was to last for twenty-two years except for the truce of Amiens in 1802-3, and it was to involve a greater proportion of the British population than any previous international conflict had done. It therefore demanded a response of some sort from an even wider cross-section of the nation than had the Revolution. War against France in the 1790s did not merely add another layer of intensity to the debate on the French Revolution. New questions were fired at an alarming rate at ministers reeling from the enormity of international events and their domestic repercussions, and they were heatedly discussed both inside and outside Parliament. These questions, concerning the causes of the war, and its purposes, nature, conduct and impact upon both Britain and France, inextricably complicated the previous debate on the Revolution and inexorably pulled it into a whole new orientation. This book is an examination of the responses of different individuals and groups of people to the conflict and the questions that it posed for them, both as distinct from the polemic on the French Revolution itself and, more substantially, as the sequel to the Revolution debate, though integrally linked to it.

This is not, therefore, a narrative account of the war, or of British diplomacy during it, but rather a study of British *attitudes* to the conflict. It is helpful, however, to have a basic grasp of the main flow of events for Britain

---

2 Among the most famous were Thomas Paine, *Rights of Man* (Part I: London, 1791; Part II: London, 1792); Mary Wollstonecraft, *A Vindication of the Rights of Men* (London, 1791); and James Mackintosh, *Vindiciae Gallicae* (London, 1791).

3 See Philp (ed.), *The French Revolution and British Popular Politics*, pp.1–6.

during the war in order to appreciate the opinions of contemporaries fully. After France had declared war on Great Britain and the United Provinces (also known as the Dutch Republic) on 1 February 1793, the First Coalition against France began to emerge. Austria and Prussia were already at war with the French Republic, since April and June 1792 respectively, and France declared war on Spain on 7 March 1793. An Anglo-Prussian treaty was signed in July, and further British treaties were made with Sardinia-Piedmont and Naples during the summer. During that first year of the war, the main British campaigns were fought in the Low Countries, in the Mediterranean, and in the West Indies, immediately establishing a pattern of overstretching scarce military resources between the European continent and British imperial possessions elsewhere. The Duke of York led the Flanders campaign of April to September, assisting the Austrian force in recapturing Valenciennes in August and then besieging Dunkirk; but his small force, unsupported by naval gunnery, was unable to withstand the French force raised by the *levée en masse*, and he had to evacuate and retreat from Dunkirk in September. In the Mediterranean, the fleets of Spain and Lord Howe combined to seize Toulon in August; but this, too, had to be abandoned in December in the face of French attack. In the West Indies, Tobago was captured, and French possession of Santo Domingo was brought under pressure.

Martinique and St Lucia were taken in 1794, as was Corsica, and the Duke of York's army continued to operate in the southern Netherlands. York had to retreat in the winter, however, evacuating most of his force from Bremen in March 1795. Meanwhile, yellow fever ravaged the troops in the West Indies; and the French defeated Austria at Fleurus, overran the Netherlands and re-established their control of Guadaloupe. In 1795, while Russia, Austria and Prussia partitioned Poland (for the third time), the First Coalition crumbled. Prussia negotiated peace with France in April, and Spain followed suit in July, leaving Austria as Britain's only major ally. The United Provinces had finally been occupied by France after its abandonment by the Austrian and British forces in the spring, and its naval fleet was seized by the French. It declared war on Britain in May.

Britain thereafter wanted to capture Dutch naval bases and imperial possessions in order to deny them to the French. In 1795 the Cape of Good Hope, Ceylon, Colombo and Trincomalee were taken, and another expedition to the West Indies buttressed the defence of British possessions and seized Demarara, Berbice and Essequibo—all formerly Dutch. Periodic but unsuccessful attempts were also made to assist the counter-revolutionaries within France, mainly in Brittany and the Vendée. Despite some success in the East and West Indies, then, the war on the European continent was no nearer to being won, and in December 1795 and March and October 1796 the British government attempted to negotiate peace with the French Republic. No acceptable settlement was forthcoming, however, and British fortunes in the conflict continued to worsen. St Lucia was retaken, and St Vincent and Grenada were won, but in October 1796 Spain declared war on Britain. The British withdrew from Corsica and the Mediterranean; and a French invasion of Ireland in December was only repulsed by the weather. The landing of a small French force at Fishguard in Wales in February 1797 led to a run on the banks in Britain, and the gold standard was abandoned shortly afterwards. The Spanish fleet was defeated by Sir John Jervis at Cape St Vincent on 14 February, and Trinidad was captured in the West Indies, but the navy mutinied at Spithead and the Nore in April and May, causing deep and widespread alarm throughout Britain. In July 1797 the government made a fourth approach to the French government to negotiate peace, but again without success. Austria, however, did settle terms with France at Campo Formio in October, leaving Britain alone in its struggle against revolutionary France.

Admiral Duncan's victory over the Dutch fleet at Camperdown on 12 October 1797 cheered British spirits somewhat; and Nelson's annihilation of the French fleet in Aboukir Bay on 1 August 1798, leaving Napoleon Bonaparte's army stranded in Egypt, was rightly hailed as a major achievement for the British war effort. Together with a large subsidy, it encouraged Russia to become an active ally of Britain. Austria, wooed with a large British loan, rejoined the conflict against France in 1799, and the Second Coalition was formed. It was short-lived. Although the French were forced to retreat in the Italian and German states, the Anglo-Russian campaign in the United Provinces between August and October was disastrous. Russia was also defeated at Zurich in September, and it withdrew from the war early in 1800. Austria was defeated by Napoleon at Marengo in June and Hohenlinden in December, and it capitulated once more in February 1801.

Isolated once again, British troops took Malta in September 1800 and defeated what was left of the French army in Egypt the following April. On 2 April 1801 Nelson defeated the fleets of the Armed Neutrality (a combination of Russia, Denmark and Sweden, resentful of British treatment of neutral vessels) at the Battle of Copenhagen. But stalemate and war-weariness now predominated, and when Henry Addington replaced Pitt as Prime Minister in March, his government immediately began to pursue peace terms with the French government, the preliminaries of which were settled in October. The final version of the Treaty of Amiens was sealed in March 1802.[4]

After the breakdown of the Amiens settlement in 1803 the British displayed a much greater degree of united hostility towards the French under Napoleon than had been elicited in the 1790s. This book explores the more

---

4 See the chronological table above, pp.x-xiv. For a concise account of the British war, see Ian R. Christie, *Wars and Revolutions: Britain 1760–1815* (London, 1982), chapters 9 and 10.

diverse attitudes to the conflict of different groups of British people in the 1790s. Support for and hostility to the war in the 1790s largely followed the division of opinion in the debate on the French Revolution: loyalists continued to support the government in its military conflict against France as well as in its ideological battle against foreign and domestic radicalism, while reformers and radicals usually opposed the conflict, because of their admiration for the Revolution and their distaste for war. This does not mean, however, that opinions on either side of the divide were uniform. 'We all unfortunately too well know', wrote Francis Plowden, Foxite lawyer and writer, in 1794,

> that at this moment we are engaged in a very bloody and desperate war with France; and yet neither in nor out of parliament can be found ten men who agree in the reasons, views, motives and objects of the war. ... so little are you at present able or willing to agree upon any one great and common point respecting the war that ... there must be a very thick mist or veil thrown over the circumstances, which are so misrepresented or withholden from our sight.[5]

This heterogeneity of opinion provoked the dialogue and was in turn perpetuated by it—an inter-genre debate carried on in government papers, parliamentary debates, newspapers, periodicals, pamphlets, the resolutions of societies and public meetings, sermons, novels, poetry and graphic prints, each reacting or replying to another. 'As always,' Norman Hampson has warned, 'the historian must choose between generalizations which are never quite true in any specific instance and an incomprehensible anarchy of individual cases.'[6] Each chapter in this book considers the dialogue within a group of people as well as their disagreements with other groups concerning the war.

The first five chapters deal with the spectrum of political opinion-groups and their reactions to the war. Edmund Burke's views were crucial to the development of the controversy on the war, as they had been to the debate on the French Revolution. He was the first in Britain publicly to advocate a war against revolutionary France; his arguments set the tone of the British debate on the conflict and remained central to it; and the book begins with a discussion of his analysis. The two succeeding chapters examine the attitudes and war-related activities of those in favour of the armed struggle against France: those of the government and King George III and those of loyalists inside and outside Parliament. Chapters 4 and 5 study the opposition to the war: the Foxite Whigs inside Parliament and their supporters, and radical politicians and 'Friends of Peace' out-of-doors. The next three chapters consider the discussion on the war

---

5 Francis Plowden, *A Friendly and Constitutional Address to the People of Great Britain* (London, 1794), pp.3–5.

6 Norman Hampson, *The Enlightenment* (Harmondsworth, 1968; 1990), pp.129–30.

that took place among various social groups. Chapter 6 examines the theological and political-theological responses of ministers of both Established and Dissenting churches; chapter 7 investigates the perceptions expressed by female writers of the decade; and the final chapter deals with the attitudes of the ordinary people of Britain and the role of public opinion in the debate on the war against revolutionary France. Ireland is not included in this analysis of British attitudes: it was united with mainland Britain only in 1801, and it had a rather different experience of war in the 1790s from that of the rest of Britain.

Such an organization of the material creates a certain degree of overlap. Chapter 2, for instance, which studies the attitudes of the government and the King, includes the views of such figures as Lord Auckland, Lord Malmesbury, Charles Long, the Marquess of Buckingham and Thomas Grenville, none of whom was a member of the administration. They have been included in this chapter, however, because they seem to fit more usefully into a study of government attitudes than into one on loyalist attitudes, because of their personal closeness to members of the government or because of their executive role in the policy of the administration. The Marquess of Buckingham and Thomas Grenville were brothers of Lord Grenville, the Foreign Secretary.[7] Lord Malmesbury, an ex-Foxite as was Thomas Grenville, committed himself to support of the war in 1793 and was sent on a diplomatic mission to Berlin in November of that year; in 1796 and 1797 he was the government's envoy in its negotiations for peace with the French Republic. Lord Auckland, another senior diplomat, was in addition a close personal friend of the Prime Minister. Charles Long was secretary to the Treasury and an ardent Pittite. Chapters 4 and 5 together form a unit on the opposition to the war, in which there is further potential for overlap. Thomas Erskine, examined in chapter 4 as a staunch member of the Foxite party and opponent of the Pitt administration, might as helpfully have been included in chapter 5 as the author of one of the most successful pacifist pamphlets of the decade, *A View of the Causes and Consequences of the Present War with France* (1797). William Wilberforce is cited both in chapter 3, as a loyal supporter of Pitt and his government for most of the decade, and in chapter 5, as a prominent ;'Friend of Peace' between December 1794 and spring 1796.

The scale of the warfare in which Britain found itself engaged was unprecedented in terms of the human and material resources it required and in terms of its eventual duration. Between 1793 and 1815 Britain lost 315,000 men

---

7 Thomas Grenville was a Foxite until the end of 1793, when he switched to support the government, as the Duke of Portland and others later did, because of his support for the war and his hostility towards domestic radicalism. See British Library, Additional Manuscripts [hereafter BL Add. MSS] 47569, ff. 30–52, Thomas Grenville to Charles James Fox, 29 December 1793.

in the wars and spent £1500 million in loans and taxes.[8] Such a conflict preoccupied British public thought; as William Windham put it, 'war seemed to have become the whole business of life'. The *Morning Chronicle* noted on 3 August 1799 that 'a great deal of war-like science' had been called forth. 'No inconsiderable portion of our annual publications is occupied with treatises on military tactics, and sermons on public affairs, with instructions for the drill of horse and foot, and heart-stirring sounds from the ecclesiastical trumpet.' Gayle Trusdel Pendleton's evidence bears out this assertion, demonstrating that the war was by far the single most-discussed topic in political pamphlet literature between 1792 and 1802.[9] Moreover, commentators of all opinions and backgrounds were impressed by a sense of the novelty and scale of the dimensions of the crisis. On the announcement in October 1801 of the signature of the preliminaries of peace, *The Times* declared that it had been 'a war which neither in its native character or object can be fitly compared with any scourge or calamity with which the earth has been visited, since the subversion of the Roman Empire, and the darkness of the middle ages'. Thomas Erskine, the Foxite MP and barrister, claimed that 'we were suddenly placed by the most extraordinary events in a new situation, both as it regarded our moral feelings as good men, and our prudence as enlightened members of civil life'.[10]

Contemporaries often described the French Revolutionary Wars as the first since the wars of religion to be fought to a substantial extent over competing ideologies, and they recognized that in this lay the unusual nature of the conflict.[11] This prompted questions concerning the nature of the conflict and therefore also its proper conduct, but it also raised the issue of the legitimacy of the British government's involvement in the war. Conservative commentators thought it vital that Britain should range itself in armed conflict against the wicked forces of licence on the continent before they invaded Britain. Lord Mulgrave succinctly expressed a common view when he told the House of Lords in December 1794 that 'the war which had been declared against us was

---

8 Colin Jones (ed.), *Britain and Revolutionary France: Conflict, Subversion and Propaganda* (Exeter, 1983), p.9. See also P.K. O'Brien, 'Public Finance in the Wars with France 1793–1815', in Dickinson (ed.), *Britain and the French Revolution*, pp.165–87.

9 William Cobbett (ed.), *The Parliamentary History of England, From the Earliest Period to the Year 1803* (London, 1806–1820) [hereafter *P.H.*], xxxv, 1440, William Windham, 2 June 1801; Gayle Trusdel Pendleton, 'English Conservative Propaganda During the French Revolution, 1789–1802', unpublished Ph.D. thesis (Emory University, 1976), p.443.

10 *The Times*, 3 October 1801; Thomas Erskine, *A View of the Causes and Consequences of the Present War with France*, 3rd edition (London, 1797), p.134.

11 Interestingly, this description of the conflict ignored the recent American war, which had clearly involved opposing ideas about the rights of governments and citizens and much discussion of these. See, for instance, H.T. Dickinson, 'Britain's Imperial Sovereignty: The Ideological Case Against the American Colonies', in idem (ed.), *Britain and the American Revolution* (forthcoming).

no ordinary war; it was a war for the annihilation of our laws, our liberties, our prosperity, our civilization, and our religion.'[12] Those who were hostile to the war, on the other hand, often argued that it was illiberal to wage war against opinions and to force one nation's views on constitutional government on another.

Despite this, historians have disagreed concerning the extent to which the war was seen by contemporaries as being fundamentally ideological. Recently, most (though not all) have tended towards discounting or downplaying the role of ideas. This study of the recorded views of the British, spoken in the Houses of Parliament, published in print, and demonstrated in various other ways, shows that most contemporary commentators did not see the conflict merely in geo-political terms. They recognized that ideological hostility had not faded away with the onset of military warfare after February 1793 and that it remained a significant aspect of the struggle. The British war against revolutionary France was naturally often supported for pragmatic and self-interested reasons. It was also opposed instrumentally, to further other ends, or for reasons of private economy and welfare. To a significant extent, however, it was both perceived to be, unusually, a conflict about political and even religious ideologies, and supported or opposed on those grounds.

This is not, therefore, to reduce British concerns to ideology alone; but it is to argue that ideas and principles were more important in British attitudes to this conflict than is often acknowledged or recognized. Equally, ideas do not operate in vacua; they need to be related to actions and events. In this war, it was difficult to separate policy from principles, or practice from ideology. Burke and ministers of religion were unusual in viewing the war from almost a purely ideological perspective. Most people were not pure ideologues: they were either active politicians with responsibilities and ambitions to fulfil or causes to promote, or they were individuals with other personal, practical stakes in the outcome of events. Their responses to the war were of course considerably influenced by factors other than ideological sympathy for or hostility to French revolutionary principles. Nevertheless, political and religious ideas also played a significant part in forming the attitudes and opinions of the politically literate sectors of British society. This book attempts to demonstrate this, and to show that a war of ideas raged in Britain over the military conflict against revolutionary France in the 1790s.

---

12 *P.H.*, xxxi, 983, Lord Mulgrave, 30 December 1794.

Chapter 1

Edmund Burke and the War Against the French Revolution

> [Burke] is the man that will mark this age, marked as it is in itself, by events, to all time.[1]

After months of mutual suspicion, fragile communications and increasing tension, Revolutionary France declared war on Great Britain on 1 February 1793. Edmund Burke, the British conservative politician and polemicist, however, had been at war against the French Revolution since the autumn of 1790, when he had written and published his hugely successful *Reflections on the Revolution in France*. This eloquent and detailed condemnation of all that the French Revolution seemed to Burke to stand for was his personal declaration of a war of ideas whose active fire would cease only with his death in 1797. The British ministry often appeared vague and even divided about the nature of the conflict and its own fundamental aims, but Burke's campaign against the French Revolution was from its inception war to the death.

Burke's hostility to the French Revolution is well known. The French Revolution was an attack on aristocratic power and privilege in France, and Burke's concern deepened as he saw signs of the revolutionary Jacobin movement spreading throughout Europe. He came to see the Revolution as an attack on the basic foundations of European civilization, which included not only the social order but also the systems of morality and belief on which that order was built.[2] The *Reflections* and the rest of Burke's battery of literary weapons against the French Revolution were therefore fired against it primarily from a

---

1 George Canning, 13 July 1797, quoted in third Earl of Malmesbury (ed.), *Diaries and Correspondence of James Harris, First Earl of Malmesbury*, 4 vol.s (London, 1844), iii, 399.

2 On Burke's views on the French Revolution, see, e.g., Frank O'Gorman, *Edmund Burke. His Political Philosophy* (London, 1973); Conor Cruise O'Brien, *The Great Melody: A Thematic Biography and Commented Anthology of Edmund Burke* (London, 1992); R.R. Fennessy, *Burke, Paine and the Rights of Man* (The Hague, 1963); Michael Freeman, *Edmund Burke and the Critique of Political Radicalism* (Oxford, 1980); Carl B. Cone, *Burke and the Nature of Politics*, vol. ii, *The Age of the French Revolution* (Kentucky, 1964); Francis P. Canavan, *The Political Reason of Edmund Burke* (Cambridge, 1960); Charles Parkin, *The Moral Basis of Burke's Political Thought* (Cambridge, 1956); Gerald W. Chapman, *Edmund Burke: The Practical Imagination* (Cambridge, Mass., 1967).

desire to preserve the old European order, especially since that of Britain was an integral part of it.

This chapter does not attempt to revise our understanding of his opposition to the Revolution in France. Rather, it explains how his hatred of the Revolution shaped his views on the *war* against Revolutionary France. This is a necessary context for the other British responses to the war discussed in this book. Burke largely set the tone for the rest of the British debate on the war, because of the early and vehement publication of his views, and because of his recognition of the French Revolution as an immensely significant ideological phenomenon. His views were instrumental in causing the British debate on the conflict to be substantially informed by ideology. The great majority of British people did not agree entirely with Burke; nor did many diametrically oppose his views by offering wholehearted support to the ideology of the French Revolution. It is also true that some denied that ideology had any part to play in the war. Nevertheless, in putting forward these opinions, they all had to respond to Burke's views in one way or another, because he had constructed a cogent ideological response to the Revolution and called for a war against it long before almost anyone else in Britain had taken the Revolution particularly seriously or recognized the possibility of war.

Burke did not limit his personal battle against the French Revolution to the *Reflections* and his wide private correspondence. He thought himself publicly 'bound to express his own sentiments with freedom and energy in a crisis of such importance to the whole human race,' as he wrote in his *Letter to a Member of the National Assembly* (May 1791);[3] and his *Appeal from the New to the Old Whigs* (August 1791), *Thoughts on French Affairs* (December 1791) and *Heads for Consideration on the Present State of Affairs* (November 1792) also denounced the Revolution and urgently insisted that the European powers intervene. Some of his pamphlets were clearly written in a specific attempt to prevail upon government policy, such as *Hints for a Memorial to be Delivered to M.M.* (1791) and *Thoughts on French Affairs*, and he even sent his son to Coblenz to try to influence counter-revolutionary tactics. Nor did his efforts to stir his country to action end with the outbreak of war, for he was rarely satisfied with the ministry's conduct of it and the national spirit often seemed to waver. He therefore continued to speak out in the House of Commons until his retirement in June 1794, and to write letters, talk to statesmen and publish his views on the war until his death, his language as colourful and pointed, as R.B. McDowell has remarked, as James Gillray's caricatures.[4] There were times and

3 Edmund Burke, 'A Letter to a Member of the National Assembly' (1793), in Paul Langford et al. (eds), *The Writings and Speeches of Edmund Burke*, 10 vol.s (Oxford, 1981ff.) [hereafter *Writings and Speeches*], viii, 308.

4 T.W. Copeland et al. (eds), *The Correspondence of Edmund Burke*, 10 vol.s (Cambridge and Chicago, 1967-70) [hereafter *Burke Corr.*], viii, p.xviii. For Burke's split from

circumstances, Burke declared in the *Appeal*, in which not to speak out was at least to connive.[5] This chapter begins by charting his growing conviction that armed conflict would be necessary and considering his reasons for this and the aims for which he thought the war should be fought. It then examines his opinions on the nature of the conflict and the manner in which it should be fought by Britain, and his reasons for vehemently opposing peace with the French Republic.

I The Menace of Jacobinism

In August 1789 Burke had expressed his initial thoughts on the French Revolution to Lord Charlemont: 'It is true, that this may be no more than a sudden explosion: If so no indication can be taken from it. But,' he continued ominously, 'if it should be character rather than accident, then that people are not fit for Liberty, and must have a Strong hand like that of their former masters to coerce them.'[6] By October 1789, his own hesitation and doubtful admiration were evaporating and he was writing to his son Richard about his concern for 'the portentous state of France—where the Elements which compose Human Society seem all to be dissolved, and a world of Monsters to be produc'd in the place of it—where Mirabeau presides as the Grand Anarch; and the late Grand Monarch makes a figure as ridiculous as pitiable.'[7]

It was not long before Burke began to view war against the French Revolution as a possibility. As early as 12 November 1789, he told Earl Fitzwilliam that he would wish to see France 'circumscribed within moderate bounds'. In his speech in the House of Commons debate on the Army Estimates, on 9 February 1790, he in fact gave it as his opinion that France need not be considered as much of a military threat for some time to come; but he also suggested that the French Revolution had 'brought on such calamities as no country, without a long war, has ever been known to suffer, and which may in the end produce such a war, and perhaps, many such.' In the *Reflections* he hinted that the British government 'may find it expedient to make war' upon the revolutionaries.[8] Burke was also the first to argue that force *must* be used

the Foxite Whigs in Parliamentary Opposition and move to supporting the Pitt administration, see chapter 4.

5 Edmund Burke, 'An Appeal from the New to the Old Whigs' (1791),*Works of the Right Honourable Edmund Burke*, Bohn edition, 6 vol.s (London, 1883-86), iii, 95. The volume in *Writings and Speeches* containing the 'Appeal' has not yet appeared.

6 *Burke Corr.*, vi, 10.

7 Ibid., pp.29–30.

8 Ibid., p.36; *P.H.*, xxviii, 353, 358, 9 February 1790; Burke, 'Reflections on the Revolution in France' (1790), *Writings and Speeches*, viii, 203.

against revolutionary France. On 25 January 1791, he wrote to a distressed member of the French aristocracy, the Comtesse de Montrond. 'Alas! Madam, it is not to me, or to such services as can come from me, that the persecuted honour of France must apply,' he told her. 'Nothing more can be said. Something must be done. You have an armed Tyranny to deal with; and nothing but arms can pull it down.'[9] From this time on, he vigorously advocated European intervention in French affairs, certain that the royalists within France were too weak to overturn the Revolution by themselves, dispersed and disarmed as they were, and equally convinced that 'no Monarchy limited or unlimited, nor any of the old Republics, can possibly be safe as long as this strange, nameless, wild, enthusiastic thing is established in the Center of Europe'.[10] He told Sir James Bland Burges that Britain must be prepared for 'very great and awful Events both at home and abroad', and expressed his astonishment that the European powers without exception had chosen to be 'mere Spectators of this scene'. By July 1791 he was becoming more impatient. Writing to Henry Dundas, the Home Secretary, he argued that 'this seems to me a moment for some decision in the foreign System so far as it regards France.—Surely a Step may be taken with great safety, great dignity and great Effect. The time for it may pass.' He told his son in August that he was sure that the revolutionaries were making preparations of some kind, and he began talking in terms of an enemy: 'Oh! let those who would [restore] the good in that Country be careful how they despise their Enemy!'[11]

Burke's view of the French Revolution was fundamental to his reasons for insisting that Britain and indeed Europe should make war upon France. The war he advocated was no typical eighteenth-century pursuit of territorial aggrandizement and power. Nor was it primarily motivated by a desire for vengeance against the foreign aggression of revolutionary France, which to him was a mere symptom of its real malignancy. He reduced the French Revolution to a system of principles which had overturned the *ancien régime* in France, and which was fast spreading to menace the peace, security and moral values of all Europe, and he insisted that it must be wholly destroyed for the future of European civilization. The French Revolution was an ideological enemy, and this was its primary danger.

The particular danger of the French doctrines of equality, reason and liberty lay in their superficial appeal to ordinary men. Burke argued that these abstract principles were a menace to political and social order because they encouraged men to seek perfection in human affairs, where it could not be

9 *Burke Corr.*, vi, 211.

10 Ibid., p.218, Burke to John Trevor, [January 1791].

11 Ibid., pp.279, 242, 280, 333, Burke to Sir James Bland Burges, [29 June 1791], to Henry Dundas, [1 July 1791], and to Richard Burke, jr., 9 August 1791.

found. In its pursuit, they overturned all else (including admirable compromises with perfection), leaving a trail of destruction in their wake.[12] The Revolution was the result of a plot hatched by a combination of philosophers, the new monied interest in France and men of letters. Their political system, based as it was on the immediate self-interest of the individual, was inherently unstable. Their professed desire for universal peace and international concord, he argued, was 'a coarse and clumsy deception': far from peace and good will to men, the French revolutionaries 'meditated war against all other governments' through systematically inciting sedition among the peoples of Europe.[13] One of the principal targets of the Revolution had therefore been France's international relations: 'The Revolution was made,' he wrote, 'not to make France free, but to make her formidable'.[14] He feared French expansion *per se*, and its upset of the European balance of power, but still more did he fear the subversion of the continent by French principles. The combination of these two threats was terrifying, for it meant the destruction of European society. The Revolution was not just the subversion of the monarchy, but a crusade against a whole way of life, against the social order which to Burke was the embodiment and bulwark of men's rights and liberties in its protection of property and the propertied.

Burke was by no means a war-monger, as his pleas for peace in India, Ireland and America had demonstrated, but he was quite clear that war was the ultimate means of justice in the world, and that this was an occasion when it was indispensable.[15] He realized that the balance of power was too often made the pretext for wars of ambition, but he constantly defended the right of a country to interfere in the internal affairs of another if it became necessary for the sake of its own security. Those who argued otherwise, he said, failed to distinguish between the promotion of sedition and rebellion in another country and the support of one side in a country already divided. He frequently referred to Vattell's *Law of Nations* (1758) for support, where it was stated that a nation trampling on the rights of other nations might be repressed by the international community; that foreign powers might help oppressed peoples against tyranny; and that, in civil war, there were two distinct powers, either of which might be assisted from abroad—all of these principles, Burke argued, were applicable to the European situation created by the Revolution in France.[16] Furthermore, by the law of civil vicinity, a man was entitled to make representation to a judge against his neighbour who had erected something on his property which was

12 See e.g. *P.H.*, xxviii, 434–5, 2 March 1790.

13 'Appeal', pp.10–11.

14 Edmund Burke, Second 'Letter on a Regicide Peace' (1796), *Writings and Speeches*, ix, 278.

15 Idem, First 'Letter on a Regicide Peace' (1796), *Writings and Speeches*, ix, 248.

16 Idem, 'Remarks on the Policy of the Allies with Respect to France' (1793), *Writings and Speeches*, viii, 500–1, Appendix.

unacceptable to him. Between nations the principle was the same, but, in the absence of an impartial judge, the 'grand vicinage of Europe', or the rest of the commonwealth, must be aware of and use its right to prevent 'any capital innovation which may amount to the erection of a dangerous nuisance', a term which might certainly be applied to the French Revolution.[17]

It was in Britain's own interests to go to war with France, Burke argued, as a self-interested safety precaution, if for no other reason. By its mere geographical position, France could affect every state of western Europe, and it had always been British policy to exercise vigilance over French external ambitions. Now those were intimately bound up with France's internal affairs; indeed, the French had made it impossible for European governments to ignore the Revolution and its principles by actively notifying them of their new domestic arrangements, an unusual step for any state to take. Since it possessed the greatest international influence in Europe, Britain was the nation which the French wished most to corrupt, in order to speed the progress of their anarchism. Revolutionary France had declared that physical and moral ties already connecting it with Savoy justified its annexation of that state; 'no doubt,' he warned, 'they will soon find out the physical and moral connexion subsisting between them and this country'. War was therefore 'a plan formed upon the ancient policy and practice of Great Britain, and of Europe ... which is ... more strongly called for by the present circumstances than by any former'.[18]

Strong measures were the more vital because of the admirers of the Revolution in Britain and elsewhere in Europe. He made no distinction between British and French Jacobins, and he thought that the British Jacobins aimed to conspire with their French counterparts to arrange an invasion of Britain and the subjugation of the nation and its government to the French Republic. Parliamentary reform might look innocent, even to some of its supporters, but it had the same tendency as Jacobinism—the complete destruction of the constitution and 'the rude inroad of Gallic tumult'. In his *Observations on the Conduct of the Minority*, he claimed of the campaign for parliamentary reform that 'Whether it is necessarily connected in theory with Jacobinism is not worth a dispute. The two things are connected in fact.'[19] The combination of an internal fifth column and French troops was the real threat to the British constitution and social order; war against France was the only alternative to a British civil war.[20]

---

17 First 'Letter on a Regicide Peace', pp.250–1.

18 *P.H.*, xxx, 71, 54–5, 13 December 1792; Edmund Burke, 'Heads for Consideration on the Present State of Affairs' (1792), *Writings and Speeches*, viii, 400.

19 Idem, 'A Letter from the Right Honourable Edmund Burke, to a Noble Lord' (1796), *Writings and Speeches*, ix, 173; idem, 'Observations on the Conduct of the Minority' (1793), ibid., viii, 443.

20 *P.H.*, xxx, 110, 15 December 1792.

According to Burke, it was also necessary for Britain to go to war against France because there was no other hope of overturning the Revolution. In his implacable hostility to French principles, he conceived the revolutionaries to have a drive equally unremitting, and he warned against hoping for signs of repentance in them. Such hopes, he thought, were tantamount to believing in the conversion of the devil himself.[21] He was also convinced that neither instability nor bankruptcy would succeed in dissolving the Revolution in France. By December 1791, French bankruptcy had run as far as it was ever likely to run, in his opinion, yet the revolution showed no signs of faltering.[22] There was therefore no hope that the French Revolution, evil, menacing, and grasping, would fail of its own accord. Only war would remove the evil at the heart of Europe, an evil which, if left, would spread to every part of the circumference, circle beyond circle, defying whatever petty defences were employed against it.[23] Negotiation with the revolutionaries, as advocated by the Foxites, was a completely inadequate means of dealing with the situation. It was extremely unlikely that the French would be persuaded to repeal the offending decrees of November and December 1792 by mere negotiation; the revolutionaries, having violated international treaties and laws as it pleased them, could scarcely be trusted to treat on any basis of law; and it would open Britain to the insult of having her ambassador sent home unrecognized. The revolutionaries were 'outlaws of humanity, an uncommunicable people'.[24]

Moreover, no successful counter-revolution could be expected from forces within France alone, due to the weaknesses of the French royalists;: their lack of internal leadership, the tyranny of the municipal republican committees and their dissipation throughout the country. Even before the execution of Louis XVI, it was plain that he was not likely to help the royalists by 'breaking their prisons, terrifying their Enemies and animating their friends'.[25] External force was necessary in order to achieve the destruction of the Jacobin government of France. It was also incumbent upon Britain to help its allies. This was partly because of treaty obligations, as in the case of the United Provinces; and partly because the European opposition to revolutionary France had no chance of victory without Britain's involvement and, indeed, leadership. Britain could not afford to sit back and hope that the other states would do the dirty work for it. It was more likely to play a fair mediating role in the alliance than any other power, since its interests were less likely to clash with those of other states, due to its

---

21 'Letter to a Member of the National Assembly', p.299; idem, Fourth 'Letter on a Regicide Peace', *Writings and Speeches*, ix, 70.

22 Idem, 'Thoughts on French Affairs' (1791), ibid., viii, 362–3. Pitt always hoped that bankruptcy would force the French to sue for peace—an over-optimistic assessment.

23 'Heads for Consideration', p.402.

24 *P.H.*, xxx, 386 (12 February 1793).

25 *Burke Corr.*, vi, 241, Burke to the Chevalier de la Bintinaye, March 1791.

geographical situation as an island and maritime power; besides, it possessed the only navy which could keep that of France in check. Without Great Britain, the cement which might hold all the other states together was missing.

Burke vehemently criticized the ministry's hesitancy to go to war. It was simply not worthwhile, in this case, to discuss, 'like sophisters', whether some evil might be tolerated for the sake of some benefit.[26] The ministry had persevered in neutrality 'with the most pedantick excess' for too long. 'If *your* hands are not on your swords, their knives will be at your throats. There is no medium,—there is no temperament,—there is no compromise with Jacobinism.'[27]

He believed that the allies' aims ought to be clear and unambiguous, in order to prevent needless bloodshed and waste in the pursuit of irrelevant ends. To this end, he wrote the *Heads for the Consideration on the Present State of Affairs* in November 1792 and his *Remarks on the Policy of the Allies with Respect to France* in October 1793. Once the allied aims had been specified, they should be pursued singlemindedly. 'Our politics want directness and simplicity', he complained in November 1793.[28] He thought that the extinction of Jacobinism in France should be the primary aim of the war against revolutionary France. The more permanent the Jacobin regime seemed to be, the more convinced Burke became that if it were not destroyed, it would destroy the whole European social order. Jacobinism, however, would not fall so long as it was pursued as a secondary object, behind the distraction of territorial ambition in the guises of indemnity and security.

Burke made it clear that in seeking the destruction of Jacobinism he did not mean that France itself should be destroyed. He was at war with Jacobinism, not France, and for him, military victory was only a necessary preliminary to the re-establishment of French society. Nor did he think the total annihilation of France desirable either for Britain or for Europe. He feared that Austria and Prussia wanted the destruction of France as a great power and that this would ruin the balance of power in Europe and lead to further war among countries preying upon France. France would be weakened sufficiently by the time Jacobinism had been extirpated not to pose a threat to the other European states; indeed, it would require to be nursed and supported rather than further drained.[29]

As to the government which should be established in France after the Jacobin regime had been crushed, Burke thought that its precise details could be determined only after the conclusion of peace. He also argued that its form was

---

26 'Appeal', p.16.

27 *Burke Corr.*, vii, 309, Burke to Fitzwilliam, 29 November 1792; ibid., viii, 104, Burke to Windham, 30 December 1794.

28 Ibid., vii, 489, Burke to Windham, 25 November 1793.

29 'Remarks on the Policy of the Allies', pp.488–9, 491.

irrelevant so long as it was stable and guaranteed property rights and justice. Nevertheless, he did have clear ideas on the form he believed would be the most likely to achieve these standards. In his *Remarks on the Policy of the Allies* (October 1793), he suggested that a military government would be necessary immediately after the end of the war 'for the energetic foundation of a lasting order'.[30] He was in fact persuaded that the only adequate form of government for the renewed France would be the 'lawful prince', that is, a restored monarchy. 'France to be anything', he wrote, 'must be a Monarchy; and a very strong Monarchy too.' Theoretical constitutions and plans bedevilled France throughout the Revolution and nothing would be of real service to it but to re-establish the old order. As time passed, he favoured less and less modification of the old regime.[31]

Burke's idea of the re-establishment of the old order, therefore, did not merely involve the restoration of the monarchy but also the restoration of property. This, he argued, followed logically and necessarily. A hereditary monarchy could not exist if nothing else was hereditary or permanent. Moreover, the re-establishment of the whole propertied order was necessary if Jacobinism were to be properly extinguished. The alternative, Burke warned, was to watch over the next twenty years the property and government of every state in Europe being overthrown as they had been in France.[32] He did, however, recognize that it would be impractical as well as impolitic to attempt to reinstate the *ancien régime* in every detail. 'That was though not so violent a State of Anarchy as well as the present. If it were even possible to lay things down exactly as they stood, before the series of experimental politicks began, I am quite sure that they could not long continue in that situation.'[33]

II The War Against the French Revolution

Burke had a very clear conception of what sort of war Britain was involved in and ought to be fighting against revolutionary France, and he was probably the first in Britain to see it in this way. He had an almost Pauline vision of wrestling 'not against flesh and blood, but against principalities, against powers, against the rulers of the darkness of this world, against spiritual wickedness in high

---

30 p.492.

31 *Burke Corr.*, vi, 480, Burke to unknown, [1791]; ibid., p.218, Burke to John Trevor, January 1791; Colin Lucas, 'Edmund Burke and the *Émigrés*', in François Furet and Mona Ozouf (eds), *The French Revolution and the Creation of Modern Political Culture*, vol. iii, *The Transformation of Political Culture* (Oxford, 1989), p.109.

32 'Remarks on the Policy of the Allies', pp.464-5; *Burke Corr.*, vii, 384, Burke to General Dalton, 6 August 1793.

33 *Burke Corr.*, vi, 480, Burke to unknown, [1791].

places', and indeed a following of 'war crusaders' collected behind him: those writers and politicians who shared many of his views on the war and often treated his writings and opinions as if they had near apostolic authority.[34]

In determining the nature of the war, Burke's first consideration was the character of the enemy. Ministers must abandon the notion that Britain was fighting the people of France, or they would be unable to fight the real enemy effectively. Britain was not involved in 'a common political war with an old recognized member of the commonwealth of Christian Europe'.[35] Rather, the conflict was primarily with the French Revolutionary *system*, not simply with French ambition or arrogance *per se*, since these were but manifestations of the revolutionary ideology in practice. The attack on the United Provinces, the attempt to upset the European balance of power and the declaration of war on Britain were all good grounds for war; but in themselves they were little more than evidence for the essential justification for war, which was the revolutionary system of France, 'in itself a declaration of war against mankind.'[36]

The contest against revolutionary France was therefore no ordinary war—it was a new kind of war. It was the first war since the wars of religion to be fought between competing ideologies, and the principles at stake were those of the old social order of Europe, rooted in the protection of property. Britain, Burke emphasized, was struggling against a set of political and religious doctrines, not just against men. Thus,

> We are in a war of a *peculiar* nature. It is not with an ordinary community, which is hostile or friendly as passion or as interest may veer about: not with a state which makes war through wantonness, and abandons it through lassitude. We are at war with a system, which, by its essence, is inimical to all other governments, and which makes peace or war, as peace and war may best contribute to their subversion. It is with an *armed doctrine* that we are at war.[37]

French arms and principles were 'things inseperable (*sic*)' and 'went as those of Mahomed, the Rights of man in one hand, and the Sword in the other'.[38]

This new type of war created a new style of warfare. It was warfare conducted without a sense of honour or integrity. No efforts would be spared by the Jacobins (who were now inured to warfare) to gain their ends, and Britain could take no conventions of eighteenth-century warfare for granted. The fanaticism of the revolutionaries alarmed Burke. He spoke of 'this dreadful and

---

34 Ephesians 6:12. For the 'war crusaders', see chapter 3.
35 Fourth 'Letter on a Regicide Peace', pp.50–1.
36 First 'Letter on a Regicide Peace', p.260.
37 Ibid., p.199.
38 *Burke Corr.*, vii, 307, 310, Burke to Fitzwilliam, 29 November 1792.

portentous energy, restrained by no consideration of God or man, that is always vigilant, always on the attack, that allows itself no repose, and suffers none to rest an hour with impunity'.[39] Crucially, this was total warfare. Revolutionary France was throwing everything it had into its war effort, and would stop at nothing to achieve its ends—it would conquer or be crushed. Burke realized this, and saw that a similar commitment from Britain would be necessary if France was to be defeated. He stressed that such a conflict as this would inevitably be long. No dangerous power in the past had ever been reduced to acceptability without a long war, and revolutionary France was no ordinarily dangerous power.

Strategically, it was incumbent upon the British administration to think the issues through properly in the light of the fact that this was a new kind of war. In his *Letter to William Elliot, Esq.* (May 1795), Burke accused the British of superficial thinking: 'People talk of war, or cry for peace—Have they to the bottom considered the questions either of war, or peace, upon the scale of the existing world? No, I fear they have not.'[40] Had the issues been considered properly, according to Burke, then military strategy would have been focused correctly and energy and resources used effectively. Since this system was based in France, the centre of western Europe, he insisted that it must be defeated there. Burke urgently wanted a military strike at Paris and the destruction there of Jacobinism once and for all before it became entrenched: 'It must be extirpated in the place of its origin, or it will not be confined to that place.' All chasing after objects elsewhere in Europe or further afield, in the East or West Indies, was therefore a waste of time and resources. This policy made sense militarily, too, he thought: 'France is strong at arm's length. She is, I am convinced, weakness itself, if you can get to grapple with her internally.'[41]

When important conquests were made in France, such as Toulon, Burke insisted that they should be held in the name of the French monarchy, although under the civil and military influence of the allies, to speed the counter-revolution and to prevent quarrels among the allies.[42] In fact, the whole conflict ought to be fought in the name of the French King. Not to recognize Louis XVII and the princes, Provence (later Louis XVIII) and Artois (later Charles X), was to acknowledge the validity of the Revolutionary government and to justify the judicial murder of Louis XVI. Burke constantly criticized the British

---

39 'Remarks on the Policy of the Allies', p.460.

40 Edmund Burke, 'Letter to William Elliot, Esq.' (1795), *Writings and Speeches*, ix, 43.

41 *Burke Corr.*, vii, 387, Burke to the Comte de Mercy-Argenteau, c.6 August 1793; ibid., p.413, Burke to Windham, 18 August 1793. Nevertheless, Burke was sometimes unable to resist giving ministers advice on which colonies should be attacked first—see the postscript to his letter to Henry Dundas of 8 October 1793 in ibid., p.446.

42 'Remarks on the Policy of the Allies', p.482.

administration for inadequately supporting the French counter-revolutionaries. He tried hard to make the British ministry see that supporting the French royalist cause was in their interests, since it gave them internal allies in France, as well as being the only just or viable means of fighting Jacobinism. The allies and the French royalists, Burke insisted, were mutually dependent. The *émigrés* in particular understood the country better and had most interest in it, but they were not nearly strong enough to effect a counter-revolution on their own. They must be consulted and employed. He estimated that there must be at least seventy thousand deprived civil and ecclesiastical property-owners; much of their force of ten thousand which had served with the Prussian troops in 1792 still existed and would willingly act again. They were also by far the best people to lead and inspire the royalists in France.[43] The fact that the conflict was in a basic sense a religious war presented another reason for using the *émigrés*. The French royalist clergy should be used to the full in helping to wipe out atheistic Jacobinism, and it had been senseless to forbid the entry of the bishop of Toulon once the port had been taken by the allies. Burke reserved severe censure for those who hesitated on doctrinal grounds to use the French Catholic clergy.

As for the conduct and management of the British political nation in waging war against revolutionary France, Burke made four main points. Britain must fight wholeheartedly; it must fight as a united nation, as far as possible; resolute leadership was vital; and public opinion must be properly managed and used.

'Humanly speaking,' Burke wrote in the *Letters on a Regicide Peace*, 'that people which bounds its efforts only with its being, must give the law to that nation which will not push its opposition beyond its convenience.'[44] It was vital that Britain should at least match the force and spirit of revolutionary France. Novelty was not the only possible source of zeal; Burke called for a passionate defence of the laws, the constitution, the institutions, the social character and the liberties of Britain, and he paced up and down the pages of his letters and publications with distressed impatience at the ministry's caution and lack of urgency. On 19 November 1793, he wrote to Sir Gilbert Elliot:

> To say the truth, I am more full of anxiety than I can well express. The operation of our remedies to the French Pestilence is slow. The Course has begun late. It is pursued without any true knowledge of its specifick Nature. It has been tardily applied—whilst the disorder moves with the pace of a Giant.[45]

---

43 Ibid., pp.474–9, 470.

44 First 'Letter on a Regicide Peace', p.195.

45 *Burke Corr.*, vii, 489.

He argued, for instance, that no physical defence could shield a country from the effects of the French example of revolutionary principles and activity. He roundly criticized the British policy of recruiting large numbers of men for home service only. This was much easier than recruiting for foreign service, and accorded with the administration's defensiveness in the middle years of the decade as Britain became increasingly isolated in the struggle against France. To Burke, however, the policy of keeping so many of the armed forces inert at home drained them of spirit and glory and, more importantly, was based on a wholly erroneous conception of how to defend the country effectively. In his view, it seemed to be a plain statement of abandoning the war and maintaining only passive defences.[46] A defensive alliance with the other European states was more foolish still, since in this their discordant interests were far more difficult to deal with than in a common offensive, which provided a clear focus.

Just as battle must be taken to the French wholeheartedly, so, second, it must be done with unity. There must be unity among the allied nations and unity within Britain itself. In the *Heads for Consideration on the Present State of Affairs* (November 1792), Burke urged the British ministry to placate, conciliate, support, encourage and stir up the other European states so that one great confederacy might be formed against France, and he continued to insist that, just as the rest of Europe was ineffective against revolutionary France without Britain's cooperation and leadership, so neither could Britain 'pretend to cope with France but as connected with the body of Christendom'. In this, Burke included the papacy and the papal states, and he wanted Britain to put bigotry aside and make use of another potential ally.[47] Indeed, religious unity was particularly important, since he regarded the allies as fighting for the very existence of ;religion, which was the basis of Europan civilization. A civil war amongst the enemies of Jacobinism would do their cause no good. All the denominations of European religion shared a common foundation, he argued, and they must all be supported, 'or they must all fall in the crash of a common Ruin.'[48] He did acknowledge the failings of the other states as allies against the Jacobins, and often denounced their conduct of the war in scathing terms—but this, he insisted, did not excuse Britain from making every possible effort to hold the confederacy together. As far as Britain itself was concerned, Burke did his best to elicit an integrated and total war effort of unity and full cooperation from the political nation, so that its whole weight might be thrown against

46 Ibid., ix, 149, Burke to Fitzwilliam, 7 December 1796.

47 'Heads for Consideration', pp.399–400; First 'Letter on a Regicide Peace', p.196; *Burke Corr.*, vii, 440, Burke to John Coxe Hippisley, 3 October 1793.

48 *Burke Corr.*, viii, 146, Burke to Fitzwilliam, 10 February 1795; ibid., viii, 130–1, Burke to William Smith, 29 January 1795. See John Dinwiddy, 'Interpretations of anti-Jacobinism', in Mark Philp (ed.), *The French Revolution and British Popular Politics* (London, 1991), p.44.

Jacobin France. He called for unity within the royal family (that is, between George III and his profligate son, the Prince of Wales), between the ministry and opposition in Parliament (so long as it was a union in favour of a full-blooded war on Jacobinism, with no compromise on the part of the ministry), and between Protestants and Roman Catholics in Ireland. He also worked hard for the coalition of the Portland Whigs with the ministry, which was eventually achieved in 1794.

Third, the political leadership of Britain in the crusade against Jacobin France was of great concern to Burke. While recognizing that they 'meant well' and were not inactive, and indeed that they formed the best administration in Europe,[49] Burke nevertheless became increasingly disillusioned with Pitt and his cabinet in their conduct of the war. By November 1796 he was telling Earl Fitzwilliam that 'Mr. Pitt, except for the direct Objects of his own power, is not a bold Politician. Even for them I do not think that Great Courage is his Character'; and three months later he wrote to French Laurence that there was little to choose between Pitt and Fox.[50] Burke's complaint was that Pitt did not declare for the anti-Jacobin cause sufficiently distinctly, nor did he pour everything into upholding the European allies and the French princes and their supporters. As J. Holland Rose pointed out, Burke's theory of the war was as inspiring as the practice of it was impossible for ministers who were contending with the disabilities of self-interested and short-sighted European allies and bitterly divided French royalists.[51] It was easy to criticize, as a spectator; in his passionate zeal for his cause, Burke seemed not to understand the exigencies of Cabinet office.

Finally, Burke was convinced of the importance of public opinion and of the need for the government to use it and control it. In 1770 he had argued that the confidence of the people was 'the great and only foundation of government'. He believed that the minds of the people (that is, he made clear, the minds of economically independent and therefore politically significant people) were as much a national resource as men, money and ships, and a resource whose significance was entirely unappreciated by the government.[52] He was persuaded of the relationship between ideas and political activities, and he realized that this was what made the French Revolution dangerous. It was therefore essential that

---

49 *Burke Corr.*, vii, 517, Burke to Lord Loughborough, 12 January 1794; 'Letter to William Elliot, Esq.', p.43.

50 *Burke Corr.*, ix, 121, Burke to Fitzwilliam, 20 November 1796; ibid., 266, Burke to French Laurence, 1 March 1797.

51 J. Holland Rose, 'The Struggle with Revolutionary France, 1792–1802', in A.W. Ward and G.P. Gooch (eds), *The Cambridge History of British Foreign Policy* (Cambridge, 1922), p.266.

52 Edmund Burke, 'On the Causes of the Present Discontents' (1770). Cf. *Burke Corr.*, ix, 119, Burke to French Laurence, 18 November 1796; ibid., viii, 124, Burke to French Laurence, [21 January 1795].

the government should make the effort to woo and hold the loyalty of public opinion for the safety of the social order. An enthusiasm for the war must be raised in the nation to counter the Jacobin fanaticism and to bear the country through the hardships of a long struggle. 'I am sure that so far from endeavouring to excite this spirit, nothing has been omitted to flatten and lower it', he lamented.[53]

When Burke wrote about how Britain ought to fight the war against France, he urged the use of new means of fighting for the sake of saving the old order of Europe. 'New wine' could not be kept in the 'old Leathern Bottles'.[54] His cry for a 'manly' leadership and his exhortations to the general political nation of Britain for wholeheartedness and unity of spirit were alike pleas for a national conviction and fervour which would subordinate everything to the supreme end of extinguishing Jacobin principles within France and from Europe. He involved the public in his struggle against the French Revolution for the sake of its numerical strength, and in this sense, he was calling for the whole nation to be employed in a total war against the French revolutionaries.

Since Burke believed war against France to be absolutely necessary and a lesser evil than allowing the French Revolution to establish itself in Europe, he had no patience with any suggestion of peace with France before Jacobinism had been utterly destroyed and the monarchy restored. His four *Letters on a Regicide Peace* were written and published in the years 1795-97 because of the attraction that negotiations with France held for the British administration during those difficult years. Much of his private correspondence was also taken up by the same concern. He argued against peace with Jacobin France on principle, on the basis of the consequences he predicted from it, and from various other pragmatic considerations.

Primarily, Burke believed that Britain ought not to make peace with revolutionary France on principle, since the original grounds for war had not been removed. Jacobinism was still alive and any termination of the war at this point would merely achieve 'a Sansculottick peace'—it would abandon mankind to the mercy of the revolutionaries.[55] The point which the British ministry and its allies seemed infuriatingly unable to grasp was that since they were not dealing with any ordinary power, the ordinary conventions of war and peace were irrelevant and ineffective. To suppose that a stable government in France would guarantee a stable peace was to betray a complete misunderstanding of the French Revolution, based on the fallacy that France's hostility to other nations proceeded from its internal anarchy, which its rulers were not strong enough to master. France was not an anarchy, although it was certainly anarchic; it was a

53 Ibid., ix, 130, Burke to Mrs. John Crewe, 23 November 1796.

54 Ibid., viii, 135, Burke to Windham, c.2 February 1795.

55 First 'Letter on a Regicide Peace', p.195.

despotism of the worst kind—'a series of short-lived tyrannies'. Burke argued that the Revolution was neither made nor sustained by the people, but was the work of a revolutionary 'cabal', and since the war was not the result of popular tumult, it followed that the arrival of relative domestic stablility and order would not necessarily produce peace with the other nations.[56] It was vital that the Revolution itself be crushed and wiped out before peace was made with France, because until that was accomplished, there could *be* no peace in any meaningful sense of the term. In peace, France would merely pursue through intrigue and proselytism what it now pursued with the sword, whereas Britain and the allies would be left with no effectual means of resistance. They were complacently waging war under an error of grotesque proportions, namely, that they could end it whenever they chose, simply by deciding to forget French crimes.[57]

Moreover, France had declared war, and her obstinate arrogance must not be met with importunate British self-abasement in seeking peace. Every fresh attempt to establish negotiations after the French rejection of Britain's first approach in 1796 could only be motivated by a masochistic desire to be mortified, so far as Burke could see, since there was no reason to believe that there had been any change in French policy. Equally shamefully, Britain's pursuit of peace with France would betray the allies. His third *Letter on a Regicide Peace* (1797) discussed and condemned the official pledge given by the British government 'in the face of all Europe' of good faith towards France, and its readiness to negotiate whenever France was willing. No European power had demanded that Britain go through such 'judicial purgations and ordeals'—no European power was remotely interested in British good faith towards France. What they desperately needed was assurances of British fidelity to the alliance against France. 'No man,' Burke wrote to Pitt, 'can more cordially pray for your bringing this arduous contest to an happy and honourable termination than I do', but the necessary prerequisite for that termination was the total extirpation of Jacobinism.[58]

Burke also argued against peace on the basis of the consequences he predicted from it. He complained that those who cried out for it did not realize what it was that they were demanding. His prognosis was indeed gloomy. Britain's very eagerness to make peace would cost it dearly, he forecast. If the revolutionaries noticed this anxiety, they would exploit it mercilessly and make Britain pay heavily for peace. Worse still, to make peace was ultimately to cooperate with the French plan for universal revolution. Not only would it remove physical resistance to the French, but it would also open the British door

56 Fourth 'Letter on a Regicide Peace', pp.86–7.

57 Ibid., p.104; 'Thoughts on French Affairs', p.352.

58 Third 'Letter on a Regicide Peace' (1797), *Writings and Speeches*, ix, 298, 317–18; *Burke Corr.*, viii, 338, Burke to Pitt, [7 November 1795].

to the Revolution. If the British government yielded to the enemy abroad, it could not hope to subdue conspirators at home. Lord Auckland had argued in his pamphlet, *Some Remarks on the Apparent Circumstances of the War in the Fourth Week of October, 1795*, that peace was quite safe, since the troubles of the French constitution must have taught the British people a healthy respect for and pride in their own constitution. Not so, retorted Burke in his fourth *Letter on a Regicide Peace*, noting the riots and the attempt on the King's life which had taken place a few days after the publication of Auckland's pamphlet. Moreover, the mass meeting held on 26 October 1795 had, he claimed, declared against the life of George III. Peace could only weaken Britain and the allies internally, much to the advantage of France.[59]

Besides contending against peace on the principle that the original grounds for war remained intact and on the basis of what seemed to him its inevitable consequences, Burke's polemical battery supplied various other arguments. The very insults returned by the French to British overtures, for instance, were cause enough for British pride to determine to stop at nothing to crush such insolence. In the first *Letter on a Regicide Peace*, Burke enumerated four stages of British approaches and their rejection by France: Bird's mission to solicit mercy for the Duc de Choiseul in 1795; the speech from the British throne and the direct message from the crown and the two Houses of Parliament offering to negotiate for peace at the end of the same year; William Wickham's mission to Basle in March 1796 to sound out French willingness to hold talks; and the shameful attempts (to Burke's mind) to achieve the mediation of the King of Prussia and the Danish minister at Paris later in that year. All had been rejected by the French on the grounds of British insincerity and bad faith; a cover, Burke believed, for the fact that the French rejected the idea of a congress and preferred to dictate the terms of peace. Later, he depicted Lord Malmesbury's return to Britain after his failed mission to establish negotiations as the return of a 'Mongrel ... whipped back to the Kennel yelping and with his Tail between his Legs.' The apparent placidity of the ministry in response to this barrage of insults was incomprehensible to Burke.[60]

He also brushed aside with contempt the various objections to the continuance of the war. Scarcity of grain and lack of resources were no reasons for peace; such notions, he wrote, were hardly worth his 'powder and shot'. Burke insisted that Britain had never been so powerful and wealthy as it now was. The public loan of autumn 1796 of £18 million ought to have been a sufficient demonstration both of the nation's ability to defend the European balance of power and of the vitality of its 'ancient spirit'. So overwhelming was

---

59 Eden (Lord Auckland), *Some Remarks*; Fourth 'Letter on a Regicide Peace', p.60.

60 First 'Letter on a Regicide Peace', pp.201–16; *Burke Corr.*, ix, 205, Burke to Windham, 25 December 1796.

the evidence of Britain's prosperity that he could only conclude that, of those who predicted economic gloom for Britain, 'I fear too many are actuated by a more malignant and dangerous spirit'.[61] Just as in the beginning of the war French force had been too much despised, so now it was too much dreaded. Britain was giving up far too easily, and making the task simple for the French revolutionaries. By displaying a willingness to negotiate whenever France should deign to do so, Britain was allowing its enemy to choose the moment of its own optimum advantage.

He accused ministry and opposition alike of being swayed by party factionalism in the urgent question of war and peace: 'This cursed Peace is at the bottom of all the mad things done by Ministry and opposition', he grumbled in December 1796. 'I see nothing short of insanity. Pitt and Fox are not contending for the Government of an independent Country, but who should be the Viceroys deputy under a French Lord Paramount.' He feared that Pitt would rather be defeated on the Rhine or the Po 'than suffer a Badgerring every day in the House of Commons', and that he might be harried into peace by the opposition.[62]

Peace with revolutionary France would for Burke have been the worst result possible, and he urged that it ought not to be debated at all; but he was to struggle to the end of his days with what appeared to him to be a willing blindness to the unspeakable dangers that such a peace would involve. 'In every other posture of things there are at least chances', he wrote; but a 'Jacobin peace' would lead to the irrevocable ruin of Britain.[63]

Burke, if by no means the sole advocate of a crusading, total war against Jacobin France, clearly had particularly strong and coherent views, and he was certainly the earliest to urge such a vision on the country. His perception of the French Revolution as an immensely significant ideological event was unusually profound, and this was widely recognized, even if most of his contemporaries did not feel able to endorse his opinions and conclusions entirely. Men of such diverse views as the Duke of Portland (who eventually joined the government and took a seat in the cabinet in 1794) and James Mackintosh (whose *Vindiciae Gallicae* (1791) and anonymous *Monthly Review* articles on the first *Two Letters on a Regicide Peace* (1796) had been arguments against Burke's position) wrote of their early admiration for his publications and the strength of

---

61 Edmund Burke, 'Thoughts and Details on Scarcity' (1795), *Writings and Speeches*, ix, 142–3; Third 'Letter on a Regicide Peace', pp.346, 350–86, 371.

62 *Burke Corr.*, ix, 179, Burke to French Laurence, 16 December 1796.

63 Ibid., vii, 148, Burke to John Wilmot, 12 February 1795; ibid., ix, 205, Burke to Windham, 25 December 1796.

his convictions.[64] 'I do not stand in need of any apology for my principles, my sentiments, or my conduct,' Burke himself wrote in the 'Letter to the Duke of Portland' which prefaced his *Observations on the Conduct of the Minority* (1793), and he continued to be completely unrepentant of his stance on the war amidst the varying hardships and difficulties that Britain faced in the 1790s.[65] As far as he could, he practised what he preached, showing particular concern for the *émigrés* in Britain—he found many of them accommodation, loans, commissions and employment; he extended his own friendship to some, and even seems to have settled some on his own land in Canada; he helped to establish and campaign for the Fund for the Relief of the Suffering Clergy of France; and he set up the school at Penn to house and educate sixty boys whose parents had fled to Britain. Conor Cruise O'Brien points out that his lack of fuss when his ally, Fitzwilliam, was recalled from the viceroyalty of Ireland in March 1795 shows how important to Burke, even in his personal life and attitudes, was the need to subordinate all to the destruction of Jacobinism.[66]

The intensity of Burke's writing on the Revolution and the war was a result of the fact that his views were not merely part of his public, professional persona, but a heavy and deeply felt personal burden. As he wrote to Fitzwilliam in 1792, 'To say that I was somewhat uneasy would but ill paint the State of my Mind'. Elsewhere, he wrote of 'a heavy weight upon my mind', 'a good deal of serious inquietude', his dread, dejection, terror, and 'absolute despair'.[67] His last years sorely blighted by the death of his son, his failure to secure the impeachment of Warren Hastings, his large debts and his failing health, Burke often seemed to identify his own troubles with the European calamity, part and parcel of the apocalyptic evil of the times.

Burke dreamed of a man of integrity, courage, determination and wisdom to lead Britain in a crusade against the French Revolution. 'How often has public calamity been arrested on the very brink of ruin by the seasonable energy of a single man!' he exclaimed again and again. 'But when and where and how is this man to appear.'[68] Pitt was a sore disappointment to him. Cautious, and bearing the ultimate responsibility without Burke's luxury of being able to look

---

64 Ibid., vii, 121–2, Sir Gilbert Elliot to his wife, [spring 1792]; ibid., vii, 447, the Duke of Portland to Burke, 10 October 1793; ibid., ix, 193, James Mackintosh to Burke, 22 December 1796.

65 'Observations on the Conduct of the Minority', p.405; see also 'Letter to William Elliot, Esq.', p.39.

66 Lucas, 'Edmund Burke and the *Émigrés*', pp.110–12; O'Brien, *The Great Melody*, pp.516–17.

67 *Burke Corr.*, vii, 309, Burke to Fitzwilliam, 29 November 1792; 'Heads for Consideration', p.402; 'Observations on the Conduct of the Minority', p.404; *Burke Corr.*, vii, 178, Burke to Grenville, 18 August 1792; ibid., viii, 363, Burke to unknown, [1795].

68 'Letter to William Elliot, Esq.', p.41; *Burke Corr.*, vi, 37, Burke to Fitzwilliam, 12 November 1789.

on and criticize, he was hardly the epic hero standing forth unambiguously against the principles and stratagems of Jacobinism. Burke urged such allies in active politics as Windham and Earl Fitzwilliam to take the moral leadership of the country upon themselves, and surely part of his frustration with his age, failing health and lack of real influence on political events was that he could not take on such a role himself.

Indeed, Burke's influence was weak where he most wanted it to be felt. He was in close contact with ministers at the beginning of the war,[69] and they treated him with patience and a good deal of civility. But he could 'distinguish between complaisance and confidence', and he feared that his practical influence on them was 'not very considerable'.[70] He had a group of followers and admirers whose projects and activities against revolutionary France were, as Colin Lucas has remarked, no more than 'private initiatives occasionally elevated by an appointment to an official post', most notably Windham's job of dealing with the *émigrés* in Britain while he was Secretary of War (1794-96).[71] Sir Gilbert Elliot, one of his more pragmatic admirers, wrote in 1793 that 'Pitt says of him that he is always right, but that it is six months before other people. Possibly this is as bad for practical purposes as being six months too late.' By 1795, Pitt was more irritable—he returned to Auckland a letter of Burke's on the government's war strategy with the remark that it was 'like other rhapsodies from the same pen, in which there is much to admire, and nothing to agree with.'[72] It was not to be until the wars against Napoleon Bonaparte in the 1800s that Burke's crusading ideas would be seen by ministers as much more than visionary 'rhapsodies'.

Yet Burke probably had more influence on British attitudes to the French revolutionary wars than he often admitted or than he is often credited with. He was frequently accused of indirectly causing the war,[73] and he became almost a stock-figure whose name was the subject both of eulogy and abuse. More accurately, in large part he set the tone of the debate on the conflict in Britain by

---

69 *Burke Corr.*, vii, 348–9, n.; O'Brien, *The Great Melody*, pp. 490, 495–6.

70 *Burke Corr.*, vii, 459–60, Burke to Col. John St. Leger, 23 October 1793.

71 Lucas, 'Edmund Burke and the *Émigrés*', p.112. See also chapter 3.

72 *Burke Corr.*, viii, 335n., quoted from the bishop of Bath and Wells (ed.), *The Journal and Correspondence of William, Lord Auckland*, 4 vol.s (1861–62), iii, 320.

73 See, for instance, Sir Brooke Boothby, *Observations on the Appeal from the New to the Old Whigs, and on Mr. Paine's Rights of Man* (London, 1792), p.80; William Fox, *The Interest of Great Britain respecting the French War*, 2nd edition (London, 1793), p.6; *Considerations on the French War ... by a British Merchant* (London, 1794), p.8; *The Evidence Summed Up or a Statement of the Apparent Causes and Objects of the War* (London, 1794), p.27; John Raithby, 'Peace' (London, 1795); also *Writings and Speeches*, ix, 14–15. Burke once confessed to feeling this responsibility himself: 'To say the Truth, I feel very awkward. I am as responsible, as a Minister, for the War, and yet in no one instance have I ... been consulted or communicated with.' (Burke to Dr Charles Burney, 14, 15 September 1793, *Burke Corr.*, vii, 423).

his ideological hatred of the French Revolution and by the breadth and vehemence of his arguments. Most of the political nation was, whether conscious of it or not, responding in some degree to his views. The *Reflections* was a great bestseller[74] and several editions of extracts from it were published, as well as selections in periodicals and newspapers; and many of the loyalist associations spread throughout the country were headed by men who had some sympathy with a Burkean view of the war and who disseminated it in crude and simplistic forms to the many ordinary people who came under their influence. Moreover, his opinions were important even in government circles. Ministers, too, had to react to Burke's views. He did not possess the executive political power to influence the actual waging of the war. But he had set the scene for the British debate on the war, and those who took part in it did so in his theatre, whether willingly or otherwise. The next chapter examines the administration's attitudes to the war and argues that ministers were more affected by Burke's stance than is often suggested.

74 Within a month of publication, 12 000 copies had been sold in Britain and editions had also been published in Paris and Dublin; the book went through five editions between its publication on 1 November 1790 and the end of December. 19 000 copies had been sold in Britain by the end of May 1791 (*Writings and Speeches*, viii, 13). The first *Two Letters on a Regicide Peace* (1796) went through eleven editions between 20 October 1796 and the end of the same year (*Writings and Speeches*, ix, 22).

Chapter 2

Government Attitudes: The Pitt Administration and George III

The driving force behind Burke's attitude to the war against France was very clearly an ideological one. By contrast, the parts played by ideology and practical power politics have long been variously weighed as motivating factors for the British government in the conflict. Some historians have argued that the administration of William Pitt had considerable sympathy for Burke's analysis of events and that, as Cyril Matheson put it, 'the struggle of the British Government with revolutionary principles became merged into the European war'.[1] Others have claimed, with John Holland Rose, that 'the war between France and Great Britain was not, for us at least, mainly a war of principle. The material issues at stake always outweighed those arising from a clash of political ideals.' T.C.W. Blanning refined the problem by recognizing that, although ideological differences create hostility, they do not necessarily lead to war and that, while opposing ideologies caused misunderstandings and miscalculations on both sides, Britain and France did not go to war over them. In his view, power and security were the fundamental concerns.[2] Other scholars have seen the problem as one of chronology, with ideology playing a more important role in the attitudes of British ministers to France either earlier or later in the 1790s.[3]

All of these explanations tend to separate the ideological aspect of the wars against revolutionary France from the government's role as an active player in them. But ideological issues and the more pragmatic issues of

---

1 Cyril Matheson, *The Life of Henry Dundas, First Viscount Melville* (London, 1933), p.173. Cf. Jeremy Black, 'The Coming of War Between Britain and France, 1792–1793', *Francia*, 20 (1993), 100–8; and idem, *British Foreign Policy in an Age of Revolutions, 1783–1793* (Cambridge, 1994), pp.460–71.

2 Holland Rose, 'The Struggle with Revolutionary France', p.256; T.C.W. Blanning, *The Origins of the French Revolutionary Wars* (London, 1986), p.206; cf. idem, *The French Revolutionary Wars, 1787–1802* (London, 1996), p.93. Norman Frank Richards, 'British Policy and the Problem of Monarchy in France, 1789–1802', unpublished Ph.D. thesis (University of London, 1954), p.66, and Jennifer Mori, *William Pitt and the French Revolution, 1785–1795* (Edinburgh, 1997), pp.134, 143, both take a similar view to Blanning.

3 Philip Schofield, 'British Politicians and French Arms: The Ideological War of 1793–1795', *History*, 77 (1992), 183–201; Peter Jupp, *Lord Grenville 1759–1834* (Oxford, 1985), pp.177, 187.

strategic interests were not so easily divided as historians have often assumed. It was not the function of government to concern itself with abstract revolutionary ideas, much though Burke would have liked it. On the other hand, it was very much the function of government to react to the activities of revolutionaries who held these ideas, particularly when those activities impinged upon British interests. Naturally, official government policy and the sympathies of individual ministers often diverged, and equally naturally both official and private attitudes changed over time as the nature and scale of the conflict changed and as the prospects of British success fluctuated.

This chapter considers the views of government ministers and King George III on their reasons for going to war against revolutionary France, the nature of the conflict, their objectives, the strategies to be adopted during it, the conditions necessary for concluding peace and the terms achieved by Britain in its eventual settlement in 1802. It does not argue that for the British government this conflict was only a war of ideas, an attempted counter-revolution. It does suggest, however, that, although strategic issues were usually uppermost in ministers' thinking, ideological issues made a substantial contribution and that they should not be removed too far from the strategic concerns.

I Entry into War: Policy and Principle

In terms of the outbreak of the war, strategic issues were undoubtedly crucial in propelling the two nations into armed conflict. Nevertheless, hostility to French Revolutionary ideology also played an important part in shaping the attitudes of the British government. The probability that it was secondary to more pragmatic considerations in causing the actual recourse to war should not lead us to ignore or depreciate its significance in reinforcing these strategic concerns. Ministers may have resisted war until French foreign policy affected Britain directly, but they were well aware that it was the external impact of the Revolution on British interests which led them into hostilities.

Great Britain and France had been habitual enemies throughout most of the eighteenth century and, by the time of the outbreak of the Revolution in France, each once again had reason to harbour resentment against the other. French opportunism and *Schadenfreude* over Britain's defeat in the American War of Independence still rankled in Britain, while the British triumph in the United Provinces in 1787 was resented in France. British ministers were also concerned about the artificial harbour under construction at Cherbourg, which was much nearer to Britain than existing harbours at Toulon and Brest, and about renewed French interest in India. Initially, however, the French Revolution held little appeal for the British government as a pretext for war. It appeared at first to ministers to be an imitation of the Glorious Revolution which as yet acted only to weaken the French state internationally. As William Grenville remarked, 'The main point appears quite secure, that they will not for many years be in a situation to molest the invaluable peace which we now enjoy.'[4] Famously, as late as February 1792 the Prime Minister, William Pitt, forecast a long period of peace: 'unquestionably,' he told the House of Commons, 'there never was a time in the history of this country, when, from the situation of Europe, we might more reasonably expect fifteen years of peace, than we may at the present moment'.[5] It was only when vital British interests were threatened that war loomed.

Pitt's administration tended to be governed in foreign affairs by two main principles: on the one hand, an inclination towards seclusion from European affairs and, on the other, a concern to safeguard British security by seeking to maintain stability in Europe, or 'the balance of power'. The dovetailing or clash of these usually determined its participation or otherwise in European matters. Public opinion united with the government's necessary preoccupation with the effects of international events on Britain in a strong desire for British isolation, an inclination only increased by the humiliation of the Ochakov fiasco of 1791, when Britain's challenge to the expansion of Russian power in the Near East had been decisively rebuffed. Ministers clung to neutrality with regard to France, and were anxious to preserve normal relations with it, until it was clear that this position had become untenable. It was believed that Revolutionary France was its own worst enemy and that its inner convulsions would weaken it sufficiently to preclude the need for a declaration of war by Britain.

With respect to British security from direct external threat, the Low Countries were of paramount importance. The upheavals in the Austrian Netherlands and the United Provinces concerned the British government far more than did the Revolution in France. It was held to be necessary that the United Provinces should be kept susceptible to British influence, in order that they should not be dominated by France and extend the cross-Channel launching-pad for French aggression towards Britain. Likewise, Austrian sovereignty in the Belgian provinces was a standard principle of British policy because of fear of French expansion up the Channel coast and interference with substantial British trading interests. So important was this that Pitt stated in 1790 that the prevention of a union of either the Austrian Netherlands or the United Provinces with France was 'worth the risk, or even the certainty of

---

4 Grenville to the Marquess of Buckingham, 14 September 1789, in the Duke of Buckingham and Chandos (ed.), *Memoirs of the Courts and Cabinets of George the Third*, 2 vol.s (London, 1853), ii, 165, quoted in John Ehrman, *The Younger Pitt*, vol. ii, *The Reluctant Transition* (London, 1983), p.47. Grenville became Foreign Secretary in April 1791.

5 *P.H.*, xxix , 826, Pitt, 17 February 1792.

war'.[6] That he meant what he said had been demonstrated in 1787, when Britain had acted decisively in concert with the Dutch Stadtholder to defeat the republican Dutch patriots and their ally, France. In 1788, Britain's entry into a Triple Alliance with the United Provinces and Prussia had increased its maritime security by guaranteeing to it the support of the Dutch navy and a safe entry into Europe for British goods in war-time.

These principles were therefore established before France declared war on Britain on 1 February 1793, and they can also be seen in the ministry's attitude to the war between France and Austria and Prussia in 1792. The British government remained carefully neutral for over three years after the outbreak of the Revolution, before tension began to build up dangerously between the two states in the autumn of 1792. Neither the Declaration of Pillnitz in August 1791, proclaiming Austrian and Prussian neutrality until other powers joined them against France, nor the eventual outbreak of war, in April 1792 between Austria and France and in July between Prussia and France, encouraged Britain to prepare for war, despite ministers' increasingly partisan sympathies. It was thought unlikely that the war would last long: Austria and Prussia would soon defeat France and restore order in Paris. According to Lord Auckland, the British ambassador at The Hague, the internal and external pressures on France were sufficient to ensure that it must 'burst like a Bomb' some day without the need for British intervention.[7]

The Prussian military failure at Valmy in September was alarming, but for the moment it was only further confirmation of the wisdom of the policy of neutrality: peace was still the safest option. The French annexation of Savoy rendered dubious earlier assurances that they were not interested in acquiring foreign territory, but it was not a direct challenge to British interests or obligations. Lord Grenville was 'thankful that we had the wit to keep ourselves out of the glorious enterprize ... and that we were not tempted by the hope of sharing the spoils in the division of France, nor by the prospect of crushing all democratical principles all over the world'.[8] Even after the defeat of the Austrians at Jemappes in November 1792, which led to the conquest of the Austrian Netherlands by France, the British ministry continued to explore every chance of peace. Auckland met secretly with General Dumouriez's agents. Charles Long was to have been sent to Paris to negotiate, but his trip was rendered unnecessary by Pitt's conference with Maret, a senior official

---

6 Quoted in Ehrman, *The Reluctant Transition*, p.49.

7 BL Add. MS 34443, f.2, Auckland to Grenville, 'Most Secret and Confidential', 1 June 1792; ibid., 34445, f.368, Auckland to Grenville, 'Most Secret and Confidential', 23 Nov. 1792.

8 Grenville to Buckingham, 7 Nov. 1792, in Buckingham, *Courts and Cabinets*, ii, 221–5, quoted in Ehrman, *The Reluctant Transition*, p.205.

from the French foreign ministry, which seemed promising as late as 2 December 1792.

Britain entered the war in February 1793 because by then the drama and implications of the events of the French Revolution were no longer regarded as belonging safely on the other side of the Channel, as they had been in 1789. The increasing violence within France, particularly that perpetrated upon the French royal family, had shocked and galvanized British opinion. It was, however, the external impact of the Revolution upon British strategic and commercial interests which led the Pitt administration into war with France. Following the evacuation of the Belgian provinces by Austrian troops on 14 November 1792, the French government declared the River Scheldt open to international navigation on 16 November, a step contrary to the 1648 Treaty of Westphalia and several major treaties thereafter, which had guaranteed it to the Dutch. This step was understood by Britain to reveal French ambitions in the United Provinces and, especially after the declaration of the National Convention on 19 November that assistance would be forthcoming for all peoples who wished to overthrow their monarchs, it was feared that the republican government sought not only to conquer Dutch territory but also to overthrow the existing regime and install an administration consonant with revolutionary principles and answerable to that of France. Steps were taken to assure the Dutch of British assistance against invasion, should it be required. On 26 November an intercepted letter written by Dumouriez arrived in London, in which he had said: 'I count on carrying liberty to the Batavians [the Dutch] as I have done to the Belgians; also that the Revolution will take place in Holland.' On the same date Brissot, in an outburst of flamboyant patriotism, proclaimed, 'We cannot be calm until Europe, all Europe, is in flames.'[9] Pitt and Grenville believed that the French were trying to force them to choose between declaring war and abandoning their Dutch ally and their own security. Grenville wrote to Auckland that he saw 'little doubt that the whole is a concerted plan to drive us to extremities'.[10]

By early 1793 circumstances seemed to show that the time was right to embark on hostilities, if war could not be averted. The Dutch seemed to be in earnest against France; Russia, Spain and several of the smaller European states were signalling their readiness to join in if Britain did. The King was increasingly in favour of a tough line against France, as was the country at large—a very different situation from that of 1791 and the Ochakov crisis. Sir James Bland Burges concluded on 18 December 1792 that the sooner war was begun the better, because public opinion was excellent, and there was 'an

---

9 Quoted in Blanning, *Origins of the French Revolutionary Wars*, pp.137, 141.

10 Ibid., p.141.

earnest desire to go to war with France'.[11] There was confidence in British power and resources in comparison with those of France, particularly in British naval power and finances. France appeared to be consumed by civil war and bankruptcy. Furthermore, while this was not an important consideration in the government's moves towards war, there was the added bonus that to do so would most probably split the Whig opposition in Parliament into those who would support the war and those who would continue to support the French.

If French aggression in the Low Countries was the primary element in Britain's entry into the war, however, it would be wrong to imagine that the philosophical menace of the Revolution was absent from the minds of minsters, either in the domestic sphere or in the arena of foreign relations. The attraction of revolutionary principles for a sector of the British population and the revolutionary tone of French foreign policy considerably increased the hostility of the British government towards the French Republic.

At first, the government had not identified the British radical movement with the French revolutionaries. In 1792, however, as British radicalism grew in strength and as the military success of the revolutionary armies forced itself on ministers' notice, it became difficult for them to separate the conquests of French arms from the spread of French doctrines, and they grew alarmed at the prospect of a radical attempt to impose French principles of government on Britain. The growth of the popular radical societies and evidence of the correspondence of some of these with the French National Convention, and reports of increasing violence within France (particularly the arrest and deposition of Louis XVI on 10 August 1792, and the September Massacres, in which some 1200 people were killed in Paris), dismayed ministers and prompted the two Royal Proclamations of May and December 1792, the first banning seditious publications and meetings, and the second calling out the militia and assembling Parliament. The building of barracks in Sheffield, Manchester, Nottingham, Birmingham, Coventry and Norwich was begun by the autumn, to accommodate troops in the event of civil unrest becoming unmanageable by ordinary restraints. A poor harvest triggered substantial domestic unrest to join the brew of French military success and British radical activity in ministers' minds. The common people in France had shown that they could be moved by political ideas as well as by hunger. Even more worrying than the actual activities of the radicals in Britain was the example they were being set by the revolutionaries in France.[12] Hence the anxiety caused to ministers by the boatloads of *émigrés* who were arriving in Britain, and increasingly so after the decree of the French Executive Committee on 25

---

11 Quoted in Holland Rose, 'The Struggle with Revolutionary France', p.220.

12 See, for instance, Dundas to the House of Commons, 13 December 1792, *P.H.*, xxx, 47.

August 1792 banishing refractory priests and after the September Massacres, in which over 200 priests were assassinated. Not all of the immigrants were clerical, and the government feared that some were agents of the republic, sent to instigate insurrection in Britain.

Its sense of foreboding was deepened by the French decrees of 19 November and 15 December promising to export the revolution by means of French arms wherever they might find support for French doctrines, and to requisition occupied countries in order to sustain revolutionary France in its military and proselytizing activities. Revolutionary foreign policy was unconventional and apparently without scruple or caution in the magnitude of its vision to impose republican government, it was feared, throughout Europe. The triumph of the French Republic in the Austrian Netherlands, its clear intention in the United Provinces, and the admiration, hope and communication with Paris it inspired in British and Irish radicals deeply alarmed the Pitt administration concerning French plans regarding Britain itself.

As T.C.W. Blanning has pointed out, the opposing ideologies of revolutionary France and Great Britain created fundamentally different criteria for assessing their mutual assets and weaknesses and therefore produced misunderstandings on both sides of the chances of success in any potential conflict.[13] On top of that, however, French foreign policy was conducted in terms of a new, proselytizing ideology, however inconsistently, while British policy continued to represent old values and traditions which emphasized balance-of-power notions of European relations. This affected not only the calculation of mutual resources for war, but also the issues over which armed conflict was begun and the manner in which the war was conducted.[14]

British ministers feared that the French government intended to transform international relations in line with its own revolutionary principles. Foreign policy, under the new French system, was formed by public debate rather than in discreet Cabinet discussions; treaties were made to conform to the universal natural rights of man rather than to the rights of nations and pragmatic balance-of-power considerations; and France intended to head a new diplomatic order in Europe in which the rights of the people against their sovereigns would be safeguarded.[15] As Grenville wrote to Auckland on 4

---

13 Blanning, *The Origins of the French Revolutionary Wars*, pp.163, 206, 208-9.

14 14 J.T. Murley, 'The Origins and Outbreak of the Anglo-French War of 1793', unpublished D.Phil. thesis (University of Oxford, 1959), pp.365–7; cf. Black, *British Foreign Policy in an Age of Revolutions*, p.465; Schofield, 'British Politicians and French Arms', p.201.

15 Black, *British Foreign Policy in an Age of Revolutions*, p.461. For a more extended account of the revolutionary practice of foreign policy and the offence it caused in Russia and the United States of America as well as in Britain, see Linda Frey and Marsha Frey, '"The Reign of the Charlatans is Over": The French Revolutionary Attack on Diplomatic

February 1793: 'It is to these views [of aggression and aggrandizement] rendered infinitely more dangerous by the principles of Anarchy with which they are connected, both in their means, and in their ultimate object, that His Majesty is to oppose a vigorous and effectual resistance.'[16] The opening of the River Scheldt in November 1792 was of little real advantage to France: it was an act of propaganda symbolic of the Convention's belief in the application of the doctrine of natural rights to international affairs. It might in fact have benefited Britain, allowing its traders to use both Antwerp and Amsterdam; but treaty obligations and the maintenance of international law were more important in the British view of foreign relations. Moreover, as a symbol of revolutionary abrogation of established rights both in external relations and in internal government, it could not be permitted to stand.

To Burke, then, France was dangerous because of its doctrines and doubly dangerous because those doctrines were armed. To the ministry, by contrast, France was a threat because it was aggressive, and doubly so because its aggression was inextricably linked to a revolutionary system of political thought. Ideology was necessary if secondary; the British government might not have committed itself to armed conflict because of French ideas, but it did go to war because of the effects of those ideas in practice. In reply to the Marquess of Lansdowne's criticism that the government was leading the country into 'a war of metaphysics', Lord Loughborough replied, 'but who were the metaphysicians? They were 120,000 French soldiers, and their cannon and bayonets were the arguments they used.'[17] It is likely that strategy was indeed primary in impelling the British government into war against Revolutionary France, but it is misleading to imply that ideological hostility therefore played only an insignificant role in the administration's attitudes. It was clearly responsible for heightening considerably the fear caused by the French seizure of the Low Countries and for widening the gap between the two states, eroding understanding not only of their respective resources but also of their manner of doing international business.

II At War With Armed Opinions

Throughout the 1790s ministers debated the nature of the war, and they did not ever come to a wholly unanimous verdict. Again, while traditional concerns were always essential, ideas continued to form a substantial part of the equation. Ministers were united, however, in beginning the conflict with what

---

Practice', *Journal of Modern History*, 55 (1993), 706-44. I am grateful to Michael Rapport for this reference.

16 BL Add. MS 34447, f.430v, Grenville to Auckland, 4 February 1793.

17 *P.H.*, xxx, 332, Loughborough, 1 February 1793.

Michael Fry has described as 'a faintly irresponsible optimism', convinced that it would be short and successful.[18] There was a sense that the British cause was right and just and destined to triumph. This optimism continued, to a greater or lesser degree, throughout 1793. Pitt admitted, for instance, that the recovery of Dunkirk by the French in December 1793 was 'a severe Check', but he was disposed to see it in the light of a spur to British exertions. On 6 March 1794 he told the House of Commons: 'There is no doubt that in the course of a campaign, the prospects of success will become more or less sanguine according to the complexion of events. But the true criterion of the success of the campaign, is to compare the general state of Europe with what it was at the commencement of the campaign.' The United Provinces had been saved; Condé, Valenciennes and Quesnoy had been seized; and, outside Europe, acquisitions had been made at the expense of France in both the East and West Indies. Whether or not they genuinely still felt it in succeeding years, ministers naturally continued to express optimism publicly concerning the outcome of the war.[19]

The only style of warfare of which the ministers had any experience was that of the more limited conflicts of the eighteenth century, and it is not surprising that they expected the present conflict to be merely another in the series. In this style of conflict, war was an instrument of diplomacy rather than a substitute for it, and it was fought for recognizable and attainable objectives. This was the warfare of Prussia and Austria, made of compromises, bargains and limited territorial aims; and, to a substantial extent, it was the warfare of Britain, based on maritime and colonial hostilities, and a limited military commitment to continental warfare via subsidies to foreign allies and Britain's own small and amateurish army, which depended on individual efforts and whose structure was highly resistant to change. It was a system which knew wars of interests, not ideological crusades. Some ministers, such as Henry Dundas, rarely saw the wars against revolutionary France in any other but a traditional light. He wrote of France in 1799, 'I am sure that country will always be the natural enemy of this, and if it is in our power we ought to use our best exertions to annihilate their naval power … we are a small spot in the ocean without territorial consequence, and our own power and dignity as well as the safety of Europe rests on our being the paramount commercial and naval

---

18 Michael Fry, *The Dundas Despotism* (Edinburgh, 1992), p.188; BL Add MS 34449, f.23, Grenville to Auckland, 8 March 1793; A. Aspinall (ed.), *The Later Correspondence of George III*, 5 vol.s (Cambridge, 1962-68) [hereafter *LCGIII*], ii, 26, George III to Dundas, 7 April 1793.

19 *P.H.*, xxx, 1485, Pitt, 6 March 1794. See, for instance, *P.H.*, xxxi, 1442–3, Grenville to the House of Lords, 30 March 1795; *P.H.*, xxxii, 142, the King's Speech, 21 October 1795; Lord Auckland, *Some Remarks on the Apparent Circumstances of the War in the Fourth Week of October 1795* (London, 1795), pp.9–12, 66-7.

power of the world.' In the following year, in the midst of his struggle to send an expedition to Egypt to defend Britain's Indian trade against the threat posed by Napoleon, he wrote to the Lord Chancellor:

> When we depart from great leading principles uniformly adhered to in the Wisdom of our Ancestors, I cannot help being jealous of what is to happen afterwards ... This is to me the more distressing, because I protest solemnly I cannot discover the temptation we were under to depart from our Antient Practice.

Likewise, the Marquess of Buckingham saw nothing new in France attempting to extend its borders and impose the power and influence of its government throughout Europe—this had been its consistent aim since the late seventeenth century.[20]

This, however, was only one side of the picture, for the opposition of the British government to French revolutionary ideology had continued after the outbreak of war in February 1793. In particular, ministers continued to oppose the impact of the Revolution on French foreign policy and its conduct. There was, firstly, a recognition that France was fighting in a new way. It was 'a military democracy, actuated by the energies, the secrecy, and the decision of despotism'. The French 'Nation in Arms' had employed 'the new invention of raising an armed force by the operation of popular tyranny', they were 'waging war with their whole substance', posing a universal threat, and the results were unpredictable to the British government.[21] It was even vaguely recognized that Britain itself might have to pursue a new kind of warfare. Auckland wrote to Pitt on 1 December 1794 to tell him that, 'exposed as we have been to a System of hostility equally new & dangerous, we seem hitherto to have pursued on our part only the old beaten ground of Warfare ... such Measures ... were not likely to prove adequate to the exigencies of the present War', and that 'it [is] expedient & even essential, to pursue the war by unusual and extraordinary Means'.[22] He declined, however, to dictate these to the Cabinet, who, he said, had access to greatly superior sources of information than he did.

The French Revolution was made animate in the language of ministers: it was a 'spirit of restlessness and intrigue', or 'the Spirit of Jacobinism', a spirit

---

20 Dundas quoted in Piers Mackesy, *War Without Victory: The Downfall of Pitt 1799–1802* (Oxford, 1984), p.13; BL Add. MS 40102, f.72, Dundas to Loughborough, 14 Sept. 1800; Historical Manuscripts Commission, *Report on the Manuscripts of J.B. Fortesque, Esq., Preserved at Dropmore*, 10 vol.s (London, 1892–1927) [hereafter *Dropmore*], ii, 390, Buckingham to Grenville, 7 April 1793.

21 Charles Long, *A View of the Relative State of Great Britain and France, at the Commencement of the Year 1796* (London, 1796), p.42; *P.H.*, xxx, 1065, Auckland, 21 January 1794; *P.H.*, xxx, 587, the Solicitor General, 15 March 1793.

22 BL Add. MSS 34453, ff. 94, 94v.

which persisted long after the fall of Robespierre and the leaders of the Jacobin club of Paris. 'It is in power alone that moderatism differs from Jacobinism,' explained Canning, 'its virulence remains unimpaired.'[23] The Duke of Portland could still describe the French government in 1798 as 'that tremendous monster'; and even Dundas warned the Commons after Bonaparte's coup of 18 *Brumaire* 1799 that the Jacobinical government of France was only at an end in terms of its form—in substance and in essence it was unchanged.[24] Ministers claimed that the war involved a battle for the fundamental principles of society. Pitt told the House of Commons on 12 February 1793 that the French had thrown down the challenge of principles 'not levelled against particular nations, but against every country where there was any form of government established ... calculated every where to sow the seeds of rebellion and civil contention, and to spread war from one end of Europe to the other, from one end of the globe to the other'. George Canning, not yet a minister, but Pitt's *protégé* and a loyal ministerialist, sounded almost Burkean when he defended the war as 'a war of passion' in January 1794.[25]

Some of this was ministerial rhetoric. But it translated into practical terms without being divested wholly of its counter-revolutionary content. The King's Speech on 30 December 1794, for instance, informed Parliament that Britain was fighting for 'the deliverance of Europe from the greatest danger with which it has been threatened since the establishment of civilized society'.[26] This might mean particularly that Britain's future economic and political welfare were understood to be in jeopardy, which it was the business of government ministers to protect; but they were jeopardized precisely because of the sort of war that France was fighting, which in turn was made possible by its revolutionary doctrines.[27]

Moreover, the war was internal as well as external, and this too cast the war in an ideological light for government ministers. The radicals continued to work and hope for political reform in Britain through 1794 and 1795, and they

---

23 Dundas to Sir James Murray, 12 September 1792, quoted in Harvey Mitchell, *The Underground War Against Revolutionary France. The Missions of William Wickham 1794–1800* (Oxford, 1965), p.26; BL Add. MS 34453, f.97v., Auckland to Pitt, 1 December 1794; Canning, *P.H.*, xxxi, 1011, 30 December 1794.

24 *LCGIII*, iii, 135, the Duke of Portland to Pitt, 5 October 1798; *P.H.*, xxxiv, 1242–4, Dundas, 3 February 1800. Towards the end of 1799, in private, Dundas did suggest that the Jacobin element of French government was declining, but Grenville rounded on him immediately—see *Dropmore*, vi, 37–9, 47, Dundas to Grenville and Grenville to Dundas, 24 and 25 November 1799.

25 *P.H.*, xxx, 347, Pitt, 12 February 1793; *The Letter-Journal of George Canning, 1793-1795*, ed. Peter Jupp, Camden IVth Series, vol. 41 (London, 1991), p.58.

26 *P.H.*, xxxi, 961.

27 In fact, many of the military policies implemented by the French Republic in 1793-94, such as the citizen army, had been suggested long before the Revolution by *ancien régime* military theorists.

tapped the unease and distress in the country caused by war-weariness and poor harvests. The naval mutinies of 1797 were believed to have been instigated by radical agents in order to weaken Britain's defences severely, moreover, and it was feared that the same activity was being industriously pursued among soldiers.[28] Since the popular radical societies claimed to subscribe to the principles of the enemy, the government was fighting enemies within as well as enemies without. Perception of the role of the Parliamentary Opposition was blurred. As part of the propertied elite, they were only hazily connected by ministers with the dangerous forces of radicalism. Yet the connection was thought real enough to be an anxiety: on one occasion, after Fox had toasted 'the people, our sovereign' at the Whig Club, Pitt wondered whether he should try to get the House of Commons to send him to the Tower of London for a spell, and in the end had him struck off the Privy Council instead.[29]

Philip Schofield has attempted to explain the new, ideological and the old-fashioned, interest-based aspects of the British government's perception of the war by chronology, maintaining that ministers, for all practical purposes, largely abandoned their opposition to French revolutionary principles after 1795. In favour of his argument, he enlists the government's first announcement of its willingness to make peace, in October 1795, and the cowing of the radical movement in Britain especially after the Two Acts of December 1795 against Seditious Meetings and Treasonable Practices, which allowed ministers to think again of British radicals and French revolutionaries as two separate threats. The stated views of Henry Dundas, Charles Long and Lord Auckland also fit comfortably into this interpretation.[30] Schofield contends that counter-revolutionary rhetoric was used in the first years of the war to justify the conflict and its conduct, and that, in turn, this rhetoric must have influenced the conduct of the war. The pursuit of peace from late 1795 onwards was also justified by ministers partly on similar ideological grounds, that is, that with the smothering of the radical movement, the war to save the British constitution had been won.[31]

This argument is quite persuasive, but not entirely convincing. Counter-revolutionary rhetoric continued to be used in the ministerial defence of the

---

28 *P.H.*, xxxiii, 798, 806-7, Pitt, 2 June 1797. On the radicals and the war, see chapter 5.

29 *Dropmore*, iv, 187, Pitt to Grenville, 5 May 1798; *LCGIII*, iii, 59, Pitt to George III, 8 May 1798.

30 See *P.H.*, xxxii, 603, Dundas, 9 December 1795; *Dropmore*, vi, 37–9, Dundas to Grenville, 24 Nov. 1799; Long, *A View of the Relative State* (1796); idem, *The New Era of the French Revolution, or, Observations Upon the Constitution Proposed in the Convention, on the Twenty-Third of June, 1795* (London, 1795); Auckland, *Some Remarks on the Apparent Circumstances of the War.*

31 Schofield, 'British Politicians and French Arms', pp.17–18, 21–2.

war and their conduct of it, especially after peace was not to be had, in 1796 or 1797; nor had it been drained of effect on policy. After the failure of the Lille talks in 1797, for example, Grenville complained that the French republican government wished 'to spread confusion over Europe, to prolong the miseries of their own country on Jacobin principles and by Jacobin means'.[32] Moreover, Schofield's analysis does not account for Grenville's increasing keenness to help the French royalists, or indeed the lack of British aid sent to them between 1793 and 1795, when the counter-revolutionary sympathies of the government are supposed to have been at their height. Certainly, after the entrance of the Portland Whigs to the Cabinet in July 1794, the government contained a significant lobby whose crusading views were not to be rapidly eroded in the manner Schofield suggests.

What Burke and other 'pure' ideologues often failed to see was that ministers were not spectators of the drama, as they were, but principal actors in it, whose strategy was constrained by a powerful enemy and by limited resources, difficult allies, and the need to justify themselves before Parliament and the nation. The need to produce viable and successful strategies inevitably shaped ministers' views of the very nature of the war. While it was for philosophers, political writers and publicists to oppose the ideological basis of the French Revolution itself, it was the task of the government to oppose that conduct which was attacking society rather than the principles behind the conduct. This did not mean that they were indifferent to those principles. Ministers were preoccupied with the balance of power in Europe, but they recognized that it was the Revolution within France which caused it to destroy that balance of power.[33] Canning told the House of Commons in 1794 that he could not 'see such nice distinctions' as that between opposing French arms and opposing French principles, since the principles propelled the arms.[34] In December 1796, in the debate on the failure of the Paris negotiations, Pitt complained of the unique and unacceptable mode of foreign relations now carried on by the French—that they held their republican laws and constitution to be the sole authority on what could happen to territory conquered by them, and that this could not be negotiable.[35] Responding to a charge of fruitlessly pitting arms against opinions in 1799, he told Parliament: 'We are not in arms against the opinions of the closet ... We are at war with armed opinions.'[36] In

---

32 *P.H.*, xxxiii, 982–3, Grenville, 8 November 1797.

33 H.T. Dickinson, 'The French Revolution and the Counter-Revolution in Britain', in Hans-Christoph Schröder and Hans-Dieter Metzger (eds.), *Aspekte der Französischen Revolution* (Darmstadt, 1992), p.258.

34 *P.H.*, xxx, 1322, Canning, 31 January 1794.

35 Ernest Rhys (ed.), *Orations on the War by William Pitt* (Everyman), pp.220, 224, 30 December 1796.

36 Ibid., xxxiv, 1051, Pitt, 7 June 1799.

effect, he was calling for a counter-revolution against French foreign policy, a major aspect of the Revolution, and the one with which the British government was principally concerned.

Clearly, not all ministers held the purely ideological aspect of the conflict in equal importance. Dundas, though willing to accept that the revolutionary character of the French government made it particularly dangerous and inimical, was chiefly concerned to weaken Britain's old rival as much as possible by winning as many French and (once the United Provinces had been conquered by France in 1795) Dutch colonial possessions as possible. His aim was the greatness of Britain, not the destruction of the Revolution.[37] William Windham, Lord Spencer and, later, Lord Grenville were much more sympathetic to Burkean, crusading ideas in support of a strategy of attacking French revolutionary principles within France itself than were Dundas and Pitt. The premier was more anxious to defeat French revolutionary ideas at work on the balance of power in Europe and to prevent the French revolutionary government from attacking other states than to destroy that government, and this view of counter-revolution became the dominant voice of the government.

III Aims

Differing views of the nature of the enemy and of the war among ministers naturally produced varying opinions about what British aims in the war should be. They were careful not to pledge themselves to anything too clearly defined, perhaps also because this might have committed them to war for an indefinite period of time until these objectives were achieved.[38] 'Security', as the Opposition MP George Tierney pointed out in 1800, was a justifiable and perennial war aim, but what exactly did it mean in practical terms? In fact, British war aims were unclear throughout the 1790s. Parliamentarians spent much time trying to define them; in November 1797 Lord Gwydir complained that 'the powers of language have been so often employed to describe the complicated nature of this war, that words have lost their effect by repetition'.[39]

The fundamental war aim was to repel what ministers claimed was an unprovoked attack on British interests by France. As Pitt said in April 1793, in a sense it did not matter what Britain's grounds for war against France were, 'for while they were discussing that principle, the circumstance that arose was,

37 Matheson, *Life of Henry Dundas*, p.186.

38 Michael Duffy, 'British Policy in the War Against Revolutionary France', in Jones (ed.), *Britain and Revolutionary France*, p.21. See, for instance, *P.H.*, xxxiv, 1046, Pitt, 7 June 1799; *P.H.*, xxxiv, 44–5, Canning, 11 December 1798.

39 *P.H.*, xxxiii, 860, Lord Gwydir, 2 November 1797.

that France had declared war against this country'.[40] This aim was taken up with renewed urgency after the failure of the attempts to negotiate a peace in 1796 and 1797—success in the conflict was necessary for survival, and it included the preservation of the British constitution. 'The war was not made to prevent France from giving herself the constitution that she might prefer; but to prevent her from giving to Great Britain, and to her allies, all the wretchedness and horrors of a wild democracy.'[41] Invasion was a very real fear, heightened by anxiety concerning a Jacobin fifth column within Britain.

Repelling French aggression also involved the preservation of the integrity of the Low Countries as well as that of Britain itself. Auckland wrote to Grenville from the United Provinces at the beginning of the war: 'Men, Commanders, Ships & Money, We could not ask for more if this Country was a part of Yorkshire; but I incline to think that it should be considered as such for the present.'[42] The British government was also anxious to restore the Belgian provinces to Austrian sovereignty, despite Austria's manifest lack of interest in recovering them. Ministers therefore wanted a restoration of the territorial *status quo ante* and of the balance of power in Europe. This held attractions for those of different persuasions concerning the nature of the war—Grenville and others of more Burkean convictions wanted to see Jacobinism at least contained within France, Dundas and those more preoccupied with material matters also wanted to see France stripped of its revolutionary prizes, while Pitt thought that it held out the best hope of a stable peace. George III was particularly anxious for the fate of his electorate of Hanover.[43] A restoration of the *status quo ante* would, moreover, defeat the ambitions of Prussia and Austria to take advantage of the conflict to seize whatever territories they could. So concerned were they, however, that the Austrian Netherlands should not remain in French hands that, in 1796, ministers compromised long-held British policy by trying to persuade Prussia to give Bavaria to Austria and receive the Belgian provinces (once they were retrieved from France) in compensation. In 1799 Grenville toyed with the idea of joining them with the United Provinces as one independent state.[44]

A secondary aim on which most of the Cabinet could unite was that of indemnity for itself and for its allies—as Pitt told the House of Commons in 1799, somewhat coyly, 'Our simple object is security, just security, with a little mixture of indemnification.' To Dundas, it was a major objective. In his opinion, Britain, having been dragged into the war most unjustifiably by

40 Ibid., xxx, 715, Pitt, 25 April 1793.

41 Ibid., xxxi, 1137, Auckland, 6 January 1795.

42 BL Add. MS 34448, f.186, Auckland to Grenville, 15 February 1793.

43 See, for instance, *LCGIII*, ii, 327, George III to Pitt, 5 April 1795; ibid., 401–2, George III to Pitt, 13 September 1795; ibid., iii, 97, George III to Grenville, 24 July 1798.

44 *Dropmore*, v, 328–9, Grenville to Sir Charles Whitworth, 27 August 1799.

France, had every reason to make the most of the opportunity to defend itself by seizing what new colonies it could, not so much for the purpose of territorial aggrandizement as for that of acquiring new markets.[45] Acquisitions of this nature were also sought simply in order to strengthen Britain's hand in future peace negotiations.

Ministers further wanted to be able to treat with a stable French government for a secure peace, and Opposition politicians were repeatedly told that Britain would not agree to negotiations until there was a firmly-established administration in France to provide some guarantee that a peace settlement would be upheld. It was hoped that this had been accomplished by the new constitution of July 1795, and in October of that year ministers began to express a willingness to treat for peace; but the triumph of the left in France in September 1797 and Bonaparte's *coup d'état* in November 1799 made this desire for a stable French government an objective of continuing relevance. 'A stable French government' was a vague demand in which ministers of all opinions could acquiesce. When it was more closely defined, however, disagreements were exposed. Pitt said in June 1793 that it could be achieved in one of three ways: if the French Revolutionary system was completely overturned from within France, if it was extinguished by external force, or if it was sufficiently weakened to render it safe to other European states.[46] Each of these solutions found advocates in the British government: most ministers would have been happy to see the first occur; Windham and Spencer pressed for the second, with the support of Grenville, Portland and George III; and Pitt leaned towards the third, while Dundas urged its adoption by the administration.[47]

Yet even those who wanted to change the revolutionary system of government in France were divided as to the form of government that should replace it. The King, and those ministers more influenced by Burke's thinking were, unsurprisingly, more decidedly in favour of a monarchical restoration. William Windham, who was Secretary for War from 1794–96 with a special responsibility for Britain's dealings with the French *émigrés* and counter-revolutionaries, expressed himself vehemently on the subject on numerous occasions.[48] The Duke of Portland also confessed himself very unhappy with the Cabinet's decision in autumn 1795 to be less committed to a restoration. Grenville was more cautious for the first few years of the war, but from late

---

45 *P.H.*, xxxiv, 1047, Pitt, 7 June 1799; ibid., xxx, 1251, Dundas, 21 January 1794.

46 Ibid., xxx, 1017, Pitt, 17 June 1793.

47 Pitt wavered on this, however; on his desire in the early years of the war for a change of government in France, see Schofield, 'English Conservative Thought', pp.192–5, 201.

48 See, for instance, BL Add. MS 37846, f.50, Windham to Grenville, 25 September 1796; ibid., 37844, f.120, Windham to Pitt, 31 January 1796.

1796 he leant increasingly towards a Burkean view of the conflict. By 1799 he believed that the restoration of the French monarchy was not only a feasible objective but also that which ought to be pursued by the European coalition: 'nothing will terminate this war but such success in France as enables us to restore the monarchy'.[49]

The British government as a whole, however, even when it came closest to backing a monarchical solution, never stipulated the exact form of monarchy, since it was recognized that it was necessary that whatever was eventually established should be widely supported within France.[50] Most ministers did not see a restored Bourbon monarchy as a *sine qua non* of peace; they vehemently repudiated suggestions from the Opposition benches that this was their goal, and they were uneasy when Lord Hood took Toulon in the name of Louis XVII in August 1793. But having laid claim to a French port, it was necessary to define British aims more clearly. In their own manifesto to the people of Toulon of 29 October 1793, they expressed a preference for a hereditary monarchy as a long-term solution.[51] This did not, however, necessarily bind the Cabinet to a restoration policy for the rest of the war. William Wickham, the British envoy in Switzerland, was instructed not to commit the government to any particular form of constitution for France in his negotiations with the constitutional monarchists in 1794.[52] Another reason for avoiding clarifying this point was the ministers' desire to use all parties who would help to attack the Republic—ultra-royalist, constitutional monarchist, or revolutionary moderate—and their consequent anxiety to offend none of these unnecessarily.

Pitt himself was willing to listen to any solution which might conceivably hasten peace, and he swung between the opinions of Grenville and Dundas, with both of whom he was very close.[53] Michael Duffy has shown that there was no significant difference over policy between him and Grenville until late 1796;[54] and, even after this, Grenville and Windham were often able

---

49 *Dropmore*, iii, 135–6, the Duke of Portland to Grenville, 23 September 1795; ibid., v, 148, Grenville to Thomas Grenville, 16 July 1795; Jupp, *Lord Grenville*, p.223.

50 See, for instance, BL Add. MS 37845, f.114, Spencer to Windham, 18 September 1793; see also Ehrman, *The Reluctant Transition*, pp.599–600.

51 PRO 30/8/334 f.192v., draft of the Toulon manifesto with Pitt's annotations; see also BL Add. MS 36808, f. 55, Grenville to Lord Bute, 19 June 1795; for doubts concerning defining a preference, see ibid., 34451, f.62v, Auckland to Grenville, 18 May 1793; PRO 30/8/140, Grenville to Pitt, 7 October 1793. See also Mori, *William Pitt and the French Revolution*, pp.159ff.

52 Richards, 'The Problem of the Monarchy', p.174.

53 See *Malmesbury Diaries and Correspondence*, iii, 521, 590–1, 1 and 24 September 1797.

54 Michael Duffy, 'Pitt, Grenville and the Control of British Foreign Policy in the 1790s', in Jeremy Black (ed.), *Knights Errant and True Englishmen: British Foreign Policy, 1660-1800* (Edinburgh, 1989). See also John Ehrman, *The Younger Pitt*, vol. iii, *The*

to persuade him to send assurances of help and more substantial aid to the French counter-revolutionary forces. But even the views of Grenville and Windham did not always match entirely; Windham was more insistent on the priority of military and material aid to the royalists over considerations of the rest of the European theatre of war. By September 1800, Dundas was having to acknowledge at least five different classes of opinion within the Cabinet: those who maintained that only a Bourbon restoration would produce European peace and British security; those who insisted on a counter-revolution in France but would not stipulate a Bourbon restoration; those who thought that the Napoleonic government had established itself sufficiently to warrant treating with it as the *de facto* power in France; those who would negotiate with France but only in conjunction with Britain's allies; and those who believed that it was no longer possible to influence France by armed force and that Britain should make peace whenever practicable, putting its own interests first.[55]

It was not, therefore, a Cabinet of pure ideologues who fought the war against France, nor indeed one of pure strategists. Rather, it was an administration struggling to find the most realistic practical solution to an unprecedented problem of international dimensions, and an administration whose antipathy to the French revolutionary system and its desire to replace it with *some* other form of government was clear, and thus too its acknowledgement that the war had an important ideological dimension.

As well as being less than transparently clear, the British war aims were badly flawed in two further ways. First, they differed from those of the other European powers engaged in the war against France. In the early part of 1793 Austria and Prussia were much more interested in attacking France itself and attempting a strike at Paris, than was Britain; but, ironically, as British ministers became more persuaded of the value of helping the French counter-revolutionaries and of the urgency of self-defence, so the rulers of the German nations became disenchanted with hostility towards France and more concerned to further their own territorial interests in Poland, which was partitioned by them in 1793 and again in 1795. Prussian ministers several times contemplated alliance with France, so little committed to the defeat of Jacobinism were they. By the time of the formation of the Second Coalition, in 1799, the only common aim was no more than one of re-establishing general

---

Continuing Struggle (London, 1996), p.64: after c. 1796 it seems that Pitt could be quite hard-headed about Grenville, to the point of contemplating Grenville's potential resignation over differences of opinion regarding peace conditions.

55 BL Add MSS 40102 ff.79–81, memorandum by Dundas, 22 September 1800. This list does not identify those who held each of these views; a rough guess might suggest that Spencer and Portland may have fallen into the first category, Grenville into the second, Dundas into the third, Pitt into the fourth, and Chatham and Camden into the last.

tranquility, and, finally, in the planning of the Dutch campaign of 1799, objectives were subordinated to strategy in an effort to achieve unity.[56] The British Cabinet disapproved of the Continental Powers using the war to rearrange the map of Europe, and they deliberately ignored continental politicking over such issues as the partition of Poland. The territory they themselves wanted was elsewhere, in the East and West Indies, and in Europe they wanted the *status quo ante bellum* to be restored.[57] Second, Britain had too many objectives not only for their own compatibility, but also for British resources to fulfil. Pitt and Grenville resented Dutch pressure to send British ships and seamen when they were sure that the Dutch could find sufficient of their own men to defend themselves.[58] Each time a new expedition was launched, the pinch was severely felt. George III wrote to Pitt on 14 September 1793, concerning the defence of Toulon: 'The misfortune of our situation is that we have too many objectives to attend to, and our force consequently must be too small at each place.'[59]

IV The Business of War

Inexperienced in military matters and ill-prepared for a conflict on any significant scale against France, the British government tended to be reactive rather than proactive in its conduct of the conflict. Certainly, as John Ehrman points out, its commitment and realism increased rapidly from the start of the war, when a mere 1500 troops were sent to Holland and confined to a day's march from their ports, whereas a year later 40,000 British and German troops were sent under the Duke of York to take part in the allied attempt to march to Paris.[60] With limited resources, however, and no clear agreement on their objectives, it was natural that ministers should in general respond to the pressure of events rather than initiate coherent strategies, despite ambitions to and perhaps delusions of control and leadership of the allied campaign. They were never so willing (nor, perhaps, so able) as France was to pay the price of unlimited war by making an absolute effort in terms of crippling taxation and a conscripted army. They consistently looked, in the 1790s, for ways in which

56 Piers Mackesy, *Statesmen at War: The Strategy of Overthrow* (London, 1974), pp.30, 35, 152.

57 As Windham wrote ruefully to Grenville on 13 February 1795, complaining of Austria's preoccupation with territorial acquisition, 'Our mouths are unfortunately stopped by our own proceedings in the West and East Indies' (*Dropmore*, iii, 19).

58 See, for example, BL Add. MSS 46519, ff.47–9, Pitt to Auckland, 2 March 1793; ibid., 37850, ff.22–7, Grenville to Lord St. Helens, 25 September 1794.

59 J. Holland Rose (ed.), *Pitt and Napoleon. Essays and Letters* (London, 1912), p.225.

60 Ehrman, *The Reluctant Transition*, pp.329–31.

the French Republic could be destroyed at minimum cost to Britain. It was a war effort dominated by politicians rather than generals, and the political leadership was neither single-minded nor decisive enough to come close to a 'total war' mentality. The desirability of overthrowing the French government, however, was perhaps a concept as near to one of unlimited war as British politicians of the time could come, despite their only delayed and partial emulation of French-style warfare. There was, nevertheless, a constant struggle between tactics of attrition and strategies of attack, for aggression was necessary to overthrow a government, but the inclination of most ministers was towards enduring the French frenzy on the Continent until it wore itself out and, meanwhile, pursuing naval warfare.

Their assessment of the value of British military involvement on the Continent oscillated, depending on the current circumstances of the war and on their individual priorities. Lord Auckland, who favoured a war of attrition, wanted the government to withdraw from all continental exertions except helping the United Provinces (before its conquest by France in 1795) and Sardinia. After the failure of the first Coalition, in 1795, the consensus was for abandoning all Continental operations and concentrating on colonial defence and acquisition, and hoping that the Republic would collapse internally. Windham disagreed, however, as he was always loath to let the French counter-revolutionaries down and give them cause to despair of aid from Britain; and Grenville maintained that France could only be beaten by a combination of allied arms and internal revolt.[61] Dundas, on the other hand, was convinced that British troops ought to be used only for efforts made for strictly British interests which, to him, pointed to colonial operations.[62]

To Dundas, the navy afforded Britain its best security for outlasting the struggle with France and its best hope for obtaining satisfactory terms at the peace negotiations. The navy was required to defend the country from invasion and to protect and sustain Britain's overseas trade and its far-flung colonies; more aggressively, it was used to destroy French ships, to blockade French ports (suffocating trade and rendering the French navy inactive), to prevent neutral ships from supplying France with military goods or from transporting French goods elsewhere and to sustain military ventures across the world. Nelson's victory at Aboukir Bay in August 1798 was crucially important, not just for the safety of British trade with India, but also because it encouraged

---

61 BL Add. MS 34453, f.99, Auckland to Pitt, 1 December 1794; *LCGIII*, ii, 400–1, Cabinet Minute, 7 September 1795; BL Add. MS 37844, f.105v., Windham to Pitt, 16 October 1795; Jupp, *Lord Grenville*, p.214.

62 Mackesy, *War Without Victory*, pp.11–12. See also BL Add. MSS 40102, ff.59–68, Dundas's memorandum on a possible expedition to Belleisle, 22 July 1800; *Dropmore*, iv, 433-5, Dundas to Pitt, [December 1798]; BL Add. MSS 40102, ff.71–3, Dundas to the Lord Chancellor, 14 September 1800.

Russia's eventual entry into the war in the following year. Pitt, too, was often persuaded by Dundas's arguments; but sometimes he was swayed by Grenville, who played down the threat to the colonies and to the Indian trade, and failed to see the value of Malta.[63] Grenville's main concern from a naval point of view was to defend the practice of regulating neutral shipping against its critics.[64] The King was also often doubtful of Dundas's colonial strategies, understanding the necessity of defence and acquisition, but believing that they diverted troops from more urgent purposes.[65]

However, because they were more concerned to defeat Jacobinism than at heart Dundas was, most other ministers recognized that France must eventually be defeated on the continent. The most usual strategy was for Britain's small army to lead expeditions on behalf of the United Provinces (in 1793–94 and in 1799), and otherwise to engage in continental military efforts through alliance with the other Powers. In 1793 the British Cabinet had hoped for a system of stable war-alliances which would share responsibilities for operations and supplies and which would be committed to continuing the war until a general peace was agreed. As usual, Britain hired large numbers of German mercenary soldiers to increase its own forces but, even with these, its total military strength was small, and its main contribution to the continental military effort was by way of loans and subsidies to the allies. Loans and subsidies, however, were rarely an unmitigated success. Britain was slow to pay instalments of its subsidies to Prussia, Austria was slow to repay instalments of its British loans, and hard feelings were not slow to grow. When loans or subsidies were not an option, ministers held out the bait of prospective territorial gains for the allies' indemnification.[66] They tried hard to accommodate the allies, for the sake of the continuation of the coalition, and much of the diplomatic correspondence of the decade was simply engaged in the tortuous process of trying to create and hold a continental alliance together.

However frustrated they themselves were with the allies, ministers developed various arguments to justify to MPs their large spending on loans and subsidies. It was traditional British policy to pay mercenaries and allies, because of Britain's relatively small population and correspondingly small

---

63 See, for instance, BL Add. MS 40102, f.81v., Grenville to Dundas, 23 April 1800; also Ehrman, *The Consuming Struggle*, pp.358, 374, 378, 380.

64 Jupp, *Lord Grenville*, p.158; *P.H.*, xxxi, 1444, Grenville to the House of Lords, 24 March 1795; BL Add. MSS 38734, ff.325–6, Grenville to Dundas, 29 November 1797. Grenville also published the *Letters of Sulpicius. On the Northern Confederacy* (London, 1801).

65 *LCGIII*, ii, 493, George III to Dundas, 3 July 1796; ibid., 121–2, George III to Dundas, 16 November 1793; ibid., 384, George III to Dundas, 19 August 1795; ibid., 553, George III to Dundas, 10 March 1797; ibid., iii, 424, George III to Dundas, 5 October 1800.

66 BL Add. MS 36808, f.24, Grenville to Lord Bute (ambassador at Madrid), 14 April 1795.

army; moreover, it saved British lives.[67] The end for which the alliances were formed was more important than the means that were used to obtain it: as Canning declared in 1794, ministers 'might with confidence tell the nation, we require this money, not to support a precarious or ideal balance of power, but to enable us to defend your government, your property, and your lives, against an enemy who is waging a war for your utter extermination!'[68] Britain's alliances might not be perfect, but they were better than none at all. Even if British hopes were not matched by dazzling military victories, simply by engaging the French armies in battle the allied armies were distracting them from untold acts of destruction. Alliances were good for trade at present, and would enable Britain to press for better peace terms in the future.[69] For public consumption, then, ministers displayed great trust in Britain's allies, although they also blamed them for Britain's misfortunes in the war when it was convenient to do so.[70]

For all the arguments in favour of Continental or maritime warfare, however, the issue of military interference within France itself was bound to play a substantial part in the government's discussions on the conduct of the war as ministers came increasingly to hope for the overthrow of the French revolutionary government, from mid-1793 onwards. At first they looked for an internal counter-revolution which, by re-establishing the Bourbon monarchy in France, would eventually lead to the restoration of general peace in Europe; but it was more realistic to recognize that external force would be necessary. Interference within France was justified in Parliament by claims that it was necessary to obtain sufficient security and reparation for the war from France and that attack was the best form of defence.

The King was naturally a supporter of a counter-revolutionary strategy. On the capture of Toulon, he wrote: 'I trust this is the real beginning of a counter revolution in France, and I am proud that history must admit that the conduct of England has struck the first essential blow in the cause of religion, law and the rights of humanity, as well as of every civilized nation.' To Windham, 'all blows not aimed at the body of France [were] thrown away',[71] and he used every argument he could think of to induce Pitt and Grenville to honour their promises of supplies to the French royalists and to commit

67 *P.H.*, xxxi, 451, Grenville, 30 April 1794; ibid., xxxi, 442, Pitt, 30 April 1794.

68 Ibid., xxx, 1320, Canning, 31 January 1794. See also ibid., xxxi, 1294–9, Pitt, 5 February 1795.

69 Ibid., xxxi, 1395, Pitt, 24 March 1795; ibid., xxxiii, Pitt, 4 April 1797. See also ibid., xxxiv, 43–62, Canning, 11 December 1798; ibid., xxxiii, 240–1, Grenville, 4 April 1797; ibid., xxxiii, 471, Pitt, 1 May 1797.

70 See, for example, ibid., xxxiii, 1341, Grenville, March 1798.

71 *P.H.*, xxx, 1016–7, Pitt, 17 June 1793; ibid., xxxi, 678–80, Earl of Mansfield, 30 May 1794; *LCGIII*, ii, 94, George III to the Prince of Wales, 15 September 1793; *Dropmore*, v, 271–2, Windham to Grenville, 10 August 1799.

themselves further to them. The French royalists could not survive on mere goodwill, and yet very little would be enough to please them. If Britain meant to win the war, surely it should utilize whatever help it could find.[72] Even if an attempt to attack France on its own ground failed, the worst that could happen to Britain was 'a necessity of making peace without accomplishing the object, that can alone make peace desireable, the overthrow of the Revolutionary Government. But is not this necessity all but incurred the moment you say, that nothing is ever to be attempted from hence in the Interior of France?'[73] Dundas, however, was willing to use British forces only to establish a secure communication with the French coast, for the purpose of transporting supplies: 'operations *in the interior* must be carried on by the French themselves'. This would leave British troops available for what, to him, were more important purposes. He pronounced himself 'a sceptic on all that subject'.[74]

Given the Cabinet's lack of united effort in one direction, it is not surprising that it tended to take an ambiguous attitude towards the French royalists. Most ministers saw the support of French counter-revolutionary activity as a device to weaken rather than to defeat France,[75] and they were reluctant to stir up insurrection until they could be sure of supporting it with a concerted allied push into France. Moreover, French ultra-royalists and constitutional royalists were bitterly opposed, and the British government was reluctant to support one group more than another. For this reason, ministers hesitated at first to ally with the *émigré* French princes, who, in any case, did not endear themselves to the British government by their arrogance and refusal to co-operate with the constitutionalists. Nor did ministers always altogether trust Frenchmen of any political persuasion to oppose any description of French government more than they opposed a British attack.[76] Wholehearted support was further denied by the government's willingness to consider treating with any form of stable French government. Government inefficiency and uncertainty combined to frustrate counter-revolutionaries intensely, as supplies failed with monotonous regularity to arrive as promised and the synchronization of uprisings and aid was never achieved. Authority was divided between British paymasters and French leaders, coordination was poor and skilled direction of campaigns consequently often failed to materialize. The British more often than not used the counter-revolutionaries in order to

---

72 BL Add. MSS 37846, f.56, Windham to Grenville, 24 October 1797; *Dropmore*, iv, 101, Windham to Grenville, 22 February 1798; BL Add. MSS 37846, f.75v, Windham to Grenville, 2 May 1799; ibid., f.170, Windham to Grenville, 1 November 1799.

73 BL Add. MS 37844, f.225, Windham to Pitt, 27 December 1799.

74 Ibid., 40102, f.5, Dundas to the Duke of York, 25 July 1795.

75 See, for example, PRO 30/8/102 f.119, Pitt to the Earl of Elgin, 16 November 1793.

76 BL Add. MS 38230, f.220, Auckland to the Earl of Liverpool, 7 July 1795.

further their own designs, Puisaye being a notable example of this.[77] Until British devotion to the counter-revolutionary cause matched French revolutionary zeal, it was unlikely to succeed.

Nevertheless, the government's intention while it held Dunkirk, Toulon and Corsica was to restore civil government to its pre-revolutionary principles; and, while British aid was usually too little and too late, it was enough at least to help sustain the French resistance until Napoleon's seizure of power in late 1799. Indeed, the resources and attention paid in increasing proportions as the war progressed to the underground war with France make it one of the major aspects of the struggle. Because Britain rarely had either a bridgehead or an army of any size in western Europe, ministers had to rely on military activity among the French population if the revolutionary government was to be overthrown. The ministry was in contact for long periods of time with the royalist Puisaye in Brittany and the constitutionalist d'André, and Grenville's agent William Wickham, based in Geneva but with contacts all over western France, worked extremely hard for the furtherance of counter-revolution. The Duke of York fired propaganda material in hollow shells into Valenciennes in the midst of his siege of the town.[78] Pitt may or may not have allowed the bribery of French officials and speculation against the *assignat* to encourage the collapse of the Republic, but it is indisputable that increasingly large sums of money were spent by the British government to support the counter-revolution in France. Each time Britain assisted the counter-revolutionary cause in France, as Ehrman notes, the government was carried a step further towards endorsing the goal of a restored monarchy.[79] For the benefit of MPs, ministers portrayed the royalists as the 'multitudes of the French nation [who] wanted only protection and support, to bring them forward to crush that convention, under which [their] evils had become insupportable'.[80] However much ministers began by using the royalists as simply another weapon in their own war against the revolutionary government of France, their assistance to

---

77 See Maurice Hutt, *Chouannerie and Counter-Revolution. Puisaye, the Princes and British Government in the 1790s*, 2 vol.s (Cambridge, 1983), esp. pp.97, 152–61, 325–7, 525; Michael Duffy, 'British Diplomacy in the French Wars 1789–1815', in Dickinson (ed.), *Britain and the French Revolution*, pp.134–6.

78 Hutt, *Chouannerie and Counter-Revolution*; Mitchell, *The Underground War*; W.R. Fryer, *Republic or Restoration in France? 1794–7 The Politics of French Royalism, with particular reference to the activities of A.B.J. d'André* (Manchester, 1965); Burne, *The Noble Duke of York*, p.57; Elizabeth Sparrow, 'The Alien Office, 1792–1806', *Historical Journal*, 33:2 (1990), 361–84; idem, 'The Swiss and Swabian Agencies, 1795–1801', ibid., 35:4 (1992), 861–84; idem, 'Secret Service under Pitt's Administrations, 1792-1806', *History*, 83 (1998), 280-94.

79 Ehrman, *The Reluctant Transition*, p.582.

80 *P.H.*, xxxi, 414, Dundas, 14 April 1794.

the royalists looked like sympathy for their aims and propelled the Cabinet further in that direction than it might otherwise have gone.

At the same time as they tried to formulate a successful war strategy, ministers were preoccupied with unrest at home and in Ireland—so much so that at times it hindered the effective waging of the war.[81] Especially before 1796, the government seriously feared an insurrection in Britain planned by the radicals in conjunction with the French Jacobins, and these fears returned in full force with the naval mutinies at Spithead and the Nore in 1797, keeping the government worried for a full three months.[82] The government passed legislation to repress sedition—the Traitorous Correspondence Act (1793), the suspension of habeas corpus (1794–95, 1798–1801), the Two Acts against Treasonable Practices and Seditious Meetings (1795), and the Combination Acts (1799–1800). Close surveillance was kept over radical activities, the small secret service collecting details from magistrates, customs officials and the post office all over the country. Spies, informers and *agents provocateur* were used; radicals were tried for sedition in Scotland in 1793–94 and for treason in England in 1794. Ehrman notes that Pitt even considered supporting legislation which would have given magistrates the power to withold licenses to preach.[83]

Furthermore, recruitment for the army and navy was a constant concern for ministers. The militia was revitalized and new Volunteer Companies were established all over the country to add to the government's strength in defending the country against external aggression and internal unrest. Volunteer Corps were sanctioned in 1794;[84] the Supplementary Militia Act was passed in 1796; the militia were introduced into Scotland for the first time in 1797; and the Defence of the Realm Act was passed in 1798, to collect details of all adult males and the service they could render the state, thus showing a shift in government policy, as Linda Colley writes, 'from seeking quality support at home to seeking it in quantity'.[85] Resort had also to be made to crimps, press-gangs, quota schemes and the Militia Volunteers Act of 1799, whereby militiamen might put themselves forward for foreign service, despite ordinary regulations restricting their use to their own counties. Dundas,

---

81 Ehrman, *The Reluctant Transition*, pp.340–2, points out that Pitt's anxieties about internal unrest in spring 1794, and the steering through Parliament of the bill to suspend habeas corpus, caused the fateful delays in sending essential instalments of the subsidy to Prussia, thus delaying the arrival of the Prussian troops till they were too late to be of any use that year.

82 See *P.H.*, xxxi, 498–9, Pitt, 13 May 1794.

83 Ehrman, *The Consuming Struggle*, p.303 n.2.

84 *P.H.*, xxxi, 89–91, 26 March 1794, 'Plan for Providing more completely for the Security of the Country'.

85 Linda Colley, *Britons: Forging the Nation 1707–1837* (London, 1992), pp.289–90; *P.H.*, xxxiii, 1357, Dundas, 27 March 1798.

however, was so sanguine that he claimed privately to be hoping for an invasion attempt, in order to prove to Britain, France and the rest of the world the independence and invulnerability of Britain.[86]

Public opinion was taken also seriously by ministers, who had been taught its power by the Ochakov crisis of 1791. The war was 'marketed' with diligence: victories were puffed, defeats were excused and strategy was justified.[87] Days of general fasts and thanksgiving were proclaimed several times a year. Propaganda was used in an attempt to deceive the French,[88] but it was mostly directed at the British public. The government sponsored a considerable number of pamphlet and tract writers, spending about £5000 in the 1790s for this purpose. Various ministers and senior government officials—Pitt, Grenville, Dundas, James Bland Burges, Canning, Hawkesbury, Loughborough, Windham, Auckland and Long—were personally involved, either in terms of patronage of writers or by their own writing for publication. The rhetoric was often Burkean in tone.[89]

By his own confession, Pitt's *forte* was fiscal rather than military, and his ingenuity in public finance was exerted to the full to pay for the war. In 1793 Britain spent £8137 million on the conflict; in 1796 the figure was £28 254 million.[90] New indirect taxes were regularly announced; assessed taxes were raised; a 'Loyalty Loan' was raised in December 1796; a Voluntary Contribution was appealed for in 1798 (to which George III himself subscribed £20,000); a new land tax was established, also in 1798; income tax was introduced in 1799; public loans were raised to finance the allies; and the National Debt rose swiftly while the sinking fund deepened. The run on the Bank in early 1797 was the only serious public scare concerning the government's ability to pull the country through financially.

There were, however, constant complaints to that effect from those who opposed the war and from the manufacturing and merchant communities, and frequent rumblings of economic distress among the lower orders. Ministers

---

86 *Dropmore*, iv, 48, Dundas to Grenville, 5 January 1798. See also *P.H.*, xxxv, 1089-90, Dundas, 25 March 1801.

87 Jones (ed.), *Britain and Revolutionary France*, p.6; Grenville wrote of his hopes of the British forces gaining 'not just Gazette victories but solid and permanent advantage' in Egypt—BL Add. MS 34455, f.460v, Grenville to Auckland, late 1801.

88 See BL Add. MSS 40101, ff.79–80, Grenville to Dundas, 17 April 1800, advising hints to be dropped to British newspapers of a false plan of action, that the French might be diverted from the real attack planned for Walcheren.

89 Pendleton, 'English Conservative Propaganda', pp.48–9, 69–122, 441. Linda Colley points out the lack of attempt made by the government to foster British national consciousness among the population ('Whose Nation? Class and National Consciousness in Britain 1750–1830', *Past and Present*, 113 (1986), 105–8), but it did make strenuous efforts to vindicate its strategy of war against revolutionary France.

90 Ehrman, *The Reluctant Transition*, pp.489, 516.

took steps to reassure them and to refute their arguments. They interfered with grain imports, exports, and prices; they collected information on its nationwide production; and they insisted on the economic buoyancy of the country despite the war.[91] 'Scarcity' was caused by poor harvests, they argued, not by the war, and it was a mark of Jacobinism to claim otherwise. Any inconvenience suffered by commerce due to the war would have been caused by the Continental conflict in any case, even if Britain itself were not involved.[92] Windham declared that he did not believe that any MP had deprived himself of anything because of war hardship, and (rather less plausibly) 'that if the rich felt no suffering, the poor also were not likely to feel any'.[93]

With respect to the management of Parliament during the war, the Pitt administration, though frequently constrained by the need to justify every move before it, was rarely in difficulties. By and large, it had the confidence of MPs, and they were, if anything, more firmly loyal in the more difficult phases of the conflict. The Foxite Opposition was troubled by internal dissension over the Regency crisis of 1788-89, the French Revolution, domestic radicalism and the war, and some of its usual adherents began to drift away to support Pitt after 1791, when Burke moved to the Treasury benches. The split was gradual and reluctant, but Pitt and his colleagues did all they could to encourage it, wooing the Duke of Portland and his followers till eventually they joined the government in July 1794, leaving a remnant of only 35 to 60 MPs loyal to Fox.[94] The government could therefore usually count on a very comfortable majority.

The strain of conducting the war and of keeping pace with continental events as well as of the domestic situation told heavily on ministers, however, and while it was a great triumph for the Pittites to have gained the Portland Whigs, this brought additional stresses to Cabinet decision-making because of their firmly crusading opinions. Lady Elliot, after meeting various ministers in the winter of 1796, wrote, 'It appears that they never agree on any point. The jealousy is so great between the old and the new party that they have no communication.'[95] The progress of the war itself was rarely very encouraging:

---

91 See [Lord Hawkesbury], *Reflections on the Present State of the Country* (London, 1796); [Charles Long], *A Temperate Discussion of the Causes Which Have Led to the Present High Price of Bread. Addressed to the Plain Sense of the People* (London, 1800).

92 Auckland, *Some Remarks*, pp.55–6; *P.H.*, xxxiv, 1445–7, Pitt, 13 February 1800; ibid., xxxiv, 1458, Windham, 13 February 1800; ibid., xxxv, 525–7, Pitt, 11 November 1800; *P.H.*, xxx, 1484, Pitt, 6 March 1794.

93 Ibid., xxxi, 1031, Windham, 30 December 1794.

94 See chapter 4 below.

95 Countess of Minto (ed.), *Life and Letters of Sir Gilbert Elliot, First Earl of Minto, from 1751 to 1806*, 3 vol.s (London, 1874), ii, 390. See also ibid., 396, Elliot to his wife, 23 May 1797; also Ehrman, *The Consuming Struggle*, pp.46–50, on Pitt's consideration of resignation in 1797.

as Auckland noted morosely in June 1794, 'it is a sad part of the Consideration that ten victories decide nothing in our favour, but that one serious defeat would probably carry the French in three weeks to the Borders of Holland at least'.[96] They were often working in the dark, from second-hand reports of events and conditions, and communications were maddeningly slow. The weather often frustrated carefully planned strategies—Grenville wryly called Sir Ralph Abercromby 'a second Jonas' who seemed to attract storms at sea, and who perhaps ought to be thrown overboard.[97] When the divisions between the allies, splits among the French royalists, a lack of proper communication and consultation between ministers and the military establishment, and rows between the army and the navy are also considered, it is clear that the government had no mean task to perform simply to keep the British war effort moving.

V Making Peace

In February 1793 Grenville had instructed Auckland that nothing but a French disavowal of all their offensive decrees, a guarantee that France would make peace with Austria, Prussia and Sardinia on reasonable terms and the renunciation of all recent French conquests would be considered by Britain as satisfactory peace terms. Conciliatory measures concerning the *émigrés* would help the process considerably.[98] The ministry's belligerent stand was gradually worn down, however, by the domestic and external pressures of unremitting warfare, until peace negotiations appeared to be a more reasonable option. By late 1794, the course of the war was discouraging, public opinion was restless and Wilberforce, a personal friend of Pitt, had decided that he must press publicly for negotiations.

Nevertheless, ministers held out until the autumn of the following year before they announced that they were ready to talk with the French government. In the debate on Wilberforce's second motion for peace, in May 1795, Pitt once more rejected it, but he hinted that a change might not be far off: 'To look for negotiation at the present moment is premature, though I look to it at no remote period.'[99] The failure of the First Coalition and of the attack on Quiberon, together with financial strains, the increasing unpopularity of the war at home and the new, more moderate, French constitution of September, encouraged the Cabinet to offer to negotiate. Auckland's pamphlet, *Some*

96 BL Add. MS 38229, f.244, Auckland to Liverpool, 23 June 1794.
97 *Dropmore*, vi, 233, Grenville to Wickham, 20 May 1800.
98 BL Add. MS 34447, f.432, Grenville to Auckland, 4 February 1793.
99 Rhys (ed.), *Orations of Pitt*, p.91, 27 May 1795.

Remarks on the Apparent Circumstances of the War in the Fourth Week of October 1795, advised ministers to seek peace, if it could be had from France on honourable terms. George III, once reconciled to the idea of a war in November 1792, remained inflexibly opposed to negotiating for peace from the outbreak of hostilities in February 1793, both in order that the Revolution should be completely destroyed and that Britain should obtain as many colonial gains as possible. Like Burke, he also thought it humiliating to have Britain's overtures for peace rejected time and time again by the revolutionaries of France. 'No disaster can make me think the treating for peace either wise or safe whilst the French principles subsist.' In July 1800, despite his hostility to the expedition to Ferrol proposed by Dundas, the King told him that, in his view, 'Anything that will keep off making peace with France till it has an established Government on which some confidence can be placed is certainly desirable.'[100] Windham was also appalled by the prospect of negotiations. 'The Moment of Peace is yet, I hope, so far distant', he wrote to Burke on 17 January 1796, 'that chance may still do much to save us from so dreadful a catastrophe: I mean of course Peace with a Jacobin Republic.'[101]

This was the crucial issue of the debate concerning peace negotiations in the 1790s. How far was it safe to treat with a revolutionary republic, which would inevitably mean granting it recognition as a valid international state? Ministers never stated categorically that they would not treat with a republic, but rather that they could not treat with the French Republic so long as it continued to flout international laws and treaties and therefore to be unreliable so far as the guaranteeing of peace terms was concerned.[102] This maintained the consistency of their stand against Revolutionary foreign policy, but it also allowed them to set negotiations on foot whenever they themselves judged the situation to be right, both internally and externally.

The ministry was always anxious that its final peace settlement with France should be a general treaty, rather than one of several separate settlements between France and all the other belligerents. Ministers knew that the French would rejoice at the opportunity to pick one Power off after another, isolating Britain in order to range all its force against it. Both in June 1796 and in June 1800, almost certain of an Austrian withdrawal and knowing that Britain could not lure Austria into persevering in the struggle by offering

---

100 J. Holland Rose, *Pitt and Napoleon. Essays and Letters* (London, 1912), pp.238–9, memorandum by George III, 27 January 1796; Earl Stanhope, *Life of the Right Honourable William Pitt with extracts from his MS. papers*, 3 vol.s (London, 1879), ii, 442, George III to Pitt, 9 April 1797; *Dropmore*, iii, 327, George III to Grenville, 4 May [1797]; Stanhope, *Life of Pitt*, ii, 455, George III to Pitt, 28 June 1800; Stanhope, *Life of Pitt*, iii, 385, George III to Dundas, 28 July 1800.

101 BL Add. MS 37843, f.94v.

102 Rhys (ed.), *Orations of Pitt*, p.55, 30 December 1794; ibid., pp.94–5, 27 May 1795.

to finance another year's warfare for it, they determined to engage in peace talks along with Austria. In any case, Auckland wrote, Britain was fighting to restore the peace of Europe in general, not to achieve petty and partial pacifications.[103] Thus, the continental alliances involved ministers in walking a tightrope between urging the European powers to continue in the war and making sure that Britain was included in the peace.

The government attempted to negotiate peace with France several times—in December 1795, March 1796, October 1796 and in July 1797—but ministers, and particularly Grenville, were pessimistic about the possibility of settlement.[104] A proposal of negotiations from Napoleon at the end of December 1799 was rejected on the grounds that his government had not yet proved itself to be any more stable than its revolutionary predecessors. Ministers had also just ratified a new Loan convention with Austria on 10 December, and they were hopeful that, this time, Britain and Austria would work in concert to achieve better results by continuing the war together than by holding talks immediately with Napoleon. Peace began to look more likely, however, as Napoleon consolidated his power; and, when the chance of another coalition looked slim, after the Austrian defeat at Marengo in June 1800, and the northern powers of Russia, Denmark and Sweden joined together in early 1801 as an armed neutrality against British interference with neutral shipping, it was not surprising that the new Addington administration of March 1801 aimed for peace from the start. The pressure of public opinion and the discouragement of Marengo had in fact caused the Cabinet to decide to agree to an armistice in September 1800. That time, Napoleon had refused the British terms.

Ministers spent much more time arguing that the war should be continued than justifying their decisions to seek a peace settlement, however. The *leitmotiv* running through all the variations on this theme was that inherent to all the French revolutionary governments was a spirit of dangerous aggression. Britain's grounds for war against France, therefore, still held. The character of Napoleon Bonaparte, for instance, was said to underline the continued vitality of Jacobinism in France, and made negotiating risky. His previous record, ministers claimed, showed him to be destructive, unreliable, perfidious, unprincipled and insincere.[105] Ministers sometimes conceded that the French government was becoming more 'negotiable',[106] but the Jacobin

---

103 Auckland, *Some Remarks*, p.66.

104 Jupp, *Lord Grenville*, pp.197, 205–7; Ehrman, *The Consuming Struggle*, pp.60–1.

105 *P.H.*, xxxv, 417–18, Windham, 9 July 1800; ibid., xxxiv, 1215–20, Grenville, 28 January 1800; *Malmesbury Diaries and Correspondence*, iv, 52–3, 64–6, 28 March 1801 and 8 April 1802.

106 *P.H.*, xxxi, 1256, Grenville, 27 January 1795; Rhys (ed.), *Orations of Pitt*, p.125, 9 December 1795.

argument could be resorted to whenever they wanted to revive support for the war.

Government ministers therefore argued along Burkean lines that, were they to conclude peace with France, it would not be a real peace in the true sense of the word, for it would be impossible for Britain safely to reduce its navy, demobilize its army, or relinquish its conquests. At best it could afford only 'a temporary and delusive repose' to Britain, 'a feverish and troubled slumber, from which we should soon be roused to fresh horrors and insults'.[107] Not only would a so-called peace with France expose Britain to physical attacks, but it would also clear the way for the more effective transportation of French revolutionary ideas to the British people, firstly because a negotiation would imply a formal recognition of the French system of government, and secondly because, in peace, it would be open to French agents to travel to Britain in numbers and to stir up sedition and insurrection. Even in 1801 Windham was arguing that though under Bonaparte's regime democratic principles were no longer operative within France itself, he was still eager to export them and so throw other countries into turmoil, ready to be conquered by his armies.[108] Negotiation would also tend to depress Britain's allies and the French counter-revolutionaries. It would inflame French pride and increase their demands, and it would eventually place the other nations of Europe at the mercy of Jacobin violence.[109]

When other arguments wore thin, ministers resorted to the voice of authority. It was the King's responsibility to make war and peace, according to the constitution, not Parliament's. It was inevitable that the government should know more about the details of the situation than anyone else could do, and it therefore was more likely to be correct in its judgement.[110] The desire of the British people for peace was no necessary reason for abandoning hostilities. Ministers took it for granted that peace was preferable to war to the majority of British subjects, but they would not believe that the country would wish them to surrender its honour, good faith and character.[111]

Periodically, however, ministers sought to negotiate with the French Republic, and they therefore had to justify the abandonment of their usual, rather Burkean, arguments against peace, both among themselves and to

---

107 *P.H.*, xxx, 1326–7, Canning, 31 January 1794; ibid., xxxi, 260, Pitt, 10 April 1794; ibid., xxxi, 1014, Canning, 30 December 1794.

108 Rhys (ed.), *Orations of Pitt*, pp.84–5, 26 January 1795; *P.H.*, xxxi, 1030, Windham, 30 December 1794; ibid., xxxvi, 107-8, Windham, 3 November 1801.

109 *P.H.*, xxx, 1019, Pitt, 17 June 1793; ibid., xxx, 1283, Pitt, 21 January 1794; ibid., Canning, 11 December 1798; ibid., xxxv, 426, the Solicitor General, 9 July 1800.

110 Ibid., xxxi, 682, Hawkesbury, 30 May 1794; Rhys (ed.), *Orations of Pitt*, p.92, 27 May 1795; *P.H.*, xxxii, 16–7, Windham, 27 May 1795.

111 *P.H.*, xxxiii, 417, Pitt, 10 April 1797; see also ibid., xxxv, 940–1, Windham, 8 February 1801.

Parliament. Peace talks could be used for tactical purposes, whether or not ministers believed a peace likely to be concluded: they could stop Austria making peace on its own with France and ceding the Belgian provinces. Ministers argued that the French people were very likely to be desperate for peace, and that they would put considerable pressure on their government to produce it. If their rulers refused it, the resulting uproar in France would seriously weaken its government.[112] It could be argued, when it suited ministers, that negotiating itself was harmless, although at other times they might argue that it was an admission of weakness. Auckland stated his opinion in October 1795 that it was 'the duty of those who conduct the war, to treat for peace whenever negociation can tend to any probable good', a comfortably vague stipulation. He expressed himself more strongly to Pitt. 'My private opinion has ever been that it is right in War to treat at all times; & that there are few Channels thro which a prudent Government may not sound the ground of pacification without risque of mischief & always with *possible* advantage.'[113]

Negotiation could also be seen as a useful domestic policy even if it failed to produce peace with France. Poor harvests in 1795 and 1799 inflamed discontent with the continuation of the war, which was a forceful motivation.[114] In 1797 ministers were particularly worried that Britain lacked the financial resources to continue in the conflict. As much as he disapproved of negotiating, even Grenville was persuaded of its value in April 1797 by this consideration.[115] Certainly, by 1801, public anxiety about the war's effects on British industry, commerce and finance, together with the likelihood that Britain could not form another, successful coalition with the European Powers against France, impelled the Addington administration to seek peace. Cornwallis wrote to his brother in November 1801 from Paris, where he had been sent to negotiate the preliminaries of peace: 'I have long considered peace to be necessary for the preservation of our Country, and I did not therefore feel myself at liberty to refuse the mission when it was pressed upon me, altho' nothing could be more disagreeable to me.'[116]

---

112 *Malmesbury Diaries and Correspondence*, iii, 452, Malmesbury to Grenville, 6 August 1797.

113 Auckland, *Some Remarks*, p.42; BL Add. MS 34454, f.37, Auckland to Pitt, 30 July 1796. See also Rhys (ed.), *Orations of Pitt*, pp.146–7, 6 October 1796.

114 Stanhope, *Life of Pitt*, ii, 439–40, Pitt to George III, 30 January 1796.

115 Mackesy, *War Without Victory*, p.120; *Dropmore*, iii, 310–11, Grenville to George III and Cabinet Minute, 9 April 1797.

116 National Maritime Museum, Greenwich [hereafter NMM], COR/60, Marquis Cornwallis to his brother, 10 November 1801; *P.H.*, xxxvi, 40, Hawkesbury, 3 November 1801; ibid., xxxiv, 83, Addington, 3 November 1801; *Dropmore*, vi, 439–40, William Wickham to Grenville, 9 February 1801.

The supporters of the Treaty of Amiens viewed it as a peace signed from necessity, and they did not necessarily approve wholeheartedly of all its provisions. Pitt had been consulted regularly and had encouraged the new ministry in constructing it. He had always been the driving force behind the government's attempts to negotiate with France in the 1790s. Malmesbury said of him that 'even when he declaimed the loudest and with the greatest emphasis for a continuation of the *war*, his real and genuine opinion went for *peace*', because of his preoccupation with Britain's financial state.[117] Now he viewed it as an honourable way out of a war that was exhausting Britain financially and one which would give Britain time to renew its strength and forces. Writing to Charles Long on 1 October 1801, to tell him that the Preliminaries had been signed, he commented: 'The Terms, tho not in every Point precisely all that one could wish, are certainly highly creditable, and on the whole very advantageous.'[118]

Dundas was relatively happy with it because it maintained British supremacy in India (although he was angry about the surrender of the Cape of Good Hope and the ambiguous situation in which Malta was left, because of the importance of British trade routes to India), and he appealed to MPs not to criticize the settlement too much for the sake of the morale and loyalty of the British people.[119] Spencer Perceval was shocked at the terms, but he too kept his fears silent out of loyalty to Pitt, as did Canning, although he disliked the peace because Addington had made it. Lord Auckland told MPs that the big picture was more important than the details—Britain had been forced into a just and necessary war and had come out, having lost nothing and gained several acquisitions.[120] Lord Mulgrave admitted that the treaty was such as to be unlikely to create such regret or humiliation in France as to provoke it to an early renewal of hostilities, and he believed that the maintenance of political unity at home was more important than criticizing the terms of the treaty. Lords St Vincent (now First Lord of the Admiralty), Moira, Cornwallis and Nelson favoured the peace.[121] The King, like most of these, supported the government rather than the peace itself, which he called 'an *experimental*

---

117 *Malmesbury Diaries and Correspondence*, iv, 50, 23 March 1801; ibid., p.53, 29 March 1801.

118 PRO 30/8/102, f.174, Pitt to Long, 1 October 1801; Ehrman, *The Consuming Struggle*, pp.562–5.

119 *P.H.*, xxxvi, 679–86, Dundas, 5 May 1802; ibid., xxxvi, 775–6, Dundas, 13 May 1802.

120 Denis Gray, *Spencer Perceval: The Evangelical Prime Minister 1762–1812* (Manchester, 1963), p.47; *P.H.*, xxxvi, 703, Auckland, 13 May 1802. See also BL Add. MSS 45279, ff.123–4, Auckland to Sheffield, 21 October 1801, for his private doubts.

121 *Dropmore*, vii, 61–2, Mulgrave to Grenville, 18 October 1801; Philip Ziegler, *Addington: A Life of Henry Addington, First Vicount Sidmouth* (London, 1965), p.126; Mackesy, *War Without Victory*, p.213.

Peace', but one that was 'unavoidable'. He had been reluctant throughout the 1790s to negotiate with France, and he did so now only from a sense that it was necessary to support the new government. He was still dubious on 5 March 1802 that France would actually sign the treaty.[122]

Lord Grenville was adamantly opposed to the settlement. He thought the government irresponsible and foolish to throw away so many of Britain's conquests, including the Cape, Malta and Egypt, to allow the British evacuation of all ports in the Mediterranean and the Adriatic, and to make no provision for the Low Countries.[123] Moreover, he could not consider the security of Europe restored until the revolutionary taint was completely washed away.[124] Windham fully agreed with him. To him, the Treaty of Amiens seemed 'the death-warrant of [his] country', and he refused to call it 'an honourable peace', since it was not even a safe peace. The colonies that had been ceded should not be thought of in mere physical and economic terms, but also in terms of the esteem and prestige they brought to Britain and the extent to which Britain was disgraced by losing them; and, in economic terms, Britain could not rely on its wealth to sustain it in Europe if it was 'scattering pearls like barleycorns' on such a scale. Like Grenville, he thought that 'Nothing ... can ... be more idle than this hope of the extinction of Jacobinism, either as an instrument to be used by France, should her occasions require it, or as a principle ever to be eradicated out of any community in which it has once taken root.' Britain had shamefully abandoned its allies, particularly the French royalists.[125]

Earl Spencer said that 'no single object of the war had been obtained, and that [Britain] had sacrificed all means of protection'. The Earl of Minto (Sir Gilbert Elliot) also agreed with Grenville, and visited him to discuss the issue of opposing the government on the treaty. Malmesbury had said in March 1801 that the measure of making peace at all at this juncture was 'unwise and weak', because of France's disproportionately strong bargaining position and continued to oppose it.[126] Thomas Grenville spoke out in the House of Commons against the peace, and the third Grenville brother, the Marquess of

---

122 *Malmesbury Diaries and Correspondence*, iv, 62–3, 26–8 November 1801; *LCGIII*, iv, 15, George III to Hobart, 5 March 1802. The treaty was signed on 27 March 1802.

123 Jupp, *Lord Grenville*, pp.309–10; *P.H.*, xxxvi, 163–70, Grenville, 3 November 1801; ibid., xxxvi, 688–97, Grenville, 13 May 1802.

124 *Dropmore*, vii, 48, Grenville to Dundas, 4 October 1801; BL Add. MS 34455 f.463, Grenville to Auckland, [1801].

125 *P.H.*, xxxvi, 13–15, Windham, 29 October 1801; ibid., xxxvi, 89, 99, 125–30, Windham, 3 November 1801; ibid., xxxvi, 742, Windham, 13 May 1802; ibid., xxxvi, 133–8, Windham, 3 November 1801.

126 Ibid., xxxvi, 160, Spencer, 3 November 1801; Minto (ed.), *Life and Letters*, iii, 229, Minto to his wife, 17 December 1801; *Malmesbury Diaries and Correspondence*, iv, 48, 60, 61, 11 March, 1 and 29 October 1801.

Buckingham, was of like mind. The Duke of Richmond, still piqued at having been replaced by Cornwallis as Master General of the Ordnance in 1795, opposed the treaty and said that peace had only been required because of the incompetent conduct of the war by ministers.[127]

The old Pitt administration, split in private on the strategy to be adopted during the war, had now split in public on the nature of the peace. Windham, persuaded by the Grenvilles not to mix the question of the restoration of the French monarchy with the general question of the peace treaty in the debates in the Commons, yet managed to give an excellent summary of the two main positions on the war and the peace. The one was aimed primarily against the Jacobin spirit of the French Revolution, the other against France as a territorially acquisitive power. Because of this confusion, he said, the country as a whole 'never knew sufficiently why it was at war', and therefore clamoured for peace incessantly, more than in any previous war. 'This error has pursued us into peace', he declared. 'No person who looked at the causes of war, could have looked at the terms of peace without alarm.'[128] Yet perhaps the Pittites and even Dundas had been closer to the Burkeans than Windham gave them credit for. They had recognized the menace of Jacobinism and they had tried to defeat it, not wholly, as he had wanted, but partially, in its external aspect, in its dealings with the world outside France.

---

127 Alison Gilbert Olson, *The Radical Duke: Career and Correspondence of Charles Lennox, Third Duke of Richmond* (Oxford, 1961), p.107.

128 *Dropmore*, vii, 66–7, Thomas Grenville to Grenville, [23–31 October] 1801; *P.H.*, xxxvi, 747–50, Windham, 13 May 1802.

Chapter 3

Loyalists and War Crusaders

'Thus, happily, the prudence of the administration, co-operating with the energy of the community, has saved the metropolis from conflagration, and the constitution from destruction', Sir George Dallas wrote in 1793.[1] This chapter considers the wartime conduct and opinions of those people in Britain who were not merely part of an acquiescent majority in the country, but who were 'energetic' in supporting Britain's war against revolutionary France. It has been argued by some historians that the conservative activists won the ideological contest of the French Revolutionary period in Britain not just because of the resilience and popularity of establishment institutions, or government repression of radicals, but in large part also because of the essential attractiveness of their arguments to the general public, as opposed to the proposals of the radicals, and because of their persuasive tactics.[2] Others have emphasized the variety and frequent ambiguity of British conservative thought and propaganda in response to the Revolution in France and the threat of domestic radicalism.[3] It is argued here that the hostility of British conservatives to French Revolutionary ideas continued during the war and substantially informed their attitudes to the conflict, although it is also recognized that their views were not uniform in ideological intensity.

The views of Edmund Burke and of the British government have now been examined, and this chapter attempts to plot the attitudes of their supporters along the spectrum of conservative thinking about the struggle against the French revolutionaries, and to show how far they were influenced

---

1 Sir George Dallas, *Thoughts upon our Present Situation, with Remarks upon the Policy of a War with France* (London, 1793), p.5.

2 See, for example, H.T. Dickinson, *Liberty and Property* (London, 1977), pp.270–318; idem, 'Popular Conservatism and Militant Loyalism 1789–1815', in Dickinson (ed.), *Britain and the French Revolution*, pp.103–27; idem, 'Popular Loyalism', pp.503–33; Ian R. Christie, *Stress and Stability in Late Eighteenth-Century Britain: Reflections on the British Avoidance of Revolution* (Oxford, 1984); idem, 'Conservatism and Stability in British Society', in Philp (ed.), *The French Revolution and British Popular Politics*, pp.169–87; J.C.D. Clark, *English Society 1688–1832* (Cambridge, 1985).

3 Thomas Philip Schofield, 'Conservative Political Thought in Britain in Response to the French Revolution', *Historical Journal*, xxix (1986), 601–22; David Eastwood, 'Patriotism and the English State in the 1790s', in Philp (ed.), *The French Revolution and British Popular Politics*, pp.146–68. See also Donald E. Ginter, 'The Loyalist Association Movement of 1792–93 and British Public Opinion', *Historical Journal*, 9 (1966), 179–90.

by Burke's opinions and by government policy. Conservative writers and activists will here be considered under the two general headings of 'loyalists', the broad mass of conservative activists who by and large supported government policy, and 'crusaders', the smaller group who campaigned for a more hardline, Burkean strategy in the war. This division is more accurately represented as a crusading subset of a loose union of conservative, loyalist forces than as two separate groups, since there was much overlap of activity and attitudes. However, to divide them in this way is not to suggest that loyalists had little or no conception that this was a war of ideas. Their support of the conflict was not merely a patriotic reaction to the threat of foreign conquest, because they claimed that conquest by Revolutionary France would not only involve loss of national sovereignty but also the toppling of the entire social and political order in Britain through the implementation of revolutionary principles. They also continued to express the fear that Revolutionary France was already trying to achieve this more insidiously, by means of British supporters of the French Revolution and their campaign for radical political reform in Britain. Like the British government, loyalists waged war not so much against the very existence of French ideas, but rather against their potential impact on Britain. They fought against the threat posed by French principles to the British constitution, and in defence of the political and social hierarchy of Britain. By contrast, crusaders tended to agree with Burke that no peace could be had until revolutionary principles were extinguished in France itself. Each of these groups is examined in turn, first in terms of their activities during the war and then with regard to their recorded and published opinions concerning it.

I Loyalist Activities

It was necessary for the governing elite, believing itself to be under threat externally from France and internally from radical activity, to be able to rely upon at least the passive support of the majority of the British people. For this, they had to enlist the active support of a significant proportion of the population, who could help them ensure a general consensus of loyalty and patriotism. The government did not resort to military conscription or excessive coercion, as the French republic did, in order to enlist support; it preferred to depend upon and, to some extent, to harness voluntary efforts on its behalf, thus leaving the social and political structure of the British state unchanged. This was only possible, however, because such active loyalist efforts were willingly made available.[4] It is difficult to tell how many of the British

4 See Eastwood, 'Patriotism and the English State', pp.150–1, 167–8.

population were 'loyalist' in this way, as opposed to merely passively loyal, uninterested, or even hostile, but loyalists were to be found throughout Great Britain. The claim that there was a remarkable surge of popular loyalism in the 1790s is not nullified, as some historians have suggested, by the economic tensions of the decade which ensured that general public opinion was unreliable as a source of government support.[5] Loyalists were, by definition, committed activists, at least for part of this decade, if not in all cases for all of it. They sought to defend whatever benefits—political, economic, religious or moral—they perceived the present social order to have conferred upon them against the common menace of Jacobinism and its British sympathisers.[6] French egalitarian principles threatened the British social and political hierarchy which, since they protected private property, loyalists believed to be advantageous to all but the very bottom ranks of society. These principles were also regarded as being hostile to the Established Churches in Britain and to the Christian religion itself, which upheld the political and social system and consoled those who were least well-off under it. Loyalists, watching events across the Channel, also judged them to be destructive of public order and morality.

From the time of the royal proclamation against seditious literature of May 1792, loyalists began rallying to support the government against domestic radicalism, by means of addresses, letters, pamphlets, newspaper articles and the establishment of hundreds, if not thousands, of Loyal Associations from 20 November 1792.[7] The loyalists had risen, almost wholly without government intervention, because of the threat to the constitution posed by British radicalism, and they were further galvanized and propelled into the public arena by the exponential increase of the domestic threat caused by French events. Far from having planned such a 'paroxysm of loyalty', ministers were

---

5 Roger Wells, *Wretched Faces: Famine in Wartime England, 1793-1801* (Gloucester, 1988), p.6. For public opinion in general, see chapter 8.

6 H.T. Dickinson, *The Politics of the People in Eighteenth-Century Britain* (Basingstoke, 1995), pp.255-6; Emily Lorraine de Montluzin, *The Anti-Jacobins 1798–1800: The Early Contributors to the 'Anti-Jacobin Review'* (London, 1988), p.15; Robert R. Dozier, *For King, Constitution and Country: The English Loyalists and the French Revolution* (Lexington, 1983), pp.78–9; Colley, 'Whose Nation?', p.114.

7 The basis of this movement was already established by the active Church-and-King opposition to the Dissenting campaign of 1790 for the repeal of the Test and Corporation Acts, however, and this, in turn, was not a new phenomenon. On the Loyal Associations and the loyalism of 1792 in general, see Austin Mitchell, 'The Association Movement of 1792–3', *Historical Journal*, 4 (1961), 56–77; Ginter, 'The Loyalist Association Movement'; Dozier, *For King, Constitution and Country*, esp. p.62; Michael Duffy, 'William Pitt and the Origins of the Loyalist Association Movement of 1792', *Historical Journal*, 39 (1996), 943–62.

incredulous at their good fortune: Grenville called it 'little less than miraculous'.[8]

By January 1793, with the trial and execution of Louis XVI, loyalist attention was increasingly focused on France as well as Britain. *The Times* continually exhorted ministers to declare war against France throughout December 1792 and January 1793: 'We had better have them as an open enemy than a perfidious neighbour, which they have long been', it advised as early as 6 December. War against France added patriotism to the loyalists' character, for it obliged them to defend the King and the British constitution not only against internal sedition but also against a foreign enemy. Military defeat of the revolutionary armies would prevent the French from menacing Britain not only on their own behalf, but also from doing so in conjunction with the British radicals. The war breathed fresh vigour into the loyalist movement, by giving it a new *raison d'être*, and this was to sustain it when, by the mid-1790s, the domestic radical threat had ebbed. Loyalist addresses now became pro-war effusions: the *Sun* reported on 1 March 1793 that the Corporation of Bridport had intimated that its subscription of £1200 'for the suppressing of Tumults and Insurrections' was now to be 'as loyally applied in increasing the Bounties to Seamen'.

Nevertheless, the loyalists' war, like that of the government, was fought on two fronts, and they continued to generate and distribute printed propaganda against radical doctrines. This propaganda was even more powerful than that written before the outbreak of the conflict, for it now associated radicalism not only with the chaos inside France but also with French aggression towards Britain. It included morality tracts, pamphlets, histories of the Revolution and the war, songs, handbills, newspapers, periodicals, sermons, novels, plays, poetry and literary reviews, directed at various classes of readers and far outdoing their radical counterparts in terms of volume, sales, variety, and social and geographical spread.[9] They were sold by booksellers or street-hawkers, or distributed freely or at a greatly subsidized rate by loyalist societies. Pamphlet production never repeated the peak of 1792, but the invasion crisis of 1797 produced nearly as many new pamphlets (about 370 compared with about 440) in that year.[10]

Some loyalist writers, such as John Reeves, Herbert Marsh and Nicholas Vansittart, were paid by the Treasury, which seemed even more concerned to defend the ministry's war policies by this means than it had been to crush radicalism before 1793. Treasury pamphlets, however, and even those written by commission for the loyalist associations, were only a small proportion of

---

8 Murley, 'Origins of the War', p.324; *Dropmore*, ii, Grenville to Auckland, 18 December 1792.

9 Dickinson, 'Popular Conservatism and Militant Loyalism', p.110.

10 Pendleton, 'English Conservative Propaganda', p.172.

the whole.[11] Much propaganda was written by minor, local figures—ministers, schoolteachers, magistrates and civil servants, often involved in their local loyalist associations—as well as by prominent national names, and pamphlets and handbills might be reproduced and adapted to serve the needs of different regions of the country.[12] Writers often felt the need to protest that they were not ministerial hirelings and that their thinking was independent.

Indeed, far from requiring the prompting and organization of government, loyalists frequently stressed the need for the efforts of individuals in the battle against domestic radicalism and revolutionary France. 'It is almost dishonourable, at a period like the present,' declared the *Sun* on 1 March 1793, 'for any man to be out of active employment in the service of his Country.' Every individual had it in his power to do some public good. Theodore Price's popular 'Job Nott' pamphlets specifically addressed various classes within the lower orders as well as the better-off—male and female artificers, 'old maids', 'young widows', the wealthy, house servants, travellers, manufacturers, overseers of the poor, farmers, and so on.[13] They believed that the British people fell into just two groups—those who fought for their country and those who fought against it. Some loyalists even tried to suggest various tactics to ministers, and for this they did not rely only upon the indirect means of their propaganda. Magistrates and many others wrote to the Home Office with their fears and recommendations, sometimes at great length, on such matters as recruitment, national defence and even international strategy.[14]

There were various other ways in which loyalists could identify with the cause of the government. Raising and contributing to subscriptions was one of the most popular means of demonstrating practical support. There were three national subscriptions in 1793: in February and March, for bounties to encourage naval recruitment, from March to July, for money to help war widows, orphans and dependants, and, in the winter of 1793-94, for funds to buy clothing and other items for the British army in Flanders. The 'king's bounty' to enlisting seamen was £5; in London, it was increased to £13 by the contributions of the City and various loyalist organizations.[15] Loyalist

---

11 Ibid., pp.399, 145–6, 357.

12 Part of [Theodore Price], *Humble Advice to Sundry Sorts of People, by Job Nott, Bucklemaker* (Birmingham, February 1793) was reprinted from [Theodore Price], *Brother Fustian's Advice to the Inhabitants of Manchester and Salford* (Manchester, December 1792).

13 [Theodore Price], *A Continuation of my Last Book, or a Back Front View of the Five Headed Monster* (Birmingham, 1798), pp.6–7; [Theodore Price], *Further Humble Advice from Job Nott* (Birmingham, 1800), pp.1–6.

14 See PRO HO 42/20–50, *passim*; also the *Caledonian Mercury*, 20 May 1797.

15 Dozier, *For King, Constitution and Country*, pp.105–11. See also PRO HO 42/24/526–v, 42/25/36, bounties offered by the inhabitants of Ashburton, 16 February 1793, and by the Totnes Loyalist Association; ibid., 42/27/131–v, 145–v, 42/28/88–9, 42/32/203, subscriptions raised by John Brookfield, 13 November 1793, by Richard Baugh, 14 November

newspapers commended these efforts and ran their own fundraising schemes. The *Sun* claimed that its subscription in aid of war widows and orphans, opened on 28 February 1793, had by 19 March 1793 raised nearly £5000, 'exclusive of the Ladies' Subscription on the same plan'. Some pamphlets declared that the profits from their sale would be given to similar causes, thus encouraging a double loyalty in their potential purchasers.[16] Later, loyalists could donate to the government's Loyalty Loan of 1796 and the Voluntary Contribution of 1798.[17] There were also loyalist meetings, addresses, street processions, banquets, demonstrations, church services, the singing of 'God Save the King' in theatres, dramatic performances on loyalist and patriotic topics, and public ceremonies on days of victory celebration and at the departures of troops and sailors for the front. Edinburgh crowds welcomed and fêted the exiled French prince, the Comte d'Artois, and his retinue during his sojourn in the Scottish capital.[18]

Some loyalists had, even before the outbreak of hostilities, proposed a further and more radical form of endeavour: military vigilance against both internal and external enemies. In February 1793, the *London Chronicle* reported that numbers of gentlemen living on the south coast of England had formed themselves into mounted patrols to defend their property against French attack. In March 1794, ministers permitted the official formation of armed Volunteer companies, to be financed, again, by public subscription. At first, these were composed almost wholly of the comfortably-off and socially respected. Such loyalists could also act as Special Constables during or after particularly alarming riots, such as the London 'crimp' riots of August 1794 or the Edinburgh 'Pike Plot' of May 1794.[19] In 1798, however, with heightened fears of French invasion, mass enlistment in the Volunteer force was encouraged. By 1805, it could boast 450,000 men, the largest organization in Britain.[20]

1793, by the Society at the Crown and Anchor, 19 January 1794, and by the *Oracle* newspaper.

16 *Desultory Thoughts on the Atrocious Cruelties of the French Nation: With Observations on the Necessity of fhe War, and a Calm Admonitory Address to all English Jacobins* (Bath, 1794) was one such pamphlet.

17 See D.G. Vaisey, 'The Pledge of Patriotism: Staffordshire and the Voluntary Contribution, 1798', in M.W. Greenslade (ed.), *Essays in Staffordshire History* (Staffordshire Record Society, 1970), pp.209–23.

18 *Caledonian Mercury*, 7 January 1796, 11 April 1796; A.J. Mackenzie-Stuart, *A French King at Holyrood* (Edinburgh, 1995).

19 John Stevenson, 'The London "Crimp" Riots of 1794', *International Review of Social History*, 16 (1971), 56; *Caledonian Mercury*, 7 June 1794.

20 Clive Emsley, *British Society and the French Wars 1793–1815* (London, 1979), p.38; Dickinson, 'The French Revolution and Counter Revolution in Britain', p.253; J.R. Western, 'The Volunteer Movement as an Anti-Revolutionary Force', *English Historical Review*, 71 (1956), 603–14; J.E. Cookson, 'The English Volunteer Movement of the French

J.E. Cookson has pointed out the greater proportion of Volunteers provided by Scotland than by England, compared with their respective populations. He suggests that, just as Scotland's role in the British empire has been seen to have contributed to its self-esteem as a partner of England, rather than as a dependent province, so too its ability to provide for its own defence in this way led not to nationalist sentiments but to a contentment with its role within the British state. In a similar way, Scottish loyalism was proud of its efforts to defend the British constitution, and sometimes compared itself favourably with English efforts. In repressing radicalism, the *Caledonian Mercury* thought, 'the metropolis of Scotland has set an example which the first provincial towns might do well to copy, and perhaps even the metropolis of England or Ireland would be unable to compete with, if brought to comparison'.[21]

There were problems with the Volunteer movement, however, for local finance and enthusiasm were not inexhaustible, especially at times when there appeared to be no tangible threat to combat; and there were uncertainties among the propertied elite concerning the political wisdom of arming such a number of ordinary people.[22] Moreover, it is likely that many enlisted in Volunteer corps less from ideological conviction than from social pressure to do so, or from motives of self-interest. Recent research has also shown that local concerns were often higher on the agenda than those of the British government, for instance in the Scottish Highlands, which contributed so many Volunteers.[23] Nevertheless, Volunteering did serve as a powerful weapon of visible propaganda by its drilling, uniforms and parades, which displayed the apparent willingness of many to take to arms to defend the political and social order which protected their property. It also provided opportunities for loyalist sermons to be preached and published, especially at ceremonies for the presentation of colours to individual companies.[24] Moreover, while individual Volunteers may not always have been highly motivated by ideological hostility

---

Wars, 1793–1815: Some Contexts', *Historical Journal*, 32 (1989), 867–91. See, for instance, also PRO HO 42/29/281–8, William Ogilvie to [Dundas], [March 1794]; Arthur Young, in *The Annals of Agriculture*, xviii (1792), 495; ibid., xxvi (1796), 516–21; ibid., xxvii (1796), 49–54, 528–38; ibid., xxviii (1797), 177–87, 441–3.

21 Cookson, *The British Armed Nation*, pp.149, 152; *Caledonian Mercury*, 2 October 1794.

22 For example, Rev. Samuel Partridge, 'Observations on a Militia of Property', in the *Annals of Agriculture*, xxi (1793), 513–16.

23 Cookson, *The British Armed Nation*, pp.68, 73ff., 237ff.; cf. Paul Langford, *Public Life and the Propertied Englishman* (Oxford, 1991), *passim*. Cookson also shows that the British government was itself often highly ambivalent in its attitude towards the Volunteers. On the Highlands, see Andrew Mackillop, *'More Fruitful Than The Soil': Army, Empire and the Scottish Highlands, 1715-1815* (forthcoming), chapter 7.

24 For example, PRO HO 42/34/118, Newcastle Military Association, 28 January 1795.

to the French Revolution, the movement itself was closely identified with the defence of the British constitution. Loyalist ideas were so often integral to the constitutions, propaganda and even names of Volunteer companies (such as the Loyal Warrington Volunteers) that it is difficult to remove loyalism from Volunteering in the 1790s.[25]

II Loyalist Opinion

Popular conservative pamphlets in the 'Rights of Man' debate were influenced by Burke's publications more in terms of their general conservative standpoint than in terms of their specific content. Their arguments were more pragmatic and populist than his.[26] A similar observation may be made of the debate on the war against revolutionary France for, in their published responses to it, loyalists tended towards a slightly more crusading line than ministers but one which was less rigid than that of Burke. While they often presented the war as an ideological crusade, therefore, they also defended the deviations of ministers from the logic of a strictly crusading strategy. Moreover, they emphasized issues which were of most direct and immediate concern to the insular British public, those which would appeal to the emotions of national chauvinism and individual self-interest, and they paid less attention to the European questions which in different ways worried both Burke and the government, and to the purely philosophical possibilities which caused Burke so much anxiety. Nevertheless, it would be misleading to suggest that loyalism began to fade out of conservative attitudes with the advent of war. It has recently been suggested that loyalism and patriotism are often confused by historians and that, during the war, loyalism was largely replaced by 'national defence patriotism'.[27] This separation is problematic, however, at least during the 1790s. Most conservative literature on the war in this decade gave a substantial amount of space to praise of the British constitution and social order by comparison with those of republican France, thus infusing a considerable element of loyalism along with that of patriotism.

Before the 1790s an ambivalent attitude towards the French had prevailed among the British people. French intellectual life and fashions were admired, particularly by the upper classes, and those who could afford it were

---

25 See, for instance, the declaration signed by each member of the Edinburgh Volunteers, printed in the *Caledonian Mercury*, 16 October 1794; James Kendrick, *Some Account of the Loyal Warrington Volunteers of 1798* (Liverpool, 1854). I am grateful to Thomas V. Jackson for the latter reference.

26 Robert Hole, 'British Counter-revolutionary Popular Propaganda in the 1790s', in Jones (ed.), *Britain and Revolutionary France*, pp.53–69.

27 J.E. Cookson, *The British Armed Nation 1793–1815* (Oxford, 1997), e.g. pp.208, 211–13, 241.

keen to travel to France. There was even some sympathy for the early stages of the French Revolution among those who would later become staunch supporters of the war against France. There was also, however, a well-established anti-gallicism at the forefront of British xenophobia, which predominated by late 1792. This had been fostered by military rivalry throughout the eighteenth century, so that France was seen as the 'natural' enemy of Britain. By the later part of the century, it was also thought by some that British admiration of French culture had gone almost so far as to approximate to cultural conquest.[28] The *Sun* declared, in tones of high glee, on 19 March 1793: 'It is glorious, it is animating to see, that the old antigallican spirit which has so often led the British Arms to fame and victory is again roused, and that it reigns with increased ardour throughout the Nation.' It had been widely expected that the French armies would be soundly defeated by the Duke of Brunswick's offensive campaign in September 1792, and loyalists were shocked when the reverse occurred. They criticized the German armies' failure severely, but they agreed that the war between France and Austria and Prussia was entirely the responsibility of an aggressive France.

Many of the arguments used by loyalists to defend the justice and necessity of the British war against revolutionary France were very similar to those used by ministers, but they were less concerned about France's violations of international laws and treaties than the government, and more preoccupied by the need to defend Britain's property, constitution, religion and commerce. They were horrified by the atrocities committed by the revolutionaries, both within France and outside it, and many, who had previously sympathized with the Revolution or had been indifferent to it, began to revile it. The massacres of September 1792 appeared to confirm that anarchy prevailed in France, and the execution of Louis XVI re-emphasized the brutality and savagery of the revolutionaries. British loyalists expressed the fear that they and their king might not be invulnerable to similar treatment. Poems, sermons and prints were produced to commemorate Louis, and some loyalists believed that Britain ought not to see such horrors perpetrated with impunity.[29]

The poverty and chaos evident in Revolutionary France were trumpeted, especially in contrast with the blessings of living under the British constitution, in order to teach the lesson that the example of France was a terrible warning to Britain and any who sought speedy political change there—

---

28 Gerald Newman, *The Rise of English Nationalism: A Cultural History 1740–1830* (London, 1987), pp.72–3.

29 E.g. William Laurence Brown, *An Examination of the Causes and Conduct of the Present War with France; and of the Most Effectual Means of Obtaining a Speedy, a Secure, and an Honourable Peace: Together with some Observations on the Late Negotiation at Lisle* (London, 1798), pp.30–1; *The Times*, 17 and 18 December 1792, 5 February 1793; [John Jones], *Sentiments on a War with France* (London, 1793), pp.34–5. See also David Bindman et al., *The Shadow of the Guillotine: Britain and the French Revolution* (London, 1989), *passim*.

No religion or laws the vile Jacobins own;
Their God they deny, and their King they dethrone;
To gain their own ends the poor people they cheat,
Then leave them to starve, not a morsel to eat.[30]

Almost more threatening to loyalists, however, especially after the war had broken out, were the fact that the French had invaded other states and had 'disorganized' the political and social order there themselves, and the fear that they might plan to do the same to Britain. The violence of the French revolutionary system (abbreviated by loyalists to 'Jacobinism') was terrible not only because of its example from within France, but also because the French were actively encouraging radicals elsewhere to follow suit and, indeed, taking a lead in imposing it on other countries. The Jacobins had failed to overturn the British constitution by underground methods and had now resorted to open warfare to achieve the same purpose. Since French principles were now being propagated by force of arms, it was necessary to resist them in the same manner.

Conservative writers defended the British government's sincerity in its initial attempt to maintain neutrality towards revolutionary France and claimed that France was the original aggressor. The British government had had no choice at all in the matter, since France had been the aggressor, showing a markedly belligerent attitude towards Britain and Europe for months before February 1793 and eventually issuing the declaration of war to Britain and Holland. Since France was implacably resolved on hostilities with Britain, prevarication and negotiation could be of no avail; at best they could only delay the conflict, perhaps until France was yet more powerful.[31]

Loyalist pamphlets and propaganda often described the war in terms of a crusade, matching government rhetoric. According to the *Sun* of 2 November 1793, it was 'a War of Virtue, Order and Religion, against Crime, Anarchy and Atheism'. 'Let us not deceive ourselves', *The Times* was still warning on 27 September 1797. 'The animosity which the Jacobins of France entertain against us, is less the consequence of that ancient rivalship which has existed between both nations, than the necessary effect of that vigorous resistance which they experience on our part, to their plan of disorganizing the civilized world.' It was a new kind of war in terms of scale, in terms of the aims of both Britain and France, and also in terms of the resources used by France and its means of carrying on the conflict. Loyalists maintained that the Revolution

---

30 *The Anti-Gallican Songster No. I* (London, 1793), p.3.

31 William Black, *Reasons for Preventing the French, Under the Mask of Liberty, From Trampling Upon Europe* (London, 1792), p.48; Herbert Marsh, *The History of the Politicks of Great Britain and France*, 2nd edition, 2 vol.s (London, 1800), esp. vol. i, pp.iii–xi, xxii.

inevitably produced war, and war of a more barbaric and uncivilized nature than before. James Rennell thought it his duty 'to impress on [every Briton's] mind, that the progress of French arms and influence in Europe must infallibly lead to this catastrophe', the establishment of a French revolutionary government in Britain.[32] They reinforced this rather Burkean argument, however, with more traditional anti-gallican justifications for war. The destruction of the continental balance of power by the revolutionaries' progress of conquest through the states of Europe was also a solid justification for war. Readers were reminded that monarchical France had also been eager to expand its frontiers, and that France harboured a permanent hatred for Britain.

Later in the war, some conservatives began explicitly to deny that it was a war about opinions, agreeing with the Treasury secretary Charles Long's 'new era' analysis of the conflict—that is, that after 1795, the ideological element had largely evaporated, leaving only the residue of French territorial greed to be dealt with. 'I confess it is not now the French revolution I dread, but French greatness', wrote Thomas Bentley in 1798.[33] Yet, like the government, many other loyalists continued to wage war against the the threat generated by the speculative opinions of Revolutionary France: a struggle not so much against democracy in France as against the aggression that that democracy ignited and against the imitation of French democratic principles in Britain. The French attempts to invade Ireland in 1796 and 1798 amid United Irishmen activity, the continued threat of a mainland invasion, the naval mutinies at Spithead and the Nore in 1797, and the reappearance of London Corresponding Society agitation in 1797 and 1798, meant that loyalists had to maintain their vigilance in the second half of the decade as well as in the earlier years of the war.

The general objective of the European war against revolutionary France, according to British loyalists, was to restore the continental balance of power. This meant dispossessing France of all its recent conquests and fencing it in inside its old boundaries. They also wanted Britain to receive indemnity in return for its expenditure on the conflict. Both of these aims, however, were usually couched in terms of the provision of a security against Jacobinism. The most urgent aims of the war for loyalists were the defence of the British constitution and the defeat of radicalism and revolutionary principles in Britain. According to the *Caledonian Mercury*, British soldiers were fighting 'to secure for us at home our Religion, our Laws, our Liberties, and our very

---

[32] James Rennell, *War With France the Only Security of Britain at the Present Momentous Crisis: Set Forth in an Earnest Address to His Fellow-Subjects, by an Old Englishman* (London, 1794), pp.10, 12.

[33] [Thomas Richard Bentley], *Considerations Upon the State of Public Affairs, at the Beginning of the Year MDCCXCVIII.* (in three parts: London, 1798), pt I, p.2. See Long, *The New Era of the French Revolution*, p.41 above.

existence as an independent and civilized nation'.[34] Loyalists feared that British radicals were fifth columnists and national enemies, and that they would be only too willing to assist a French invasion, in the hope of seeing a republic established in Britain. The most effective way, therefore, of guarding the British constitution and crushing radical hopes would be by overturning the French revolutionary regime. The loyalists were more divided, however, on the question of whether or not the restoration of the French monarchy ought to be an objective of the war, reflecting ministers' doubts and disagreements. In response to Opposition accusations that the ministry harboured this aim, loyalists tended to deny it hotly and to insist that it was merely a preference, particularly after 1795, when the ministry had expressed its willingness to treat with any stable government in France.[35] When not under Opposition fire, however, loyalists might advise that the restoration of the Bourbon monarchy would be the best way of re-establishing peace and stability in France and Europe.[36]

In terms of the justification, nature and aims of the conflict, then, loyalists tended to present it as a war for the defence of the British constitution against French and British Jacobinism. With regard to the actual conduct of the war, their main themes were optimism, support for the government and its measures, and suggestions for improving home defence. Loyalist writers usually expressed optimism regarding not only the final outcome of the war, but also respecting individual campaigns and expeditions, since they were concerned to vindicate government strategy. The newspapers were particularly constant in their hopefulness. Over a week after the evacuation of Dunkirk (which *The Times* could hardly bring itself to mention), the *Sun* still clung to the hope that its capture 'may yet probably be numbered amongst the acquisitions of the Campaign'.[37] It was often argued that France must collapse, sooner or later, from the rigours of the revolutionary warfare she pursued, especially because of the depreciation of the *assignat* and because of the republic's requisitioning of resources and manpower. British and allied successes were loudly celebrated as they happened, and constantly listed to cheer and convince doubters. The European allies might sometimes suffer losses and defeats, but British soldiers, and especially British sailors, were always to be praised. Even during the agony of the mutinies of 1797, the worst that was said of the great majority of the sailors involved was that they must

---

34 30 September 1793.

35 Ibid., 20, 21, 24 September 1793, 5 October 1795.

36 William Playfair, *Thoughts on the Present State of French Politics, and the Necessity and Policy of Diminishing France, for Her Internal Peace, and to Secure the Tranquillity of Europe* (London, 1793), p.60; *P.H.*, xxxiv, 1533, Charles Yorke, 21 February 1800.

37 The *Sun*, 17 September 1793, and also 24 September 1793.

have been misguided and deluded. Britain, in fact, was crucially important in the European struggle against revolutionary France, according to the loyalist writers. It had stood in the breach for civilized society, saving it from the revolutionary torrent, and Pitt was lauded and honoured for his leading role as 'the *Saviour of Europe*'. One pamphleteer went so far as to predict that 'France herself, if ever that country can be grateful, will one day own the obligation [to Britain] as all Europe does now.'[38] Above all, and more than ever, the monarchy was the focal point of conservative ideology. George III symbolized British stability and rectitude against French republican chaos and violence and, later, against Napoleonic 'treachery' and 'tyranny'. The loyalist press took great pride in royal ceremonial during the war, and even greater pride in the active involvement of members of the royal family in the armed forces.[39]

Loyalist writers defended both the government's domestic tactics and its international strategy. They called insistently for political unity within Britain behind the Pitt administration during the war, and they were loud in their disapproval of the Foxite Opposition in Parliament. Without internal unity, warned one, 'we shall ... perish like other great empires, who fell more from the internal wounds of civil discord, than the lasting victories of invading enemies'.[40] A common plea in loyalist recommendations for dealing with the internal enemy was for a moral reformation among the British people in general, that British morality might shine the brighter against French and radical immorality, and that it might be found deserving of victory over both enemies by God. Many loyalists thus identified themselves with the existing 'reformation of manners' movement.[41]

---

38 [Thomas Richard Bentley], *Considerations upon the State of Public Affairs at the Beginning of the Year 1796* (London, 1796), pp.96–7.

39 Vincent Carretta, *George III and the Satirists From Hogarth to Byron* (Athens and London, 1990), pp.505–13; Marilyn Ann Morris, 'The Monarchy as an Issue in English Political Argument During the French Revolutionary Era', unpublished Ph.D. thesis (University of London, 1988), pp.238–82; Linda Colley, 'The Apotheosis of George III', in *Past and Present*, 102 (1984), 97–129. I argue (ch. 8) that graphic satires generally fit more usefully into an analysis of public opinion than into one of activist loyalism, but Carretta's argument here applies equally to loyalist writing. See also *The Anti-Gallican Songster*, i, 14–15; *The Times*, 5 February 1793; the *Sun*, 28 February 1793, 12 September 1793; and Marilyn Morris, *The British Monarchy and the French Revolution* (New Haven and London, 1998).

40 Dallas, *Thoughts Upon Our Present Situation*, pp.62–3.

41 For the reformation of manners movement, see Joanna Innes, 'Politics and Morals: The Reformation of Manners Movement in Late Eighteenth-century England' in Hellmuth (ed.), *The Transformation of Political Culture*, pp.57–118; Richard A. Soloway, 'Reform or Ruin: English Moral Thought during the First French Republic', *Review of Politics*, xxv (1963), 110–28; and M.J.D. Roberts, 'The Society for the Suppression of Vice and its Early Critics, 1802–1812', *Historical Journal*, 26 (1983), 159–76. For loyalist concern in the 1790s, see Thomas Lister, *Opposition Dangerous* (London, 1798), pp.19–20; [Theodore Price], *More Advice from Job Nott* (Birmingham, 20 February 1795), p.4; John Bowdler, *Reform or Ruin: Take Your Choice!* 5th edition (London, 1798); Hannah More et al., *Cheap Repository Tracts* in *Works*, 6th edition, 11 vol.s (London, 1853), vol.s i–iii.

Conservatives feared French republican emissaries, so they approved of repressive measures to minimize their impact on the country (the Aliens Act of January 1793 and the Traitorous Correspondence Act of May 1793), and also the legal measures taken to suppress British radical activity. These might look tyrannical at first sight, it was acknowledged, but they existed for the protection of the liberty of British subjects. Indeed, in her survey of English conservative propaganda during the 1790s, Gayle Trusdel Pendleton estimates that 'Popular opinion would probably have approved considerably more repressive legislation than Pitt requested', and she notes that measures of suppression were endorsed in at least 130 different pamphlets.[42]

Loyalists also maintained that scarcity of grain and commercial problems were not caused by the war. Other explanations were provided, such as the corrupt activities of monopolists, the divine wrath presently resting on the nation, a simple supply and demand imbalance, and the sway held by materialism and luxury over the country. Nicholas Vansittart pointed out that the Continental war would have affected British trade whether or not Britain had participated.[43] The various financial measures adopted by ministers to pay for the war were defended more or less without complaint. If the country supported the war, it must be prepared to pay for it and to make retrenchments if necessary.

The large sums of money spent by the government on the allies were therefore defended on the grounds that they were a necessary way to harass and wear France down, and that they were cheap at the price. Moreover, if the rest of Europe did not band together against France, the revolutionaries could much more easily defeat each individual nation. The *Sun*, on 18 September 1793, was particularly optimistic—the union of the allies, it claimed, was 'indissoluble'—but other loyalists also expressed great confidence and trust in the allies, more, one presumes, in partisan bombast than in real faith, particularly as they easily switched to blaming the allies and praising the unique virtues of Britain as the occasion demanded.

Despite their support for the army and navy, the loyalists were eager to suggest various improvements in the regulation of both forces. They were not enthusiastic about crimping and the press-gang. Some tried to resign their readers to making the best of a bad system; others suggested that a national system of recruiting should be established instead. Representations were also made that courts-martial were in need of reform, that demobilized soldiers and sailors must be paid before being dismissed, and that young sailors required some form of formal education; but the government's scheme for building

42 Pendleton, 'English Conservative Propaganda', p.284.

43 Nicholas Vansittart, *Reflections on the Propriety of an Immediate Conclusion of Peace*, 2nd edition (London, 1794), pp.53–5.

barracks for soldiers in Britain received applause from loyalists, who were glad that soldiers would be more readily available in the event of civil unrest but also relieved that they could be kept by themselves, out of trouble.

Most loyalist writing was concerned with defensive measures and with the threat of invasion. Newspapers periodically reported the sighting of preparations being made on the French coast for an attack on Britain, either as a diversionary tactic or in real earnest. The general attitude of loyalists was a mixture of confidence that a French invading force would be 'destined to feed the fishes of our seas', but that, none the less, extensive preparations ought to be made in case the French should make the attempt and indeed to persuade them not to do so.[44] Domestic artillery and cavalry should be substantially increased, so that the defending forces would be considerably superior to the invaders; light cavalry forces should also be formed, to move around the country when necessary; and fishing boats should be armed and fully manned. More signal towers and ammunitions batteries ought to be built, and groups of expert marksmen, such as sportsmen and gamekeepers, should be gathered.[45]

The .i.strategy of interference within France did not receive a great deal of loyalist comment, but those who discussed it were generally supportive. They quoted writers on the laws of nations; they argued that France had interfered in numerous other countries, that attack was the best form of defence, that the ministry only undertook such a repugnant strategy reluctantly, and that France had shown itself unfit to take political decisions for itself. In any case, Britain had been invited into France by the French counter-revolutionaries. Attitudes to the *émigrés* were more mixed. Some approved of the help given to them by the British government and by individual British subjects; others thought that they should be employed in the British armed forces, but not paid bounties, since they ought to have sufficient other incentive to fight the Revolution.[46] The strategy of giving substantial financial aid to the counter-revolution in France received only limited support.[47]

Except between 1796 and 1797 and after October 1801, when the ministry was attempting to negotiate a settlement with France, loyalists allowed little of their natural desire for peace to show in their discussions of the issue, except in private letters, or in poems and songs which placed the

---

44 [Bentley], *Considerations on ... Public Affairs ... 1798*, pt. I, p.65.

45 *Thoughts on the Defence of These Kingdoms* (London, 1796), pp.49–53; NMM, MEL/6, Capt. A. Blair to John Bruce, 3 March 1798; ibid., MEL/9, Col. W. Fullarton to the Duke of Portland, Sept. 1796.

46 [Jones, John], *Remarks on a Pamphlet Published as Mr. Fox's Speech, at the Opening of the Parliament, Including Some Observations on the Nature and Causes of the Present War* (London, 1793), pp.82–3; the *Sun*, 19 November 1796; *P.H.*, xxxi, 373, William Baker, 11 April 1794; *The Dutch Expedition Vindicated*, pp.17–23.

47 [Bentley], *Considerations on ... Public Affairs ... 1798*, pt. I, pp.23–31; *The Times*, 24 January 1794.

blame for the continuance of the war squarely on French shoulders. Instead, they argued that France should initiate talks, having been the original aggressor, but they expressed grave doubts that the French government had any intention of doing so. It had never demonstrated any interest in peace and, even should that change, its word was hardly to be trusted, in view of the violated treaties and professions of good faith trailing in its wake. Loyalist writers and MPs bristled with rage at the 'insolence' of the French rulers towards Great Britain—particularly the insulting treatment and dismissal of Lord Malmesbury at Paris in 1796—and they insisted that Britain, defended by its splendid navy, had no need to make a humiliating peace by bowing and scraping to such an arrogant and depraved rival. Such a peace had no chance of lasting. The Earl of Morton 'professed himself exceedingly hurt at the idea of this country stooping to sue for peace'.[48] Until Jacobinism was no longer a threat, it would be necessary to press on with vigorous warfare. It was possible to wage war with anarchy, but not to make peace with it.[49] Only military victory was likely to secure a real peace. The ministry's rejection of Bonaparte's offer of negotiations in December 1799 was stoutly defended; the French Consul himself was vilified as ambitious, unscrupulous and Jacobin, and his government condemned for being as precarious as its predecessors. 'It is a willing error to think we have refused a Peace', declared *The Times*.[50]

Very occasionally, strictures were delivered by war-weary or crotchety loyalists in Parliament on the Pitt administration's attitude to peace or its handling of negotiations; and there was some lack of confidence in the new administration under Henry Addington when it took office in March 1801.[51] By and large, however, these arguments against negotiation changed little over the decade, except for the periods 1796-97 and 1801-2, when loyalists felt more relaxed about letting their own desire for peace show, since ministerial policy openly sought at least negotiations if not a settlement. These attempts allowed loyalists to argue with confidence that the British government was sincere in seeking peace and that the responsibility for continuing the conflict rested with France. They also, however, felt obliged to justify these attempts to halt the conflict after so many declarations that it was vital to continue to wage it vigorously. Those loyalists who subscribed to the 'new era' theory that, after the fall of Robespierre, the French government had become much more moderate and stable, could reason that it was no longer necessary to engage in

---

48 *P.H.*, xxxi, 969, the Earl of Morton, 30 December 1794.

49 [Bentley], *Considerations on ... Public Affairs ... 1798,* pt. II, pp.45, 79-88.

50 *The Times*, 23 January 1800.

51 *P.H.*, xxxi, 991, the Duke of Leeds, 30 December 1794; ibid., xxxiii, 425–6, Thomas Tyrwhitt Jones, 10 April 1797; ibid., xxxv, 885, the Earl of Fife, 2 February 1801; ibid., xxxv, 936–7, Henry Bankes, 3 February 1801; ibid., xxxv, 1106, Earl Temple, 25 March 1801.

ideological warfare, for the conflict had again become a traditional eighteenth-century battle for territorial aggrandizement between Britain and France which could be ended whenever both sides agreed on a stalemate. The *Sun*, for instance, trenchantly criticized Burke for arguing against the ministry's attempts to negotiate with France in 1796-97, in his *Letters on a Regicide Peace*, as 'Quixotic', 'intermeddling' and pernicious to the national interest—though, like the government and other loyalists, it sometimes reverted to talk of an ideological war against French and British Jacobins after the peace talks had failed.[52] Others simply reasoned that, successful or not, peace negotiations could be used to rally the nation behind the government.

It was recognized by loyalists that British insistence on an indemnity and on the liberation of the Belgian provinces from French rule in any peace terms would cause an obstacle to a settlement, but they maintained Britain's right to demand both for the sake of its future security. *The Times* was indignant at the charge of greed laid by some against this concern: 'The War ... is not as we have been perfidiously told, "a War for Spice Islands and Sugar Colonies". This is a language not to be endured. For all men feel it is a War for existence itself.'[53] Some were consequently disappointed by the eventual settlement of peace at Amiens and its distinctly lightweight character with regard to indemnification; but many rejoiced full-heartedly in it, praising its 'moderation', and *The Times* discreetly refused to arbitrate between the divided views of ministers and ex-ministers.[54]

III The War Crusaders

For most loyalist writers, popular and otherwise, the main inspiration was the government's presentation of events and its justification of its conduct, a view of affairs which was considerably coloured by Burke's thinking, yet differing significantly from it. There was, however, a small minority of pamphleteers and journalists—some who were in fact Treasury-paid—who clearly agreed with Burke's opinions on the war much more closely than most, and whose writings reflected his influence much more truly.

While both loyalists and these 'war crusaders' recognized the French Revolution to be 'the common enemy of all governments, and of all establishments, religious and civil',[55] most loyalists, influenced by government doubts and divisions, were far from certain that the primary object of the war

---

52 See the *Sun*, 7, 12, 13 and 15 October 1796.

53 *The Times*, 12 September 1801 and also 21 July 1801.

54 Ibid., e.g. 29 April and 17 May 1802. On ministerial disputes, see pp.61–3 above.

55 *The Anti-Jacobin Review and Magazine; or, Monthly Political and Literary Censor* [hereafter *A-JR*], ii (January 1799), 12.

ought to be the defeat of the Revolution in France and the restoration of the ancient French monarchy. They might have preferred this outcome, but ultimately they were prepared to treat for peace with any stable form of French government. Burke, on the other hand, was quite sure of the need for a thorough restoration of the French monarchical regime, and the crusading pamphleteers were to be found much nearer to his camp than to the government's. The ministry and the loyalists were more concerned about the outworking of the French Revolution than with principles in the abstract; that is, they were preoccupied with the impact of Revolutionary ideas on French foreign policy and on British radicalism. Burke and the war crusaders, although very conscious of these revolutionary products, were principally fixated by the fear of the original principles of liberty, equality and fraternity, and with the threat to the social order and to property all over Europe. 'In nations, as in individuals, principles are the main springs of action', wrote John Bowles; 'every thing else that influences human conduct is accidental, and takes its colour and direction from principles.'[56] They thought that these principles could only be stamped out properly by the removal of the government they had created in France.

Almost to a man, they had until late 1792 supported the government's policy of isolation, neutrality and non-interference in French internal affairs, being much more concerned about the 'Rights of Man' debate in Britain than with the international situation. They were probably alerted to the volatility of Franco-British relations more directly by the general panic which gripped British loyalists in the winter of 1792-93 than by Burke's pre-war writings. Burke was almost alone in his interest in international politics and in his foresight regarding the war but, once they were convinced of the imminence of armed conflict, crusading pamphleteers and politicians were attracted to Burke's views on it and began to propagate them themselves.[57]

Probably most war crusaders, as the most militant of the conservatives, were connected with the government in one way or another. John Bowles, for instance, was a paid Treasury writer from 1792: he was paid sums of Secret Service money on at least two occasions, he was also made a Commissioner of Bankrupts and, in 1795, he was given one of the five places on the Commission for the sale of Dutch prize ships. By the mid-1790s, when his

---

56 John Bowles, Article IV, *A-JR*, ii (January 1799), 86–7.

57 H.T. Dickinson, 'Britain and the Ideological Crusade Against the French Revolution', in L. Domergue and G. Lamoine (eds.), *Actes du Colloque international* (Toulouse, 1992), pp.166–7; Philip Schofield cites two early pamphlets which agreed with Burke's insistence that Britain must interfere in France internally: [Graham Jepson], *Letters to Thomas Payne, in answer to his late publication on the Rights of Man. By a Member of the University of Cambridge* (London, 1791), pp.51–9; and *Modern Madmen; or, the Constitutionalists Dissected. By Solomon Searchem, Esq.* (London, 1792), pp.21–50. See Schofield, 'British Politicians and French Arms', p.187 n.16.

writing career was at its height, he had abandoned the legal profession.[58] Arthur Young, agricultural improver and author of the successful pamphlet, *The Example of France A Warning to Britain* (February 1793), was patronized by Pitt himself: he was made Secretary to the Board of Agriculture.[59] John Gifford received a Treasury pension and two consecutive police magistracies, and he probably edited the Treasury-funded *True Briton* newspaper as well as the crusading *Anti-Jacobin Review and Magazine*.[60] These war crusaders therefore owed certain obligations to the government. They were probably by choice also of a more loyalist and patriotic, sometimes even jingoistic, disposition than was Burke. Nevertheless, they were much more firmly gripped by the purely ideological aspect of the war than were most loyalists. They clearly had a great deal of sympathy for Burke's view of the war, one more rigid and less compromising than that of the Pitt administration, and they were perhaps more prepared to criticize the ministry than were most loyalists. Yet neither were they all simple copyists of Burke. They hated the French Revolution with a passion that could hardly have been manufactured on demand, and which caused them to develop personal emphases in their writings. They were 'Burke's fellows, not his followers, in the cause'.[61]

The chief grounds for war in crusading eyes were the doctrines of the French Revolution. Their false and abstract ideas of liberty and sovereignty threatened to act as a universal solvent to destroy the long-established habits of civil and religious subordination which formed the strongest ties of society and the very basis of true freedom by enabling the supreme power in a state to maintain itself with the least possible degree of coercion. In promoting resistance to and the subversion of all legitimate authority, French principles invited gross violence and great instability, which necessitated rule by force; they also must be overthrown by force.

After it was published in 1797, the war crusaders tended to subscribe to the Abbé Barruel's conspiracy theory of the French Revolution and the wars it produced, a theory which fitted well with Burke's own ideas on the genesis of the Revolution. This was, as Bowles wrote, 'a deep and vast conspiracy against all the ancient institutions of Europe, civil, political, and religious', focused on the French Revolution, but instigated decades earlier by the propagation of

---

58 Chatham Papers, PRO 30/8, vol.229, pt.2, ff.291a, 292a. These list subsidies to Bowles of £15 on 18 July 1792 and £100 on 10 November 1792. He also wrote to Henry Dundas in late 1793, reminding the Home Secretary that he had declined the offer of a place under the Police Bill of 1792 and asking for the position of Register in Chancery for the island of Barbados (PRO HO 42/27, ff.836–v.).

59 Pendleton, 'English Conservative Propaganda', p.115.

60 de Montluzin, *The Anti-Jacobins*, p.26.

61 Pendleton, 'English Conservative Propaganda', p.256; see also Emma Vincent, '"The Real Grounds of the Present War": John Bowles and the French Revolutionary Wars 1792-1802', *History*, 78 (1993), 416–20.

Voltaire's infidel philosophy and fed by 'licentious' German writings. Politically, the movement incited sedition, disturbance and rebellion wherever it could against the existing authorities.[62] When the Revolution eventually burst out, the Jacobins were thus able to spread their false principles much more easily and openly. The French Republic took possession of peoples who accepted the Revolution and declared war on those who did not. Armed force, therefore, was not the first tactic resorted to; before that came the stirring of civil discord, the incitement to insurrection, and the weakening and dissolution of social, religious and moral ties.

The presence of French agents and incendiary literature in Britain before war broke out seemed to prove the existence of the plot. Evidence that it was succeeding was furnished by the British radical addresses to the National Assembly, the outpourings of propaganda from the radical presses, the establishment of radical clubs and societies and the experiment of the British Convention in 1793. Not only were the revolutionary doctrines propagated earnestly by the French, they were also clearly contagious. Thus, when they had once been accepted by some British subjects, they became naturalized (and this the more easily in Britain since they could be seen to derive directly from Lockean principles) and were energetically promoted by native Britons. Only the creation of Loyal Associations across the nation had averted catastrophe.[63] John Gifford later defended ministers for their adherence to neutrality until February 1793, as Burke would not have done, on the grounds that this proved French aggression beyond all question; but others, such as Bowles and Earl Fitzwilliam, rather chided them for their slowness to act against France, although they could not claim Burke's consistency in this, since they had not urged the government to wage war before its outbreak.[64]

While it was important that the balance of power should be restored in full in Europe, the chief aim of the war, according to crusaders, must therefore be the universal defeat of these revolutionary principles. This would ensure the adequate defence of the British constitution, along with all other legitimate constitutions, and, crucially, it would entail the downfall of the illegitimate

62 Abbé Augustin de Barruel, *Mémoires pour servir à l'histoire du Jacobinisme* (1797); [John Bowles], *Letters of the Ghost of Alfred, Addressed to the Hon. Thomas Erskine, and the Hon. Charles James Fox, on the Occasion of the State Trials at the Close of the Year 1794, and the Beginning of the Year 1795* (London, 1798), p.49; idem, *Reflections on the Political and Moral State of Society at the Close of the Eighteenth Century*, 2nd edition (London, 1801), pp.125–7.

63 John Gifford's *A Short Address to the Members of the Loyal Associations, on the Present State of Public Affairs* (London, 1798), told the Loyal Associators that they had 'judiciously converted the Stream of Democracy into a Current of Loyalty' (p.10).

64 John Gifford, *A Letter to the Hon. Thomas Erskine; Containing Some Strictures on His View of the Causes and Consequences of the Present War with France*, 4th edition (London, 1797), pp.18–20, 45–50, 54–5; Bowles, *Reflections ... at the Close of the Eighteenth Century*, p.38; *P.H.*, xxxi, 673–4, Earl Fitzwilliam, 30 May 1794.

French Revolutionary regime. The existence of a republican government in France, wrote Arthur Young, was 'the establishment of eternal hostility against all real liberty, and consequently that of Britain'. The prevention of the further progress of the revolutionary system would be entirely insufficient, according to Bowles: 'The malady is not of a nature to admit of palliatives, and a relapse will be inevitably fatal.'[65] He himself, despite a cautious rider to the effect that Britain could not insist on any specific form of government in a counter-revolutionized France, was a vociferous advocate of a restored Bourbon monarchy, maintaining that the whole *ancien régime* must be re-established (though it need not return with all its abuses and corruptions), that only a restored monarchy would be capable of holding it all together, and that the monarchy was the form of government best suited to the French people.[66] Other war crusaders also made clear their strong preference for a restored monarchy. Gifford believed that the interest of Europe 'evidently demanded the restoration of the ANCIENT MONARCHY', and Earl Fitzwilliam was confident that 'By the restoration of monarchy, every thing would fall again into its place.' Others, such as Young and Jacques François Mallet du Pan, a Franco-Swiss *émigré*, concentrated on the need for stable government after the destruction of the Revolution, and refused to commit themselves wholeheartedly to any particular form.[67]

To the war crusaders, then, this was very much a war of ideas, and it was vital to grasp the true nature of the enemy in order to fight it successfully. The French Revolution, not its military armies, was the primary foe. The Jacobins had transformed their whole degraded nation into 'a camp bristling with bayonets', drunk with induced frenzy and bombast.[68] Yet their decrees were more dangerous than the military threat. Bowles struggled hard to describe the energy of the Revolution and its apparent self-will. Driven by a 'maniacal rage', it was 'like Fire which can only be kept alive by the constant accession of fresh fuel' and, if Britain continued to ignore its real causes, it would be no more in that country's power to resist the Revolution's effects than to combat

65 Arthur Young, *The Example of France a Warning to Britain*, 4th edition (London, 1794; first published 1793), p.210; John Bowles, 'Postscript to "The Real Grounds of the Present War with France"', in *The Retrospect* (London, 1798), p.80.

66 John Bowles, *Objections to the Continuance of the War Examined and Refuted* (London, 1794), pp.71–6; idem, *Farther Reflections Submitted to the Consideration of the Combined Powers*, 2nd edition (London, 1794), pp.23–4, 31–3, 39, 43, 62[F]; idem, 'Postscript to "The Real Grounds"', in *The Retrospect*, pp.80–3.

67 John Gifford, *A Letter to the Earl of Lauderdale, Containing Strictures on his Lordship's Letters, to the Peers of Scotland* (London, 1795), pp.171–2; *P.H.*, xxxi, 675, Earl Fitzwilliam, 30 May 1794; Young, *The Example of France*, p.40; Jacques François Mallet du Pan, *Considerations on the Nature of the French Revolution; and on the Causes which Prolong its Duration* (Dublin, 1794), pp.69–72.

68 Jacques François Mallet du Pan, *Dangers Which Threaten Europe* (London, 1794), pp.12, 51–4.

those of a tornado or earthquake. Even the revolutionary leaders—including Bonaparte himself—had no power to control it. It was a torrent rushing behind them and, 'while they seem to drive, they themselves are driven'.[69] Jacobinism, moreover, was not less to be feared at home than abroad: 'your internal enemies are many', wrote one pamphleteer, 'and are more dangerous, because suspected but by few, and hard to be distinguished from friends.... you breathe the same air, you dip in one dish, you drink from one cup with traitors'. Just because they had not yet committed such excesses as their French counterparts had did not mean that their intentions ought to be underrated—they would yet imitate the French Revolution in Britain if they could.[70]

Uniquely, this was a war of extermination—either the French monster of anarchy must perish, or all the thrones, governments, society and religion of Europe collapse. War was essential to the very existence of Jacobinism, and Jacobinism could fight with weapons unknown to ordinary warfare: the energy of Revolution, the total material and human resources of the French nation, the lack of any ordinary restraint or scruple. In 1798 Gifford published a pamphlet entitled *A Short Address to the Members of the Loyal Associations, on the Present State of Public Affairs*, which described a conservative's nightmare vision of Jacobin plans for Britain, should revolutionary France triumph in the war, listing the names of well-known radicals (including Paine, Horne Tooke, Thelwall, Hardy and Muir) as members of the Directories to be formed for England, Scotland and Ireland, and the various measures they would carry through, such as the dispersal of the British navy between France, Holland and Spain, leaving only a few ships each to England, Scotland and Ireland.

Crusaders advocated many of the same strategies for conducting the war against France and against British radicals as the loyalists did, but, because they were adamant that the revolutionary government must be overthrown, they also insisted upon an allied military attack within France itself. 'The Anarchical Monster must be pierced in his vitals, or he will never be destroyed,' declared Bowles. This was just and necessary, for France interfered within other countries and their governments, and this was the only effective and permanent way to guard against it.[71] Colonial expeditions simply wasted troops which could be used more effectively at the heart of the matter. Full support for and use of the French counter-revolutionary forces were urged, for the crusaders believed that their need for allied help was mutual. There was no

---

69 Bowles, *The Real Grounds of the Present War with France*, 2nd edition (London, 1793), p. 70; idem, *A Third Letter to a British Merchant*, pp.8, 53; idem., *Farther Reflections*, p.9; idem., *Reflections ... at the Close of the Eighteenth Century*, pp.107–8; idem, *Reflections on the Political State of Society at the Commencement of the Year 1800* (London, 1800), pp.95–7.

70 *The Voice of Truth to the People of England, of all Ranks and Descriptions, on Occasion of Lord Malmesbury's Return from Lisle* (London, 1797), pp.7, 18–39.

71 Bowles, *Farther Reflections*, p.45.

rational prospect that France could be reduced to order without the efforts of the French people themselves. The vast majority of the French population was impatient to be rescued from the crippling yoke of the Revolution; once given courage by allied support, they would rush forth to break their chains. The Combined Powers should recognize Louis XVII (and later, his uncle, Louis XVIII) as the hereditary King of France. The clergy and nobility must also be protected and helped, since they were essential to any restoration of the old system in France, both in terms of their places in the social structure and, in the case of the clergy particularly, of their value in restoring a sense of morality to the country. Mallet du Pan, as befitted an *émigré*, was more aware of the potential difficulties of this policy than most—the fears which would grip the French population of allied plundering and of the return of the abuses of the *ancien régime*—but he was certain that it was the only way to defeat the Revolution.[72] The allied powers must also learn to follow up their victories properly, especially those achieved on French territory, for they were too prone to lose their advantages through failing to reinforce and press on quickly enough.

Crusaders were, then, more prepared to differ from ministerial policy than were loyalists, because of their strong conviction that there was only one strategy capable of defeating revolutionary France. They treated the government's failures somewhat more gently, however, than did Burke. They were willing to allow that, if this was a just and necessary war, ministers were not ultimately responsible for its success, and they were as much concerned to defend them against Opposition accusations than they were to press their own criticisms.

The characteristic by which war crusaders could most easily be distinguished was that of their attitude to peace negotiations. Again, the crusaders used many of the arguments rehearsed by ministers and loyalists against peace, but loyalists were almost always relieved when ministers attempted to treat with the French government and defended them for doing so. Crusaders' reactions to negotiations with revolutionary France always ranged from disapproval to horror. To them, the grounds of war—which were to do with the survival of society and civilization rather than with the usual petty causes of irritation—still held, and so it was appalling to contemplate an abandonment of the struggle. Jacobinism was still a threat; by the later 1790s, it might have lost many of its adherents, but many others were incurable, and every country in Europe was plagued with those who were infected and those who were its dupes. It had had an amazingly successful ten years by the turn of the century, having overthrown half the governments of Europe, and it had no reason to be discouraged. The fall of Robespierre did not herald the dawn of

---

72 Mallet du Pan, *Considerations*, pp.46–9, 66–9.

'moderation' in the Republic, or anything like it—the methods of different French revolutionary governments might change, but their object remained constant. It ought to be unthinkable for Britain to recognize the French Republic:

> Though we cannot controul the course of events, nor direct the chances of war, yet I cannot foresee any situation to which we can possibly be reduced, so disastrous as to extort from us an acknowledgement of the French republic; an acknowledgement pregnant with such infinite danger as almost to amount to a political suicide.[73]

For war crusaders, this must be a war to the death.

Despite these views, most war crusaders—Earl Fitzwilliam being a reliable exception—were at least more willing to contemplate the possibility of peace than Burke had been, because of their greater concern to defend the ministry. Bowles argued that ministers were entitled to the plea of necessity in their decisions at various times to offer to negotiate, since public opinion was so heavily in favour of such action. In his *Reflections at the Conclusion of the War* (1801), he urged the proper use of the defences of the country during peace-time, trying to reconcile the crusading instincts which warned him that a mere military peace with the revolutionary Republic would be no true peace, with his loyalty to the ministry which was in the process of concluding the terms of peace. In like manner, John Gifford advised the retention of the Alien Bill during peacetime, and its vigorous enforcement.[74]

As for the eventual settlement of 1801-2, Bowles declared that the ministers had done very well in embarrassing circumstances; but he was little satisfied with the so-called peace in prospect. Rejoicing over the two islands which Britain had been permitted to keep was like a man rejoicing that he had saved a few days' provisions from a fire which was threatening to burn down his home, for however honourable Britain's own terms, the balance of power in Europe had been virtually surrendered. Worse still, the peace had left the French monarchy overthrown. Dr Laurence was less amenable still, and told ministers that they had laid themselves open to 'the most serious charge of misconduct' and that the treaty was 'most fatal to the country'.[75]

---

73 Gifford, *Letter to the Earl of Lauderdale*, p.171.

74 Bowles, Article I, *A-JR*, i (August 1798), 134; idem, *Reflections at the Conclusion of the War: being a Sequel to 'Reflections on the Political and Moral State of Society, at the Close of the Eighteenth Century'*, 2nd edition (London, 1801), pp.43, 46, 58; Gifford, *Letter to the Hon. Thomas Erskine*, p.103; Gifford, *A Second Letter to the Hon. Thomas Erskine* (London, 1797), p.39.

75 Bowles, *Reflections at the Conclusion of the War*, pp.5, 7–8, 35–7, 43; *P.H.*, xxxvi, 145, Dr Laurence, 3 November 1801; ibid., xxxvi, 674, Dr. Laurence, 12 May 1802; also ibid., xxxvi, 806-7, Dr. Laurence, 14 May 1802.

Geoffrey Carnall has suggested that 'What other people were haunted by as an occasional bad dream, was for [Burke] a habitual nightmare',[76] and this is a helpful spectrum on which to see British loyalists and crusaders in the 1790s. Very few people, if any, were driven to the same state of desperation by the French Revolution as Burke was, and consequently few viewed the war with the same inflexibility. Some of those who knew him well, such as Earl Fitzwilliam and Dr Laurence, probably came closest to him in unrelenting crusading opinions. Bowles, Gifford, Young and other crusading pamphleteers had greater obligations to defend the ministry's conduct of the war, and probably greater loyalist sympathies of their own, but they also suffered from the nightmare of a world revolutionized by Jacobinism badly enough to diverge clearly from the ministerial line in their views of the aims and nature of the conflict, their ideas of how it should be waged and their attitudes towards peace. Loyalists, too, were captured by horrible visions, though of a slightly different nature. Their nightmare was less of a world or even a Europe revolutionized and more of a Britain in thrall to radical politicians and levelling economists. A French invasion was a variation on this theme which occurred with increasing frequency as the threat from domestic radicalism diminished, but this was a dream which could be banished by the prospect of peace. The visions of crusaders could only be intensified by such a prospect.

---

76 Geoffrey Carnall, *Robert Southey and His Age: The Development of a Conservative Mind* (Oxford, 1960), p.9.

Chapter 4

The Opposition to the War (I): The Foxite Whigs

Opposition to the British government's war against revolutionary France fluctuated, as different groups at different times found it in their interests to be counted part of it or not. The conflict was actively opposed in a consistent way for three main reasons: party politics, support for the French Revolution and pacifism. These motivations overlapped in the anti-war reasoning of any individual or group of people, but, while Foxite Whigs inside Parliament and their sympathisers outside it tended to be motivated considerably by party political opposition to the conflict, the arguments of radical politicians were dominated by their desire for 'French principles' to be permitted to spread unhindered, and the liberal 'Friends of Peace' emphasized the evil nature and consequences of war in general. This chapter and the next will examine the views of these three groups of anti-war activists, leaving the consideration of the more sporadic demonstrations of popular opposition to the conflict to chapter 8.

By their attitudes to the secession of the Portland Whigs in 1794, to the French Revolution in general, and to the aims, conduct and cessation of the war, the Foxites showed themselves to be as concerned to defeat Pitt as to preserve peace with France. However, it is also clear that their complaints about the war were made at least partly because of their sympathy for the principles and achievements of the first two or three years of the Revolution in France. Party was undoubtedly extremely important in the Foxite view of the conflict. But the Foxite position, no less than that of their loyalist opponents, was substantially shaped by the notion that this was, at least in part, a war of ideas. Even when they criticized the government for pitting armed force against ideas, this was to some extent due to the fact that they disagreed with the government's ideas and claimed to support those of revolutionary France. This chapter examines the opinions of the Foxite Whigs in Parliament and their supporters out-of-doors, considering why and then how they opposed the conflict. It begins, however, by considering those former allies of Fox, the Portland Whigs, and their journey from parliamentary opposition to membership of the government because of their support for the war against revolutionary France.

I The Portland Whigs

The rapidly changing events during the war against France made choices more difficult for the Opposition Whigs as well as for the ministry and, if the government was unclear in its war aims, the Opposition of 1792–94 was clearly divided in its attitudes to the war itself. Because of its direct impact upon Britain, the conflict forced a polarization of political attitudes even more sharply than had the Revolution. It had become a matter of national security and fence-sitting could no longer be an option for Opposition or independent MPs. The problem was complicated for the Whig Opposition in Parliament by the decision they had to make over the relative importance of the existence of a parliamentary opposition and the issue of national security. For some, such as Charles James Fox, the existence of an opposition in Parliament to the Pitt administration was of such fundamental importance that it helped to shape their views on the war. For others, national security came first, and they eventually made the difficult choice of leaving the opposition benches to support the government.

Fox could not bear the idea of 'suspending opposition for the purpose of giving strength to Government', even during a war, particularly since the government was led by William Pitt, who had been used by George III to overthrow the Fox-North coalition of 1782–83.[1] This injustice remained a root of great bitterness. A considerable number of those who remained with him did so partly because of their eagerness for parliamentary reform—younger men, such as Charles Grey and Samuel Whitbread—while their less radical elders continued in opposition for much the same reasons as Fox, having been with him in Parliament through the struggle for office of 1782–84. They may have been less enthusiastic for parliamentary reform in Britain (William Adam opposed Grey's motion calling for it in May 1793), but their hostility towards British or allied interference in French affairs led them to condone republicanism in France.

On the other hand, those MPs, who at various stages between 1791 and 1794 abandoned their support of Fox and eventually came to support Pitt, and who became known as 'the Portland Whigs', saw the menace to the welfare of Britain in the 1790s as an essentially different entity to the danger posed by the influence of the crown in the 1780s. The major enemy then had been the influence of the Court on British political life. Now, it seemed to these Opposition MPs, a greater foe threatened, in the shape of revolutionary principles armed by Frenchmen and welcomed by British radicals. In the face of these it was not only prudent, but necessary, to cease fighting the lesser antagonist and to join forces against the common enemy. To Fox and his

1 BL Add. MS 47565, f.163, Fox to Adair, 29 November 1792.

friends, the British war against France was not a struggle against any serious threat, but merely another symptom of corruption in British high places, which remained the real foe. The Duke of Portland and various other erstwhile allies of Fox, however, sympathised with Burke's fear of French ideas and they increasingly agreed with his crusading views on the conflict. They therefore had progressively less in common with Fox as the war began to dominate political debate in Parliament and in the nation at large. In August 1791 Burke (who had himself previously been close to Fox) published *An Appeal from the New to the Old Whigs*, condemning the 'new Whig' principles of Fox, Sheridan and their followers and vindicating the 'old Whig' principles of those who thought as he did about the Revolution and its excesses. Pitt reinforced Burke's strategy, declaring in Parliament that in the matter of 'fundamental principles', he was in complete agreement with Burke.[2]

While the conservative Opposition Whigs were attempting to persuade Fox of the dangers of the French Revolution, the younger members of the party were trying to gain his sanction for their support for its principles. In April 1792 they formed the Association of the Friends of the People with the object of campaigning for parliamentary reform in Britain.[3] Fox did not join the society, but, on the other hand, neither did he disown it. This caused the conservative Whigs great concern. 'I am very sorry to see that Fox has taken a part in their support, although he has not signed the Association; but he might just as well have signed it as made the speech he did yesterday', Sir Gilbert Elliot wrote to his wife on 1 May.[4] They continued to hope that the increasing violence of events in France would shock Fox into agreeing with their perspective on the Revolution. That perspective was not yet clearly defined, an indecision in which the conservative Whigs were hardly unique. While Thomas Grenville and Earl Fitzwilliam wanted to suspend systematic parliamentary opposition, but were not yet convinced that Britain ought to prepare for war against France, Windham agreed with Burke that the country should be made ready to defend itself and even perhaps to assist the Combined Powers on the Continent. Portland himself was prepared to sympathize with the Austro-Prussian invasion of France, but it was unclear what he thought about a possible British intervention in the European turmoil.

By December 1792 they were sufficiently alarmed by the political turmoil outside Parliament to agree, at least tacitly, with the ministry's calling out of the militia and summoning Parliament. In the debate on the Address of

---

2 *P.H.*, xxviii, 372–3, Pitt, 9 February 1790; Ehrman, *The Reluctant Transition*, ch.6, esp. pp.184–93.

3 For its founding declaration, membership and address to the British people, see *P.H.*, xxix, 1303n.

4 Minto (ed.), *Life and Letters*, ii, 17–18, Elliot to his wife, 1 May 1792; *P.H.*, xxix, 1312, Fox, 30 April 1792. See also *Malmesbury Diaries and Letters*, ii, 454, 9 June 1792.

Thanks to the King, on 13 December, Windham defended the right of a nation to interfere in another's internal affairs if its own interests were affected. Viscount Stormont went further and declared his support for the government for the purposes of resisting French principles. 'I cannot shrink from, or elude that duty [of defending the British constitution], by saying to myself, "I do not like these ministers; I wish the administration was in different, and, as I may think, in abler hands"', he told the House of Lords. 'It is not this or that minister, this or that denomination of men, that I join upon occasions like this. I range myself under the broad banner of the constitution.' Lord Fielding followed suit in the Commons. On 31 December Sir Peter Burrell and the Marquis of Titchfield (Portland's son) supported the ministry in the Commons debate on the Army Estimates.[5] Lord Loughborough accepted the seals of office as Lord Chancellor on 18 January 1793 and, after the declaration of war in February, Windham and perhaps twenty-five other Whigs joined some independent MPs to form a 'Third Party', also known as 'the Alarmists', to support the government in its conflict against France, while reserving their judgement on other matters and on the actual conduct of the war.[6] They agreed with Burke that the government's strategy was not nearly close enough to a consciously counter-revolutionary line.

These MPs appeared to hope that they differed with the Foxites only on the war and that this might soon be resolved. They found themselves on the horns of a dilemma, unable in their position to defend the government's strategy or to attack its conduct of the war. Some, however, such as Sir Gilbert Elliot and Lord Malmesbury, had recognized even before the outbreak of war that to remain in awkward opposition could only be a temporary solution and that it would be necessary to break with Fox completely and give formal support to the government, because the issues surrounding the war had become 'truly the just criterion of public conduct and connection'.[7] Elliot unhooked himself in April 1793, declaring himself at the service of the ministry, and was eventually appointed the British Commissioner at Toulon in September of that year, after some negotiation and manoeuvring. Malmesbury likewise accepted a diplomatic mission to Berlin in November 1793.

Portland and his followers took longer to overcome their deep-seated distrust of Pitt, which, like Fox's, dated from the events of 1782–84, and had

---

5 *P.H.*, xxx, 39–40, Windham, 13 December 1792; ibid., xxix, 1572–3, Viscount Stormont, 13 December 1792; ibid., xxx, 9–10, Lord Fielding, 13 December 1792; ibid., xxx, 191, Burrell and Titchfield, 31 December 1792. Later in the debate (col. 213), indeed, Titchfield declared that the ministry ought to have acted sooner.

6 Frank O'Gorman, *The Whig Party and the French Revolution* (London, 1967), pp.117, 126–8; Jupp (ed.), *The Letter-Journal of George Canning*, p.114.

7 *P.H.*, xxx, 160, Earl Spencer, 22 December 1792 is a typical apologia for a Whig now voting with the government on the war.

been reinforced by their objections to his conduct of the war. For some time they were unwilling to admit that the difference between them and the Foxites was one of principle and more than one of interpretation.[8] They rarely spoke in Parliament, supporting neither Pitt nor Fox. But the war did not end conveniently after one campaign and, in January 1794, Portland and his followers opted to follow the 'Third Party' formula of separation from Fox and systematic opposition, granting their support for the war, but as yet no systematic support for the administration. They were involved in the Volunteer movement from the spring of 1794; but it was not until July, after lengthy talks and various concessions, that they were finally persuaded to overcome their dislike of Pitt and their objections to his war strategy sufficiently to join the administration, having decided that the ministry required to be stiffened by their greater resolve against revolutionary principles and activities. 'If We decline taking our share of responsibility in the present moments the danger with which this Country and all the Civilised World are threatened must be unavoidable and greatly increased,' wrote Portland.[9] It was clear that he and his supporters had shifted sides wholly because of their ideological hostility to the French Revolution and, indeed, that their hatred of Revolutionary principles had had to be sufficiently great to overcome their considerable party political reluctance to move. In the reconstructed administration Portland himself became Home Secretary, Windham joined the War Office, Fitzwilliam became Lord President of the Board of Trade, Lord Spencer took up the Privy Seal and Lord Mansfield was made a Cabinet Minister without portfolio. Various other marks of favour and patronage were also conferred on the Portland Whigs and, with regard to policy, Portland received assurances that the British government aimed at the restoration of the French monarchy.

II Foxite Opposition to the War: Party and Principle

The seceders were regretted rather than condemned by Fox. He wearily told his nephew, Lord Holland, that he would prefer to retire from politics altogether, but that 'this could not be done, and there therefore remains nothing but to get together the remains of our party, and begin, like Sisyphus, to roll up the stone again, which long before it reaches the summit, may probably roll down again'. Some of his remaining followers were less forgiving, and angrily

---

8 See *LCGIII*, i, 650–2, the Duke of Portland to the Prince of Wales, 21 January 1793.

9 Wentworth Woodhouse MSS, f.31b, the Duke of Portland to Earl Fitzwilliam, 14 June 1794, quoted in O'Gorman, *The Whig Party*, p.196.

denounced the Portland Whigs.[10] The traffic within Parliament, however, though hardly equal, was by no means one-way. The Foxite party also received support in opposition from a few former Pittites who were hostile to the war, such as William Smith, who was a member of the Friends of the People and who had been instrumental in arranging Pitt's talks with Maret in December 1792.[11] The Marquess of Lansdowne, not previously an admirer of Fox, fell out with Pitt over his non-inclusion in the Cabinet and opposed him over the war, and by late 1792 he and his son, the Earl of Wycombe, had decided to throw in their lot with Fox.[12] Moreover, the Duke of Grafton, William Wilberforce and Henry Duncombe all opposed the government at various times on the issue of the war.

The Foxite rump was, nevertheless, a relatively small group of MPs—Frank O'Gorman estimates it at some sixty-six MPs, less than half of the old opposition group, and L.G. Mitchell describes it as 'no longer an opposition but a pressure group'. Fox also realized in 1794 that all was 'not quite in harmony' within it and that increased party spirit would have to be fostered through the experience of the split with the Portland Whigs.[13] It had been only over the past decade that organized and consistent opposition to government was becoming recognized as legitimate, by way of the turmoil of 1782–84 and the Dissenting campaign of 1790 for the repeal of the Test Acts. Opposition to the British war against revolutionary France was a further significant factor in the formation and consolidation of the institution of a party of opposition in Parliament. Fox led his followers in a campaign marked as much by hostility to ministers as by opposition to the conflict itself. On 12 December 1792 Fox declared that 'there was no address at this moment that Pitt could frame, he would not propose an amendment to, and divide the House upon'. His opinion had not changed by October 1794. 'This war must grow to be disliked by all classes of people, as much, or more than the American war,' he wrote, 'and we may profit, as a party, by such an opinion becoming prevalent.'[14]

---

10 Lord John Russell (ed.), *Memorials and Correspondence of Charles James Fox*, 4 vol.s (London, 1853–57), iii, 65–6, Fox to Lord Holland, 9 March 1794; *A Letter to the Greatest Hypocrite in His Majesty's Dominions* (1794), an open letter to Loughborough; also *P.H.*, xxx, 1240–1, Sheridan, 21 January 1794.

11 Richard W. Davis, *Dissent in Politics 1780–1830. The Political Life of William Smith, M.P.* (London, 1971), pp.51–102; Murley, 'Origins and Outbreak', p.264. O'Gorman, *The Whig Party*, pp.253–4, lists other MPs who were not recognized to be associated with Fox but who often voted with him during the 1790s.

12 Henry Richard, Lord Holland, *Memoirs of the Whig Party During My Time*, 2 vol.s (London, 1852), i, 43–4.

13 O'Gorman, *The Whig Party*, pp.129, 253; L.G. Mitchell, *Charles James Fox* (Oxford, 1992), p.141; Russell (ed.), *Memorials*, iii, 66, Fox to Holland, 9 March 1794.

14 Ehrman, *The Reluctant Transition*, pp.54–6; *Malmesbury Diaries and Correspondence*, ii, 475, 12 December 1792; Russell (ed.), *Memorials*, iii, 89, Fox to Holland, 5 October 1794.

There had been no direct defensive necessity for Britain to go to war against France, it was argued. France, wrote an anonymous pamphleteer, 'can have no interest but to get rid of the frightful burthen of her foreign war, and to look to her deranged internal affairs, which will soon fix and fascinate all her regards'.[15] As for the question of Dutch security, the Whigs were scornful that the French breach of the Scheldt should constitute a serious ground for war. Protection of their river was a Dutch affair: the British alliance could not be expected to stretch to cover such a trivial issue, which would undoubtedly result in a long and arduous conflict. Therefore, Foxites argued, ministers must have had another purpose for engaging in hostilities. This notion was built up by some Foxites until it assumed the proportions that the conspiracy theory of the French Revolution beloved of the war crusaders was later to do. The Opposition theory of the war was that it was a despotic crusade waged by the absolute monarchs of Austria and Prussia against the newly-born republic of France, and it was deeply shameful that Britain had aligned itself with the cause of despotism rather than with that of liberty. Benjamin Vaughan, a member of Lansdowne's circle, had provided a detailed description of this autocratic crusade in his *Letters, on the Subject of the Concert of Princes, and the Dismemberment of Poland and France, By a Calm Observer* (1793), which had been published first as a series in the *Morning Chronicle* between 20 July 1792 and 25 June 1793. As early as 25 July 1792 he had asked: 'are they [Austria and Prussia] not acting upon a deep plan, long concerted, and profoundly secret? ... a conspiracy (which will eventually become one against the whole human race) is begun, such as was never begun before ... a *revolution*, as extraordinary as that of France, is under issue'. Vaughan did not implicate the British government as a full and deliberate member of this conspiracy, but he warned against allowing Britain to become associated with such wickedness, albeit unwittingly.[16] Fox and his followers, nursing old political grievances against George III and anxious to emphasize their credentials as traditional Whigs who were hostile to the corruption of executive power, developed this idea. In it they saw an explanation for the revolutionary violence of August and September 1792: the despots of Europe had harassed the Revolution into perversity. From the beginning of the war they declared that, encouraged by Burke and his writings, Britain had intentionally joined a 'Crusade of Kings', not a war of the people.[17]

---

15 *Comments on the Proposed War with France, on the State of Parties, and on the New Act Respecting Aliens* (London, 1793), pp.32–3.

16 Vaughan, *Letters on the Concert of Princes*, p.79. See also his *Two Papers by the Calm Observer, not printed in the collections of his letters extracted from the Morning Chronicle* (London, 1795), re-publishing letters first printed in August and September 1792.

17 For example, *Considerations on the French War, in which the Circumstances Leading to it, its Object, and the Resources of Britain for Carrying it on, are Examined, in a*

The Foxites mocked all government attempts to convince them that there were other and justified reasons for the war. They played hard on the ministers' difficulty in defining the specific objects of the war. They pressed ministers to admit that the real aim of the British government and its allies was to re-impose the monarchy on the French people, especially after Lord Hood's declaration in favour of Louis XVII at Toulon in September 1793. This was something that the despotic Combined Powers had no right to do and in which Britain, with its long tradition of liberty, ought to have no role. 'We who banished the race of Stuart, are fighting to restore the race of Capet, we who reformed the national religion and rejected popery, are fighting to continue its abuses!' one pamphleteer wrote.[18]

In their opposition to the war, the Foxites spoke often of the strategic advantages and superior resources they supposed France to possess over those of Britain and its allies. One reason for this, they explained, was the revolutionary state of France, which freed its treasury from dependence on ordinary fiscal limitations and allowed it to wage war with the whole capital of the nation. 'What a spectacle of energy does not the Republic of France display at this moment!' enthused the *Morning Chronicle* of 13 September 1793.

> The animating cause in which they are engaged has so roused and invigorated their minds, that what they could never accomplish under the reign of Despotism, they now achieve—they shew themselves a match for all the world. Such ever will be the result of a contest for Freedom.

On the other hand, Britain's national debt was immense and, while revenue from commerce had been expanding steadily, this had been paralysed by the war, which further drained British funds by the huge loans and subsidies paid to the allies, while ministers continually promised the people that French finances were in such a state of collapse as to make the end of the war imminent. 'Pitt, I really believe, is weak enough to think that the French cannot go on much longer, and they, on the other hand, have but too good grounds for thinking that we cannot,' Fox wrote to Holland in February 1796.[19]

Opposition writers and MPs also exposed what they represented as the adverse effects of the war upon Britain's internal circumstances. 'Pittism' became a clichéd term of abuse denoting a system of misrule dating back to Pitt's entry to power in late 1783. In the present instance, as in the American conflict, the government was charged with 'gambling with its people' in

---

Letter, to the Rt. Hon.ble William Pitt, By a British Merchant (London, 1794), pp.22–4; *P.H.*, xxx, 372-3, Fox, 12 February 1793; ibid., xxx, 1467, Whitbread, 6 March 1794.

18 *Considerations on the French War*, p.34.

19 Russell (ed.), *Memorials*, iii, 130, Fox to Holland, 18 February 1796.

kindling a blaze of deceived popular hysteria for a war they were waging in order to corrupt the liberal British constitution for their own personal gain, rather than for the defence of the nation. The real domestic object of the war was the extension of the influence of the crown, by the expansion of patronage in new contracts and posts, and this was the reason for their inability to inform the public of the specific object of the conflict. It was also the issue which caused the greatest hysteria in the opposition press: 'THE EXCESS OF THIS INFLUENCE IS THE CAUSE!—THE INCREASE OF THIS INFLUENCE IS THE OBJECT OF THE WAR!!!' screamed one pamphlet.[20]

The ministry was charged with robbing the British people of their civil liberties. Sheridan mocked ministers in the Commons in 1801: 'You have gagged the people, and bound them hand and foot; and then you say, look how quiet they are.'[21] The alarms raised in November 1792 had been whipped up on purpose in order to prepare the public mind for repression and war. In the Traitorous Correspondence Bill of March 1793 ministers infringed the liberty of commerce of British subjects. Opposition MPs and writers denounced the sedition and treason trials, the repeated suspension of habeas corpus, the 'Two Acts' of 1795, and the loan to Austria made by ministers in 1796 between parliamentary sessions, and therefore without Parliament's consent.

In justification of these criticisms, the Foxites maintained that Burke and those who agreed with him were yielding to hysteria and irrationality concerning the extent of the radicalism threat within Britain. Nothing had been proved to support the ministers' assertions of insurrection and riot in late 1792, claimed Sheridan. Dennis O'Bryen argued that it was a 'libel against the people' to think that there was any considerable number of people who wanted to change the 'genuine' British constitution. The public conception of 'French principles' had been grotesquely manipulated into the notion that all reformers wanted to level all property and institute economic equality. As for the very few extreme radicals in Britain, the Foxites warned the government that war only encouraged them. 'War is the parent of Discontent, and Discontent is the nurse of Revolution. A continuance of hostilities will produce the times which Mr. Burke describes, and then, as in France, it will be too late to Reform,' warned Daniel Stuart.[22]

Foxite commentators warned that if Britain should emerge victorious, it was unlikely that the ministry would fall, and the increased crown influence of

---

20 *War with France!* p.23.

21 *P.H.*, xxxv, 934, Sheridan, 2 February 1801.

22 Ibid., xxx, 524–33, Sheridan, 28 February 1793; Dennis O'Bryen, *Utrum Horum? The Government; or, the Country?* 5th edition (London, 1795), p.64; Daniel Stuart, *Peace and Reform, Against War and Corruption. In Answer to a Pamphlet, written by Arthur Young, Esq., entitled 'The Example of France, a Warning to Britain'*, 2nd edition (London, 1794), pp.105, 136.

war-time would not diminish and might even increase, because greater patronage might be available through new colonies conquered during the war. Ministers might be irremediably corrupted by their despotic Austrian, Prussian and Russian allies. To avert these evils, the remedy proposed by the Opposition, alongside a speedy settlement of peace, was a reformation of manners. This was a common cry in the 1790s, but in Foxite party terms it stood for the eradication of corruption in political high places. Mr. Curwen told the Commons in 1797 that

> He was not for a change of administration, which should have only for its object the putting one man into the place of another. The country would gain nothing by such a change. The change must be total, not of men, but of system. The immense influence of government must cease.

Fox was represented as a 'martyr of liberty' in contrast to the corrupt ministry and Court: as Stuart put it, 'He undauntedly struggled to avert the calamities of war; he did not succeed: But he succeeded in what was of much more immediate importance perhaps, in shielding the remaining liberties of the English people.'[23] More explicitly, they bayed for the removal of the Pitt administration from office and its replacement by Fox and his friends.

It is evident, therefore, that the war was in part simply the context in which they made their calls for a change of ministry. Fox wrote in 1800 to Grey that 'the incapacity of Ministers, rather than peace with Denmark or with France &c. ought to be the point principally pushed out of doors, and, to a certain degree too, within'.[24] Motions were moved in Parliament specifically calling for the dismissal of Pitt himself.[25] Another tactic was to call for Parliament to be resolved into a Committee on the State of the Nation, to inquire into Britain's circumstances under the present government.[26] Such calls continued to be made even after Pitt and his Cabinet had resigned in

---

23 *P.H.*, xxxiii, 602, John Christian Curwen, 19 May 1797; Stuart, *Peace and Reform*, p.120.

24 BL Add. MS 47565, f.17v, Fox to Grey, 1800.

25 *P.H.*, xxxiii, 183–5, the Earl of Suffolk, 27 March 1797; ibid., xxxiii, 595–6, Harvey Christian Combe, 19 May 1797; ibid., xxxiii, 735–44, 766–9, the Duke of Bedford, 30 May 1797; ibid., xxxiii, 1313–20, the Duke of Bedford, 22 March 1798; ibid., xxxv, 697–710, Thomas Tyrwhitt Jones, 4 December 1800.

26 Ibid., xxxi, 1408–9, Fox, 24 March 1795; ibid., xxxi, 1434–9, Guilford, 30 March 1795; ibid., 1449, Lansdowne, 30 March 1795; ibid., xxxii, 902–11, Grey, 10 March 1796; ibid., xxxv, 405–10, Charles C. Western, 9 July 1800; ibid., xxxv, 602–16, Tierney, November 1800; ibid., xxxv, 871–5, Earl Fitzwilliam and the Earl of Suffolk, amendment to the Address of Thanks, 2 February 1801.

February 1801.[27] Sheridan affected indignation when it was suggested that the Opposition's motivation for criticizing the ministry might be party politics and the desire to taste power:

> It is too much to see such men, covered equally with crime and shame, besmeared at once with blood and mire, erect their crests, and boldly demand support from the country, because they have endangered it, and attempt to proscribe as factious traitors, those who have fruitlessly endeavoured to save it.[28]

Nevertheless, despite the high content of party politics in Foxite polemic on the war, their opposition to the conflict was not wholly instrumental or manipulative. It was characterized by considerable sincerity, too, for the Foxite Whigs were also motivated by their own support for the French Revolution itself. They welcomed its early achievements, and they could not see why these should be a cause for alarm in Britain, far less for war against France. Many of them were inclined to support the French partly because of their personal connections with France. Fox himself was enchanted with the Revolution in its initial stages. He responded to it more wholly emotionally and less intellectually than Burke did, joyfully praising its acclamation of freedom and its condemnation of despotism. He associated the events of the Revolution in France with those of the Glorious Revolution in England a century earlier, with the American Revolution and (if not explicitly) with the Whig struggle of 1782-84, seeing only its attack on despotism and corrupt Courts and not its tendency towards an unstable democracy.[29] He continued to support the more moderate Girondin party when the Jacobin violence which so dismayed him was propelled into the ascendancy in Paris.

War against France was grossly unpalatable to these Whigs, and they declared that it was both unnecessary and undesirable, defending the revolutionaries' international activities against government and loyalist charges. It was unnecessary because France posed no danger to Britain. Democratic opinions had made very little progress in Britain, and French arms were directed elsewhere. France was anxious to preserve peace with Britain, and it was in too great a state of turmoil to be in a position to harm its powerful rival. It invaded only the territories of its declared enemies. War might in fact accelerate the circumstance which ministers were apparently so eager to prevent: the extension of radical opinion within Britain, and the aggrandizement of France. The Foxites regretted the Austro-Prussian war of

---

27 Ibid., xxxv, 1051–67, Grey, 25 March 1801; ibid., xxxv, 1169–79, the Earl of Darnley, 20 March 1801.

28 Ibid., xxxii, 1255, Sheridan, 2 November 1796.

29 Mitchell, *Charles James Fox*, chs. 6 & 8.

1792 against France, and sympathized with France; and although they were shocked by the events of August and September in France, they were delighted by the retreat of the Duke of Brunswick and the Prussian army. Fox wrote to Lord Holland that 'no public event not excepting Saratoga & York Town, ever happened that ever gave me so much delight. I would not allow myself to believe it for some days for fear of disappointment.'[30]

The Foxites did not divide Parliament on the announcement of the outbreak of Franco-British hostilities, but they continued to argue that the conflict was unnecessary. Britain ought to have welcomed the Revolution in France as the downfall of a government characterized by restless intrigue and love of warfare, and as a development that surely augured well for international commerce. They were adamant that the French, harried by German armies and anxious about their domestic state, had not wanted war with Britain and that it could have been avoided by negotiation. Their declaration of hostilities had simply been a pre-emptive strike after clear evidence of British hostility, such as the British refusal to mediate between France and the German powers in June 1792, the recall of Lord Gower, the British ambassador, from Paris, the violation of the 1786 commercial treaty, the Alien Act and the expulsion of the French envoy, Chauvelin, from London.

As the war progressed, the Foxites actually appeared to delight in allied reverses, and to indulge in grim unsurprise at British failures. In part this was due to their obsession with hoping for the fall of the ministry, which might possibly be produced by sufficiently bad military performances. The *Morning Chronicle* reported on 27 September 1793, with more than a hint of suppressed pleasure, that it was more than likely that America would join the war on the French side if it continued into 1794. Of the British expedition to Noirmoutier in September 1795, Fox wrote:

> Violent as the wish may sound I had much rather hear that they were all cut to pieces than that they gained any considerable success, for in the latter case the war may be prolonged to the utter destruction of both countries and to the total extinction of all principles of liberty and humanity in Europe. I think nothing can show the complete infatuation of our Government so much as this desperate expedition, which I believe as well as hope has not the smallest chance of success.[31]

---

30 BL Add. MS 47571, f.17v, Fox to Holland, 12 October 1792. Two years earlier, Earl Stanhope had even urged alliance with France—ibid., xxviii, 898, Stanhope, 26 November 1790.

31 BL Add. MS 47572, f.81, Fox to Holland, 10 September 1795.

However, he and his party did little to allay suspicions of francophilia. Opposition Whigs publicly condoned those revolutionary excesses which privately caused them real distress.[32] They accused conservatives of exaggerating the extent of these atrocities, and claimed that there were understandable excuses for them. One of the most popular explanations was that the Revolution had unleashed so immense a supply of energy, previously pent-up under absolutist oppression, that it could not immediately be brought under control. It was regrettable, but only natural, that those who had suffered such inhumanities at the hands of royal despotism should have to vent their fury when it became possible for them so to do. Only a minority of Frenchmen had supported the execution of Louis XVI, and Britain itself had executed Mary, Queen of Scots and Charles I. Nor were the human rights records of the allies, and other nations with which Britain was associated, by any means clean. The unbearable pressure brought to bear upon the fledgling republic by the hostile armies surrounding it was surely another factor to be taken into account. French excesses were therefore no justification for Britain to wage war against the Revolution; as one writer asked, 'why are *We* to be punished for *Their* crimes?'[33] They also supported British radical politicians tried for treason in 1794 and 1798. Thomas Erskine pleaded in vain that 'a man may be a friend to the rights of humanity and to the imprescriptible rights of social man, which is now a term of derision and contempt, that he may feel to the very soul for a nation beset by the sword of despots, and yet be a lover of his own country'.[34] The King wrote to Pitt in April 1797 about the recent Budget debate in Parliament: 'I think Mr. Fox's attempts to aggravate the difficulties must, if any further proof was necessary, convince every impartial man that from personal pique at me and my Administration he is become an open enemy of his country.'[35] Fox and his associates did not actually want to see the defeat of their country, but in their enthusiasm for republican France, hyperbole sometimes caused them to think the unthinkable: 'Much as I deprecate the idea of a conquest,' wrote William Williams, 'I so entirely differ

---

32 See, for example, BL Add. MSS 47571, ff. 11–19, Fox to Holland, 20 August 1792, 3 September 1792, [September 1792], 12 October 1792.

33 *War with France! or, who pays the reckoning? In an Appeal to the People of England! Repentance may come too late!* (London, 1793), p.30.

34 Thomas Erskine, speech at the trial of Thomas Hardy (1794), in James Ridgway (ed.), *The Speeches of the Hon. Thomas Erskine when at the Bar, on Subjects Connected with the Liberty of the Press, and against Constructive Treasons*, 4 vol.s (London, 1810), iii, 457. Many graphic satires portrayed the Foxites as Jacobins, e.g. Gillray's 'French-Telegraph making Signals in the Dark' (26 January 1795), BMC 8612.

35 *LCGIII*, ii, 566, George III to Pitt, 27 April 1797.

with Mr. Burke, that I would rather ten thousand times see my country a department of France, than a province of any other nation.'[36]

The arguments against war in general were not difficult to make. It was always a great evil, Opposition writers and MPs pronounced. Wars were perhaps inevitable in former, savage ages. 'But now, in these civilized and enlightened times, war can always be avoided with honour by a state powerful like England.' Indeed, war hindered the progress of civilization. It ought never to be engaged in 'until after every effort and speculation have been employed to repel its approach', censured Erskine. Fox told the Commons that war was detrimental to the general morality and humanity of the peoples involved; it calloused their hearts and minds to a state of indifference to cruelty and horror. Those who supported the war were reminded also of the hardships it produced for ordinary people. It was easy, claimed the Duke of Bedford, for ministers to expend other people's blood and treasure, untouched by their distresses. Many poems and songs were published in opposition journals and periodicals lamenting the sorrow of war-widows.[37]

In the present case, the Opposition argued that war was no practical answer to the ill-effects, imaginary or otherwise, of the French Revolution on Europe. Like religion, politics ought not to be propagated by the sword. Force could not ultimately achieve a desirable state of affairs. It was hardly beneficial to 'cut [Frenchmen's] throats to prevent their dying of rot'. Moreover, as the Duke of Bedford pointed out in the debate on the government's rejection of Bonaparte's offer to negotiate in January 1800, as long as the conflict lasted, France was not likely to become more stable and peaceful.[38]

Furthermore, any intentions the British government had to interfere in France and with its form of government were regarded as unjustifiable. No state, the Foxite Whigs argued, had the right to interfere in another. They were unconvinced by Burke's justification of interference in France by the law of civil vicinity, in his *Letters on a Regicide Peace*.[39] The civil case, argued Ralph Broome, presupposed an established rule of law which laid down what was and what was not a nuisance, and this was decided by a judge and based on past experience. The case of the French Revolution was entirely new, and it remained to be seen if the republican government of France was more injurious

---

36 William Williams, *A Reply to Mr. Burke's Two Letters on the Proposals for Peace with the Regicide Directory of France* (London, 1796), p.34.

37 *War with France!* pp.28–9; Erskine, *View of the Causes and Consequences*, p.114; *P.H.*, xxxi, 404–5, Fox, 17 April 1794; ibid., xxxi, 993–4, Bedford, 30 December 1794; poems in Betty T. Bennett, *British War Poetry in the Age of Romanticism, 1793–1815* (New York and London, 1976), pp.179–81, 153–4, 156, 253, 267–9.

38 William Williams, *Rights of the People; or, Reasons for a Regicide Peace ... with a few anticipating strictures upon Mr. Burke's long promised letters against a Regicide Peace* (London, 1796), p.65; *P.H.*, xxxiv, 1223, Bedford, 28 January 1800.

39 See pp.13-14 above.

to its international neighbourhood than the previous government; moreover, there was no impartial judge between nations as there was between individuals. Even if the interference were undertaken for the good of France, it was still a violation of principle, and it also might furnish other, less unselfish, nations with warrants for abuse.[40] Opposition writers were quick to point out the inconsistency involved in complaining that the French were seeking to spread their own opinions on government to Britain and at the same time planning to 'carry fire and the sword into the heart of France' in order to impose another form of government upon it by force.[41]

This line of argument did lay the Foxite Whigs themselves open to a charge of inconsistency: it was difficult for them to take successfully the moral high ground of insisting that wars of principle should not be fought, since they clearly favoured the ideology of the French above that of the allies and ignored or excused French aggression in Europe. They too often identified French principles with all that was good in philosophy and humanity:

> If these are the men who are to be extirpated everywhere, and especially in *France*, I am sure it will be impossible, unless those who feel it their interest to extirpate them, also feel themselves strong enough to destroy humanity, truth, philosophy, nay, the Heavens themselves.[42]

It was also awkward because of the violence and terror and blatant illiberality with which 'French principles' were increasingly associated. The Opposition therefore pointed to the example of Poland, which Russia, Austria and Prussia had shamelessly invaded and plundered and partitioned for their own advantage. Why was Britain interfering in France because of its violence towards other countries when she had not acted to halt the progress of the allies in Poland? The Foxite Whigs complained also about allied 'war crimes' against the earlier revolutionaries Lafayette and Dumouriez, both Whig heroes of the Revolution. Fox challenged the House of Commons in April 1793: 'If, as he feared, this war was undertaken against principles, let us look to the conduct of Germany, Russia and Prussia and, if the spirit of chivalry was so alive amongst us, see if there were no giants, no monsters, no principles against which we had better turn our arms.'[43] Nevertheless, Foxite sympathy

---

40 [Ralph Broome], *Strictures on Mr. Burke's Two Letters, addressed to a Member of the Present Parliament* (London, 1796), p.53; Vaughan, *Letters on the Concert of Princes*, pp.ii, vi–vii.

41 For example, O'Bryen, *Utrum Horum?* p.60.

42 J.G.A Pocock, *Virtue, Commerce and History* (Cambridge, 1985), p.285; Horatius Publicola, *The Prospect Before Us!!! Or the state of France in the month of August, 1794* (London, 1794), pp.89–90.

43 *P.H.*, xxx, 724, Fox, 25 April 1793.

for revolutionary France and hostility to Britain's war against it make it clear that the Opposition was motivated not only by party politics, but also by ideological partiality.

III Criticising the War and the Peace

Besides disputing the legitimacy of the war, Opposition Whig MPs and writers also found fault with the government's handling of the conflict and they called frequently for peace to be negotiated with the French Republic. Sometimes they simply grumpily listed French successes, failed British and allied campaigns and sums of money spent to date and made gloomy prognostications for the success of the allied war in the light of these facts. Delays and incompetence were severely censured, and the responsibility was always laid at ministers' feet, never with the British forces or their commanders. Even when the British troops or fleets won victories, the Opposition complained that the advantages were squandered by an administration inept in matters of strategy. Like loyalists, the Opposition seemed bewildered by the naval mutinies, which seemed to be 'inconsistent with the brave, generous and open character of British seamen', but, unlike loyalists, they were sure that 'the country were to look to the ministers for the great cause of all this', for not having provided sufficiently good conditions for the sailors.[44]

Another constant Opposition complaint was the expense of the war. They mentioned national debt increases in tones of horror, and predicted ruin for Britain if another war should arise before there had been time to heal the nation's finances from the ravages of the present one. The government was condemned for the weight of taxes it was imposing on the lower classes. The conflict also robbed essential British agriculture of farm labourers, who were pressed into the navy or the army, and great numbers of whom were killed. It dried up commerce and drove British manufacturers out of business and labourers out of work. The greatest extravagance complained of by Opposition MPs, however, was the subsidies and loans granted by the British government to its allies. Fox accurately forecast in 1794 that when other powers saw Prussia's successful blackmailing of the British ministers to provide money in return for its armies, they would do likewise and he warned that Britain would end up bearing the whole cost of the war. It was complained that the King of Prussia and the Austrian Emperor were not to be trusted to fulfil their military obligations or to repay loans fully and on time. 'Our allies', observed

44 *P.H.*, xxxiii, 487–8, Sheridan, 8 May 1797.

Lansdowne in March 1795, 'appeared to be allies only for the purpose of taking our money.'[45]

On the possible invasion of Britain by the French, Opposition writers and MPs divided their comments between doubts that the government had provided adequately for the defence of the country and patriotic certainty that the British people would be more than a match for any invading force. Dennis O'Bryen solved the equation by arguing that a French invasion could never succeed against an armed and united British people, but that while the country remained torn by discontent and division under the Pitt administration, it was in grave danger from any such attack.[46] Certainly, the Foxites would have assisted in the defence of the country had an invasion occurred. Fox told Grey in 1799 that he did not want to cooperate until an invasion actually arose, so that the government might not have any further encouragement for their repressive measures, but that in the event all who were able should exert themselves 'to the utmost' against the French.[47] Sheridan spoke on 20 April 1798 in support of a spirited and united opposition to any French invasion, earning the rather stiff thanks of Pitt—George III, having heard earlier of Sheridan's intention to speak in this vein, had instructed Pitt not to welcome his support too warmly: 'any compliments would disgust friends, and certainly are not necessary; indeed, I should wish some intimation might be made that this change of language was very late'.[48]

Since the Opposition could not criticise the armed forces, because of the patriotic attitude they wanted to display, they raised constitutional matters concerning them instead. They argued that British Dissenters and Roman Catholics ought to be permitted to become officers in the army and navy, since they had long shown their loyalty to their country in times of national crisis, and now that French and Irish Catholics were being employed by the government in this capacity. They complained that ministerial measures to strengthen home defence, by increasing the numbers of the militia and by instituting the Volunteers, were unconstitutional and might prove to be the beginnings of a standing army, the traditional Whig symbol of court corruption. When only the propertied were enlisted in the Volunteers, the Opposition worried about the strengthening of the aristocracy at the expense of the people and of the crown. When the Volunteers were widened in 1798 to include all able-bodied men, aristocratic members of the Opposition

---

45 Ibid., xxxi, 442–51, Fox, 30 April 1794; ibid., xxxi, 1445, Lansdowne, 30 March 1795.

46 O'Bryen, *Utrum Horum?* pp.74, 77.

47 BL Add. MS 47565, f.4, Fox to Grey, [1799]; cf. *P.H.*, xxxii, 1216–23, Fox, 18 October 1796. See also the *Morning Chronicle*, 13 October 1796.

48 *P.H.*, xxxiii, 1424–8, Sheridan, 20 April 1798; ibid., xxxiii, 1428–9, Pitt, 20 April 1798; *LCGIII*, iii, 49, George III to Pitt, 21 April 1798.

complained that the landed classes had been deprived of their traditional privilege of raising their own local defence forces. Ministers were accused of raising the alarm of invasion simply in order to be able to increase the number of troops within Britain. These fears were further substantiated by the erection of barracks to house regular army troops on duty within Britain. The voluntary subscription which was established to pay for the Volunteers was opposed because it would lead to social intimidation and invidious personal distinctions and because it was unconstitutional. Rather, it was suggested, a new tax should be imposed, to be levied on placemen and the holders of sinecures.[49] The Opposition also claimed that keeping foreign soldiers within Britain was unconstitutional too, and might lead to the formation of a standing army. This issue was raised by the temporary installation of Hessian troops in barracks in Hampshire and on the Isle of Wight in 1794, and by the employment of French *émigré* regiments in the British army.

These Opposition criticisms, however, laid their authors open again to the charge of double standards and, in consequence, of engaging in factious party politics. In order to be able to criticize Pitt and his Cabinet on as many grounds as possible, they wanted to be able both to oppose the war altogether, for the various reasons already outlined, and to find fault with the way in which ministers conducted it. It was not necessarily inconsistent to complain that the war was both undesirable and badly managed; but it was difficult to complain quite so much as the Opposition did about the conduct of various campaigns in a war with which they were supposed to disagree altogether, without being found guilty of criticizing for its own sake. Finding fault with the conduct of the war in its first year had the added appeal of being a potential means of retaining the support of the Portland Whigs.[50] The *Morning Chronicle* of 22 February 1793 summarized well Whig thinking on the war, containing in a nutshell doubts of the necessity of the war, claims to patriotism, criticism of ministerial management and calls for a change of administration:

> However we may have got into the war, the war must be supported. This country cannot, must not see the French extend their maritime frontier through the whole Dutch territory; but if we are to avert this fatality, we must begin by addressing the Crown to remove the Ministers, whose imbecile councils, in bringing us into the calamity, give us no confidence in their talents to conduct it.

Peace was constantly demanded by the Foxites, who did not support the continuance of the conflict at any stage in the 1790s. If there had been a

49 The *Morning Chronicle*, 27 December 1796; *P.H.*, xxxi, 165–9, George Harrison and Thomas W. Coke, 8 April 1794.

50 See BL Add. MS 47569, f.15, Fox to Adam, 18 September 1793.

justifiable motive for going to war in the defence of the Dutch, they argued, the British government ought to have made peace with France after the French troops had been evacuated from Holland in 1793. War was a greater evil and a greater source of evil than peace with revolutionary France, since either failure or success was dangerous to Britain's welfare. Defeat would establish a great military republic in the heart of western Europe, hostile to Britain, while success would destroy a valuable market for British manufactures and strengthen the bastions of European despotism. Even a humiliating peace would be better than further military disasters and infamy. 'We have sacrificed much to experiments of war,' stated the *Morning Chronicle* wearily on 25 October 1799; 'why may we not sacrifice a little to experiments of peace?'

The Foxite Opposition was adamant that the French government sincerely desired peace. Peace was too great a blessing for it to refuse, for it would allow it to restore order and peace within the nation. Violent speeches were made in both the French and British legislative assemblies and these, it was argued, should not be seen as reliable barometers of attitudes towards peace. Fox was sure that the French people were anxious for peace and that this must influence their rulers.[51] The Opposition claimed that public opinion in Britain was also very largely hostile to the war and eager for peace. 'It is said, as a proof of the popularity of the War, that 1500 recruits were raised last week in Manchester,' reported the *Morning Chronicle* of 22 February 1793. 'Alas! is it not rather a proof, that the war has already suspended the looms of Manchester?'

Sometimes, especially after Napoleon's rise to military and then political power, members of the Opposition confessed that they no longer approved of the French system of government, but they claimed that Britain had no chance of changing it and should therefore abandon the conflict.[52] It was better to make peace before Britain was beaten into it. Britain was in danger of making the same mistake as it had in the American war, that of underestimating the enthusiasm and commitment of the republican people for their new government, and the French people had considerably more resources and experience of arms than had the Americans. Not only did France have a powerful army but it had become an armed nation. Britain's small force, often abandoned by its allies and threatened by neutral nations, could expect to make little military impact upon it. Britain, said Lansdowne, had become a 'Don Quixote' figure, fighting a crusade against the French windmill.[53] Surely

---

51 Russell (ed.), *Memorials*, iii, 184, Fox to Holland, October 1800.

52 *P.H.*, xxxiii, 1535–8, Lansdowne, November 1798; ibid., xxxiv, 1052, Tierney, 7 June 1799.

53 *P.H.*, xxxi, 459, Lansdowne, 30 April 1794.

negotiations by themselves could do no harm, and might even strengthen Britain's fighting position.

However, the Opposition was sceptical of the government's sincerity in offering to negotiate for peace after December 1795. Ministers had 'peace in their mouths, while they made preparations for war'.[54] But the Foxites criticized the administration's strategies in negotiating and in setting up negotiations as calculated to delay and to frustrate the French—the lack of full negotiating powers held by Lord Malmesbury in 1796; his return as the British envoy in 1797, although it was known that the French distrusted him; the use of the title of King of France in referring to the Comte de Provence; the continual reproaching of France as the initial aggressor. Ministers were charged with making excuses to carry on a war which kept them in power. Their reasons for not negotiating were all self-generating: they required a stable *enough* government in France, *enough* security and *enough* indemnity to give them confidence that a settlement would be adhered to.[55]

'I am convinced that this ministry cannot make any peace without incredible sacrifices,' wrote Fox in February 1796, privately conceding French as well as British obstinacy. 'The minds of the two Governments are so hostile to each other, and their mutual diffidence so rooted, that it must be next to a miracle, if they can agree till absolute necessity forces them.'[56] Nevertheless, he and his supporters insisted that if peace were to be made, it would be necessary to conciliate the French. Britain must acknowledge the French Republic and restore all its conquests as the price of peace, though some conceded that France should also renounce some of its conquests. All Britain's conquests should be viewed 'as dust in the balance' compared with the blessings of peace. Such concessions might disgrace ministers, but they would not humiliate the country.[57]

On the whole, the Foxites were pleased with the treaty of Amiens. They were delighted that the war had been stopped by an inglorious peace, having achieved none of the objects for which it had been claimed to be fought. 'The Triumph of the French government over the English does in fact afford me a degree of pleasure which it is very difficult to disguise,' Fox told Grey. The navigation of the Scheldt had not been re-closed; Savoy, Holland and Belgium had not been rescued from revolutionary France; the government of France had not been restored to a monarchical form; in short, Europe was not 'delivered'

---

54 *P.H.*, xxxii, 716–17, Grey, 15 February 1796.

55 Vaughan, *Letters on the Concert of Princes*, pp.352–4; *The Evidence Summed Up*, p.34; Williams, *A Reply to Mr. Burke's Two Letters*, pp.22–3; Erskine, *View of the Causes and Consequences*, pp.94–5; *Strictures on the Overtures of Peace*, pp.24–5; *P.H.*, xxxiv, 1226, Bedford, 28 January 1800.

56 Russell (ed.), *Memorials*, iii, 130, Fox to Holland, 18 February 1796.

57 Erskine, *View of the Causes and Consequences*, pp.107–12, 116, 123–4.

from the French Revolution. In general, therefore, the Foxites sanctimoniously mixed approval of the fact of peace with resignation to such peace terms as had been accepted. As Sheridan summed up, damning the settlement with faint praise:

> This, Sir, is a peace which every man ought to be glad of, but no man can be proud of. It is a peace involving a degradation of the national dignity, which no truly English heart can feel with indifference. It was a peace, which the war had a tendency to lead to, as its necessary result. The war was one of the worst wars in which this country was ever engaged: and the peace is, perhaps, as good as any man could make, under the circumstances in which the country was placed.[58]

The peace had been made too late to prevent much of the evil of war or much French aggrandizement, but it was better to be made now than later still. The Earl of Carnarvon, however, joined disappointed supporters of the war in condemning the terms as wholly inadequate to the safety and glory of Britain. He told the House of Lords that 'our negociators [had] ineffectually surrendered the interests of the country'. Lansdowne also had reservations about the concessions Britain had made, and he thought that another war was probable before too long.[59]

IV Opposition Tactics

In pressing their views on the war, the Foxites relied chiefly on a combination of parliamentary opposition and the press, backed by any other support they could persuade to cooperate. The opposition press was heavily used throughout the decade, although it was never so successful as the conservative press in terms of sheer volume of output and distribution. London newspapers which remained faithful to the Whigs were the *Morning Chronicle*, the *Telegraph*, the *General Advertiser*, the *Gazetteer*, the *Courier* and the *Morning Post*. Parliamentary speeches of Opposition MPs were well circulated—Fox's published speeches and Erskine's pamphlet, *A View of the Causes and Consequences of the Present War with France* (1797) sold particularly well, Erskine's *View* going through nine editions in its first week and forty-eight editions altogether. Opposition pamphlets sometimes replied directly to pro-war tracts, especially those written by Burke, though Daniel Stuart's *Peace*

58 BL Add. MSS 47565, ff.51–v, Fox to Grey, 22 October 1801; *P.H.*, xxxvi, 17, Sheridan, October 1801.

59 *P.H.*, xxxvi, 188, Carnarvon, 3 November 1801; ibid., xxxvi, 712–7, Carnarvon, 13 May 1802; NMM, DUC/7, Lansdowne to Admiral Sir John Duckworth, 19 October 1801.

and Reform (1794) was addressed in reply to Arthur Young's *The Example of France a Warning to Britain* (1793), and, not to be outdone in pedantry, the historian William Belsham wrote two pamphlets in point-by-point reply to Herbert Marsh's loyalist accounts of the causes of the war.[60] Like conservative propaganda, opposition publications were designed to reach different levels of readership, ranging from handbills and short, pithy tracts to lengthy, densely argued pamphlets.

In Parliament, the Foxites continued to divide Parliament even when they had no chance of defeating Pitt, ostensibly to record their opinions and their efforts to halt the conflict, but also to maintain a sense of party and perhaps to win over some war-weary Pittites. But they were forced to admit the defeat of this tactic, and in 1797, Fox and many of his parliamentary supporters seceded from Parliament in protest at their lack of impact on government policy. Whitbread, Tierney and Smith remained at Parliament, attending more regularly than ever and continuing to criticize government war policy; Sheridan often turned up and others drifted back; but Fox himself stayed away until 1801. It was a move he had contemplated as far back as April 1795, and it is hard to resist the conclusion that he enjoyed the privacy he was afforded by the secession. He explained to his supporters in 1800 that his views appeared to be unacceptable, but that he was too old to change them, and so he would remain in seclusion from Parliament. Erskine assured them that Fox would return to Westminster whenever he thought he had any chance of success.[61] 'Always remember', Fox told Grey in the same year, on Grey's request that he attend a debate on the Irish union,

> that the original ground of retiring was not the questions likely to be agitated were unimportant, but that our attendance in Parliament upon them was useless, and because useless in some measure hurtful as tending to deceive the country into an opinion that the House of Commons was still a place in which it was worth while to try the effect of argument and reason.[62]

Lord Holland thought that the secession was less successful than it might have been because it was not complete and because it was overshadowed almost immediately by the naval mutinies, but that it did disconcert Pitt and deprived

---

60 William Belsham, *Remarks on a Late Publication, Styled the History of the Politics of Great Britain & France* (London, 1800); idem, *Reply to the Rev. Herbert Marsh's Vindication of a Late Work, Styled a History of the Politics of Great Britain and France* (London, 1801).

61 Fox, *Mr. Fox's celebrated speech with the proceedings at the Shakespeare Tavern, on Friday, October 10, 1800, etc.* (London, 1800), pp.18, 20–1.

62 BL Add. MS 47565, f.24, Fox to Grey, 1800. See also ibid., 47569, ff.99–100, Fox to Wilberforce, 21 February 1799, for remarks in a similar vein.

him of a lever with the King who could be less easily persuaded that measures were either impossible or necessary because of Parliament.[63] It also naturally weakened the Foxite voice of opposition on the war.

Opposition writers and MPs often called for the public to make the goverment aware of its disapproval of the war. The *Morning Chronicle* of 12 January 1793 published a very early call to public action against the war: 'If the people are foolishly supine on this occasion, they may thank themselves for the burdens which must be the inevitable consequence. When the war is once entered into, it will be too late to deprecate its effects.' The Opposition Whigs also cooperated with some activities organized by Friends of Peace. Indeed, the petitions against the war in 1795 and against the 'Two Bills' as part of a malevolent 'war system', and the Addresses to the throne requesting peace and the dismissal of ministers in 1797, were initiated by the Foxites and supported by the liberals locally.[64] The Foxites failed to develop this strategy, however. Fox himself was increasingly disillusioned with public willingness to protest against the war and against the government. At the beginning of January 1795, as the petitioning movement gathered momentum, he wrote with some excitement at the prospect of such a show of strength in the country. In November 1795 he thought that the 'higher classes' of British society were disappointingly universal in their support of Pitt's repressive measures, but that he and his party were popular among the lower classes. During the secession, however, he despaired of the public 'spirit'. In 1801 he wrote to Grey: 'till I see that the publick has some dislike (indignation I do not hope for) to absolute power, I see no use in stating in the House of Commons the principles of Liberty and Justice'.[65] However, his own lack of activity and interest almost certainly discouraged others from initiating or supporting anti-war petitions and meetings, and so the Foxite opposition to the war lost momentum and energy.[66]

Fox and his allies inside and outside Parliament certainly opposed the British war against revolutionary France and criticized its handling by the government because of their political concern to undermine Pitt's policies and to bring down his government. This resulted in the further development of a

---

63 Holland, *Memoirs*, i, 91–2.

64 For example, the Edinburgh petition of December 1795, which collected 8000 signatures in the space of four days against the Two Bills and in support of a call for peace. The petition was organized by Henry Erskine, who lost his position of Dean of the Faculty of Advocates in Scotland over the issue, and it was presented in Parliament by his brother Thomas.

65 BL Add. MSS 47569, ff.54–6, Fox to ?, 2 January 1795; Russell (ed.), *Memorials*, iii, 126, Fox to Holland, 15/17 November 1795; BL Add. MS 47565, f.38, Fox to Grey, 1801.

66 J.E. Cookson, *The Friends of Peace: Anti-War Liberalism in England, 1793–1815* (Cambridge and New York, 1982), p.162; Mitchell, *Charles James Fox*, p.145; see also Cookson, *Friends of Peace*, p.197.

party system at Westminster, but it also meant that the Foxites could not focus singlemindedly on the war itself as a discrete issue. Nevertheless, they also opposed the conflict because of their enthusiasm for the original principles and achievements of the French Revolution. To this extent, they too were gripped by the notion that this was a war of ideas, and they themselves characterized it as such, claiming that the British government had joined battle on the wrong side. Radical and pacifist writers and activists, as the next chapter shows, opposed the conflict from different standpoints, but they, no less than the Foxites, also had to respond to Burke's conception of the war as a struggle over ideas.

Chapter 5

The Opposition to the War (II): Radicals and Friends of Peace

If Opposition writers and MPs were hostile to the war because they were hostile to William Pitt as well as for ideological reasons, radical politicians and the liberal 'Friends of Peace' had other concerns which led them to oppose it no less vehemently, but usually with little or no cooperation from each other or from the Foxites. Radicals opposed it because they were sympathetic to the French Revolution and because they wished to see its doctrines spreading unhindered. Their enthusiasm for the Revolution was stronger than that of the Foxite Whigs: they approved of the Jacobin government as well as its predecessors, and they only began to doubt the French Republic when Napoleon Bonaparte rose to power. They also criticized the conflict for imposing great hardships on many ordinary people. The radicals' arguments were more consistent and less weighed down by opposition for opposition's sake than those of the Foxites, but they also used the war to further their primary concern to demand parliamentary reform and, in particular, the extension of the franchise. Just as the loyalists were hostile to French Revolutionary ideology , and especially so as it appeared to threaten the British constitution, so the radicals acclaimed that ideology, and particularly so because it supported the cause of parliamentary reform in Britain. The Friends of Peace were the group who most singlemindedly opposed the war itself. They did not oppose it, however, out of agreement with French Revolutionary principles, but rather because they disputed British loyalist and crusading ideas. Fundamentally, they opposed war in general because of the moral and religious objections they held towards it; but they were also hostile to this particular conflict because of the injustice they perceived in the British grounds and conduct for it. The radicals, therefore, were deeply caught up in the British war of ideas, though they largely aligned themselves opposite the British government; and while the Friends of Peace rejected the validity of a war over ideology, they had perforce to take part in the British ideological debate in order to repudiate the conservative analysis. The opposition to the war within Parliament has been considered in the previous chapter; this chapter expands on anti-war attitudes by examining the views of these extra-parliamentary activists.

I The Radicals

The radicals were hostile to the conflict against France mainly because they supported the French Revolution. They admired its heroism and defended its purpose:

> The People of France had for many centuries groaned under the most horrible despotism that the human imagination can conceive ... To overthrow this villainous combination of the FEW against the liberty, property, and happiness of the MANY, in the year 1789, the whole Nation actuated as it were by one general impulse, rose up, 'hurled the Tyrant from his throne', and established the RIGHTS OF MAN.[1]

It appalled them to see an attempt to overturn this great triumph, and they ardently supported revolutionary France in its struggle against Austria and Prussia in 1792. Delegates and addresses were sent by radical societies to encourage the National Convention, and clothing, shoes, blankets and ammunition were sent to help the 'soldiers of Liberty'. The London Corresponding Society (LCS) address to the National Convention expressed regret that the British army was not fighting alongside the French: 'Our hands are bound, but our hearts are free, and they are with you.'[2] Sheffield radicals staged a massive demonstration to celebrate Prussia's defeat in September, roasting a whole ox, quartering it, and taking it through the town to be given to the poor and the debtors in jail, cheered by a crowd and cannon-fire; and an effigy of the Duke of Brunswick was executed on Kennington Common in London. The French victory at Jemappes and Dumouriez's entry into Brussels in November and December 1792 respectively stimulated celebrations in Perth and Dundee.

In the autumn and winter of 1792 the radical societies of Britain grew and multiplied rapidly. The reports sent home by French envoys of the Paris National Convention implied that the British government would be unable to oppose the French Republic's strategy in Europe, such was the enthusiasm in Britain for radical opinions, and the myth gained currency in Paris that Britain was on the verge of a highly successful revolution of its own. To some extent the pre-war optimism of the British radicals themselves supported this view. The LCS told the National Convention: 'Frenchmen, you are already free, but Britons are preparing to be so.' Other declarations to the Convention and the Jacobin Club of Paris assured the French that the British people would not

---

1 [Daniel Isaac Eaton], *Extermination, or an Appeal to the People of England on the Present War, with France* (London, 1793), pp.4–6.

2 The full address is printed in Albert Goodwin, *The Friends of Liberty: the English Democratic Movement in the Age of the French Revolution* (London, 1979), pp.501–3.

allow their government to go to war. This was not a deliberate attempt to deceive the French; the Edinburgh radical William Peddie wrote in the same month to a friend, 'I am of opinion with you, that it must end in a Republic. The soldiers will not fight against a Republic, but should they, France will send over 80,000 to help us.'[3] Handbills and pamphlets were published in Britain, arguing against a war against France on the basis of the hardships and misery it would cause.

In fact, however, although much more numerous and well-organized than ever before, British radicals were only a small minority of the population, and they were not well co-ordinated. Many societies were quite small and short-lived; Dissenters, Whigs, and working-class societies had very little contact with each other; local issues often preoccupied provincial societies; and few had a degree of hostility to the existing order in Britain approaching that of the revolutionaries in France—the great majority called for reform rather than for revolution. The general public alarm of early December stimulated by the government's summoning of Parliament and calling out of the local militia showed how weak the support for radicalism really was in Britain and how ready the population was to rally to the call for loyalism.

When war broke out between Britain and France, the radicals in Britain nevertheless continued to support the Revolution in France against the allied powers of Europe, which now included Britain. They approved of Jacobinism and defended it throughout the decade in their publications. Atrocities were explained by the enormity of the cataclysm: 'It could not be expected', wrote Joseph Towers, 'that so enormous a system of civil, ecclesiastical, and aristocratical tyranny, as that of which the old government was composed, could be so completely overturned, without very violent convulsions.' William Fox's *Thoughts on the Death of the King of France* (1793) did not condone the execution of Louis XVI, but it argued that it was a totally unjust cause of war. Those who executed him had been simply the last link in a long chain of events, of which the real initiator had been the old government itself, by its injustice and abuse of power. John Thelwall even tried to question whether there was any link at all between the violence and the Revolution itself. 'If the excesses cannot be proved, either logically or experimentally, to have been connected with the *principles*, coincidence of time is nothing to the purpose, and the one cannot be said to have produced the other.'[4] Like opposition

3 LCS address quoted from the *London Chronicle*, 12 November 1792, cited in Emsley, *British Society and the French Wars*, p.14; PRO HO 102/7, William Peddie to Robert Purvis, 21 November 1792, quoted in Murley, 'Origins and Outbreak', p.175. On radicalism in the 1790s, see also H.T. Dickinson, *British Radicalism and the French Revolution 1789–1815* (Oxford, 1985).

4 [Joseph Towers], *A Dialogue Between an Associator and a Well-Informed Englishman, on the Grounds of the Late Associations, and the Commencement of a War with France* (London, 1793), pp.22–4; William Fox, *Thoughts on the Death of the King of France*

writers and MPs, radicals blamed the war on Pitt and the Combined Powers of Europe, and they criticized its counter-revolutionary objects. The radical lecturer at Sheffield on the fast-day of 1794 claimed that the war being waged against France was a kind of spiritual persecution, which often advanced rather than hindered good causes, such as the establishment of Christianity.[5]

Radicals therefore continued to support the French armies, now fighting against those of their own country. They toasted 'the Armies of Liberty' and used French revolutionary phrases, songs and symbols—*Ça ira*, the *Marseillaise*, trees of liberty, Jacobin oaths, the title of 'citizen' and the denunciation of tyrannical kings. They used the title 'Convention' for the national meeting of radical society delegates in Edinburgh in November and December 1793, and they imitated French procedures and terminology in it. They insisted that the British government ought to recognize the French Republic formally: William Fox argued that denying its existence could not prevent it from existing and that, by making war against it, the government was recognizing it *de facto*.[6] Wordsworth's *The Prelude* recalled his mixed feelings after the French victory at Hondeschoote on 8 September 1793:

> Exulted, in the triumph of my soul,
> When Englishmen by thousands were o'erthrown,
> Left without glory on the field, or driven,
> Brave hearts! to shameful flight. It was a grief,—
> Grief call it not, 'twas anything but that,—
> A conflict of sensations without name ....

Robert Southey wrote in October 1799 to Humphry Davy of his joy at continuing French success: 'Massena, Buonaparte, Switzerland, Italy, Holland, Egypt, all at once! the very spring-tide of fortune! It was a dose of gaseous oxide to me, whose powerful delight still endures.'[7]

The allied war effort was in fact deemed ultimately hopeless by radical commentators. The dreadful power of France had been demonstrated in the first campaign, and it could not be assumed that Britain would always be victorious by some fixed law of nature. France was never easily subdued, and it had been strengthened immeasurably by the enthusiasm of the people for their new freedom. Britain, marching from defeat to defeat, from rash projects

---

(London, 1793); John Thelwall, *Sober Reflections on the Seditious and Inflammatory Letter of the Right Hon. Edmund Burke, to a Noble Lord. Addressed to the Serious Consideration of his Fellow-Citizens* (London, 1796), p.69, 85–6, 95.

5 *Fast Day at Sheffield. A Serious Lecture Delivered at Sheffield; February 28, 1794. Being the Day Appointed for A General Fast; to which are added A Hymn and Resolutions*, 4th edition (London, 1794), pp.8–9.

6 William Fox, *The Interest of Great Britain, Respecting the French War*, 2nd edition (London, 1793), p.16.

7 William Wordsworth, *The Prelude* (1850), x, 285–90; Carnall, *Southey*, p.48.

to acute losses, ought to be moved to caution by these repeated warnings, instead of which the government appeared to be convinced that the French struggle was the last convulsion of an exhausted state. Radicals mocked British and allied military failures. The lecturer at the Sheffield Fast-Day in 1794 compared 'the leagued Despots' to the kings who conspired against 'the immortal Joshua': 'yet all could not overcome him, but victories upon victories he gained, and in one campaign not less than thirty-one kings he slew'.[8]

But the radicals opposed the war not just for its attack on the French Revolution, but also as an evil in itself. They insisted that there was no such thing as 'natural enemies' and, as Richard Price had done in his 1790 *Discourse on the Love of Our Country*, they extolled the virtues of universal brotherhood. A nation was just one member of the family of the human race, and it could flourish only within the harmony and welfare of the whole. War was 'altogether a solecism in commercial politics'; it was also 'unworthy of rational Beings, and utterly repugnant to ... the Christian Religion'.[9] It was particularly odious when it was waged against opinions; it was persecution and, as such, detestable. This was particularly significant to British radicals, who believed that they along with the French revolutionaries were being persecuted for their opinions by the British government and its war. It could not be a means of justice, according to Thelwall, since might was not necessarily right: it was rather a means of revenge, desolation, conquest, ambition, plunder, corruption, murder and oppression.[10]

The radicals also called for an end to the war because of their primary objective, which remained political reform in Britain. The resolutions taken by the Sheffield radicals in February 1794 began by denouncing the war, but ended by declaring that 'the People have no remedy for their Grievances, but a REFORM IN PARLIAMENT'. Likewise, the resolutions adopted by the LCS on 29 June 1795 at St George's Fields demonstrated that, although 'the Friends of Reform [were] indeed the Friends of Peace', the war to the radicals was just one of the many distresses brought upon the people by a corrupt government, if a major one, and that it was only likely to be halted by parliamentary reform, the panacea for all these ills.[11]

Government ministers, according to radicals, exploited the conflict in order to suppress civil liberties in Britain. They believed that they were

---

8 *Fast Day as Observed at Sheffield*, pp.6, 11.

9 *The Voice of the People* (printed for R. Lee), pp.2–3; *Fast Day as Observed at Sheffield*, pp.7, 11 no. 1.

10 John Thelwall, *The Rights of Nature*, 2 vol.s (London, 1796), i, 67, 86; ibid., ii, 7–8.

11 *Fast Day as Observed at Sheffield*, p.11 no. 11; *Account of the Proceedings at a General Meeting of the LCS*, pp.12 no.s 1–3, pp.13–14.

suffering an English 'reign of terror' under Pitt, 'the English Robespierre'.[12] In June 1795 the LCS reprobated the war's sole purpose of annihilating the liberties of France and Britain. Trade and commerce would recover after the war, but, warned Mrs. Barbauld, 'the stab, which our liberties have suffered, is not susceptible of so speedy and effectual a remedy'.[13] The Sheffield radicals passed resolutions stating that the government's policies of quartering Hessian troops temporarily in Britain and of building barracks around the country were a menace to British liberty: the Hessians might at any time be let loose upon British subjects, and the barracks might be designed to house more foreign mercenaries for the same purpose. Daniel Isaac Eaton reported that a Hessian soldier had stabbed an Englishman in a street quarrel, and inferred that they had all been brought over 'to cut the throats of Englishmen'. The LCS resolutions of April 1794 included two against the employment of French *émigrés* in the British armed forces for the same reason, and against impressment into the forces. Wordsworth and Coleridge reprobated the government's use of spies and informers, and the suspension of habeas corpus. John Thelwall saw the violent interruption of his lectures in Yarmouth and elsewhere in 1796 by naval press-gangs as merely a symptom of the malady. Something was rotten in the state of Denmark: 'I cannot but conclude that the brutal conspiracy ... originated with higher authorities that the commanders of two or three frigates and sloops of war. The system of terror is still to be supported.'[14] If the continental despots were successful in their war against France, having already crushed the Polish revolution, according to radical commentators, they might next turn upon England, the home of revolutionary ideas through Locke and later political thinkers, including Burke himself.

---

12 Clive Emsley, 'An Aspect of Pitt's "Terror": Prosecutions for Sedition During the 1790s', *Social History*, 6 (1981), 155. At least, said Thelwall, 'the *French* Robespierre was no *apostate*' (*Sober Reflections*, p.75). For an example of popular radical complaint about Pitt, see *A Full, True, and Particular Account of the Birth, Parentage and Education, Life, Character and Behaviour of that most notoriously notified Malefactor Willy Pitto* [n.d.].

13 *Account of the Proceedings at a General Meeting of the London Corresponding Society, convened by public advertisement, and held in an inclosed field, behind the Long Room, Borough Road, St. George's Fields, on Monday, the 29th of June, 1795* [London, 1795], p.12 no.3; [Mrs. Barbauld], *Reasons for National Penitence, Recommended for the Fast, Appointed February XXVIII, 1794* (London, 1794), p.32.

14 *Fast Day as Observed at Sheffield*, p.11, no.s 4–7; Daniel Isaac Eaton, *Politics for the People*, II:7, 15 March 1794, quoted in Erdman, *Blake*, p.278; *P.H.*, xxxi, 492-3; Alan G. Hill (ed.), *Letters of William Wordsworth. A New Selection* (Oxford, 1984), p.17, Wordsworth to William Matthews, 8 June 1794; Coleridge, 'On the Present War', in *Conciones ad Populum or Addresses to the People* (Bristol, 1795), printed in Lewis Patton and Peter Mann (eds.), *The Collected Works of Samuel Taylor Coleridge*, 16 vol.s (Princeton and London, 1970ff.), i:*Lectures 1795 on Politics and Religion*, 60-2; John Thelwall, *An Appeal to Popular Opinion, Against Kidnapping & Murder; Including a Narrative of the Late Atrocious Proceedings, at Yarmouth. Second edition, with a Postscript; containing a Particular Account of the Outrages at Lynn and Wisbeach* (London, 1796), pp.6, 52.

'Then Britons! be assured, that in fighting against France, ye are fighting against yourselves, that if the liberties of France are lost, your own, such as they are, will not long survive.'[15]

The government was further castigated for the war by the radicals because of its expense and its adverse effects on trade and living standards. Like the Foxite opposition, the radicals criticized the government's conduct of the war, but they did this more consistently with their hostility to the war than the Foxites did. Much of their anti-war protest was based on its effects on ordinary poor people, and their main specific criticism related to individual policies which inflicted hardship on these people. The Birmingham Corresponding Society told the Society for Constitutional Information in November 1793 that 'Mr. Pitt's "War of Humanity"' had 'almost utterly annihilated our Trade in the Town'. Daniel Isaac Eaton was indignant that 'such enormous subscriptions' had been raised for the French *émigrés* 'at a time when an immense body of our own Poor are absolutely starving'; but, he added sarcastically, 'the Poor of England are not *Noble!!!*' Joseph Gerrald criticized the government for squandering the increased revenue from war taxation on three new boards (for India, agriculture and exchequer bills) while industry was crippled.[16] Thomas Holcroft condemned Windham for his refusal to believe that the poor felt any hardship from the war. Windham had ignored the slaughter and bereavement of war, the unemployment, low wages, high prices, high taxes and high poor relief contributions. In times so full of terror and dismay, Holcroft asked, 'will men suffer to be told that the war is not felt? Is it possible that a perversion of truth and reason so incredible as this can be real?' Coleridge reprobated Arthur Young's opinion that the scarcity was a mark of divine chastening on the nation rather than a direct result of an unjust and unnecessary war. 'Famine' was unknown, wrote one pamphleteer, where there was no war, for nature was never so severe as to refuse to supply people's real needs. He linked this with Pitt's decision in 1793 to forbid the export of corn to France and concluded that he was attempting to starve both France and Britain into submission.[17]

---

15 [Eaton], *Extermination*, p.9.

16 The Birmingham Corresponding Society quoted in Emsley, *British Society and the French Wars*, p.30; [Eaton], *Extermination*, p.12n.; Joseph Gerrald, *A Convention the Only Means of Saving Us From Ruin. In a Letter, Adddressed to the People of England* (London, 1793), pp.62–3.

17 Thomas Holcroft, *A Letter to the Rights Honourable William Windham, on the Intemperate and Dangerous Tendency of his Public Conduct* (London, 1795), pp.38–41 (for Windham's remark in the Commons, see p.56); S.T. Coleridge, 'Review of a Pamphlet by Arthur Young Entitled "The Question of Scarcity Plainly Stated"', in the *Morning Post*, 27 March 1800, printed in Erdman (ed.), *Works of Coleridge*, iii: *Essays on His Times in The Morning Post and The Courier* (1978), 238; *The Wrongs of Man* (printed for R. Lee), pp.2–3.

War was, to radicals, a game for kings, princes and their ministers and one that ruined ordinary people. 'Despots delight in war, to them 'tis sport, A Royal Game—their subjects lives the stake.' Courtiers, said the Sheffield lecturer, delighted in children's toys (ribbons, stars and garters) and nicknames (titles). One pamphleteer suspected that the government had entered the conflict simply because the Duke of York, 'anxious to make a splendid parade of his *great military talents*', had cried out for a war. Joseph Gerrald surveyed the wars of the eighteenth century to show that 'they might have been avoided by negotiation, instead of being decided by arms; that they arose, not from the jarring interests of two peoples, but from the ambition and avarice of courts, and, that at the end of each war, the situation of the people was always much worse than at the beginning of it'. *The Blessings of War*, one of the selections of 'Extracts from Pigott's Political Dictionary' printed for Richard Lee, bitterly defined 'Life' as 'a state of existence to be sacrificed by the *lower* orders of society whenever kings and ministers think proper—witness the reeking plains of Flanders'.[18] The government was also criticized by radicals for its appointment of public Fast Days. Morality, it was said, ought not to be conflated with wicked governmental interest. The idea of the rich fasting was ridiculed, and it was pointed out that many of the poor fasted of necessity and not as a religious observance. Radicals constantly demanded peace, and they questioned whether ministers were sincerely working towards it.

Some radical pamphlets and meetings applauded the efforts of the Foxites in Parliament for 'supporting the public in opposing the war'.[19] Others criticized them roundly for merely charging the ministry with a feeble prosecution of the war, instead of refusing to cooperate with voting for supplies, and demanded that they secede, instead of laying themselves open to the accusation of guilt by association.[20] The degeneration of the British people towards 'slavery' was often lamented. Coleridge printed in the *Morning Post* of 11 April 1796 two Remonstrances from Wilkes and the City of London to the King in 1775 against the 'tyrannical measures' pursued against America, and asked 'Where has the spirit of the Citizens of London fled, and why do they not NOW address the Throne in similar language?'[21] Sometimes these sentiments could be phrased as direct condemnation of the King or even threats addressed to him. In *The Song of Los*, Blake blamed the King as the villain

---

18 *The Blessings of War* (printed for R. Lee: London, [1795]), p.2; *Fast Day as Observed at Sheffield*, p.4; *The Rights of Princes* (printed for R. Lee), p.7; Gerrald, *A Convention the Only Means of Saving Us From Ruin*, pp.7–8, 8–38; *The Blessings of War*, p.3.

19 Lovett, *The Citizen of the World*, pp.16–17, 32; *Fast Day as Observed at Sheffield*, p.11 no.s 8, 9.

20 Gerrald, *A Convention the Only Means of Saving Us from Ruin*, pp.118–9.

21 Printed in Erdman (ed.), *Works of Coleridge*, iii, 205–8.

whose policy resulted in 'famine from the heath'.[22] Sometimes the King himself was protected from direct attack in radical publications by the use of the 'evil ministers' argument; but his coach was physically attacked while he travelled to open Parliament on 29 October 1795, and it had to be bullet-proofed for the following year.

Since warfare was evil, soldiering was an evil profession and likened by radicals to a butcher's trade in human beings. 'Soldiers have no privileges, no rights, no feelings of humanity to guide them to action, no sentiment of regard for their fellow-men! They are a distinct order, kept apart, that all sensibility, all sympathy for the sufferings of others with them may be extinct.'[23] While the radicals criticized the soldiers' profession, however, they pitied them as ordinary men who had been bribed or forced into a dangerous position. Coleridge published excerpts from soldiers' accounts of campaigning life in *The Watchman*, emphasizing the misery of cold and danger, fever, inept and corrupt medical staff, Austrian atrocities and allied plundering.[24] Better conditions were demanded for soldiers, especially after demobilization. The system of recruitment by crimps and the press-gang, and their methods of promising glamour, offering bribery, promoting alcoholism and resorting to kidnapping, were all condemned. Radicals were also convinced that sailors were not necessarily so loyal to the government as conservatives claimed. John Gale Jones claimed to have spoken to a naval officer, who had told him that sailors were motivated more by the sense of danger or fear of punishment than by loyalty, that for them it was only a job and that they did not think about the justice of the cause in which they fought. The Navy to them was not 'the wooden walls of Britain', but 'a floating hell'.[25]

The anti-war activities of the radicals centred on trying to inflame and use popular discontent. Indeed, their anti-war activism was simply another strand of their reformist strategy. They used food riots, probably not in the way that anxious conservatives imagined—by hoarding grain to force disturbances—but at least to stir people up and to impress public opinion with a sense of widespread discontent.[26] In a similar manner, they sought to make

---

22 William Blake, *The Song of Los* (1795), 6:9, 15–22, in Geoffrey Keynes (ed.), *Blake. Complete Writings with Variant Readings* (Oxford, 1969), p.247.

23 *The Blessings of War*, pp.5, 6–8.

24 Coleridge, 'Interesting Narration relative to the Campaign of 1794 and 1795', and 'Farther Particulars Relating to the Campaign of 1794 and 1795' in the *Watchman*, 19 and 27 April 1796, printed in Patton and Mann (eds.), *Works of Coleridge*, ii: *The Watchman*, 238–41, 282–4.

25 John Gale Jones, *A Sketch of a Political Tour* (London, 1796), quoted in Morris, 'Monarchy as an Issue', p.169.

26 Clive Emsley, 'The Impact of the French Revolution on British Politics and Society', in Ceri Crossley and Ian Small (eds.), *The French Revolution and British Culture*

political capital out of public war-weariness and hostility to the war. Poverty, unemployment, crimping and pressing, and food shortages were the main grounds on which they opposed the war in publications after 1793, and distress seems to have been a significant recruiting force for the radical cause. The British radical movement was small and without political power, so it had to depend on the moral weight of public opinion. Since the war was an almost universal experience, it helped the radicals, as Mark Philp suggests, to develop a language of protest that was widely understood.[27] Sometimes these demands became conflated by rioting crowds or bill-posters, so that they cried for peace and bread 'or a King without a head'.[28]

Some radicals used the war as a direct means of demonstrating the *de facto* involvement of the people in government policy and urging their active participation in making that policy. Mrs. Barbauld's pamphlets on Fast Days made the connection between national guilt and the responsibility of each individual in the nation for the deeds of the nation. William Williams made a similar point. When their British ancestors put the power of making war and peace in the hands of their executive government, he explained, it was a delegation of trust, not an absolute authority conferred, because the people themselves bore the burden of blood and money required. Government ought to be participated in by all. At its mass general meeting of June 1795, the LCS warned the British people 'not to fall into those fatal errors which have so frequently misled our ancestors, nor rest your expectation on that delusive phantom—a Change of Ministers! ... YOUR CHIEF, PERHAPS YOUR ONLY HOPE, IS IN YOURSELVES!'[29]

Radicals voiced their anti-war sentiments in periodicals such as the *Analytical Review*, the *Monthly Review* and the *Critical Review*. With regard to pamphlet literature, it has been argued that radicals seem to have made less effort than conservative propagandists to cater for the market at the lower end of the social scale. On the other hand, it has also been claimed that this is relative, for their publications were more accessible to a mass audience than

---

(Oxford, 1989), pp.47–8; John Bohstedt, *Riots and Community Poltics in England and Wales 1790–1810* (Cambridge, Mass. and London, 1983), p.171.

27 Mark Philp, 'The Fragmented Ideology of Reform', in Philp (ed.), *The French Revolution and British Popular Politics* (Cambridge, 1991), pp.62, 66, 89.

28 Emsley, 'The Impact of the French Revolution', p.53.

29 [Mrs. Barbauld], *Sins of Government, Sins of the Nation; or, a Discourse for the Fast, Appointed on April 19, 1793. By a Volunteer*, 2nd edition (London, 1793); [idem], *Reasons for National Penitence*, esp. pp.5–6; William Williams, *A Reply to Mr. Burke's Two Letters on the Proposals for Peace with the Regicide Directory of France* (London, 1796), p.49; *Account of the Proceedings at a General Meeting of the London Corresponding Society ... on Monday, the 29th of June, 1795*, pp.5–7.

ever before.[30] In terms of the war debate, it seems probable that, while there were some radical handbills, posters and pamphlets aimed directly at the lower orders, they relied more on stirring up existing discontent by word of mouth, personal activism, demonstrations, petitions and meetings. Sometimes radicals went so far as to try to persuade soldiers to their political views—Edinburgh radicals were arrested in autumn 1792 for distributing seditious medals to soldiers; the Scottish Friends of the People tried to encourage fencible regiments to revolt; it was widely believed that radicals had a hand in instigating the naval mutinies of 1797; and a young man was hanged in Bolton in September 1801 for trying to seduce two dragoons from their duty.[31]

They had mixed feelings about a possible French invasion. Often their rhetoric seemed to look forward to such an event, but it is unlikely that many would have supported it in reality. The *Sheffield Iris* was unsympathetic to the French forces. The meeting of the LCS broken up by Bow Street Magistrates on 19 April had been discussing what they should do if the French landed; many thought they ought to help the Volunteers, and one prominent member was reported as having argued that the Society should help to repel them, because they seemed 'more desirous of establishing an extensive military despotism, than of propagating republican principles'.[32] On the other hand, Gilbert Wakefield and others warned the government that invasion would not pose the French much of a problem. John Gale Jones, on the day the Two Acts were passed, said that, in the present circumstances, 'should the French invade our Coasts, I would not take up a Musket to oppose them. I would not assist the French to invade this Country, nor would I resist them; for if I am to be a Slave, it matters not whether I be the slave of an English, or of a French Tyrant.' Likewise, Thomas Spence avowed that, if confronted by French invaders, he would 'throw down [his] musket saying let such as the Duke of Portland, who claim the country, fight for it, for [he was] but a stranger and sojourner, and [had] neither part nor lot amongst them'. Others, particularly the United Irishmen, but also some radicals in the large towns and cities of the mainland, were ready to join the French and were impatient for their arrival.[33]

---

30 Pendleton, 'English Conservative Propaganda', p.164; Philp, 'The Fragmented Ideology of Reform', p.70.

31 John Brims, 'The Scottish Democratic Movement', unpublished Ph.D. thesis, University of Edinburgh, 1983, pp.554–5; John Prebble, *Mutiny: Highland Regiments in Revolt, 1743–1804* (London, 1975); Bohstedt, *Riots and Community Poltics*, p.143.

32 Emsley, *British Society and the French Wars*, pp.68–9; idem, 'The Impact of the French Revolution', p.55.

33 Gilbert Wakefield, *A Reply to the Bishop of Llandaff* (1798), quoted in Emsley, *British Society and the French Wars*, pp.69–70; William Fox, *Thoughts on the Impending Invasion of England* (London, 1794), pp.12–16; PRO HO 42/37/454, John Gale Jones, 18 December 1795; Thomas Spence, *The Restorer of Society to its Natural State* (London, 1801), reprinted in H.T. Dickinson (ed.), *The Political Works of Thomas Spence* (Newcastle-upon-

Radicals had traditionally assumed the character of 'true' patriots, associating themselves with the mythical history of Anglo-Saxon freedom and a Norman oppression continued still by the present governors of Britain. A handbill published in Sheffield and Nottingham in December 1792 arguing against going to war was signed 'Sydney', associating itself with the seventeenth-century radical Algernon Sydney and the radical interpretation of the Glorious Revolution which Burke's *Reflections* had been at pains to refute—that of the triumph of the sovereignty of the British people over their governors.[34] During the war, radicals continued to appropriate this character. They lost support, however, because they had gained a pro-French and therefore anti-British image. This was, of course, principally because Britain was at war with France, and radicals supporting France appeared to be anti-patriotic, but it was ironic that their patriotic label had been gained earlier in the century by their denunciations of aristocratic imitation of French fashions and their consequent anti-French associations. Clearly, their anger had always been directed against the elite, just as it was now in their opposition towards war against the anti-aristocratic French Revolution, but the superficial message of anti-France had suddenly become pro-France, and it was a severe handicap to their success in Britain.[35] Although they claimed that conservatives deliberately distorted their case, their tendency to alternate between republican rhetoric, in support of the French revolutionaries, and declarations supporting the British monarchy, which reflected their reforming background and, probably, the actual views of most radicals in Britain, produced understandable confusion among loyalists as to their real intentions.[36]

Despite intimidation of the radicals by the rise of patriotic loyalism, the suppression of the Edinburgh Conventions, the sedition and treason trials, and the 'Two Acts' of 1795, the LCS still had a membership at the end of 1796 a third greater than it had had in 1793,[37] and clandestine groups of United Englishmen and United Scotsmen were active from 1797. John Thelwall warned in 1796 that, despite a cowed appearance, the radical movement, or 'the manly spirit of Britain', 'is not dead but sleepeth', and that should it be provoked by further tyrannical outrages, either the old champions of the cause

---

Tyne, 1982), p.79. See also Bohstedt, *Riots and Community Politics*, p.191; PRO HO 42/40/325, possibly an oath of the United Englishmen, swearing 'as far as in me lies ... to assist the French in landing to free this country'.

34 *War!* (Nottingham, 31 December 1792; Sheffield, 20 December 1792 in PRO HO 42/23/633). See also 'To the Inhabitants of Nottingham', signed 'Hampden', in the British Library collection of songs and broadsides at 648.c.26.

35 Newman, *The Rise of English Nationalism*, pp.230–1; Hugh Cunningham, 'The language of patriotism', in Raphael Samuel (ed.), *Patriotism: The Making and Unmaking of British National Identity*, vol. i, *History and Politics* (London and New York), pp.57–89.

36 Morris, 'The Monarchy as an Issue', p.89.

37 Emsley, *British Society and the French Wars*, p.68.

would 'resume their neglected arms', or others would step forward to take their place.[38] Against this must be balanced those who, like Wordsworth, Coleridge, Southey and Blake, reluctantly stopped opposing the war after the rise of the autocratic rule of Napoleon Bonaparte and his demonstrated lack of respect for representative government such as that of the Swiss cantons. The radicals' reactions to the peace of Amiens in 1802 was probably mixed. The war had ceased: Thomas Hardy wrote to Napoleon in 1802, 'Now peace reigns on earth and this is the work of Frenchmen.'[39] Nevertheless, they had suffered a decade of hounding and suppression.

Ultimately, radical activists were more concerned with making war on political 'tyranny' in Britain than with opposing the government's war against France. They began by opposing the war out of sympathy for the French Revolution and in the context of their hostility to conservative ideology, but their interest in it became more instrumental as time passed and as their opportunities to persuade people of their views on it became more limited, with government restrictions on their activities. The 'Friends of Peace', on the other hand, opposed the government chiefly because they opposed the war against revolutionary France.

II The Friends of Peace

The 'Friends of Peace' were a group of liberal men spread throughout the country and, although they were not a formally constituted body, they had formed a network over previous years by their association in opposing various issues such as clerical subscription to the Thirty-Nine Articles, the Test and Corporation Acts, the American War and the slave trade, and by ties of family, friendship, religion, intellect, profession and business. Based mainly in London and in the north of England, but with contacts nationwide, they formed the real leadership of the anti-war protest. Many of them were Dissenters, hostile to what they saw as a Pittite 'Tory' high-church party, although some were liberal Anglicans; most were 'rational' Christians, stressing the importance of the mind, reasoning and human potential above faith, emotion and human sinfulness, but Evangelicals were also involved. They supported the parliamentary Opposition Whigs, but while the link was strengthened by bonds of friendship and obligation, it was strained by the suspicion of the Friends of Peace that the liberalism of the Whig MPs was superficial. They opposed the war from two main standpoints: they opposed war in general on grounds of

---

38 John Thelwall, *Sober Reflections on the seditious and inflammatory letter of the Rt. Hon. Edmund Burke, to a noble Lord, addressed to the serious consideration of his fellow citizens* (London, 1796), p.10.

39 Emsley, *British Society and the French Wars*, p.92.

morality and religion, and they had specific ideological and practical objections to this conflict against France in particular.[40]

Various supporters of Pitt joined the liberal protest against the war at one point or another. William Smith has already been mentioned as one who changed to consistent and ardent support of Fox because of the war, and the Duke of Grafton did the same. William Wilberforce, the slave trade abolitionist, was a more celebrated example. A close friend of Pitt, he refused to join the Foxites in their condemnation of the causes of the war, but his antipathy to armed conflict in general, and pressure on him as a renowned humanitarian, led him to call for negotiations in 1795.[41] L.G. Mitchell has written, in the context of the split of the Whig party, that 'the issue of the war had so neatly divided up politics, that few politicians would have the agility to leap from one side to the other'.[42] Wilberforce was one of those few. The end of 1795 brought a government pledge to seek negotiations whenever it was consistent with British honour, and this, together with a conviction that the responsibility for the failure of the 1796 and 1797 peace talks was French, allowed him to support ministers again with a clear conscience, although he was, unsurprisingly, accused of cowardice and inconsistency by other anti-war protesters.[43]

While some Friends of Peace were inclined to believe that the French Revolution was part of the general progression of the world towards enlightenment and harmony, they did not sympathize with the French armies as did the Foxites and radicals. Wilberforce was far from being a Foxite, although he sometimes joined forces with them, and while he might have wanted peace with France he continued to advocate war against Jacobinism at home. He opposed the withdrawal of British troops from St Domingo in 1797 because it would be ceding ground to French republicanism in a war which the British government now appeared to be willing to end. He also supported the government's decision in 1800 to refuse negotiations with Bonaparte, if

---

40 Cookson, *The Friends of Peace*, pp.1–3, 5, 14–15, 20. This section relies heavily on Cookson's work.

41 See *P.H.*, xxxi, 1016, Wilberforce, 30 December 1794; ibid., xxxi, 1237, Wilberforce, 26 January 1795; ibid., xxxii, 1–9, Wilberforce, 27 May 1795. For pressure on him to vote against the war, see, for example, R.I. and S. Wilberforce (eds.), *The Correspondence of William Wilberforce*, 2 vol.s (London, 1840), i, 107–12, 139–48, Stanhope to Wilberforce, 5 December 1794 and Jeremy Bentham to Wilberforce, September 1796; 'Sonnet to W. Wilberforce', in the *Cambridge Intelligencer*, 28 February 1795, printed in Bennett, *War Poetry*, p.148.

42 Ehrman, *The Reluctant Transition*, p.380; L.G. Mitchell, *Charles James Fox and the Disintegration of the Whig Party 1782–1794* (Oxford, 1971), p.228.

43 See, for example, *An Appeal to the Moral Feelings of Samuel Thornton, Rowland Burdon, Hawkins Brown, Esq.rs, and to Every Member of the House of Commons who Conscientiously Supports the Present Administration. In a Letter to William Wilberforce, Esq.* (London, 1797), esp. pp.38–9.

privately and reluctantly, because he thought it better to wait for the result of the Austrian negotiations with him.[44] Others protested their attachment to the British political order, perhaps in an attempt to gain a better hearing for their recommendations. One writer introduced his pamphlet with the explanation that although he advised a policy of seeking peace with France,

> he was not an admirer of French principles, or an approver of French proceedings.... On the contrary, he has contemplated with almost uninterrupted disapprobation, every proceeding of the French people since the month of July 1789, and every principle from which those proceedings were deduced, or upon which they have been defended.[45]

The Friends of Peace were also prominent in encouraging the Volunteer Corps at the time of the 1798 invasion scare (and again in 1803–5), since they believed that self-defence was wholly justified. They served in the Volunteers themselves, wrote essays in their favour and preached sermons to them.

These 'Friends of Peace' did not therefore argue against the war out of any great ideological sympathy for the French Revolution. Rather, to these men of liberal views, war was a power-game between small ruling elites which brought no benefit to the mass of society which might outweigh its horror and distress. Peace and harmony between nations were not only desirable but entirely possible, if only governments would subjugate their own ambitions to the furtherance of the good of their people. Christian arguments demonstrating that war was intrinsically wrong were predominant in the anti-war protests. These were based firstly on fundamental Christian beliefs, which Evangelicals tended to stress. As a God of love, God had commanded men not to kill one another, but rather to love their enemies. War was directly contrary to the order and harmony of His creation, and therefore unnatural in man, showing him at his worst. To wage war was flagrantly to disobey God as well as to cause great suffering in human society. It might be used by God for purposes of national judgement and chastening, but the correct response was not the continuation of fighting, but the settlement of peace and the reform of the abuses in society which had offended Him, such as the slave trade.[46]

Second, 'rational' Dissenters usually emphasized arguments based on a particular Christian view of the universe, using history and nature as well as biblical exegesis. They argued that men lived in an ordered universe in which a benevolent God was in complete control, and in which human society ought to

---

44 R.I. and S. Wilberforce (eds.), *Correspondence of Wilberforce*, i, 209–10, Wilberforce to J. Hare Naylor, 5 July 1800.

45 *Considerations on the Principal Objections Against Overtures for Peace with France* (London, 1795), p.iv.

46 Cookson, *The Friends of Peace*, pp.32-3.

progress continually. As men's knowledge of the created universe extended further and further, so also would they advance in virtue and happiness, since by means of their powers of reason, they would understand what was good for them and what was not. God Himself was actively intervening to assist the progress of good, and so evil would eventually be eliminated by the cooperation of human reason and divine wisdom. War was therefore an eradicable evil, however much its horrors pointed to the contrary, and it would ultimately be rejected altogether by men.[47] The Rev. Vicesimus Knox, Master of Tunbridge School and Rector of Runwell and Ramsden Crays, Essex, argued that, while war was understandable in 'native barbarians', because of their lack of culture, knowledge and religion, it was unacceptable that 'a state justly pretending to all the polish of cultivated manners, and professing the purest Christianity' should wage war—it was 'mischievous, flagitious, and detestable, without one alleviating circumstance'.[48] While Evangelicals underlined the depravity of the human race in general, and rational Christians stressed the corruption of the powerful and the need for immediate reforms, both were therefore agreed that war was a social and moral evil which was fundamentally wrong. Anti-war poetry stressed the misery of war and the advantages (commercial, political and, above all, domestic) of peace.

The liberals, however, were opposed not only to war in general, but also to this particular war, as unnecessary and unjust. Most admitted that, while aggressive war was inexcusable, a nation had the right to act in self-defence, although even this narrow definition of a 'just war' was rejected by some 'high' pacifists (including many Quakers) who argued that no war was justifiable or lawful. Those who allowed that defensive war could be justifiable rehearsed many of the same arguments as the Foxite Whigs and the radicals to demonstrate that the British war against revolutionary France was not defensive, and that Britain and its allies were perpetrating an unnecessary and impractical aggression on France. They therefore rejected the Burkean legitimation of the war, which argued that it was an ideologically defensive conflict from the British standpoint.

The liberals went on to reprobate what they perceived to be the unjust conduct of the war by the British government. Gilbert Wakefield protested that British cruelty and atrocity in prosecuting the war was worse than French violence, and that the British government ought to remove the plank from its own eye before it sought to remove the speck in the eye of the French government. The execution of one individual (Louis XVI), he suggested, was hardly more terrible than Pitt's alleged scheme to starve twenty-five million

47 Ibid., pp.5–6, 31.

48 Vicesimus Knox, Preface to 'Antipolemus; or, the Plea of Reason, Religion, and Humanity, Against War. A Fragment; Translated from the Latin of Erasmus' (1795), in *Works*, 7 vol.s (London, 1824), v, 417.

men, women and children by refusing to export British corn to France. Another pamphleteer criticized the object he supposed the allies to have of partitioning France, the encouragement of civil discord within France by Britain's support of the counter-revolutionary cause and the alleged forgery and circulation of assignats within France by Pitt.[49]

The adverse effects of the conflict on Britain were further adduced by Friends of Peace to support their case against it. One of their principal arguments, chiefly since it drew support from other quarters of the anti-war lobby, was that the war would have a ruinous effect on the British economy. The conflict was said to enrich 'a race of harpies, contractors, commissaries and stock-jobbers' at the expense of what the liberals regarded as the virtuous, enterprising and valuable middle classes of society.[50] The flat rate of the 1799 Income Tax was especially attacked for its failure to take any account of individual financial circumstances, thus falling more heavily on the productive classes of society, rather than upon the non-productive, ostentatious rich. The Friends of Peace also criticized the war for aggravating periods of 'scarcity' due to harvest failure, since it was necessary to send a certain amount of grain to the army and navy, and since the war disrupted the importation of foreign grain. Furthermore, it vastly increased the National Debt and seriously unsettled confidence in public credit. They often failed to match the chronology of price movements to their arguments, and their statistics were often either faulty or insufficient, but they made good rhetorical capital from it. 'Let others talk of glory; let others celebrate the heroes, who are to deluge the world with blood,' wrote William Frend; 'the words of the poor market woman will still resound in my ears, We are sconced three-pence in the shilling, one-fourth part of our labour. For what?'[51] Economic disaster was gloomily predicted by the liberals throughout the 1790s, until in 1801 work was published which convincingly demonstrated that Britain had achieved an impressive rate of growth during the eighteenth century and was showing no signs of economic collapse, even in the midst of an expensive war. Nevertheless, they gathered support from industrial and trading interests in the north of England which were badly hit by the effects of the war.

Friends of Peace lamented the increase in the numbers of soldiers and sailors. Knox maintained that 'the whole of the military system is much

---

49 Gilbert Wakefield, *Remarks on the General Orders of the Duke of York to his Army, on June 7, 1794* (London, 1794), pp.8, 20–4; *Letter to Wilberforce*, pp.30-5.

50 *Five Minutes Advice to the People of Great Britain, on the Present Alarming Situation of Public Affairs: in which the good policy of immediate hostilities with France is candidly investigated. By a Citizen of London* (London, 1792), 6–7, 18–19

51 William Frend, *Scarcity of Bread. A Plan for Reducing the High Price of this Article, in a Letter Addressed by William Frend to William Devaynes, Esq.* (London, 1793), pp.1–5.

indebted for its support to that prevailing passion of human nature, pride'. It encouraged the ambition and vanity of members of the squirearchy, who became captains and bribed volunteers to enlist in order to further their own careers of sycophancy. Wakefield reminded his readers that the occupation of a soldier was largely made up of 'rapine, blasphemy, blood, and carnage', which was incompatible with a Christian's profession. The system of recruiting by means of crimps and the press-gang was naturally also deplored by them. William Frend forecast riots if the system was not abolished, and Knox thought the practice little better than slavery, hiring and selling 'images of God ... to do the work of butchers'.[52]

The liberals called, as many conservatives did, for a moral reformation alongside peace. Wilberforce later wrote of Pitt, 'If only he had tried to "govern by principle", he would have succeeded. And then the whole British body politic would have been cleansed and strengthened. Even so great a cataclysm as the French Revolution would have left it unshaken.'[53] Branded unpatriotic for their refusal to support the war, they insisted on a public right to challenge the government concerning the justice and necessity of the conflict. William Roscoe, the Leeds anti-war campaigner, wrote of a moral patriotism that differed from blind and ugly bigotry:

> Every pretended patriot, every proud and ignorant individual, can cry out for war, and urge on his neighbour to the work of destruction; but where is the man who will oppose himself to the national madness? ... He who would dare to attempt this is indeed a patriot.... The truth is, that a patriot must be a virtuous man, and a virtuous man will not commit or encourage injustice for the sake either of himself or others.[54]

J.E. Cookson sees the expression of the grievances of a non-elite as the source of the intensity of much of this anti-war argument.[55] Like the Foxites and radicals, the Friends of Peace attacked what they claimed was corruption in high places, but they broadened it to include not only government ministers but also all within the governing classes of society. Dror Wahrman has

---

52 Vicesimus Knox, 'The Spirit of Despotism' (1795), in *Works*, v, 250, 252; Wakefield, *Remarks on the General Orders*, pp.29–30; Frend, *Scarcity of Bread*, p.6; Knox, 'The Spirit of Despotism', pp.202–3.

53 Quoted in Robin Blackburn, *The Overthrow of Colonial Slavery: 1776-1848* (London, 1988), p.152.

54 Henry Roscoe, *The Life of William Roscoe* (London, 1833), pp.298–9, 431–3. See also Raithby, *Peace*, pp.1, 32–3.

55 Cookson, *The Friends of Peace*, pp.26–9, 151. The argument becomes increasingly clear in the 1803–15 phase of the conflict, when northern manufacturing interests were much more involved in the anti-war campaign. See also Knox, 'The Spirit of Despotism', p.243.

recently argued that this apparent socio-political reality was in fact only an idiom of political rhetoric. The idiom of a 'middle class' was a device used, consciously and unconsciously, by the non-radical anti-war protesters in the 1790s to emphasize their political moderatism at the same time as their disapproval of the conflict. The fact that the liberal opponents of the war used the notion of a virtuous, rational middle class and the problems caused to its members by the conflict in their writings and speeches against the war does not, according to Wahrman, prove that there was in fact a coherent social and political middle class which collectively and self-consciously opposed the war.[56] Conservatives and radicals described British society in dualistic terms instead; and the opponents of the war did not have a monopoly on the middle strata of society, members of which supported both sides of the war debate.

Wahrman's analysis of this particular element of the war debate is both fascinating and useful. To examine the polemic through this one lens alone, however, results in some over-simplification. For instance, although he criticizes Cookson for too easily identifying Dissenters, the emerging industrial interest, the provincial interest and the middle class all as one and the same group of people with a largely common political mind,[57] he himself implies much the same kind of identification of the Foxites and the Friends of Peace. It has been suggested here, however, that while there was often substantial political overlap between the two groups, they should also be distinguished clearly in terms of the composition and motivation of much of their anti-war argument. Moreover, Wahrman does not try to prove that the social make-up of the great majority of liberal anti-war protesters was anything but middle-class, even if they did not include all members of the social middle.

The Friends of Peace urged that every opportunity should be taken to negotiate an end to the conflict. 'Is it discussion of opinions we fear? and war the remedy!' exclaimed David Hartley of Bath. 'The obvious imputation from such affectation of timidity, would be, a charge of conscious deviations from the national interest, which the alarmists were anxious from unostensible motives to conceal.' Wilberforce argued at the end of 1794 that the worst of French Jacobinism was spent, and it should no longer be used as an excuse for not negotiating. France was beginning to display signs of moderation once more. 'He thought it a very important duty in every war', he told the Commons in May 1795,

> not only to take care that in the commencement it was just and necessary, but to look out also from time to time, for every opening which might be given for the conclusion of it; to see whether the

---

56 Dror Wahrman, *Imagining the Middle Class. The Political Representation of Class in Britain, c.1780–1840* (Cambridge, 1995), e.g. pp.59–60.

57 Ibid., p.39.

> original motives for it continued—whether our country, whether that of the enemy, whether the state of other powers, and the general circumstances of the times, made it still needful to pursue the path we were treading.[58]

Even if the government of France was still unstable, that was no reason not to hold talks with it. That was an argument morally false, according to John Raithby, for it was an obvious pretext—Britain never considered the stability of the Turkish government when treating with it, despite its permanent instability.[59] The dangers of risking the insecurity due to an unstable French government were hardly as great as those involved in continuing the war, argued Wilberforce. 'He was ready to allow that an extensive peace establishment was a great evil; but surely it was speaking of it in too strong terms to put it on a level with a state of actual war.'[60]

The practical tactics of the Friends of Peace were those best adapted to channelling the diverse strands of hostility to the war. One of the most successful was the development of the concept of a 'war interest' and a 'war system'. It was an all-purpose charge against the government under which various complaints and interest groups could unite—Foxite Whigs, radicals (as they used anti-war protest in their own campaign for political reform, so perhaps they themselves were used), industrial and trading interests hard-hit by the conflict, Dissenters who thought themselves unfairly ostracized from the ecclesiastical and political order and ordinary people who wanted to protest against high prices and shortages of grain. This was an adept way of focusing their various sectional grievances against the war and the establishment. Town corporations (such as Norwich and Nottingham), county meetings (such as those of Northumberland, Durham and Yorkshire) and Dissenting and Methodist chapels which were sympathetic were harnessed to the cause and used to propagate anti-war views. Anti-war chapels used national Fast Days not to protest against the establishment by non-observance of them but rather as a platform from which to voice anti-loyalist sympathies. Public meetings were held, and occasionally the liberals attempted to convert loyalist meetings to their views. Petitions for peace were virtually impossible in the fervently loyalist atmosphere of the early years of the decade, but they were organized in 1795, 1797 and 1801, when there was greatest discontent with the war. The petition organized in Edinburgh in 1795 collected 8000 signatures within four

---

58 David Hartley, *Argument on the French Revolution* (Bath, 1794), pp.4–5; *P.H.*, xxxi, 1016–17, Wilberforce, 30 December 1794; ibid., xxxiii, 2, Wilberforce, 27 May 1795.

59 John Raithby, *Peace. Reasons why Terms of Peace should be offered to the French Nation. Addressed to the inhabitants of Great Britain, through the medium of their representatives in Parliament* (London, 1795), pp.72–3.

60 *P.H.*, xxxi, 1023, Wilberforce, 30 December 1794.

days. The Yorkshire petitions of 1801 gathered some 30,000 signatures. The liberal press, one of the most powerful weapons available to the Friends of Peace, was also used to great effect. The Whig and radical London newspapers and periodicals provided the basis of liberal pre-eminence in the press, and there were dozens of liberal provincial papers and periodicals, including the *Manchester Herald*, the *Sheffield Register*, the *Leicester Herald* and the *Leeds Mercury*.[61]

With quiet persistence, the Friends of Peace began a campaign against the war in the 1790s that would continue and develop greatly in the post-Amiens phase of the conflict. They harnessed various political, religious and commercial groups to their support whenever they could, including the political opposition groups of Foxites in Parliament and radicals outside it. The hostility of both Foxites and radicals to the war was sometimes instrumental, thinly veiling ulterior motives. By means of their religious and moral primary opposition to the war itself, however, and their great skill in channelling many diverse protests against the Pitt administration into an anti-war discourse, the Friends of Peace took the leadership of the campaign against the British government's war against France in the 1790s. Ironically, unlike the Foxites and the radicals, the Friends of Peace did not oppose the conflict because they sympathized to any great extent with the revolutionaries in France. None the less, they too entered the British polemic on the ideological nature of the war simply by denying that such a characterization of the conflict legitimized it.

---

61 Cookson, *The Friends of Peace*, *passim.*

Chapter 6

Churchmen: Political Preaching, Patriotism and Pacifism

The whole spectrum of political standpoints on the war has now been examined, from war crusaders to radicals and pacifists. The following three chapters proceed to explore cross-sections of society, rather than groups of people who held broadly similar opinions on the conflict: ministers of religion, female commentators on the war, and the broad mass of British public opinion. Given the continuing importance of religion to the great majority of the British people in the eighteenth century, it is not surprising that religious arguments contributed significantly to the political debates of the period. In particular, it has been shown that ministers of religion took a great interest in the French Revolution and in its British repercussions, and that their reactions to it contributed significantly to the rise and fall of the influence of their different church denominations.[1] This chapter is not so much concerned to re-examine ecclesiastical reactions to the Revolution, as to consider the theological-political responses to the *war* of churchmen of different denominations.

It has been shown in previous chapters that religious arguments were used by laymen both to support and to oppose the British government's war against revolutionary France. Conservative writers of the 1790s not only endlessly repeated religious doctrines and reasoning enjoining submission and loyalty to

---

1 J.C.D. Clark, *English Society 1688–1832: Ideology, Social Structure and Political Practice during the Ancien Regime* (Cambridge, 1985); idem, *Revolution and Rebellion: State and Society in England in the Seventeenth and Eighteenth Centuries* (Cambridge, 1986); idem, *The Language of Liberty 1660–1832. Political Discourse and Social Dynamics in the Anglo-American World* (Cambridge, 1994); Robert Hole, *Pulpits, Politics and Public Order in England, 1760–1832* (Cambridge, 1989); idem, 'English Sermons and Tracts as Media of Debate on the French Revolution, 1789–99', in Philp (ed.), *The French Revolution and British Popular Politics*, pp.18–38; Nancy U. Murray, 'The Influence of the French Revolution on the Church of England and Its Rivals', unpublished D.Phil. thesis, (University of Oxford, 1975); John Brims, 'The Covenanting Tradition and Scottish Radicalism in the 1790s', in T. Brotherstone (ed.), *Covenant, Charter and Party. Traditions of revolt and protest in modern Scottish History* (Aberdeen, 1989), pp.50–62. See also John Gascoigne, 'Anglican latitudinarianism, Rational Dissent and political radicalism in the late eighteenth century', in Knud Haakonssen (ed.), *Enlightenment and Religion: Rational Dissent in Eighteenth-Century Britain* (Cambridge, 1996), pp.219–40; Emma Vincent, 'The Responses of Scottish Churchmen to the French Revolution, 1789–1802', *Scottish Historical Review*, 73 (1994), 191–215.

the government, 'as a last, fine-meshed net to catch those who had eluded the looser weave of the secular arguments',[2] but they also justified the war in religious terms. Influenced by Burke, by probably a majority of British clergymen, and later by the Abbé Barruel and Professor John Robison, they argued that the atheist Republic posed a threat to the institutions and teachings of religion in Britain and throughout Europe. While religion was perhaps less used by radicals than by conservatives to validate their constitutional theories, both radicals and Friends of Peace used religious arguments to oppose the war, claiming that armed conflict was fundamentally in breach of the spirit and teachings of Christianity; some, indeed, opposed it primarily from a religious standpoint.

Religious polemic on the war was generally used by loyalist and pacifist laymen in combination with political arguments, and mostly in a supporting role. By contrast, sermons preached by churchmen on the subject of the conflict naturally usually emphasized a theological reading of the situation and made less attempt to persuade their audiences with secular political reasoning. The theology and political theology, of various colours, were not new, as the widespread use of them by lay writers testifies; but the warfare of the 1790s, and the urgency and breadth of its impact upon society, were unprecedented in British experience. It seems likely that ordinary local ministers were more concerned with the war than with the French Revolution itself (as distinct from the general issues of domestic loyalty and submission which the Revolution highlighted). The diary of 'the Country Parson', the Rev. James Woodforde, has much more to say about the practical effects of the war on an ordinary churchman's life and work than it does about the Revolution, which seems to have disturbed him greatly only in so far as it harmed the French King and Queen.[3]

Churchmen therefore rushed to apply well-established theological principles to the conflict and to lead their congregations and readerships in what they believed to be sound Christian thinking and responses. Questions such as the moral and theological justifications for war and patriotism were raised and answered, and eternal issues were emphasized in the light of the cruelties of war. The nature of the conflict, and such grounds for it as related to religious and moral issues, were discussed in terms of a theological understanding of the nature of God and of man, and in terms of a political theology of society, the State and the international community. The conduct of the British government's war effort was rarely examined. The majority of churchmen tended towards quite a Burkean loyalist position, but all the major political stances on the

---

2 Hole, *Pulpits, Politics and Public Order*, p.101.

3 John Beresford (ed.), *The Diary of a Country Parson: the Reverend James Woodforde, 1758–1802*, 5 vol.s (Oxford, 1924–31), iii, 124, 146, 280, 281, 396, 397–8; ibid., iv, 2–4, 12, 21–2.

conflict had their clerical proponents and theological underpinnings. As in the controversy on the Revolution, therefore, so in the argument over the war: the responses of churchmen to the war did not constitute a new debate on it, but rather another layer of national discussion, another language of discourse.[4]

By appointing several Thanksgiving and Fast Days each year to be nationally observed, the government displayed its concern to benefit from both the propaganda potential of the vast network of loyalist preachers across the country, and the public legitimation of the war which theology could provide. This chapter examines the wide support given by the Established Churches for the war and the varying opinions of Dissenting ministers, based on their political theology and its application to the war, and the attitudes and actions this led them to urge upon their congregations. It shows that ecclesiastical arguments on the war, although politically diverse, were deeply imbued with the conviction that this was a conflict about competing ideologies.

I The Established Churches

The theology, political theology, and ecclesiastical and political concerns of Established Church ministers in England and Scotland, led most of them to accept the inevitability of war in the present world and to support the British government in fighting the present one against revolutionary France, and to call for religion, virtue, loyalty, patriotism and endurance to be practised by the British people in response. Liberals and Evangelicals within the Established Churches, however, were sometimes less vocal in their support, and a small minority expressed opposition to the war.

The theological doctrine most important to the understanding of most ministers concerning war in general was probably that of divine Providence, 'the firm and deep foundation of true religion'. God ruled over the world, not remaining remote or aloof from its affairs, but intervening according to His will and purposes. The Rev. Dr Alexander Carlyle of Inveresk wrote in 1794: 'The Almighty governs the world, not merely by general laws, but by constant superintendence and frequent interposition', and he illustrated this from the history of the Jews and of Christianity.[5] As for the nature of man, most

---

4 Hole, *Pulpits, Politics and Public Order*, p.7; idem, 'English Sermons and Tracts', pp.30–1.

5 Charles Moss, *A Sermon, Preached Before the Honourable House of Commons, at the Church of St. Margaret, Westminster, on Wednesday, March 7, 1798, Being the Day appointed by His Majesty's Royal Proclamation, to be observed as a Day of Solemn Fasting and Humiliation* (London, 1798), p.7; Alexander Carlyle, *National Depravity the Cause of National Calamities, a sermon from Jeremiah 6:8* (Edinburgh, 1794), p.3. *Pace* Boyd Hilton, the doctrine of Providence was not peculiar to Evangelicals in the 1790s—cf. Boyd Hilton, *The*

Establishment preachers emphasized his fallen condition. He had been created in the image of God, and so given high dignity; but man's refusal to submit to God and His demands had marred God's image in him and made him capable of gross wickedness. Sin was 'the cause of all national evils, and if persisted in by any people, will provoke the Almighty *to cause his soul to depart from them*'.[6] Because God was actively interested in and intervened in human affairs, it was natural that rebellion against Him should result in chastisement. In the case of nations, this usually came in such forms as weak and unstable government, irreligion, economic depression and war. National repentance in such dark times was not only possible, but necessary, in order to regain God's favour. Texts such as Jeremiah 18:8 were quoted: 'If that nation, against whom I have pronounced, turn from their evil, I will repent of the evil that I thought to do unto them.'

War was therefore validated by Establishment clergy first on the grounds that it was simply a fact of life after the Fall. Wars would not 'cease in all the earth' until the end of time; they were part of the general suffering and misery of human life caused by sin, and they could not be eradicated until sinful human beings were no more and the new heaven and the new earth were established. Second, while some wars were waged from 'a variety of sinister and unrighteous motives', others, particularly those undertaken in self-defence, were just and necessary, and Christians need feel no shame for being involved in them.[7] 'God not only gave us life and property,' argued William Vincent,

> but implanted courage in our breast, as well as other qualities of the mind; and if our life or property is in danger, we have the same right to defend them against the enemy who would kill us, as against the wild beast which would devour us.... I am persuaded no command of God forbids, no precept of the Gospel condemns, military service in the cause of justice.[8]

Age of Atonement: The Influence of Evangelicalism on Social and Economic Thought, 1795–1865 (Oxford, 1988).

6 Carlyle, *National Depravity*, p.9.

7 Richard Valpy, *A Sermon, Preached August 13, 1798, Before the Reading and Henley Association, the Woodley Cavalry, and the Reading Volunteers, at the Consecration of the Colors of the Reading Association* (Reading, 1798), p.4; John Hampson, *Observations on the Present War, the Projected Invasion, and a Decree of the National Convention for the Emancipation of the Slaves in the French Colonies* (Sunderland, [1793]), pp.5–6.

8 William Vincent, 'A Sermon Delivered in the Church of St. Magnus, London Bridge, November 25; and in the Church of Allhallows the Great and the Less, Thames Street, December 16, 1798; Before the Associated Volunteer Companies, in the Wards of Bridge, Candlewick, and Dowgate', in *Sermons on Faith, Doctrines, and Public Duties*, 2 vol.s (London, 1817), i, 290–1.

Preachers thought themselves justified in discussing political subjects from the pulpit. Since God was active in society, they argued, religion was essential in order to please Him and to ensure the social and political well-being of any state. Moreover, as 'the great cement of society', religion could go further than the law, reaching men's inward thoughts as well as their outward actions, restraining the wicked and encouraging the good. Human nature was so corrupt that government alone was unable to restrain it. 'When men agree to cast off the fear of God, they will seldom long accord in any thing else', warned the Evangelical John Newton. The Rev. Dr Thomas Somerville of Jedburgh stated that 'without religion ... no civil government can be maintained or supported'.[9] Even those, such as John Erskine (another Evangelical), who acknowledged that ministers did not have the detailed facts necessary to advise politicians, insisted that they should emphasize the general maxims of virtue and prudence which ought to guide the actions of politicians.[10] Such political preaching was held to be especially necessary at a time of national emergency or when the King appointed special Thanksgiving and Fast Days to be observed nationwide. Some bishops voiced concern at the numbers of non-resident clergy in their dioceses, and the consequent loss of good influence in the parishes concerned. The General Assembly of the Church of Scotland regularly assured the King of its clergy's undeviating perseverance in their exertions to preserve sound doctrine and to advance genuine piety, for the benefit of public order.

Establishment ministers were influenced not only by these theological and political-theological positions, however, but also by three current fears that they held concerning the Revolution in France and the Church and State in Britain. First, ministers were extremely hostile towards the French Revolution's attacks on the Christian religion, and they feared for the acceptance of Christian theology in British society. The rationalism and deism of Enlightenment philosophy seemed to be at the root of the dislocation in France, and the Revolution's atheism and confidence in man's inherent reason, virtue and perfectibility directly challenged Christian belief. 'The contest, in the present day', wrote William Laurence Brown of Aberdeen, 'is not between one particular form of religion and another, but between the existence of any religion

---

9 Alexander Carlyle, *The Love of Our Country, explained and enforced in a sermon from Psalm 137: 5, 6* (Edinburgh, 1797), p.23; John Newton, *Motives to Humiliation and Praise. A Sermon, Preached in the Parish Church of St. Mary Woolnoth, Lombard-Street, on December 19, 1797. The Day of General Thanksgiving to Almighty God, for Our Late Naval Victories* (London, 1798), p.16; Thomas Somerville, *The Effects of the French Revolution* (Edinburgh, 1793), p.89.

10 John Erskine, *The Fatal Consequences and the General Sources of Anarchy: a Discourse on Isaiah 24:1–5* (Edinburgh, 1793), pp.10–11.

whatever, and the total extirpation of it.'[11] Many believed that political reform and religious free-thinking went hand-in-hand; overt worship of reason in Paris and Paine's blasphemous attacks on Christianity drew the cry of 'the Church in danger', rallying even Evangelicals within the Establishment in Britain. Richard Watson, the Latitudinarian bishop of Llandaff, told the clergy of his diocese in 1798 that it was necessary for them to beware of 'wicked Teachers, who are creeping in among the common people, and attempting, by profane writings and evil communications, to unchristianize the world'.[12]

Second, like other conservatives in the 1790s they were fearful of political insurrection and domestic anarchy, and they believed that it was better to err on the side of caution, repressing anything which might lead to the subversion of law and authority, and clinging to the emblems and products of civilization as they knew it. Since man was fallen and imperfect, restraint was necessary. Hole shows that discussion of various forms of government and legitimate means of changing a government disappeared from political-theological discourse very quickly after the French Revolution erupted and that it was replaced by a greater emphasis on order and control.[13]

Third, they were anxious that the relationship of Church and State might change at the expense of the influence of the Established Church. The Dissenters' campaign in 1787–90 to have the Test and Corporation Acts repealed and full toleration granted was unsuccessful, but it nevertheless called into question the relationship of the Church of England with the State. The triumph of the Established Church was by no means a foregone conclusion in 1787; and the second House of Commons vote on repeal, in 1789, lost by only twenty votes. The fears inspired by the French Revolution among the landed interest achieved a defeat for repeal of 294 votes to 105 in 1790, but the Anglican clergy could not know how long such support for them would last, and they were thus encouraged to support the government loudly throughout the 1790s to prove their crucial importance to it.[14] The Church of Scotland was legally independent of the State, unlike the Established Church of England, but the Moderate party in the Kirk, dominant in the General Assembly for so much of the later eighteenth century, was increasingly feeling the heat of Evangelical

---

11 William Laurence Brown, 'A View of the Present Times,', in John Leland (ed.), *A View of the Present Times, with regard to religion and morals, and other important subjects* (London, 1798), p.492.

12 Richard Watson, 'A Charge Delivered to the Clergy of the Diocese of Landaff, in June 1798', in *Miscellaneous Tracts on Religious, Political, and Agricultural Subjects*, 2 vol.s (London, 1815), i, 148–52, 134–5.

13 Hole, *Pulpits, Politics and Public Order*, pp.97, 128 and *passim.*

14 Murray, 'The Influence of the French Revolution', pp.21–2, 310; G.M. Ditchfield, 'The Parliamentary Struggle over the Repeal of the Test and Corporation Acts, 1787–1790', *English Historical Review*, 89 (1974), 551–77.

(or 'Popular') attack and advance, and they felt justified in looking for government assistance in return for their public support of the government.

These theological, political and ecclesiastical ideas and fears determined the views of Establishment churchmen on the French Revolution, on loyalty to the government and on the war. Many churchmen did not condemn the Revolution immediately, however; like many others in Britain, they underwent a tidal change in their attitudes towards it. William Robertson, Moderator of the General Assembly of the Church of Scotland from 1762–80, at first denounced Burke's *Reflections* as 'ravings', and Thomas Somerville called it 'the ranting declarations of aristocratic pride'. Thomas Hardy wrote of the Scottish ministers' initial response to the Revolution: 'We saw a great people reclaiming the inheritance of men, and boldly aspiring to be free.'[15] Their idea of 'the inheritance of men' was considerably more limited than that of the radicals, however, and, for this reason, they did not think themselves inconsistent when they changed, around 1792, to denounce what the Revolution had become. By then it could no longer be regarded as moving towards a moderate, constitutional monarchy as many of them had hoped, and its malevolence towards the Roman Catholic Church in France was already clear.[16] Others were happy to assume that the Revolution was divine retribution for the French having taken the American side in the War of Independence, while others still reacted with hostility almost immediately. William Jones, the curate at Nayland, Suffolk, famous for his 'John Bull' letters of 1792, denounced the French Revolution publicly in 1789, as did George Horne, the Dean of Canterbury Cathedral and, like Jones, a Hutchinsonian High Churchman. Bishops Samuel Horsley and Beilby Porteus privately recorded their antipathy in early 1790.[17] From late 1792 onwards, however, Establishment clergy were largely united in their condemnation of the Revolution for its violent overthrow of Church and State, and for its assault on public and private morality.

Given their fear of popular disorder and revolt, their anxiety concerning Church-State relations and their condemnation of the theories and practices of the French Revolution, Establishment churchmen were largely loyal to the government. 'From what I can learn,' Dundas told Pitt in 1794, 'the [Scottish] clergy with very few exceptions are all right in their dispositions.'[18] Resolutions

---

15 Robertson and Somerville quoted in J.D. Brims, 'The Scottish Democratic Movement in the Age of the French Revolution', unpublished Ph.D. thesis (University of Edinburgh, 1983), pp.59, 75; Thomas Hardy, *The Patriot* (Edinburgh, 1793), p.4. On England, see Hole, *Pulpits, Politics and Public Order*, p.99.

16 The Civil Constitution of the Clergy was passed in July 1790 and Louis XVI was deposed in August 1792.

17 Hole, 'English Sermons and Tracts', p.19; idem, *Pulpits, Politics and Public Order*, pp.161–2. Horsley was a High Churchman; Porteus is less easily categorized.

18 Chatham Papers, PRO 30/8/157/1/144, quoted in Fry, *The Dundas Despotism*, p.179.

and addresses were passed throughout Britain at the national, diocesan, synod, presbytery and parish levels; loyalty was preached; and radical tendencies among parishioners were checked if possible.[19] Preachers defended not only the British constitution but also the current administration and its policies, and they argued that political reform might well be possible later, at a more opportune time, so benevolent and virtuous was the present government.

The war against revolutionary France was interpreted ideologically by Establishment churchmen, from both Burkean and purely theological standpoints. Burke's writings greatly influenced the view which saw the French Revolution as particularly concerned to destroy religion and its institutions and, thereby, all social restraint and public order. Most of the rest of Burke's analysis was also accepted. The French revolutionaries were described as inherently evil men ('*enthusiasts* in wickedness', Dr Thomas Horne insisted), propagating principles destructive of all civilization and harmony. The conflict was therefore ideological in nature. Britain was fighting to defend all right and just principles of religion, society and government. It was, said Robert Nares (a High Churchman), 'a War to assert your Right to do your Duty, and obey the Will of God'.[20] Most Establishment ministers had little difficulty in arguing that it was a just and necessary war: it had been undertaken in self-defence against revolutionary armies with a mission to subvert all order, government, religion and property in Britain and throughout Europe by force. The General Assembly regularly declared to the King their 'full approbation of this necessary exertion of public force'.[21]

Preachers called also, however, for reflection and meditation on current affairs in the light of Scripture, for a proper discernment of 'the signs of the times'. It was important, insisted William Jackson, to learn 'not from the imaginations of our own hearts, but from the word of God, the fit estimates which humility and piety will lead us to make', concerning European events.[22] The Revolutionary opposition was often described in terms of spiritual enmity, the embodiment of hostility and evil, against which only steady virtue and faithfulness could prevail. Many subscribed to the conspiracy theory first hinted at by Burke's *Reflections on the Revolution in France* in 1790 and developed by the Abbé Barruel and by Professor John Robison of Edinburgh University in

---

19 See Thomas Somerville, *My Own Life and Times, 1741-1814* (Edinburgh, 1861), pp.266–7.

20 Thomas Horne, *A Sermon, Preached Before the Chiswick Military Association, on Sunday, Sept. 2, 1798* (London, 1798), p.7; Robert Nares, *Man's Best Right: A Solemn Appeal in the Name of Religion* (London, 1793), pp.45–7.

21 For example, 'Address to His Majesty on the subject of the present War' (1794) in the *Acts of the General Assembly* (Edinburgh).

22 William Jackson, *A Sermon, preached before the Honourable Society of Lincoln's Inn, on Wednesday, Feb. 25, 1795; Being the Day appointed by His Majesty's Proclamation for a General Fast* (Oxford, 1795), p.5.

1797, of the French Revolution having been hatched by continental philosophers plotting against the Christian religion. Some, displaying a degree of paranoia, thought that the Dissenters and Methodists were also participants, for the sake of destroying the power of the Established Churches.[23]

The doctrine of Providence was also applied to the war by almost every sermon preached on it. 'I am grieved to observe', wrote the Evangelical Rev. Thomas Robinson, 'that the attention of many is fixed only on second causes; as if the War ought not to be considered in the light of a dispensation from God, since it may have originated from the wrong administration of our public affairs.' The conflict had begun and would only end at the instance of God, who also controlled its procedure. The Form of Prayer appointed for the Fast Day on 8 March 1797, acknowledging the defeat by stormy weather of the French attempt to invade Ireland, thanked Him for 'what appears to us a Providential Interference—when the Winds and Storms, fulfilling Thy Word, dissipated that mighty Armament, which threatened the Peace of our Sister Kingdom'.[24]

It was a short step from this to claim that God was on Britain's side. Many saw Britain as the new Israel, God's favoured nation. The Rev. John Hampson of Sunderland, preaching on the reign of good King Hezekiah, a time when Israel was threatened by the ferocious Assyrian troops of Sennacherib, asked his congregation:

> Is there any man so blind as not to perceive the parallel? or can anything be more congenial than the language of this blasphemous Assyrian and that of our modern Reformers upon the Continent? Judea was invaded in the reign of one of its best princes, and in the moment of its prosperity. This Country was never more wisely and mildly governed, nor was it ever so prosperous as on the eve of the present war.[25]

The identification of Britain with Old Testament Israel was also taken seriously, at least as a tool of propaganda, by the highest religious and secular authorities. When George III went to St Paul's Cathedral in December 1797 to offer thanks for the naval victories gained by the British fleet, the parallel was made visual. Military banners captured from the defeated French were brought to the

---

23 Murray, 'The Influence of the French Revolution', pp.58–9, 75–6. Bishop Randolph of Oxford, according to Hole, was the exception who proved the rule (Hole, *Pulpits, Politics and Public Order*, pp.154, 170–2).

24 Thomas Robinson, *A Serious Exhortation to the Inhabitants of Great Britain with Reference to the Approaching Fast* (first published Leicester, 1795; this edition, Edinburgh, 1797), p.10; *A Form of Prayer To Be Used In all Churches and Chapels ... upon ... the Eighth of March next, being the Day appointed by Proclamation for a General FAST and Humiliation before Almighty God* (London, 1797), p.9.

25 John Hampson, *A Sermon Preached in St. John's Chapel, Sunderland, on Friday, April 19, 1793, being the day appointed for a General Fast* (Sunderland, 1793), p.8.

Cathedral by the King to testify to God's goodness to Britain in direct imitation of David, King of Israel, who had once laid the spoils of his victories before the Lord in the Temple at Jerusalem.[26]

Many Establishment ministers believed that the Providential purpose of the war was to chasten an immoral and irreligious France and, by so doing, to serve a warning to the rest of Europe. Following Scriptural precedent, many also thought that France was being used as the divine scourge for the rest of Europe, while suffering punishment for its own iniquities. William Jones of Nayland saw France as 'the man of sin' prophesied in 2 Thessalonians. This seemed a sufficient explanation for Britain's lack of military success in the war, and it in turn was explained by Britain's own immorality and irreligion. William Agutter listed perjury, blasphemy, duelling, 'notorious sedition and secret treason', 'the want of subordination in all ranks of society' and neglect of religion as some of the sins rife within Britain which made it an object of the divine wrath. John Newton added persecution of Methodists, the oppression of native peoples in British colonies, national pride and vanity, and the slave trade (in which, as he freely admitted, he had once played a very active part).[27] Only a few could help their country by fighting for it or by advising its rulers; everyone could help it by practising religion, loyalty and virtue. Evangelicals in particular vigorously criticized the irreligion and extravagance of the upper classes. Gerald Newman has seen an 'Evangelical anti-conspiracy' in this movement for moral reformation: 'The "reaction against the French Revolution" was genuine enough, but it also marvelously camouflaged those moral revolutionaries who, following John Brown, had thirsted for decades to transform, nationalize, level, and make uniform their country's institutions.'[28] It seems more likely, however, that while some may have enjoyed having a self-righteous dig at the elite, most of the preaching against upper-class idleness and conspicuous over-consumption was rooted in simple moral outrage. Establishment churchmen, orthodox, high, or Evangelical, feared rather than favoured social levelling.

With these Burkean and Providentialist views on the war, most Establishment churchmen had no hesitation in calling for religion, virtue, loyalty and patriotism to be practised by the British people. The British ought to be grateful to God for their peculiar status as his favoured nation, which secured to

---

26 This was spelled out in the *Form of Prayer To Be Used In all Churches and Chapels ... upon ... Tuesday, the Nineteenth of December next, being the Day appointed by Proclamation for a General Thanksgiving to Almighty God* (London, 1797), p.6.

27 William Agutter, *Observations on the General Fast of the Year 1796* (London, 1796), p.8; Newton, *Motives to Humiliation and Praise*, pp.7–25. On millenarianism and apocalypticism among Establishment ministers as well as Dissenters, see W.H. Oliver, *Prophets and Millennialists: the uses of biblical prophecy in England from the 1790s to the 1840s* (Auckland, 1978), chapter 3; and J.A. Oddy, 'Bicheno and Tyso on the Prophecies', *Baptist Quarterly*, 35 (1993), 81–9. I am grateful to David Bebbington for these references.

28 Newman, *The Rise of English Nationalism*, p.235.

them social harmony and blessing through their constitution, and it was insisted that 'A people eminently distinguished by the favour of heaven, ought certainly to be a religious people.'[29] Churchmen called for fasting, repentance and reformation, since it was clear to them that many in Britain fell far short of these virtuous standards. Fast Days were appointed by the King and his Privy Council, and were an established part of British war efforts in the eighteenth century. Ministers pointed to instances in Scripture where God withdrew His wrath and prevented disasters from happening to people in response to their repentance and fasting, such as the Ninevites under the influence of Jonah's preaching, and drew the conclusion that similar measures now might stay the divine chastening presently upon Britain. Some ministers even spoke of the war as a blessing: James Landon, Charles Moss and William Agutter believed that the magnitude of the cataclysm had awoken Britain from its state of slumber in moral decline and ingratitude for its assets, and that the war had isolated Britain from the French disease. 'As salt preserves meat from putrefaction,' wrote Agutter, 'so War has been our preservation against moral contamination: it has been our bulwark and protection.'[30]

Having called for diligence in religion and virtue, most Establishment ministers also preached loyalty, as a particular virtue. It was the duty of every good British citizen not only to practise Christianity faithfully, but also 'to abhor the opinions and conduct of the fanatical sect [of French revolutionaries], and to oppose them to the utmost of his power', and 'to strengthen the hands of government by yielding a willing and ready obedience to his lawful superiors'.[31] The blessings of living under the British constitution were underlined, and it was explained that, in return for the protection of their lives and property, people owed submission and obedience to the government. Sermons were still being preached before the Houses of Commons and Lords respectively on 30 January in 1786–91 and 1793–95 to commemorate the so-called 'martyrdom' of Charles I, thus reinforcing the value attached to the monarchy by the Church of England. The clergymen appointed to preach before MPs and peers in 1793–95 did not miss the opportunity to draw the parallel between the execution of Charles I and that more recently of Louis XVI, and to emphasize the heinousness of the crime of regicide.[32] Radicalism, rebellion and

---

29 Alexander Black, *National Blessings Considered and Improved, in a Sermon, preached on Thursday, November 29, 1798* (Edinburgh, 1798), pp.27–8.

30 William Agutter, *An Address to Every British Subject on the Late Important Victories* (London, 1798), p.3.

31 William Laurence Brown, *The Spirit of the Times Considered. A Sermon, preached in the English Church at Utrecht, February 13, 1793, the day appointd by the States for the General Thanksgiving, Fasting and Prayer* (London, 1793), pp.23, 32.

32 Horsley, *Sermon Before the Lords Spiritual and Temporal* (1793); Vernon, *Sermon Preached Before the Lords Spiritual and Temporal* (1794); Madan, *Sermon Before the Lords Spiritual and Temporal* (1795); Hay, *Sermons Before the House of Commons* (1793, 1794,

revolution were regularly condemned, and the point was heavily emphasized that ordinary people rarely benefited from them and often suffered as a result. Richard Munkhouse went so far as to insist that the common people had 'no immediate concern' with matters of political administration, and that they ought not to interfere with or even discuss them, since they were 'alike far beyond the sphere of their action, and above the reach of their comphrehension'.[33] While many Church of England ministers encouraged the establishment of Sunday Schools as a method of civilizing and restraining the lower orders, many ministers in the Church of Scotland thought them a dangerous innovation promoted by itinerant preachers (*alias* political and religious radicals) for the propagation of their evil ideas and banned them, in 1799.

Finally, along with religion, virtue and loyalty, Establishment ministers exhorted their congregations to practise patriotism. Hugh Blair of Edinburgh and Alexander Carlyle of Inveresk both preached sermons entitled *On the Love of our Country* after Richard Price's famous discourse of 1789, arguing the very opposite to his exhortation to world citizenship and the Revolutionary principle of *fraternité*. To love the French as much as the British, scorned Blair, would be like loving strangers as much as one's own wife and children.[34] Prayers were said to supplicate God for British victory: 'Convince our enemies that we are thy people; and that thine arm, stretched out, can set at naught the most daring designs against our peace.'[35] In their efforts to inspire patriotism, ministers spoke to people's emotions as well as to their minds, appealing to all that might tug at them—family, tradition, religion, the desire for glory, fear of French depredations, the threat of judgement, personal pride.

In the names of religion, virtue, loyalty and patriotism, then, ministers called civilians and soldiers alike to endurance while the war lasted. Those who remained at home were urged to pay their taxes willingly: a Briton's religious faith and political liberty ought to be even more important to him than his property, according to Munkhouse.[36] They sympathized with those who

---

1795). The anniversary was missed in 1792 and 1796–99 because Parliament was still in recess on 30 January in those years, but interestingly it was also missed in 1800, although Parliament was sitting over 30 January that year, and the practice appears to have been more or less discontinued after that. Elsewhere it was continued: a sermon was preached on 30 January 1800 before a congregation at Oxford University (Landon, *Sermon Before the University of Oxford*).

33 Richard Munkhouse, *A Sermon, Preached ... on ... November 29th, 1798; Being the Day Appointed for a General Thanksgiving* (London, 1799), p.19.

34 Hugh Blair, 'On the Love of Our Country' (Edinburgh, 1793), in *Sermons*, 5 vol.s (London, 1818), v, 129. See also Evan Radcliffe, 'Revolutionary Writing, Moral Philosophy, and Universal Benevolence in the Eighteenth Century', *Journal of the History of Ideas*, 54 (1993), 221–40.

35 *A Form of Prayer ... General Fast* (19 April 1793), pp.6, 7.

36 Richard Munkhouse, *A Sermon, preached ... on December 19th, 1797. On occasion of a General Thanksgiving* (London, 1798), pp.41–2.

suffered most from the 'scarcity' of grain and high prices, but they denied that these had been caused by the war. Prayers were said for the return of plenty, and the better-off were urged to economize on luxuries and to help the poor by making nutritious food cheaply available to them. Ministers praised those who enrolled in the militia, the Volunteers or the regular armed forces. Heaven's highest places, encouraged Carlyle, were reserved for those 'who have deserved well, or have died in the service of their country'.[37] Sermons were preached before Volunteer companies, often at services of dedication of their colours, exhorting them to conduct themselves in faith and with patriotism and valour, and commending them to the rest of the community.

Congregations and readers were encouraged to prepare for, but not to be afraid of, a French invasion. Ultimately, ministers claimed to place their faith in God to deliver Britain from such an incursion, but they pointed also to the public spirit of the nation, shown both in the courage and skill of the navy and home defence troops and in the general population and their love for their country. Bishop Horsley told his clergy not to participate themselves in armed service, either with the regular army or with the local militia, simply because they were not likely to make good soldiers. They would do more good in the event of an invasion by supervising the evacuation of the weak and helpless and the livestock and by helping to destroy buildings in the path of the enemy. They should 'level the Musquet or trail the Pike' only in a dire emergency.[38]

For all their apparent bellicosity in their loyalty to the government and in their hostility to revolutionary France, Establishment ministers, like the great majority of the population, were eager to see the restoration of peace and they reminded their listeners of the principle of loving one's enemies. Many were delighted with the peace settlement at Amiens, thinking, as William Vincent did, that they had 'lived to see a great nation renounce Christianity and embrace heathenism; and again revert from heathenism, to submit once more to the empire of the Gospel'.[39] Evangelicals were particularly pleased, since they believed that Catholicism had been irreversibly overthrown in France, making clear the way for 'pure religion' once the madness of official atheism had passed, and they expressed great optimism for the future of Christianity in France until Napoleon's Concordat with the Pope was signed in 1803.[40] There were some who voiced anxiety, however. Bishop Horsley did not think that a

---

37 Carlyle, *Love of our Country*, p.33.

38 Quoted in Hole, *Pulpits, Politics and Public Order*, p.170. The idea of even this level of involvement 'hurried and affected' Parson Woodforde 'a great deal indeed' (Beresford (ed.), *Diary of a Country Parson*, v, 329, 6 August 1801).

39 Vincent, 'A Sermon preached before the Honourable House of Commons ... on Tuesday, June 1, 1802, being the day appointed for a General Thanksgiving' (London, 1802), in *Sermons on Faith*, i, 325–7.

40 Murray, 'The Influence of the French Revolution', pp.279–81.

real peace could last for any length of time, since the strength of French power by the settlement contained in it 'the seed and germ of everlasting wars'. He dreaded 'the revival of the spirit of Jacobinism in this country', pointing to a symptom of it in those who urged Britain to concede much in order to pacify France.[41]

Liberal churchmen and Evangelicals within the Established Churches tended, if sometimes reluctantly, to retreat from protests and demands for ecclesiastical and political reform during the war—the liberals because of the association of religious liberalism and radicalism with political radicalism, and Evangelicals because of their own conservative reactions to the threat to religious and secular authority posed by the armies of revolutionary France. Sometimes the patriotism of Evangelicals was qualified, however. They, more than mainstream churchmen, claimed to place their trust in the prayers of Christians and the mercy of God rather than in the British government and its fleets and armies. As William Stafford explains, their strong sense of sin worked for obedience to the government but against national pride: 'because of man's wickedness the state is essential; but characteristically their pride in their native land is reduced by their sense of its depravity'.[42] Evangelicals such as John Newton, Thomas Scott and Thomas Gisborne, while basically loyalist, were nevertheless suspicious of the war, because all war was harmful and destructive and because this war was undertaken in alliance with corrupt papal monarchies in part to restore Roman Catholicism in France. They also continued to press for reforms such as the abolition of the slave trade and to acknowledge that moderate political reform was needed and should be carried through at a more opportune time.[43]

It is also true that a minority of Establishment ministers opposed the British wars against revolutionary France in the 1790s. The Rev. J.H. Williams, vicar of Wellsbourn in Warwickshire, was not convinced that the political state and order either of Europe or of Britain had warranted it, and he pointed out that even if it was favoured by general consent, it was not true that the opinion of the majority was always right. War caused gross damage to the morals of individuals and of nations: it attacked piety, fostered hatred, threatened loyalty to the government and King and was generally hostile to the spirit of the gospel.[44] These ministers sometimes suspected that religion was being used for secular

---

41 *P.H.*, xxxvi, 179–82, the Bishop of Rochester, 3 November 1801.

42 William Stafford, 'Religion and the Doctrine of Nationalism in England at the Time of the French Revolution and Napoleonic Wars', *Studies in Church History*, 18 (1982), 386–8.

43 See also Andrew Mackillop, *'More Fruitful Than The Soil': Army, Empire and the Scottish Highlands 1715–1815* (forthcoming), chapter 7, on the conflict of Evangelical religion with militarism in the Highlands.

44 J.H. Williams, *Two Sermons Preached on the Public Fasts of April 1793 and February 1794* (London, 1794), pp.22–64.

political purposes, and they were indignant. They disagreed with the obligation they felt themselves under to display political loyalty and, in particular, to conduct Fast Day services for the support of the war. Vicesimus Knox said that this was an odious rendering of religion subservient to secular ambition, and Williams deeply resented 'the not being suffered to do our own business in our own way'. It was wrong to go to war for the sake of religion, according to Richard Watson, even if the French were attempting to destroy Christianity. It would be better to try to convert them than to kill them.[45]

Nevertheless, the great majority of Establishment churchmen remained loyal to the government and supported it in its war against revolutionary France, because of their Burkean condemnation of the theories and practices of the French Revolution and their conviction that the French Republic constituted a spiritual enemy. They also feared popular disorder and revolt in Britain, and the weakening of Church-State relations, and they constituted a major instrument of propaganda in encouraging their congregations and readership to imitate their loyalty.

II Dissenters and Seceders

Although 'rational' Dissent seems to have declined in England in the 1790s, at least in terms of the fears it held for the orthodox Establishment, Evangelical Dissent enjoyed considerable growth, both in England and in Scotland. Between 1788 and 1794, 1872 Dissenting meeting-houses were registered in England and 610 Dissenting licences to preach were granted at quarter-sessions. Between 1795 and 1801, the figures were 3378 and 1318 respectively.[46] 'Dissent' in Scotland is more accurately divided into Secession churches (Burghers, Anti-Burghers, Relief Church and Reformed Presbyterians) and Dissenting churches (Episcopalians, Roman Catholics, Baptists, Independents and Methodists). This reflected the distinction between, respectively, those churches which split from Established presbyterian government only after 1690 and retained some degree of similarity in terms of doctrine and church government, and those which had never been part of it and which were organized along quite different lines.

---

45 Knox, 'Preface' to 'Antipolemus', p.421; Williams, *Two Sermons*, pp.vi, vii; *P.H.*, xxxi, 1267, the Bishop of Llandaff, 27 January 1795. On Watson, cf. p.140. Having opposed the war for the above reasons until 1798, he then published his view that, since the French had refused to make peace in 1796 and 1797, their threat towards Britain had been made plain and the war had become just and unavoidable (Richard Watson, *An Address to the People of Great Britain* [London, 1798], p.11; idem, *Anecdotes of the Life of Dr Watson, Bishop of Landaff*, 2nd edition, 2 vol.s [London, 1818], ii, 1–26).

46 Murray, 'The Influence of the French Revolution', pp.153–4, 160, 201; Deryck Lovegrove, 'English Evangelical Dissent and the European Conflict 1789–1815', *Studies in Church History*, 20 (1983), 263.

'Rational' Dissent also grew in Scotland in the 1790s, with the first Unitarian congregation established in Montrose in 1792, and spreading to Dundee, Forfar and Arbroath in 1795.

Denominational politics were as significant in determining the attitudes of Dissenters to the war as they were in forming those of Establishment ministers. The identification of the Establishment with government policies tempted some to woo the support of political dissenters and, in so doing, they became more politically nonconformist themselves. In the case of the New, or Kilhamite, Methodist Connexion, this meant splitting away from the Church of England and the main Wesleyan body. Many, however, despite their dislike for what they believed to be a powerful and corrupt Establishment, were sufficiently disturbed by the political and religious radicalism of some within their own sect or denomination, or of those in rival sects, to give limited support to the political and religious authorities during the war. Methodism presents an interesting amalgam of Establishment and Dissenting attitudes in the 1790s, a decade of flux for its followers. After the death of John Wesley in 1791, Methodists struggled with his desire that they should remain within the Church of England, some preachers wishing to bow to popular demand for Methodist celebration of the sacrament. The great majority of Methodist preachers, however, remained within the Church of England during this decade, partly because of government pressure for a demonstration of their loyalty, partly due to their own fear of popular radicalism among Methodists, and partly because of their continuing adherence to Wesley's loyalism.[47]

A majority of Dissenters, in fact, were not gratified by the French Revolution after its initial stages. John Young, Anti-Burgher minister of Hawick, like so many others, had been deeply disappointed by the degeneration of the French Revolution into violence, through the dissolution of the National Assembly, the Constitutional Assembly, which had 'acted as so many children', to the Convention, which was 'an assembly of bloodsuckers, who seemed to feast themselves with the miseries of their fellow-men'.[48] The Revolution became particularly abhorrent when it renounced Christianity. Some were convinced that the conspiracy theory of the Revolution was true, and even the politically radical Dissenters of the *Analytical Review* 'found unacceptable what [they] judged to be the flippant and irresponsible manner in which French

---

47 For Methodism in the 1790s, see W.R. Ward, *Religion and Society in England, 1790-1850* (London, 1972), chapter 2; John Walsh, 'Methodism at the End of the Eighteenth Century', in R. Davies and G. Rupp (eds), *A History of the Methodist Church in Great Britain*, vol. i (London, 1966), pp.278–308; David Hempton, *Methodism and Politics in British Society, 1750–1850* (London, 1984), chapter 3.

48 John Young, *A History of the Commencement, Progress, and Termination of the Late War Between Britain and France* (Edinburgh, 1802), p.2.

philosophers dismissed Christianity out of hand'.[49] Even most Unitarians were part of a pious and strict nonconformist religious culture and believed that fundamental religious and moral principles should be taught to the masses.

Nor were Dissenters as unwilling to prove their loyalty as the government often assumed. Leading Seceding ministers in Scotland met with Robert Dundas, the Lord Advocate, to assure him of their desire to smother radicalism in their congregations and clergy. Scottish Episcopalians could, after their Relief Act of 1792, be relied upon to support the state; but Seceders and English Dissenters also defended the constitution and preached the importance of religion, submission and patriotism. Loyal addresses were regularly sent to the King, public statements of their loyalty were made, allegations of radicalism among their numbers were investigated. 'Give none occasion to the world, who observe you,' admonished Alexander Shanks, the Burgher minister of Jedburgh, 'to call you an ill-humoured and ill-principled sectary, disaffected to the welfare and prosperity of that country in which you are fed and protected.'[50] Thus, their sermons had a two-fold purpose: to persuade their Seceding hearers and readers to be peaceful, blameless subjects in order to improve the reputation of the churches; and to convince anyone else who might read them, particularly anyone in authority, that Seceders were neither seditious nor even deserving of suspicion.

Of conservative political sermons published in England between 1789 and 1802, Roman Catholics seem to have produced more than Protestant Dissenters: Gayle Trusdel Pendleton has traced 98 and 51 respectively. Catholics were, of course, horrified by the course of the Revolution in France. Bishop Hay in Scotland argued that 'to stop the progress of a set of furies, open and professed enemies to God and man and to prevent the spreading of their contagious and diabolical doctrines, which carry devastation and misery wherever they go, is surely a common cause of humanity'.[51] At first, some Catholic gentlemen were reluctant to join Volunteer corps because of the political restrictions on Catholics, and, similarly, they were often unwilling to enlist in the regular army, because as Catholics they would have to obtain annual indemnities to be allowed to serve in it. It seems, however, that their reluctance was also motivated by more widely-held objections to military service, such as the necessity of spending time away from family and business; and the continuation of the domestic and foreign threats eventually persuaded some to overcome their

---

49 Brian Rigby, 'Radical Spectators of the Revolution: the Case of the *Analytical Review*', in Crossley and Small, *The French Revolution and British Culture*, p.69.

50 Alexander Shanks, *Peace and Order Recommended to Society* (Edinburgh, 1793), p.8.

51 Pendleton, 'English Conservative Propaganda', p.208; Hay quoted in Christine Johnson, 'Developments in the Roman Catholic Church in Scotland 1789–1829', unpublished Ph.D. thesis (University of Edinburgh, 1980), p.150.

scruples and to participate in armed loyalism, both in the Volunteers and in regular regiments.[52]

With regard to the war itself, Britain was again sometimes pictured as the new Israel, God's favoured nation, but more often the conflict was interpreted by Dissenters as the divine chastening of Britain and Europe for their irreligion and immorality. Providence, as for Establishment ministers, was a cardinal doctrine. Archibald Bruce claimed to see God's hand at work, using the war as a scourge not only on Britain in general, but also on the Established Church of Scotland in particular, for its spiritual tyranny, its considerations of interest and its elevation of human laws and customs above the precepts of Scripture. Fasting, repentance, prayer and faithfulness to the teaching of Scripture were necessary if real peace was to be restored. 'We need repentance and reformation,' warned the London Presbyterian Abraham Rees, 'and whilst the war is prolonged, we shall not be exempt from fear and danger.'[53]

Many Evangelical Dissenters in fact were unwilling to publish on political matters. James Bradley discovered no sermons on political topics published by any English Dissenters in 1796–97.[54] John Young was attacked, not only by his own anti-Erastian congregation, but also at presbytery and Synod levels of the Anti-Burgher church for publicizing his politically conservative views, expounded in his *Essays on the Following Interesting Subjects* (1794). Rather than engage in political discussions and become embroiled in party allegiance, many Evangelicals chose to embrace millenarianism or to plunge into intense evangelistic work. Not all millenarian interpretations of the French Revolution and its aftermath were as wild and fantastic as those of Joanna Southcott of Exeter, or those of the naval officer Richard Brothers, who prophesied the fall of the British monarchy if the war was continued, announced himself the Prince of the Hebrews and commanded George III in God's name to hand over his crown and authority. Other, more cautious and scholarly, studies were published, meditating on the likeness of the present convulsions to the events that Scripture predicted would precede the end of time. James Bicheno, the radical Baptist minister and schoolmaster of Newbury, published at least six works on this subject between 1793 and 1817, adapting his interpretation of biblical prophecy to events as they came to pass. Joseph Priestley emphasized

---

52 M.Y. Ashcroft, *To Escape the Monster's Clutches*, pp.30, 52–3; correspondence of the Huddlestons of Sawston, Cambridgeshire CRO, e.g. 488/C2/H5, HD19; 488/C3/B10, B41, B56, B57, HR2, HR3, P34. I am grateful to Professor Clive Emsley for these references.

53 [Archibald Bruce], *A Serious View of the Remarkable Providences of the Times* (Glasgow, 1795), p.41; Abraham Rees, *The Privileges of Britain. A Sermon, preached at the meeting-House in the old Jewry on Thursday the 29th of November 1798, being the day appointed for a General Thanksgiving* (London, 1798), pp.30–4.

54 J.E. Bradley, *Church, Clergy and Counter-Revolution in England, 1789–1800* (a paper presented at the annual conference of the American Society for Eighteenth-Century Studies at New Orleans in April 1989), p.6.

the deliverance of the oppressed which the millenium would bring. Most, however, as Deryck Lovegrove comments, restricted themselves to expressing 'the more circumspect if somewhat imprecise conviction that Christ's reign was rapidly approaching'.[55]

Missions, foreign and domestic, became very popular in the wake of the French Revolution. The decline of papal power in Europe, together with the collapse of French power overseas, presented a great opportunity for missionary enterprise, and Dissenters were very actively involved in this work. In 1792 the Baptist Missionary Society was formed by William Carey, followed in 1795 by the London Missionary Society, in 1798 by the Glasgow Missionary Society, in 1799 by the Church [of England] Missionary Society, and in 1801 by the Scottish Missionary Society. This work was publicized by the *Missionary Magazine* in Scotland and the *Evangelical Magazine* in England. Domestic missions were engaged in by Independents and Baptists in England, Charles Simeon and Rowland Hill embarking on long and arduous preaching tours, and by the Relief Church and the Haldane brothers (via the Society for the Propagation of the Gospel at Home, which they founded in 1797) in Scotland. Sunday Schools soon spread to most of the larger towns, as well as to many smaller places. Unions to organize itinerant preaching were increasingly established after 1795, and Dissenting ministers and students in Huntingdonshire paid evangelistic visits to the French prisoners of war held there.[56] Sometimes gospel tracts were distributed which made direct reference to the war, such as one published in Yarmouth in 1798, which at first sight appears to be a simple piece of government recruiting propaganda, but which, from the texts printed beside each exhortation, quickly proves to be a pamphlet recruiting instead for the army of Heaven.[57]

It must also be noted, however, that even the loyalty of politically conservative Dissenters was, at best, qualified, and that a significant proportion of Nonconformists held anti-war views. By its very nature, Dissent was anti-establishment, and some ministers were quite open about their liberal or radical political views.[58] Mark Wilks, a Baptist minister in Norwich, reminded his audience in 1791 that 'Jesus Christ was a Revolutionist', and he went on to

---

55 Lovegrove, 'English Dissent and the European Conflict', p.269; Oliver, *Prophets and Millennialists*, chapter 3; Oddy, 'Bicheno and Tyso'. See also Iain McCalman, 'New Jerusalems: prophecy, Dissent and radical culture in England, 1786–1830', in Haakonssen (ed.), *Enlightenment and Religion*, pp.312–35; David Hempton, 'Evangelicals and Eschatology', *Journal of Ecclesiastical History*, 31 (1980), 179–94.

56 Lovegrove, 'English Dissent and the European Conflict', p.269.

57 *An Alarm to the Public, and a Bounty Promised to Every Loyal Subject, Who Will Come Forward to Repel the Enemy. Arms and Accoutrements Provided For Every Man, Gratis* (Yarmouth, 1798).

58 For the background to Dissenting attitudes at the end of the eighteenth century, see J.E. Bradley, *Religion, Revolution and English Radicalism* (Cambridge, 1990).

express the view that 'the French Revolution is of God, and that no power exists or can exist, by which it can be overthrown'. Wilks later preached sermons to help raise money to pay for the defence of Thomas Hardy, John Horne Tooke and John Thelwall at their trials for treason, and he also helped to organize the Norwich petition against the Two Bills of 1795.[59] James Bicheno and Archibald Bruce also defended the French Revolution as a battle for civil and religious liberty, and Bruce condemned the Loyal Associations as 'guilty of an outrage on the constitution of their country, as well as on the rights of their fellow-subjects', for intimidating people into acquiescing in their views and measures, and often causing disturbances of the peace in the process.[60] Alexander Kilham, founder of the New Connexion of Methodists, believed that the spiritual equality of all men before God granted the right to an equal voice in the regulation of their church to all the regenerate. Hutchison of Paisley was attacked by some in his Relief Church congregation for his enthusiasm for the rising liberties of France and his hostility to British attempts to crush them.[61] Several Seceding ministers attended the Edinburgh Conventions of 1792–93.[62] Unitarian preachers such as Joseph Priestley, Richard Price and Thomas Fysshe Palmer were well known advocates of reform.

Not all Dissenting ministers, therefore, supported the armed struggle against revolutionary France, and a significantly higher proportion of them openly opposed it than was the case in the Established Churches. It was argued that war was directly contrary to the teachings and spirit of Christianity and to the interests of civilization, and that it was the means of sending many unconverted souls to hell. Bruce held that 'the approved citizen of Zion is one who shutteth even his ears from hearing of blood', which was the pietistic line

---

59 On radicalism in both Wilks and Norwich, see C.B. Jewson, *Jacobin City* (Glasgow and London, 1975).

60 Hole, 'English Sermons and Tracts', p.23; James Bicheno, *The signs of the times: or, The overthrow of the papal tyranny in France, the prelude of destruction to popery and despotism; but of peace to mankind*, 4th edition (London, 1794), pp.38–41; Archibald Bruce, *A Peaceable Declaration of the Sentiments of a Number of Presbyterians in Scotland, relative to the War between France and Great-Britain* (Edinburgh, 1797), pp.ii–x; idem, *A Brief Statement and Declaration of the Genuine Principles of Seceders, respecting Civil Government; the Duty of Subjects; and National Reformation: and a Vindication of their Conduct in reference to some late Plans and Societies for Political Reform; and the Public Dissentions of the Time. Proposed and Read in a Meeting of the General Associate Synod in Scotland* (Edinburgh, 1799), p.66; Brims, 'The Covenanting Tradition', pp.54–7.

61 Walsh, 'Methodism at the End of the Eighteenth Century', pp. 307–8; Brims, 'The Covenanting Tradition', p.52; G. Struthers, *History of the Rise, Progress, and Principles of the Relief Church* (Glasgow, 1843), pp.381–3.

62 William Kirkland, 'The Impact of the French Revolution on Scottish Religious Life and Thought, with special reference to Thomas Chalmers, Robert Haldane, and Niel Douglas', unpublished Ph.D. thesis (University of Edinburgh, 1951), on Niel Douglas; Brims, 'Scottish Democratic Movement', pp.105–13.

favoured by Quakers and anti-war Baptists.[63] Many Dissenters held to a politically neutral line, expressing only horror at war in general and exhorting Christians to pray for the return of peace and to do good wherever possible. Rational Christians did not always follow Richard Price and William Godwin in rejecting all sentiments of patriotism, but they often argued from love of country to love of mankind in general, rather than stopping at the shores of Britain as Establishment ministers often did. Partial affections, it was taught, were necessary only as concessions to man's weakness and limitations, and they ought to produce general benevolence in those who held them.[64]

The fundamental reason why some Protestant Dissenters objected particularly to the war against revolutionary France was their unshakeable anti-Catholicism.[65] They had been thrilled by the overthrow of the Catholic Church in France: as James Bicheno put it, appearances seemed to indicate 'that this will be a fatal stroke to the Papal usurpations and to the reign of despotism'. He interpreted this very specifically as the slaying of the first Beast mentioned in the book of Revelation. Britain, in trying to help restore it to power, was therefore fighting on entirely the wrong side in this Armageddon. Archibald Bruce took the same view, looking back with longing to the days of the Protestant alliance of Britain, the United Provinces and Prussia. 'In such days of shaking and alarm,' he warned, 'Protestant nations can only be safe by stedfastly maintaining the reformation they have attained.'[66] Some Establishment publications had criticized Roman Catholicism and applauded its downfall in France, but such hostile millenarianism came mainly from Dissenters.

For these reasons, then—that this was a war in opposition to liberty, that it was being fought in support of Catholicism, and that all war was an evil—some Dissenting churchmen insisted that Britain ought to repent and withdraw from the war. They protested against the use of fasting to encourage political loyalty: it was not the task of true servants of God to amuse their congregations with 'courtly panegyrics on the excellency and purity of our government in church and state' and 'virulent invectives against their neighbours, whose sentiments, about public measures, may differ from their own'.[67] Instead, they used Fast

---

63 M.R. Watts, *The Dissenters*, vol. 2 (Oxford, 1995), p.350; Bruce, *Brief Statement*, p.61; PRO HO/42/24/274–v, the Quakers' petition to the King on 27 January 1793 to ask him to intervene to prevent a war.

64 Lovegrove, 'English Dissent and the European Conflict', p.267; Stafford, 'Religion and the Doctrine of Nationalism', pp.384–6.

65 See Colin Haydon, *Anti-Catholicism in eighteenth-century England, c.1714–1780. A political and social study* (Manchester, 1993).

66 Bicheno, *Signs of the Times*, pp.iii, 19–20, 72–3, 113–14; Bruce, *Brief Statement*, pp.79–80.

67 James Bicheno, *A Word in Season: or, a Call to the Inhabitants of Great Britain to Stand Prepared for the Consequences of the Present War. Written on the Fast-Day, Feb. 25, 1795* (London and Edinburgh, 1795), p.3.

Days to preach their own conviction that the war was unjust and unnecessary, which, as Cookson points out, explains why there was so little non-observance by Dissenters.[68] Lay and clerical Dissenters played a very active role in the anti-war movement throughout the decade, and while expressed antipathy to the war was not the norm even among Dissenting churchmen, it was much more common among them than it was among Establishment ministers.

III Impact

Four main factors, therefore, influenced the attitudes of British ministers of religion to the war against revolutionary France: theology, political theology, ecclesiastical politics and political ideology in response to the French Revolution. Religious radicalism of the left *or* of the right tended towards political radicalism and opposition to the war, while religious moderation or conservatism tended towards loyalism. Ideological hostility to or sympathy for the French Revolution was clearly significant in determining churchmen's views on the war. As the government's function was to respond to French principles on the ground, so the clergy's natural sphere, like Burke's, was in the realm of pure ideas. They easily agreed that this was a war about ideologies, principles and values. Government inducements to loyalty should not be overlooked, as a further possible motivation, but it is impossible to say how many they actually persuaded to preach loyalty, since they were usually given to ministers whose political inclinations were likely to have been conservative already. Henry Dundas was particularly assiduous in courting Scottish ministers of different persuasions: 'perhaps if I was to name what circumstance was of the most essential importance to the peace of the country, I would name the influence of the clergy over the people properly exercised', he told Pitt. Moderates and Evangelicals in the Establishment received royal chaplaincies, and the Episcopal and Catholic Churches received relief and subsidies.[69]

How far did their preaching affect the ordinary people? The impact of conservative and radical literature in general on public opinion will be considered in chapter 8, but the churches held a particular significance war-time as leaders and foci of national sentiment and as a source of comfort for the anxious and the bereaved, despite the gradual erosion of the influence of Establishment religion by the Enlightenment, by the beginning of industrial urban growth, and by clerical neglect.[70] The combined loyalism of the majority of the clergy of most

---

68 Cookson, *Friends of Peace*, p.137.

69 Fry, *The Dundas Despotism*, p.179.

70 On eighteenth-century clerical neglect, see Peter Virgin, *The Church in an Age of Negligence: ecclesiastical structure and problems of church reform, 1700–1840* (Cambridge, 1989).

denominations at such a time of national emergency undoubtedly had some impact. The number of published loyalist sermons was probably only a small proportion of the whole and many more taught conservative principles without referring directly to the war, or even to the French Revolution. Sermons were an unusually powerful means of communication, in that they reached the literate and illiterate alike and could claim the support of the highest possible authority. The pulpit was a most effective platform, particularly when combined with the written word. Bradley ranks the Anglican clergy with the best of politicians and government pamphleteers, and many of their Scottish counterparts could also be commended for their consistency and force of argument. Attendance was high on national Fast and Thanksgiving Days, since these were regarded as times of great symbolic significance. Printed sermons could have a wide circulation: 10,000 coarse and 1000 fine copies of George Hill's *The Present Happiness of Great Britain* (Edinburgh, 1792) were distributed.[71] Nevertheless, it is open to debate how much success the conservative sermons had in converting those with reformist or radical inclinations to patriotism and submission, or, on the other hand, how many otherwise loyal citizens were persuaded to oppose the war by pacifist or radical sermons. It seems likely that, in general, the most that sermons could achieve politically was to confirm people in their own attitudes by giving them Scriptural and ecclesiastical backing; but it is also possible that their strongly ideologically-based teaching encouraged those who received it to conceptualize the conflict as one of ideas.

---

71 Brims, 'Scottish Democratic Movement', p.357.

Chapter 7

Women at War: British Women and the Debate on the Wars Against Revolutionary France 1792-1802[1]

> As sailors in a storm throw overboard their more useless lumber, so it is but fit that the *Men* should be exposed to the dangers and hardships of war, while we remain in safety at home. They are, generally speaking, good for little else but to be our bulwarks.[2]

Thus 'Sophia' sought to justify the masculinity of the military profession, while stating her case for *Woman Not Inferior to Man* in 1739. In 1793 war was as imminent a problem for British women as it had been for 'Sophia', and one which kindled similar anxieties about gender and spheres of operation.

The conservative writer Laetitia Matilda Hawkins claimed in her *Letters on the Female Mind* (1793) that most British women knew very little about the Revolution or the war:

> The whole world might be at war and yet not the rumor of it reached the ears of an Englishwoman—empires might be lost, and states overthrown, and still she might pursue the peaceful occupations of her home; and her natural lord might change his governor at pleasure, and she feel neither change nor hardship.[3]

Yet the impositions of this war upon the British people in terms of military participation, vulnerability to a French invasion and liability for providing the

---

1 A substantially similar version of this chapter was published under the same title in *Enlightenment and Dissent*, 15 (1996), 3–32.

2 Quoted in Virginia Sapiro, *A Vindication of Political Virtue. The Political Theory of Mary Wollstonecraft* (Chicago and London, 1992), p.261. 'Sophia' has been variously suggested to have been Lady Mary Wortley Montagu (by Sapiro, loc. cit.) and Lady Sarah Fermer (in *Notes and Queries*, 1897), but there is not enough evidence to prove her identity (Janet Todd [ed.], *A Dictionary of British and American Woman Writers, 1660-1800* [London, 1984], p.292).

3 Laetitia Matilda Hawkins, *Letters on the Female Mind*, 2 vol.s (London, 1793), ii, 194.

material resources required to finance the war effort brought the conflict directly into the lives of most British women as well as men. In terms of direct military involvement, however, women could at most be spectators, not actors, in the drama. Eighteenth-century warfare was a fundamentally male-dominated phenomenon. As necessary spectators, therefore, their views hold interest in the context of the war debate. What did women think about the conflict, and how did they express their opinions? Moreover, how does their involvement in the war debate fit into the historiographical model of 'separate spheres' of influence and activity for men and women in the 1790s?

The difficulties of attempting to assess the significance of the written attitudes of British women to the wars against revolutionary France are largely concerned with lack of evidence. Those women who left detailed written records of their opinions on the conflict were usually exceptional people as well as unusual women for their time, and they are few in number. Furthermore, men wrote much of the literature directed at women. *The Lady's Magazine* and other periodicals for women were edited by men and mostly written by men; and, while several pamphlets were signed by 'an Englishwoman' or 'Britannia', the text suggests that they were written by men. For these reasons, the following sections rely mostly on texts whose authorships are reasonably certain.

Yet the question of female views on the war is important enough, though generally neglected, to be considered seriously on the basis of what evidence there is. Their opinions were naturally often very similar to those of men, but it is arguable that, whatever part of the social or political spectrum they represented, women consistently emphasized certain issues and concerns. Moreover, not only were they trying to answer the questions posed also for men by the conflict but, in a war which had a direct impact on a very wide cross-section of society over such a long period of time, they also struggled with the question of their own role in a society at war. This chapter examines women's contributions to Britain's pamphlet debate on the conflict, as well as journals and letters written by women, in order to gain insight into women's views on the war. In doing so, it also tries to shed light on the ways in which they conceptualized desirable female behaviour during the war. It ends by examining men's attitudes towards women's participation in the conflict and in the debates surrounding it.

I Joining the Debate

Over the last two decades historians of gender and class have explored the significance of the concept of separate spheres in British society from the mid-eighteenth century to the mid-nineteenth century, and they may be said to have fallen into two similar but distinct camps on the subject. While developments in medical thinking over the late seventeenth and eighteenth centuries were vital to the theoretical justification of patriarchy in nineteenth-century Britain,[4] some historians have identified the period from the 1790s to the 1830s as a crucial phase in the development of separate spheres in practice for British men and women. This, they explain, was partly due to an increasing separation of workplace and home in this period, with the development of industrialization. An increasingly well-off middle class, faced with the choice of women remaining at home or going out to work, could afford the luxury of leisured wives, and wished to be seen to be able to afford it. The growing influence of Evangelical values was also significant. Their role in the anti-slavery campaigns had won the Evangelicals sympathy and arguably gave greater credibility to their crusade to increase morality in public and private life. An important element in this endeavour was their promotion of the role of the wife and mother in creating the home as a safe haven, out of the corrupting influences of public life. Moreover, the alarm created by the French Revolution, in which French women participated in some of the most radical events of the first four years, together with fears that similar tumultuous social and economic change might overwhelm Britain also, caused conservatives to cling ever more tightly to the 'traditional' social order in which women were subordinate and remained modestly in the background, in the private sphere of life, while men took responsibility for the public sphere of work, politics and leadership.[5]

Others agree that this period witnessed great public anxiety concerning women's participation in public life, but they point out the limitations of the separate spheres lens for viewing British society in this period. They argue, for instance, that separate spheres had long characterized British society and that it was not new to this period. Others contend that the separation of the spheres was more prominent in ideology and rhetoric than in practice and that the public roles of women were at least surviving, if not, indeed, growing in this period.[6]

---

4 Anthony Fletcher, *Gender, Sex and Subordination 1500–1800* (New Haven and London, 1995).

5 Catherine Hall, 'The Early Formation of Victorian Domestic Ideology', in S. Burman (ed.), *Fit Work for Women* (Oxford, 1979); Leonore Davidoff and Catherine Hall, *Family Fortunes: Men and Women of the English Middle Class, 1780–1850* (London, 1987); Mary Poovey, *The Proper Lady and the Woman Writer: Ideology as Style in the Works of Mary Wollstonecraft, Mary Shelley, and Jane Austen* (Chicago and London, 1984), pp.x–xvii, 1–35; Cynthia L. White, *Women's Magazines, 1693–1968* (London, 1970), pp.32–41. For a comparative view of the position of women in revolutionary France, see Olwen H. Hufton, *Women and the Limits of Citizenship in the French Revolution* (Toronto, 1992).

6 Neil McKendrick, 'Home Demand and Economic Growth: A New View of the Role of Women and Children in the Industrial Revolution', in McKendrick (ed.), *Historical Perspectives: Studies in English Thought and Society in Honor of J.H. Plumb* (London, 1974), pp.152–210; Karl von den Steinen, 'The Discovery of Women in Eighteenth-Century English Political Life', in Barbara Kanner (ed.), *The Women of England* (Hamden, Conn., 1979), pp.229–58; Mitzi Myers, 'Reform or Ruin: "A Revolution in Female Manners"',

Linda Colley, for example, has recently argued that the French wars both underlined the perceived functional differences between men and women and yet enlarged the actual boundaries of women's activities. She suggests that the fund-raising, sock-knitting and banner-sewing activities engaged in by British women during the war were not just a socially acceptable extension of the 'traditional female virtues of 'charity, nurture and needlework' into the military sphere, but rather 'the thin end of a far more radical wedge', because they demonstrated that these domestic skills possessed 'a public as well as a private relevance'.[7] This chapter examines women's contributions to the printed debate on the war, rather than their practical contributions to the war effort or their demonstrations in opposition to it. These publications broadly support Colley's conclusions. Women took a serious interest in the issues and ideas raised by the conflict as well as participating in war-time activities; and they ventured to express their opinions in print to a much greater extent than had been the case in previous wars. At the same time, however, anxieties expressed in print by both men and women concerning the proper roles of women seem, if anything, to have been heightened by the experience of the war.

Women were clearly affected by the conflict against revolutionary France both directly and profoundly but, on the whole, they responded practically on the margins of military activity. They were rarely involved in the physical defence of the country, although local women appear to have played a significant part in the defence of Fishguard during the French landing of 1797. A few women did sail with warships during operational voyages, either illegally as passengers or stowaways, or legitimately as nurses. Where they extended the boundaries of their participation in public life, they nevertheless adhered to socially acceptable 'feminine' channels of activity, such as sewing, knitting, making presentations and donations, wearing commemorative jewellery and accessories, and generally supporting male activity.[8] Their engagement in the

---

Studies in Eighteenth-Century Culture, 11 (1982), 199–216; Linda Colley, *Britons. Forging the Nation 1707–1837* (Yale, 1992), pp.237–81; Dror Wahrman, '"Middle-Class" Domesticity Goes Public: Gender, Class, and Politics from Queen Caroline to Queen Victoria', *Journal of British Studies*, xxxii (1993), esp. 408–9; Hannah Barker and Elaine Chalus (eds), *Gender in Eighteenth-Century England: Roles, Representations and Responsibilities* (Harlow, 1997); R.B. Shoemaker, *Gender in English Society 1650–1850* (Harlow, 1998). See also Elizabeth Fox-Genovese, 'Placing Women's History in History', *New Left Review*, 133 (May/June 1982), 5–29; on women in France, see Darline Gay Levy and Harriet B. Applewhite, 'Women of the Popular Classes in Revolutionary Paris, 1789–1795', in Carol R. Berkin and Clara M. Lovett, *Women, War, and Revolution* (New York and London, 1980), pp.9–35.

7 Colley, *Britons*, pp.261–2.

8 On these activities, see Colley, *Britons*, pp.237–8, 277–81; R.W. Chapman (ed.), *Jane Austen's Letters to Her Sister Cassandra and Others*, 2 vol.s (Oxford, 1932), i, 65, Jane Austen to Cassandra Austen, 2 June 1799; Sophia Sarah Banks's collection of broadsides and newspaper cuttings in the British Library, LR.301.h.6, ff.55–70; Valpy, *Sermon Before the Reading and Henley Associations*, pp.33–4; D.G. Vaisey, 'The Pledge of Patriotism: Staffordshire and the Voluntary Contribution, 1798' in M.W. Greenslade (ed.), *Essays in*

pamphlet debate on the war was, however, possibly the most radical wartime activity in which women were involved, no matter how conservative the contents of some of their publications, for not only did they express their views in print to a considerably greater extent than had been the case in any previous war, but this also demonstrated that, contrary to widely expressed opinion, women were able and willing to discuss publicly and intelligently a political phenomenon such as war and its issues. Publications by women such as Hannah More and Mary Wollstonecraft were substantial contributions to the war debate and its propaganda,[9] and other women, such as Fanny Burney, Hester Piozzi, Helen Maria Williams, Anna Laetitia Barbauld, Mary Robinson and Amelia Opie, through novels, poetry and overtly political writings also made serious contributions to the general discussion about the current turbulence of world affairs.

By the late eighteenth century, it was becoming increasingly acceptable, if still far from easy, for women to publish their writings on matters of religion, morality and education, as well as novels and poetry. Mary Poovey suggests three factors which advanced their progress: the demise of literary patronage after 1740, which made anonymous publication possible; the appearance of the 'Bluestockings', who included Hannah More among their number, and who became role models, preserving their reputations untainted while simultaneously publishing for profit; and the trend towards philosophical empiricism and 'sentimentalism', emphasizing individual feelings, imagery and observation, a style of writing to which women were thought to be particularly suited.[10] The involvement of a small but significant number of women in the printed debate on the war in the 1790s should therefore be seen in the context of an increasing body of female writers in Britain; yet the clear political content of this polemic marks out their participation in it as a more radical step. These women believed themselves to be at liberty to comment publicly on the 'masculine' question of war and peace. Their writing was also set in the contexts of increasing political

---

Staffordshire History (Staffordshire Record Society, 1970), esp. pp. 214, 220–2; *Caledonian Mercury*, 16 December 1793, 5 July 1794.

9 Hannah More, *The Cheap Repository Tracts* (London, 1795–98); idem, *Remarks on the Speech of M. Dupont* (London, 1793); Mary Wollstonecraft, *Letter on the Present Character of the French Nation* (London, 1793); idem, *An Historical and Moral View of the Origin and Progress of the French Revolution; and the Effect It Has Produced in Europe* (London, 1794). For recent research on other areas of political activity engaged in by women in the later eighteenth century, see the essays by Elaine Chalus and Amanda Foreman in Barker and Chalus (eds), *Gender in Eighteenth-Century England.*

10 Poovey, *The Proper Lady and the Woman Writer*, pp.35–8. See also Bridget Hill, *The Republican Virago: The Life and Times of Catharine Macaulay, Historian* (Oxford, 1992), pp.130–48. For women writers in the seventeenth and early eighteenth centuries, some of whom managed to support themselves financially by their writing, see Anne Laurence, *Women in England 1500–1760: A Social History* (London, 1994), pp.172–6.

activity among both men and women of the middle classes and of the turbulent climate induced by the war.

II Women, War and Ideas

Unsurprisingly, most women were convinced that war was, in general, an evil which ought to be avoided if at all possible; similarly, however, they were also generally imbued with the same Francophobia as characterized the average British male in this period. Ward Hellstrom and Warren Roberts have detected a markedly Gallophobic bias in Jane Austen's novels, particularly through her characterization of certain individuals (Wickham in *Pride and Prejudice*, the Crawfords in *Mansfield Park* and Frank Churchill in *Emma*, for example) with classic 'French' personality traits, such as frivolity, urbanity, polish, moral carelessness, deviousness and wilfulness, as opposed to the plain 'English' virtues of her heroes and heroines. *The Lady's Magazine* continued to carry reports on the fashions current in Paris whenever it could, despite the war; but women were part of a population which by and large supported its government in the conflict against the French Republic.[11] Mrs Jane Webb of Plymouth, anxious to prove the loyalty of the great majority of the whole British population, female as well as male, wrote:

> all ranks of people, with a spirit becoming Britons, are arming for our internal defence.... may we not say the whole kingdom is the school of Mars; the ladies are zealous, and in many places have presented those new-raised corps with colours.[12]

Hester Piozzi, as so often, colourfully captured the ambivalent attitude of many: 'The Times are sadly out of Joynt indeed, the War ruinous, & Peace a peril that I hope we shall be spared; for as things now stand We have a Right to keep French men from our Island by Alien Bills &c.'[13]

Women writers did, however, distinguish this war from other eighteenth-century wars against the French. Naturally, both supporters and opposers of the conflict were found among them, as they either either opposed or admired the

---

11 Ward Hellstrom, 'Francophobia in *Emma*', *Studies in English Literature*, v (1965), 607–17; Warren Roberts, *Jane Austen and the French Revolution* (London and Basingstoke, 1979), pp.31–42; see also Marilyn Butler, *Jane Austen and the War of Ideas* (Oxford, 1975); *The Lady's Magazine*, May and October 1798 (vol. 29), June, September, November and December 1799 (vol. 30).

12 Mrs. Jane Webb, *A Letter to His Grace the Duke of Portland, on the Late Alarming Parties in the Country, by Mrs. Webb* (Plymouth, 1795), pp.12–13. I am grateful to David Wilkinson for this reference.

13 Katherine C. Balderston (ed.), *Thraliana. The Diary of Mrs. Hester Lynch Thrale (later Mrs. Piozzi) 1776–1809*, 2nd edition, 2 vol.s (Oxford, 1951), ii, 904–5.

French Revolution. Some, such as Hannah More, were quite convinced of the justice of the war. In what war, she asked, 'can the sincere Christian ever have stronger inducements, and more reasonable encouragement to pray for the success of his country, than in this?' It was a war fought not for revenge or conquest, but for the defence of Britain's king, constitution, religion, laws and liberty ('in the sound, sober, and rational sense of that term'). British aims in the hostilities, according to most pro-war literature, were clearly the protection of British blessings; some women followed a more Burkean, crusading line and were, like More, of the opinion that Britain's best, and perhaps only, security lay in the utter destruction of the Revolution and its doctrines and the restoration of the monarchy in France.[14] This might include their own particular security as women. Mrs Richard Wyatt told the Havering Volunteers: 'As fathers, husbands, brothers, relations and friends, our sex and our children have every natural and well-founded reason to hope, for all the protection in your power, under God, that zeal, affection and courage, can yield.'[15]

Other women continued to support the French Revolution and therefore opposed the British war against France. Because of the increasing diffusion of the knowledge and understanding of political principles, Mary Wollstonecraft believed that it was possible to be confident of an approaching era of peace and reason, in which war would be abandoned as irrational and brutish.[16] The arguments used by female anti-war pamphleteers mirrored those of their male counterparts, although they were more likely to condemn *all* war as futile and immoral, as well as the present war as unjust and unnecessary. Wollstonecraft denounced war as an adventure pursued by the idle rich. The Dissenting writer Mrs Barbauld insisted that the language of 'natural enemies' was absurd, 'as if nature, and not our own broad passions, made us enemies ... and yet this language is heard in a Christian country, and these detestable maxims veil themselves under the semblance of virtue and public spirit'. People ought to think less about glorious heroes returning home and more about the maimed, the bereaved, the orphaned, the mental agonies of war and the ravages it inflicted upon countries (of which Britain, geographically isolated from the Continent, was complacently ignorant).[17]

---

14 Hannah More, *Remarks on the Speech of M. Dupont, with a prefatory address in behalf of the French Emigrant Clergy* (1793), in *Works*, 3 vol.s (London, 1847), ii, 407; see also Mrs. Piozzi in Balderston (ed.), *Thraliana*, ii, 932 and Miss Patterson's speech to the Poplar and Blackwell Volunteers as reported by the *Times*, 6 June 1799 (Banks Collection, f.64).

15 Banks Collection, f.57; cf. Colley, *Britons*, pp.254, 256.

16 Wollstonecraft, *An Historical and Moral View*, p.17.

17 Ibid., p.23; [Mrs. Barbauld], *Sins of Government, Sins of the Nation; or, a Discourse for the Fast, Appointed on April 19, 1793. By a Volunteer*, 2nd edition (London, 1793), pp.22–4, 28–30.

Within this framework of political ideas, women on both sides often articulated similar concerns. They tended, for example, to develop moralistic or religious standpoints on the war, so articulating views on a political subject in an acceptably female mode.[18] They frequently rejected as arrogant and unjustified the notion that Britain was a favoured nation. Britain was not so pure, wrote Mrs Barbauld austerely, that it could afford to see itself as an instrument of divine justice. Its trade in African slaves and its conquests in India were crimes at least as heinous as any France had committed, and it had wilfully encouraged the aggression of the European states towards one another. Fanny Burney agreed. 'We are too apt to consider ourselves rather as a distinct race of beings', she told readers of her *Brief Reflections*, recognizing that English chauvinism was a major obstacle to helping the *émigrés*.[19] Miss Berry disliked her enforced wartime restriction to Britain and the insularity of her countrymen: 'All the other cities, and courts, and great men of the world *may* be very good sort of places and of people, for aught we know or care; except they are coming to invade us, we think no more of them than of the inhabitants of another planet.'[20]

Hannah More's pamphlet, *Remarks on the Speech of M. Dupont* (1793), made the connection between atheism and radical politics: 'it is much to be suspected, that certain opinions in politics have a tendency to lead to certain opinions in religion'. Mrs Piozzi also saw the war in a fundamentally religious light, but hers was a much more apocalyptic vision. Distinguishing first from second causes, she perceived the first, cosmic cause of the French Revolution to have been the turbulence which is the preparation for Antichrist. In May 1795, she noted in her journal:

> a complete Famine, and three raging Factions are now devouring Paris, Poland is become a mere Desart deluged with blood, Insurrections in Rome and Naples threat those unhappy States with calling in the French directly, whilst Russia & the Porte prepare for instant war.—And is not the End of all to be expected? What other Signs would this adulterous Generation have?[21]

---

18 Cf. Colley, *Britons*, pp.277, 280.

19 [Mrs. Barbauld], *Reasons for National Penitence, recommended for the Fast, appointed February XXVIII, 1794* (London, 1794), pp.4, 16; [idem], *Sins of Government*, p.25; Fanny Burney (D'Arblay), *Brief Reflections Relative to the Emigrant French Clergy: Earnestly Submitted to the Humane Consideration of the Ladies of Great Britain* (London, 1793), p.12.

20 Lady Theresa Lewis (ed.), *Extracts of the Journals and Correspondence of Miss Berry from the year 1783 to 1852*, 3 vol.s (London, 1865), ii, 70, Miss Berry to Mr. Greathead, 2 August 1798.

21 More, *Remarks on the Speech of M. Dupont*, pp.402, 405–6; Balderston (ed.), *Thraliana*, ii, 929.

Female writers, whether conservative or radical, Anglican or Dissenting, agreed in urging moral vigilance on the nation, since they believed that the war ought to be viewed in a religious light; that Britain had no great cause for complacency concerning its own standing with heaven; and, above all, that it was highly desirable from the point of view of domestic social order. 'John Bull is a fine Fellow,' claimed Mrs Piozzi, 'but if not well *fed* he will *roar*.' She disapproved both of measures taken by the rich that were guaranteed to irritate the poor (such as the closure of the London brewhouses in 1795) and measures taken by the poor to redress their grievances against the rich (such as the handbill posted on church doors in Streatham '*demanding*, not *requesting* Relief for the lower Orders').[22] The reform of political grievances, Hannah More insisted, would be insufficient to render the British 'a happy people'; for that, a reformation of manners would be necessary. Mrs Jane West, in her *Tale of the Times* (1799), wrote approvingly of contemporary moral instructors who 'would not ascribe the annihilation of thrones and altars to the arms of France, but to those principles [such as the French sanctioning of divorce] which, by dissolving domestic confidence, and undermining private worth, paved the way for universal confusion'.[23] Helen Maria Williams, like Mary Wollstonecraft an admirer of the French Revolution, was horrified by tales of atrocities perpetrated by British officers upon Italian patriot prisoners of war, which she felt to be a great stain on British honour.[24] So depressed was Mrs Piozzi about the moral state of the nation that, in 1800, she told her friend Mrs Pennington that the government 'must leave off appointing such solemnities' as national fasts, since 'the time is over when they did any good'. Mrs Barbauld, whose pamphlets of 1793 and 1794 were written especially for national Fast Days, was also caustic in her denunciation of their use. 'We cannot subsidize the Deity, as we have subsidized his majesty of Sardinia', she warned.[25]

Women writers did not often comment on the actual conduct of the war. Mrs Piozzi, Miss Berry and Helen Maria Williams were the most interested in its events and in the conduct of British strategy, but they did not often offer sustained examination of these aspects of the conflict. Miss Berry, who was as well informed, however, as any private individual, male or female, was frequently scathing of the government's strategy in the United Provinces. 'How

---

22 Balderston (ed.), *Thraliana*, ii, 842; ibid., ii, 920, 909; Oswald G. Knapp (ed.), *The Intimate Letters of Hester Piozzi and Penelope Pennington 1788–1821* (London, 1914), p.180, Mrs. Piozzi to Mrs. Pennington, 21 August 1799.

23 More, *Remarks on the Speech of M. Dupont*, p.391; West, quoted in Butler, *Jane Austen and the War of Ideas*, p.105.

24 Helen Maria Williams, *Sketches of the State of Manners and Opinions in the French Republic, towards the close of the eighteenth century. In a Series of Letters*, 2 vol.s (London, 1801), i, 198.

25 Knapp (ed.), *Letters to Mrs. Pennington*, p.188, Mrs. Piozzi to Mrs. Pennington, [April 1800]; [Barbauld], *Sins of Government*, pp.7–9, 30–3.

Holland is now to be saved I do not see,' she wrote to Horace Walpole on 28 September 1794; 'and how we are to be safe when it is gone, I as little see; and how and why the D. of York stays to have half his army destroyed, and the other half driven home, I still less see.' 'I have long been perfectly convinced', she later wrote, 'by several circumstances that have come to my knowledge, of the entire and disgraceful ignorance of our Ministers as to foreign politics.'[26]

Fears of invasion, however, were often expressed. Mrs Piozzi wrote a short *Address to the Females of Great Britain* and translated General Dumouriez's pamphlet, *Tableau Spéculatif de l'Europe* (1798), to raise the invasion alarm among the apparently complacent upper ranks of British society: by then, she thought that 'Invasion was a fear no longer fashionable', and when the Irish rebellion erupted later that year, she saw it as a severe mortification of British vanity.[27] Fanny Burney was not one of those who were sanguine about the prospect of an invasion. Her beloved sister, Susannah, had moved to Ireland with her husband in 1796, and since the threat to Ireland was always greater in the 1790s than that to England, Burney was continually anxious for her sister's safety.[28]

Colley has suggested that 'in the wars against Revolutionary and Napoleonic France, as in so many later conflicts, British women seem ... to have been no more markedly pacifist than men', despite the assumptions of history.[29] This may have been true in terms of their practical support for the war, but the expression of a desire for peace was a characteristically female emphasis. Men might stand to gain from war, as professional soldiers and sailors, armaments manufacturers, cloth and leather manufacturers, shipbuilders and contractors. These interests might benefit women indirectly, too, but women seem to have been more influenced by thoughts of the darker side of war and its adverse consequences for individuals and families, or at least to have felt more able than men to admit to such influences. Mrs Piozzi endorsed this view. 'Female politicians', she wrote, 'confide in negotiation. Elizabeth of England, Isabella of Spain, hated war, and took every possible method to avoid it; while Queen Anne's natural ardour to conclude the peace of Utrecht cost her almost her life.' Hannah More, for all her conviction of the justice of the conflict on Britain's part and sympathy for crusading opinions, was fatigued by 1797: 'I say nothing of war, because I am weary of the word, nor of peace, because I

---

26 Lewis (ed.), *Berry Correspondence*, i, 441, Miss Berry to the Earl of Orford, 28 September, 1794; ibid., ii, 102, Miss Berry to Mrs. Cholmeley, 28 October 1799.

27 Piozzi, *Retrospection*, ii, 527.

28 Hemlow (ed.), *Burney Journals and Letters*, iii, 273, Fanny Burney to Mrs. Phillips, 10 February [1797].

29 Colley, *Britons*, p.262.

lose all hope of it.'[30] Songs and poems lamenting the miseries of war and sighing for peace were common, such as the sonnets to peace and war published in *The Lady's Magazine* of 1799. These were not always simple diatribes against the horrors of conflict. Amelia Alderson's *Ode, Written on the Opening of the Last Campaign* (1795), might be described as a pragmatic cry for peace. Preferring an immediate cessation of hostilities, but recognizing that this call was unlikely to be heard on its own merits, the poem prays not only for immediate peace but also for victory against France in the coming campaign, in the hope that this may hasten peace.[31]

Mrs Piozzi did have doubts about the eventual peace settlement at Amiens. Admitting that, like everyone else in Britain, she was glad of the peace for material reasons, she nevertheless deplored what to her was a peace bought for the indulgence of British avarice and which allowed the French to reorganize the map of Europe and persuaded Britain to abandon its allies to their fates. Georgiana, Duchess of Devonshire, was much more sanguine and perhaps more typical: 'Peace! Peace! Peace! ... I must rejoice in spite of all the alarmist long faces.'[32]

Female writers of all viewpoints, therefore, stressed the moral and religious aspects of the conflict, emphases consistent with the accepted private or 'female' sphere of writing. In discussing the nature of the war, women writers were also often accused of 'emotionalism' in their writing. It is true that they often vented their personal emotional responses to the Revolution itself. They were particularly fixated by French atrocities and the sufferings of individuals; whereas male writers, by and large, wrote about these only for a purpose, chiefly that of inspiring loyalty to the British government through fear, female writers and readers seemed to be genuinely transfixed by them. Many women were deeply affected by the trial and execution of Louis XVI,[33] but it was not only the sufferings of royalty which fascinated women, or were thought to fascinate them. *The Lady's Magazine* carried such items as 'The Dying Soldier;

---

30 Piozzi quoted in McCarthy, *Hester Thrale Piozzi*, p.221; R. Brimley Johnson (ed.), *The Letters of Hannah More* (London, 1925), p.132, Hannah More to Mrs. Boscawen, 1797.

31 See Bennett (ed.), *British War Poetry*, pp.137–8.

32 Balderston (ed.), *Thraliana*, ii, 1030–1; Bessborough (ed.), *Georgiana Corr.*, p.248, the Duchess of Devonshire to her mother, [31 March 1802].

33 See, for example, Ralph M. Wardle (ed.), *The Collected Letters of Mary Wollstonecraft* (New York and London, 1979), p.227, Wollstonecraft to Joseph Johnson, 26 December 1792; also poems written by Mary Robinson, Charlotte Smith and Eliza Daye for *The European Magazine*, *The Scots Magazine*, *The Universal Magazine*, and *The Gentleman's Magazine*, printed in Betty T. Bennett (ed.), *British War Poetry in the Age of Romanticism: 1793–1815* (New York and London, 1976), pp.74–6, 81–2, 91–4. Also Bindman et al., *The Shadow of the Guillotine*, pp.22–4, 47–53, 134–43.

a Fragment' and 'Verses from the French; written by a French Prisoner, as he was Preparing to go to the Guillotine'.[34]

It is not necessary, however, to see all subjective female writing about the Revolution as warm-hearted romanticism. Virginia Sapiro argues that Wollstonecraft's heated style in her *Vindication of the Rights of Men* (1791) was all part of her response to Edmund Burke, who had himself written in a subjective and often violently colourful style. Wollstonecraft was simply replying in kind or, perhaps, even criticizing his method by parody rather than responding to the substance of his argument alone.[35] Furthermore, when women wrote 'sentimentally' about the Revolution or the war, it was often because, for various reasons, they elevated the private aspects of events over the public. Wollstonecraft's *Vindication of the Rights of Woman* was, on one level, a call for radical political thought to be extended beyond the public politics of government institutions into the private politics of the home. Women writers acknowledged this female prioritization of the private: the heroine of Helen Maria Williams' little tale, *Madeleine and Auguste* (1792), perceived the chief implication of the Revolution's liberation of all Frenchmen to be that every Frenchman must surely be free to marry the woman he loved. The lady of the house in Charlotte Smith's novel, *The Banished Man* (1794), was able to talk of politics, but she chose not to be interested in them except insofar as they could advance her own family members.[36]

A preoccupation with individual public figures was a natural by-product of this concern for the personal in female writing and opinions. Lady Wallace was clearly fascinated by General Dumouriez—'this wonderful little hero'—while Helen Maria Williams was infatuated with Napoleon, 'the benefactor of his race'.[37] Other women were more fascinated by what they believed to be the Corsican general's ferocity and brutality, and with what particulars of his early history and present lifestyle they could glean from the press. Mrs Piozzi was vehement, viewing the name 'Napoleon' as a corrupted form of the word 'Apollyon', which means 'Destroyer': the apocalyptic name for the devil.[38] The

---

34 *The Lady's Magazine*, 29 (July 1798), 325, 328. See also Pendleton, 'English Conservative Propaganda', p.216.

35 Sapiro, *A Vindication of Political Virtue*, pp.191–202.

36 Helen Maria Williams, *Letters from France: Containing Many New Anecdotes Relative to the French Revolution, and the Present State of French Manners*, 2nd edition (London, 1792), pp.174–5; Charlotte Smith, *The Banished Man*, 4 vol.s (London, 1794), ii, 110–11.

37 Lady Eglantine Wallace, *The Conduct of the King of Prussia and General Dumourier Investigated by Lady Wallace* (London, 1793), p.125; Helen Maria Williams, *A Tour in Switzerland, or a View of the Present State of the Governments and Manners of those Cantons, with comparative sketches of the present state of Paris*, 2 vol.s (London, 1798), ii, 56–7.

38 Hester Lynch Piozzi, *Retrospection: or a view of the most striking and important events, characters, situations, and their consequences, which the last eighteen hundred years*

superhero for pro-war writers was Horatio Nelson, particularly after his victory over the French fleet at the Nile in 1798. *The Lady's Magazine* published a biographical sketch of the admiral, together with 'an elegant Engraving' of his ship engaging two larger Spanish ships off Cape St Vincent in 1797.[39] He became a focus for the cult of heroism which had grown among women in particular in Britain over the preceding five years, though this was adulation at a distance. Nearer at hand, as Jane Austen noticed, in *Pride and Prejudice*, were those soldiers barracked around the country, parading in their fine uniforms and attracting much female attention—another way, personal and small-scale, in which women could involve themselves in a society at war. Austen did not describe this situation with approval, however—rather, in Lydia Bennet's downfall, she showed what could happen as a result of billeting soldiers among the civilian population.

Aside from the personal inclination of some women writers to focus on the private and particular at the expense of the public and the general, this tendency was entirely in keeping with the views of late eighteenth-century society on what women ought to be interested in. It was deliberately encouraged, as Mary Poovey points out, by the male editors and journalists of women's literature. Literature addressed to women laid much less emphasis on reporting facts than that directed to men and was of a much more emotional or moralizing strain. 'The implicit assumption', as Poovey notes, 'is that women's quick passions will be more effectively engaged by such formulations'; they were expected to be more emotionally than intellectually responsive.[40] Women were not supposed to be concerned with public affairs, and their emphasis on the personal, private side of public events may well have been the valve they used in order to be able to comment on the war at all. Some clearly felt this constraint more than others—radicals such as Wollstonecraft and Williams felt no shame in commenting freely on the war; the conservative Austen and Burney were much more restrained, but this does not mean that they were unaware of the public arena of political events or unable to express opinions about it, as Austen showed in her subtle comment on the government policy of creating military barracks.

Female writers suggested other ways in which British women could contribute to the war effort. They especially instructed each other to contribute good domestic management and, thus, money to the British war effort. Hannah More's *Remarks on the Speech of M. Dupont* was prefaced by an 'Address in Behalf of the French Emigrant Clergy' which was particularly directed at a female audience, urging them to make small retrenchments in their domestic

---

have presented to the view of mankind, 2 vol.s (London, 1801), ii, 523–4. See Revelation 9:11.

39 *The Lady's Magazine*, 29 (November 1798), 483–5.

40 Poovey, *The Proper Lady and the Woman Writer*, pp.16–19.

economy and especially in their own fashion expenses in order to be able to give more to this cause. Fanny Burney admitted that charitable giving was not an exclusively female virtue, but she argued that women's demands on their own money were less serious and pressing than those of men, and that their response to her appeal might therefore be swifter and more general.[41] Neither conservative nor radical female writers, however, advocated the idea of female soldiers. Dumbarton working women declared that

> it is not in their province to defend their country by arms, but they will give their money in so good a cause; and if their husbands, brothers, or fathers, are called to meet the enemy, they will do every thing in their power to make them fight with zeal in the cause of their country, of religion, and virtue.[42]

While Hannah More wanted to 'prevail on beauty, and rank, and talents, and virtue, confederating their several powers, to exert themselves with a patriotism at once firm and feminine, for the general good', this was intended only in the sense of moral influence, for she immediately went on to insist that she was not 'sounding an alarm for female warriors, or exciting female politicians', for she hardly knew which of the two was 'the most disgusting and unnatural character'. Wollstonecraft might well have wanted to see female politicians—she certainly wanted women to study politics and to have a greater involvement in it—but she insisted that while she wished to see 'the bayonet converted into a pruning-hook', she would not advise women to 'turn their distaff into a musket'.[43]

But the fact that they themselves were discussing the public, political issue of war, however conformably to the female sphere, was new and it provoked disapproval from male readers and discomfort among the female writers themselves. In discussing women's role during the conflict, women writers often acquiesced in the notion of separate spheres for men and women, particularly since warfare was such an overwhelmingly male-dominated activity. In this arena above all, a woman's sphere was almost wholly confined to the private, the domestic and the small-scale—the public arena, the acknowledged sphere of the significant and the substantial, was for men. 'Till Amazonian virtue is again the fashion, we shew better in peace than in war, at home, in our

---

41 More, *Remarks on the Speech of M. Dupont*, pp.377–80; Burney, *Brief Reflections*, p.7.

42 *Caledonian Mercury*, 10 March 1798.

43 More, *Strictures on the Modern System of Female Education* (London, 1799), in *Works*, iii, 14; Wollstonecraft, *A Vindication of the Rights of Woman* (1792; London, Everyman, 1985), pp.160, 162.

closet or our nursery, than in the field of battle', admonished Laetitia Hawkins.[44]

Other female writers struggled more than Hawkins appeared to with the question of their commenting on the war. In the heat of the invasion crisis of 1798, Hester Piozzi's *Address to the Females of Great Britain* appealed to women to cease behaving like children and statuettes in such a crisis as the present struggle against France:

> Nobody hinders [women] from being wise or strong, Learned or brave; nor does any one ... pretend to like them better for being weak, ignorant or pusillanimous. You are therefore ... called upon, to act rationally, & steadily: & to maintain that Place among reasonable Beings we have so often heard you urge a Claim to.

Yet she elsewhere claimed that she was 'no Politician ... nor either think much or care about publick Concerns'. She had learned, as William McCarthy comments, to dissemble her 'unfeminine' interest in politics.[45] In fact, she worried that she had learned to camouflage it too well: of her *British Synonymy* (1794), which used political affairs to illustrate many of its definitions, she wrote, 'I am only afraid the title may prove a millstone round its neck: no one will think of looking for Politics in a volume entitled *British Synonymy*.'[46]

Fanny Burney protested against a female involvement in public political debate. She told Princess Mary that she had deliberately left political ideas out of her novel, *Camilla* (1796), because 'they were not a *feminine* subject for discussion' as well as because she believed that steering her readers clear of politics altogether was doing them a better service even than inculcating them with her own conservative ideas on the subject. She also thought it necessary to preface her *Reflections on the Emigrant French Clergy* (1793) with an 'Apology' to justify the entry of a woman into public affairs on the grounds of 'tenderness and humanity'. Yet enter that arena she did: her preface went on to argue that while it was generally right for women to remain in the background, on this occasion it was more proper for them to come forward to offer their help to the *émigrés*.[47] Likewise, Hannah More felt compelled to defend her entry into political polemics: at the beginning of her preface to her *Remarks on M. Dupont's Speech*, she too justified her boldness by the emergency facing the country. Throughout the pamphlet, she claimed not to be 'entering far into any

---

44 Hawkins, *Letters on the Female Mind*, i, 118.

45 Quoted in McCarthy, *Hester Thrale Piozzi*, pp.210, 234.

46 Knapp (ed.), *Letters to Mrs. Pennington*, p.101, Mrs. Piozzi to Mrs. Pennington, 2 December 1793.

47 Burney, *Brief Reflections*, pp.iv–v; Katharine M. Rogers, *Frances Burney. The World of Female Difficulties* (New York and London, 1990), p.4.

political principles'.[48] It is true that her conservative case was specifically based on religious principles, but this was typical of much conservative literature on the war, and More's argument was clearly extended to be applied to political submission and loyalty. She also actively encouraged the distribution of conservative propaganda, and she wrote a great many of the famous *Cheap Repository Tracts* herself. Helen Maria Williams wrote self-deprecatingly of her former ignorance of and lack of interest in public affairs, but explained that she had been stimulated to write by her 'love of the French revolution'.[49]

All these women were in some way claiming that the extraordinary nature of the present times justified their self-directed extension of the female sphere of influence from the private and the domestic into the public and the political. It was true that it was professedly the extremity of threatened revolution in Britain and actual warfare with France which drew them into public activity and permitted their acceptance in this role by society, and that the implication (doubtless often sincerely meant) was that after the return of peace and domestic order, they would shrink back out of the realm of public political comment. Yet even though they had dressed their political views in 'feminine' and often apologetic moral and religious clothing, a precedent had been created. In the nineteenth century women continued to debate and campaign on social and political issues, such as the movements for the reformation of manners and the Chartists' aims, and against slavery, Catholic emancipation and the Corn Laws.

III Male writers, women and war

What did British male writers think about women's involvement in the wars against revolutionary France? Of those who expressed any opinion at all, some simply used gender to characterize men's attitudes to the war and to incite them to particular responses; some saw a passive role for women in the war effort; others were willing to allow them, or even demand from them, a more active participation; and various tactics were employed to steer women towards perceiving their war role in particular ways. To some extent, since war had always been a male-dominated phenomenon, the use of gender identities in war-rhetoric was not new; but because women were participating in and against the war effort and in the war debate to a greater extent than in previous conflicts, gender was used more frequently in public rhetoric on engagement in the war and also discussed frequently as a current issue.

---

48 More, 'Remarks on the Speech of M. Dupont', p.407.

49 Helen Maria Williams, *Letters written in France, in the Summer of 1790, to a Friend in England: Containing Various Anecdotes Relative to the French Revolution; and Memoirs of Mons. and Madame du F_*, 3rd edition (London, 1792), p.108.

The concept of woman as weak and helpless, physically, mentally and emotionally, was used to denigrate different responses to the war. Both pro-war and anti-war writers dubbed their opponents' position as effeminate and, by implication, unworthy. Dennis O'Bryen charged the government with a 'feminine' cowardice, in resorting to slander against France rather than relying in a 'manly' way solely on the military force of the nation, pitted against that of France. It boded ill, he pointed out, for the success of peace negotiations that the British government and its hirelings should continue to insult and vilify the power it could not conquer.[50] It was more usual, however, for war to be represented as virile and peace as effeminate. One author scornfully dismissed peace-campaigning as an 'effeminate and womanish longing'.[51] Recruitment literature appealed to masculinity, offering ways in which to assert it, such as the physical training and discipline necessary for the work of a soldier or sailor, and providing a reason to undertake the dangers and hardships of battle—the protection of women and children, man's natural role. By implication, not to serve one's country in this way was to leave one's masculinity open to doubt. 'Who can call himself a *Man*,' asked 'Job Nott' rhetorically, 'who can pretend love for women, who will not prepare or assist in some way to thrust such villains from his Country's shores.'[52] This taunt was reinforced by unfavourable comparisons of British men both with supposedly effeminate Frenchmen and with British women.[53]

Almost all writing by men that considered the position of women in wartime assumed and reinforced an environment of separate spheres for men and women, but often these were spheres in which there was a contribution of some sort which women could make towards the successful outcome of the conflict. Some writers viewed this contribution as fundamentally passive. As well as providing a reason for men to fight for their country, women could be seen as a reward for men who had fought valiantly. Their approval and their safeguarded and faithful chastity were held up as prizes for military courage and service. In a more abstract sense, they were sometimes seen as goddesses or

---

50 Dennis O'Bryen, *Utrum Horum? The Government; or, the Country?* 5th edition (London, 1796), pp.29–31.

51 *Reasons against National Despondency; in refutation of Mr. Erskine's View of the Causes and Consequences of the Present War. With some remarks upon the supposed scarcity of specie* (London, 1797), pp.104, 167.

52 [Theodore Price], *A Continuation of My Last Book, or a Back Front View of the Five Headed Monster. By Job Nott, Buckle-Maker* (Birmingham, 1798), p.6; see also Arthur Young, *The Example of France, a Warning to Britain*, 4th edition (London, 1794; first published 1793), p.144.

53 E.g., BMC 8435 and 8436, Gillray, 'A Republican Beau' and 'A Republican Belle' (10 March 1794); the *Sun*, 24 September 1793; BMC 9314, [Woodward] and Isaac Cruikshanks, ['Female Opinions on Military Tactics'], ([1798/9]); *The Times*, 1 February 1793 and the *Sun*, 11 February 1794, both reporting births to French soldiers.

figureheads, either for the nation, or for particular groups of soldiers, sailors, or Volunteers. This perhaps made it peculiarly appropriate that they produced and presented the banners and flags which were to be carried at the head of regiments and corps of soldiers, which could come to symbolize their benefactors, rather in the manner that ladies' tokens had been worn centuries previously at jousts.[54] Female figureheads could be either homely or exalted: 'Mrs Bull' (an innovation of the American revolutionary era), or 'Liberty' or 'Britannia'. 'Britannia' symbolized both the country and womanhood, both in need of defence. By never taking part in battle, even in defence, she encapsulated the position of women within the war propaganda. She watched the conflict from the safety of her island or from the heavens, and her weapons appear to be decorative and symbolic rather than for practical use.[55]

Other war commentators were prepared to permit women a more active role in the British war effort. One of the most frequently expounded contributions of this sort was the moral significance of women. In part, this was to be seen as a contribution to military morale, in women's faithfulness to their absent husbands. It was also claimed to be a much more fundamental force in society. For John Bowles, the government war propagandist, as for many others, the most important attribute of a woman was her chastity, and not only that, but its very appearance also, must be jealously guarded. Thus it was that he saw in the current fashion for women to wear lower necklines than he thought modest, 'a much more formidable enemy than Buonaparte himself, with all his power, perfidy, and malice', for female modesty was 'the last barrier of civilized society'.[56]

Colley notes that the chastity of women was taken particularly seriously by propagandists in this war against revolutionary France because it was a way of scoring points against the enemy, whose women, it was suggested, were somewhat less than chaste.[57] The role of women as childbearers was naturally exalted in time of war, when the size and health of the population was a particularly significant issue. For centuries, however, anxieties had been voiced

---

54 See, for example, Col. Parker of Maidstone, as reported in the *Sporting Magazine*, 73 (October 1798), 33–4 (Banks Collection, f.57).

55 Stella M. Ni Ghallchóir Cottrell, 'English Views of France and the French, 1789–1815', unpublished D.Phil. thesis (Oxford, 1991), pp.113–16; Marina Warner, *Monuments and Maidens: The Allegory of the Female Form* (London, 1985), pp.xix–xx.

56 John Bowles, *Remarks on Modern Female Manners, as Distinguished by Indifference to Character, and Indecency of Dress; extracted from 'Reflections Political and Moral at the Conclusion of the War'* (London, 1802), pp.5, 12.

57 Colley, *Britons*, pp.250–3. See, for instance, *Desultory Thoughts on the Atrocious Cruelties of the French Nation: with Observations on the Necessity of the War, and a Calm Admonitory Address to all English Jacobins. By a loyal subject to the King and Constitution of Great Britain* (Bath, 1794), pp.64–6; 'A Word to the Wise', *The Anti-Gallican Songster*, i (London, 1793), p.6.

concerning the possibility of wives tainting their husbands' lines of inheritance by marital infidelity.[58] This explains why, in the war-time prints and literature which depicted women as potential victims of Frenchmen, their treatment was highly ambivalent. Some propaganda showed them simply as objects of purity and beauty to be protected and sheltered from the contamination and plundering of the French. Some, however, showed them as unreliable and unscrupulous, revoltingly eager for the attentions of Frenchmen and greedy for the potential material gain involved in these transactions.[59] In the second case, the fear was not so much for the violation of the women as for the contamination of the British line, and therefore British property and liberty, by a French attack.

Suitably feminine contributions were good domestic management, the donation of money and tending the sick and wounded.[60] Another role admitted to women by even the sternest conservatives was that of encouraging their men to fight for their country. 'Job Nott' suggested that women could be 'stirring up young men to be public spirited protectors of their fair country-women', and, he added, 'you can laugh at those who hang back.' Arthur Young argued that if the influence of British women were thus extended, he was sure that it would send 'thousands with ardour to the standard'.[61] Men refused, however, to entertain the idea of yielding their traditional prerogative in the defence of the country to women. 'Chamberpot defence' was the most that was generally allowed to women by the graphic satirists—beyond that, it was men's work.[62] 'A hen is a repectable animal when she is feeding or brooding her chickens,' 'Thomas Bull' told his cousin 'John', 'but in a cockpit she is ridiculous.'[63] In 1803 'The Projector' wrote in *The Gentleman's Magazine* of his genuine concern that women were being wasted as a potential military resource and that, were they

---

58 Poovey, *The Proper Lady and the Woman Writer*, pp.5–6; Cottrell, 'English Views', p.138. See also Fletcher, *Gender, Sex and Subordination*, *passim*.

59 See, for example, BMC 9725, Cruikshank, 'Thoughts on the Invasion!' (27 August 1801).

60 The *Sun*, 27 November 1799; *Caledonian Mercury*, 26 February 1798; *The Times*, 11 March 1795, quoted in Clive Emsley, *British Society and the French Wars 1793–1815* (London, 1979), pp.51–2; [Theodore Price], *Further Humble Advice from Job Nott* (Birmingham, 1800), pp.5–6; William Cobbett (ed.), *The Parliamentary History of England, from the Earliest Period to the Year 1803* (London, 1806–1820), xxxiii, William Windham, 24 April 1798.

61 [Price], *A Back Front View*, p.6; Arthur Young, *National Danger and the Means of Safety* (London, 1797), p.30.

62 An exception was BMC 8432, [Nixon], 'French Invasion or Brighton in a Bustle' (1 March 1794), which showed old women among others helping to repel the French; but this was a mocking comment on the quality of national defence, rather than an encouragement to female involvement in it.

63 *A Letter to John Bull, Esq. From His Second Cousin Thomas Bull, Author of the First and Second Letters to his Brother John* (London, 1793), p.35.

suitably trained and educated for the task, women might be equal if not superior to men as soldiers; but this, of course, remained a highly controversial claim.[64]

Finally, and particularly so in view of all these concerns, female pamphleteering on the issue of the war was also a questionable activity. Some male writers approved heartily of well-known conservative female writers such as Hannah More: 'MISS HANNAH MORE APPEARS to be another Instrument in the hand of Providence to benefit Mankind, and I hope she will go on in her labour for the public good, and not be diverted from her object by the sneers', wrote 'Job Nott'. Fanny Burney's *Brief Reflections Relative to the Emigrant French* was favourably reviewed in the *British Critic*, the *Monthly Review*, the *Critical Review* and the *European Magazine*.[65] Men were often doubtful of the value or propriety of women publicly airing their views on political subjects, however. Richard Polwhele thought that it had been just tolerable in the past, when they had been few and far between—then, a female writer had been 'esteemed a Phenomenon in Literature' and sure of a favourable reception among the critics simply because she was a woman. Now there were so many of them that they had grown complacent and bold, and no longer could they charm critics by self-deprecating acknowledgements of their own 'comparative imbecility'.[66] The *Sun* noted on 24 September 1795: 'The Comedy which Mrs Inchbald has ready, we hope to find devoid of all political allusions; and if so, her Muse, we doubt not, will receive and deserve a liberal patronage.' Readers of *The Lady's Magazine* in October 1799 were left in no doubt as to the impropriety of women either participating in the war or commenting publicly on it:

> Women were created to be the companions of man, to please him, to solace him in his miseries, to console him in his sorrows, and not to partake with him the fatigues of war, of the sciences, and of government. Warlike women, learned women, and women who are politicians, equally abandon the circle which nature and institutions have traced round their sex; they convert themselves into men.[67]

---

64 'The Projector, XXI', in *The Gentleman's Magazine*, ii (1803), 715, quoted in Cottrell, 'English Views', pp.109–11.

65 [Price], *Further Humble Advice from Job Nott*, p.7; Hemlow (ed.), *Burney Journals and Letters*, iii, 40 n.2.

66 Richard Polwhele, *The Unsex'd Females; A Poem, Addressed to the Author of the Pursuits of Literature* (New York, 1800; first published 1798), p.19n.

67 *The Lady's Magazine*, 30 (October 1799), 450–1.

IV Conclusion

Only a minority of women engaged heavily in patriotic activism, and an even smaller proportion published their views on the war. These naturally reflected their social class and their era in the attitudes they revealed, and they clearly identified with the notion that this was, at least in part, a war of ideas. Yet it is clear that women's writings also had identifiably characteristic concerns and emphases in the issues they discussed. Female writers were universally horrified by the violence and cruelties of warfare and, while they could be as chauvinistically British as male writers, they also noticed and rebuked this attitude more often than men did. They were generally more concerned with the personal and the private than with the massed and the public. Most did not comment much on the British government's conduct of the war, but some of those who did showed themselves to be as well-informed as most male observers. Peace was, if anything, an event still more desired by women than by men, whatever their political stance. While some women clearly sympathized with their stance, none seemed to be war crusaders of quite the intensity of a Burke or a Windham, ready to sacrifice all possibility of peace until monarchical government was restored in France, however much they might wish for such an outcome.

It is also true to say that it was a war which offered women a substantially greater opportunity to become involved in its issues and activities than any previous conflict had done. This was partly because it was such a long war and involved such a great proportion of the British population. It had a direct impact on ordinary women as well as on professional male soldiers and sailors. This was also a war in which more emphasis was consciously placed on ideological issues than any since the wars of religion and, since the intervening period had seen an escalation both of the press and of literacy and more recently of professional women writers, there was more place for women to become actively involved. Yet the British debate over the conflict also reinforced the rhetoric of separateagenda for men and women, since those women who ventured to express their opinions publicly, whether in print or otherwise, tended to articulate their views through developing notions of separate spheres and acknowledged their validity.

Chapter 8

The Voice of the People? Public Opinion and the Wars Against Revolutionary France

The growth of popular interest in domestic politics, and the need for popular cooperation with the government's measures if Britain were to wage a successful war against revolutionary France, meant that the 1790s saw both loyalists and opposition politicians concerned to measure and to manipulate or control public opinion. The question immediately raised is, of what did public opinion consist? Who were 'the public' and what were their opinions? Were they Burke's 'people', a political elite of around 400,000, or could they be said to include the population of Britain? Late eighteenth-century public opinion has been variously defined as consisting of the electorate (as the section of the nation with whose opinions politicians were most concerned); all those who read newspapers and whose views were thereby shaped and reflected in newspaper columns; and all the extra-parliamentary classes of society. Since the war against revolutionary France was not an abstract political question affecting only the traditionally politically literate classes, this chapter concerns itself with the broad mass of the middling and lower ranks of society.[1]

Most people were probably only aware of and concerned with the conflict in so far as it affected their own lives; but many more were thus affected, either directly or vicariously, than had been the case even in the American war little more than a decade previously. There were troops stationed around Britain in substantial numbers; militia ballots required lists of all men within a certain age-range; and the Volunteers created further military visibility and experience. Sea-ports were constantly busy, and those who lived near the coast must have been aware of the threat of a French invasion. 'A great meeting at Reepham today', reported Parson Woodforde of Norfolk on 23 April 1798, 'respecting all People

1 J.A.W. Gunn, *Beyond Liberty and Property. The Process of Self-Recognition in Eighteenth-Century Political Thought* (Kingston and Montreal, 1983); Hannah Jane Barker, 'Press, Politics and Reform: 1779–1785', unpublished D.Phil. thesis (University of Oxford, 1994), pp.267–8, 273; H.T. Dickinson, *The Politics of the People in Eighteenth-Century Britain* (London, 1995); Mark Philp, 'Thompson, Godwin and the French Revolution', *History Workshop Journal*, 39 (1995), 97; David Eastwood, 'E.P. Thompson, Britain and the French Revolution', ibid., 83.

arming themselves &c. against an Invasion of this Country from the French &c. which is much talked of at present by all kinds of People especially the poor.'[2] War taxes affected everyone; and bonfires and illuminations to celebrate victories were held all over the country. The information and views of much of the population were probably very crude, but no less valid for that.

How is it possible to know the views of ordinary people two hundred years ago? Some left behind diaries, letters and memoirs; another measure of educated opinion is the vast array of caricatures and other graphic prints published on the war (including maps printed in newspapers)—evidence of an intense public interest. Barker suggests that the opinions expressed in late eighteenth-century newspapers, especially the London press, reflected the attitudes of their readership to a significantly greater extent than is usually allowed, largely due to market economics. Caricaturists and graphic satirists set out more self-consciously to reflect as well as to shape public reactions to the events and implications of the war.[3] Indeed, the character of John Bull was appropriated and further developed by them in this decade as a representative observer of home and foreign affairs: a common Englishman outside the governing classes, typically urban or rural middle-class, but sometimes artisan, and, importantly, neither loyalist nor reformer, but equally critical of both the government and the Foxite Whigs. He represented the patriotism of common sense rather than either unthinking submission or factious opposition, and he was a figure abused by both government and Opposition.[4] Clearly, it is far easier to discover the views of the literate classes than those of people who could not leave a written record of their opinions, but some impression may also be gained from the various activities in which people became involved because of the war, although it is as difficult to know their motives for participation as it is to be sure of the motives of politicians and others whose attitudes have been recorded.

This chapter seeks to trace popular pro-war, anti-war and uncommitted opinion and behaviour, and the influences on public opinion. It shows both the

---

2 John Beresford (ed.), *The Diary of a Country Parson: the Reverend James Woodforde, 1758–1802*, 5 vol.s (Oxford, 1924–31), v, 113–14, 23 April 1798; see also ibid., v, 115, 25 April 1798.

3 George (ed.), *Catalogue of Political and Personal Satires*, vi, p.xi; ibid., vii, p.xi; H.T. Dickinson, *Caricatures and the Constitution, 1760–1832* (Cambridge, 1986), pp.13–15, 19–20; John Brewer, *The Common People and Politics, 1750–1790s* (Cambridge, 1986), pp.45–7; Barker, 'Press, Politics and Reform', p.266.

4 Diana Donald, *The Age of Caricature* (New Haven and London, 1996), pp.157–62; George (ed.), *Political and Personal Satires*, vii, pp.xvii–xviii. For examples of radical Bull family letters, see *A Few Words, but No Lies; from Roger Bull to his Brother Thomas* (London, 1792), and [Ann Jebb], *Two Penny-Worth of Truth for a Penny; or a True State of Facts: with an Apology for Tom Bull in a Letter to Brother John* (London, 1793), which are both replies to the loyalist *One Penny-Worth of Truth from Thomas Bull to his Brother John* (London, 1792).

volatility of the British public in its reactions to the war, and its limited engagement with the ideological issues which were debated by the polemicists and which have been discussed in this book. Whereas the politically literate and activist were clearly influenced by the conception of this war as a conflict over ideas, the majority of ordinary British people showed no evidence that their views were more than marginally coloured by the competing ideologies at stake. Although it is occasionally possible to trace impressions made by the ideological conflict, their attitudes and behaviour were usually more pragmatic and personal. This naturally produced swings of opinion, depending on circumstances such as the success of the British armed forces at any given time.

I Popular Support for the War

A consideration of popular pro-war behaviour during the 1790s may help to bridge the gap between David Eastwood's heterogeneous popular patriots and their many, ambiguous and unreliable reasons for patriotic action, and Robert Dozier's militant loyalists, criticized by Eastwood for their simple delineation as a uniformly solid group of government supporters.[5] Chapter three considered the activities and opinions of committed conservative activists; here the much less reliable and much less constant patriotism of the rest of the population, which from time to time reinforced the vigour of the activists, is examined. Popular pro-war opinion was stimulated by three broad categories of factors: the impact of active loyalism, direct individual profit and the influence of specific issues relating to this particular war against revolutionary France. This section discusses these influences and their effects in turn in an attempt to examine the evidence for public support for the British government's cause in its struggle against the French republic.

Naturally, the conservative elite hoped that the role of active loyalism would be significant in promoting popular conservatism and support for the war. Their clear advantage over the forces of opposition was the inherent traditionalism of the majority of the population, which buttressed the monarchy, the landed hierarchy and the Church of England—the political and social establishment. There was a lack of genuine and reliable mass support for radicalism among the population. Widespread contentment with, or at least acquiescence in, the existing order meant that suggestions of possible change to a familiar system were greeted with suspicion, particularly such a violent and chaotic change as was demonstrated by the revolution in France. In other words,

5 Eastwood, 'Patriotism and the English State', p.147; also Cookson, *The British Armed Nation*, *passim*.

most people in Britain did not appear to question that they had an interest in the continuation of the *status quo*.

The vast outflow of conservative propaganda may well have had some effect in convincing, or at least assuring, those who could read it. Pamphlets, tracts and broadsides were written to suit both middle-class and lower-order readers, and the ideas of Burke and other popular conservative writers such as Bowles and More were repeated frequently in loyal addresses. The *Anti-Jacobin Review* sold 2500 copies weekly, a substantial sale for such virulent loyalism.[6] While Pendleton urges caution concerning the use of the term 'popular literature', arguing that literature for 'the real masses' was largely apolitical, she also refers to research which shows that the French Revolution provoked a great number of loyal statements in mass literature, after two centuries of popular lampoons on the royal family and the Church, thus indicating that the majority of the population at the bottom end of the social scale were not oblivious to events played out on the international political stage.[7] Pamphlets written locally may well have had more impact in their communities than more famous and complex publications; and propaganda such as free public dinners, victory celebrations, military parades and church sermons needed no literacy at all. The social intimidation practised generally and locally by militant loyalists may also have had some effect, though equally unmeasurable: aside from stopping the mouths of the more prudent radicals, it may well have persuaded some to display loyalty more ostentatiously than they might otherwise have done, if at all.

Certainly there were many mass demonstrations of loyalty and support for the war, involving great numbers of ordinary people, which must have been stimulated by government and loyalist publicity and propaganda. There were huge numbers of loyal addresses, resolutions and petitions sent to the King—many more than their radical counterparts, although it naturally took substantially more bravery to organize a reformist or anti-war petition than one applauding the activities of the government. Loyalist and pro-war addresses were sent from towns, counties, religious bodies, universities, magistrates, manufacturers, merchants, Volunteer and militia corps, theatres, clubs and societies. These were no doubt usually organized by active loyalists, but they carried substantial numbers of signatures—11,000 on one from Liverpool and over 8000 on one from the Merchant Taylors Hall in December 1792, and 2500 on one from Portsmouth and Portsea in November 1798—which suggests that non-activists were also involved, whether voluntarily or under pressure.[8]

Subscriptions also attracted the support of many ordinary subjects. The fund established by the Association at the Crown and Anchor Tavern for the

---

6 Emsley, *British Society and the French Wars*, p.66.

7 Pendleton, 'English Conservative Propaganda', pp.162–4, referring to Robert Collison, *The Story of Street Literature, Forerunner of the Popular Press* (London, 1973).

8 See the *London Gazette*, 18–22 December 1792 and 10–13 November 1798.

relief of sailors' wives and children received support not just from other Loyal Associations, but also from 'ladies of fashion', philanthropists, church congregations, Eton College, town and county corporations and army regiments; the *Observer* claimed on 10 March 1793 that so widespread an activity must be an 'irrefutable attestation' of the war.[9] The 1798 Voluntary Contribution, largely because of the threat of invasion, raised £2,826,000, only a little less than the tripled assessed taxes did.[10] Substantial local subscriptions were also collected to fund public military parades and dinners for soldiers stationed in the vicinity on such occasions as the King's birthday.

Crowds were involved in activities such as burning effigies of Thomas Paine and pro-war street demonstrations, too many all to have been hired or manipulated by the elite.[11] Wealthier people had other opportunities to demonstrate their support for the war. Ladies wore decorative items of dress to express their loyalty—'King and Constitution' favours in their hair or caps in 1792, 'Camperdown bonnets' in 1798. A graphic satire of 1799 ridiculed the fashion among London fops of feigning war-wounds when the British army returned from Holland.[12]

Recruitment was a major opportunity for ordinary people to show practical support for the government and the war. There were 35,000 regular British troops in 1793; by 1795 there were nearly 125,000, and the 1790s in general saw the highest returns from recruitment for the eighteenth century. The combination of the bounty, natural patriotism and the anticipated excitement and drama of military life attracted a substantial number of men to the Volunteers and the supplementary militia as well as to the army and the navy. William Rowbottom of Oldham reported a 'universall pant for glory' as well as financial hardship among enlisting local weavers. One Scotsman serving in the rank and file at the siege of Valenciennes in 1793 wrote home to his mother of his desire to 'do more yet for my King & Country's saik'. Clive Emsley has estimated that ten per cent of all adult British males served in the regular armed forces during the whole 1793–1815 period, and that this proportion rises to one-sixth if the Volunteers and militia are included.[13] While it is true that rather more of these served after 1802 than before, it is undeniable that very substantial numbers of

---

9 Dozier, *For King, Constitution and Country*, p.109. See also ibid., pp.148, 164; and Beresford (ed.), *Diary of a Country Parson*, iii, 380, 19 October 1792, for a clerical subscription in aid of French *émigré* clergy.

10 Vaisey, 'The Pledge of Patriotism', p.223.

11 Dickinson, 'Popular Conservatism and Militant Loyalism', p.119.

12 Beresford (ed.), *Diary of a Country Parson*, v, 129, 25 July 1798; BMC 9447, [Cawse], 'The Bond Street Battalion—or the Hospital Staff from Holland!!!' (18 November 1799).

13 Emsley, *British Society and the French Wars*, pp.37, 74, 133; Aspinall, *LCGIII*, ii, 86, Corporal George Robertson to his mother, 1 August 1793.

British men participated in the military defence of their country even before the Peace of Amiens.

The bounties and wage increases offered to enlisting soldiers and sailors raises a second motivation for ordinary people to demonstrate support for the war: the expectation or experience of direct profit.[14] Professional soldiers and sailors were one group who fell into this category. Others who profited from the conflict were industrialists who manufactured woollen goods, boots and shoes, iron, copper, arms and ships. Workmen in certain trades were also able to benefit from the increased demand for their labour in wartime. Joseph Farington noted in 1795 that 'Caulkers & Shipwrights who understand their business well can get twenty shillings a day.—In peaceable times, they can earn when paid by the piece, half a guinea a day.'[15] It was even reported that the town of Okehampton had been 'much improved by the French prisoners on parole—one of the blessings of war!'[16] This type of self-interest could generate genuine support for the war among those whom it benefited. However, self-interest could also stimulate pro-war behaviour which was not necessarily indicative of much or any real pro-war sentiment, which will be discussed below.

Third, certain events and aspects of the war against France encouraged pro-war behaviour from ordinary people. The execution of Louis XVI on 21 January 1793 had a huge impact on British people. Immediately after the first news of it arrived, on 23 January, theatre performances were cancelled and calls for war were made, both in street demonstrations and in the press. Chauvelin, the French envoy, wrote to his superiors that he could not so much as leave his house 'without being exposed to the insults and ignorant ferocity of that part of the nation that is still called here the mob'.[17] The horror and curiosity created by the news of the execution were still lingering on 23 March 1793, when the *Sun* advertised a five-foot high model of a guillotine on show in London and reported it to be a great public attraction. The popularity of George III grew, and he became a national asset to be defended against a nation of regicides. The frequent references to the execution of the French king in conservative propaganda throughout the decade suggests that it was an issue which continued to raise anti-gallican sentiment. Caricaturists often portrayed George III as synonymous with John Bull, the representative of the ordinary British people.[18]

---

14 See the *Caledonian Mercury*, 25 February 1793, 11 May 1797, and the *Bee* (Edinburgh), 6 March 1793, on the efficacy of bounties for the recruitment of sailors.

15 Greig (ed.), *The Farington Diary*, i, 92, 22 February 1795.

16 A.D. Harvey, *English Literature and the Great War with France* (London, 1981), pp.4–5.

17 Pendleton, 'English Conservative Propaganda', p.373. See also Bindman et al., *The Shadow of the Guillotine*, pp.22–4, 47–53, 134–43.

18 See, for example, BMC 8458, [Cruikshank], 'John Bull Humbugg'd alias *Both-Eared*' (12 May 1794) and ibid., 8664, 'Billys Hobby Horse or John Bull Loaded with Mischief' (6 July 1795).

Popular xenophobia and, in particular, anti-gallicism were hardly new characteristics of the British people. In the 1790s, however, atheism and republican chaos replaced Catholicism and absolute monarchy as the French converse of British Protestantism and mixed government, inflaming the popular sense of ideological rivalry. With the outbreak of war, traditional British pride and suspicion of the French became hostility and downright bigotry among the British population. Revolutionary France was associated with blood, destruction, licence, wickedness and impiety. Previous images of the French as foolish and ragged were superimposed on the ideology of warfare in graphic prints and caricatures.[19] This did not mean that the French threat was taken lightly, however; prints often emphasized the strength, aggression and atrocities of the enemy and, in the later 1790s, Napoleon was seized upon as the embodiment of the rapacious French revolutionary enemy.[20] Wariness of the impoverished *émigrés* was described among different classes of people, from the fashionable world of Joseph Farington to the humbler one of the Rev. James Woodforde, although they were apparently fighting a common enemy with the British.[21]

The other side of British anti-gallicism was a pride in Britain itself, an instinctive patriotism, another useful tool for pro-war propaganda and displayed in many of the prints. The outbreak of hostilities produced a natural flow of patriotism, especially since the French had declared war, and many probably expected an early success. London theatre audiences had been singing a popular verse celebrating the opening of hostilities with France for a week before they were actually declared. Robert Dozier quotes the *Sussex Weekly Advertiser* of 14 March 1793, a paper not always wholly in approval of government measures: 'never was there a war in which the spirit of the nation seemed more roused and interested than the present'.[22] Victories achieved by the British army or navy were powerful stimulants to pro-war sentiment and behaviour: the national anthem and other patriotic songs were sung by audiences at the theatre, illuminations were made and street celebrations were held. After the difficult year of 1797, the victories at the Nile and Minorca lifted the public spirit and increased public tolerance for the continuation of the struggle. 'Even the sensation produced by ... untoward events, such as the stoppage of the Bank, was mitigated by that darling and most natural subject of English exultation, Great Naval Victories', Lord Holland wrote. Sheridan agreed: 'If ever man

---

19 For example, BMC 9355, Gillray, 'Egyptian Sketches' (12 March 1799).

20 On Napoleon, see BMC 9431, [Cawse], 'Satans return from Earth Discovered in Council' (30 November 1799).

21 Greig (ed.), *The Farington Diary*, i, 3, 21 July 1793; ibid., pp.14–15, 9 November 1793; ibid., p.182, 3 January 1797; Beresford (ed.), *Diary of a Country Parson*, v, 206, 20 July 1799.

22 Dozier, *For King, Constitution and Country*, p.111.

loved man; if ever one part of the people loved another, the people of this country love the seamen.'[23]

A more powerful motivation still to support the war was the real threat of a French invasion. It was probably this which stimulated so swift and so generous a response to the government's appeal in December 1796 for a Loyalty Loan; and it is hardly surprising that the Duke of York was able to report to the King that 'nothing could exceed the zeal and loyalty which has been shewn by all the people' at Fishguard when the French attempted to land there in February 1797. In the ports and hinterland of Edinburgh in 1796–97, when invasion fears were running high, fishermen offered to man gun-boats, and farmers and postmasters offered their horses and carts as transport for troops and their baggage. Later, dockworkers offered to be trained in the use of shoreguns.[24] However, the King himself noted in 1801 that 'the not having had any [recent] attempt of invasion has certainly in a great measure cooled the ardour and dilligence [*sic*] of the Volunteer Corps and perhaps of the embodied militia'.[25] Songs attempting to inspire courage and loyalty in the face of this threat reminded their listeners of famous English victories over France in the past, such as Poitiers and Crècy. Prints expressed both apprehension concerning the horrors which might be produced by a successful revolutionary invasion and at the same time the conviction that a French invasion could never succeed: the defending and triumphant British soldiers were often pictured as humble labourers, or with wooden limbs.[26]

Serving officers, especially those belonging to the social elite, were sometimes very conscious of the ideological nature of the war. Vice-Admiral Collingwood was emphatic that this was 'not a war of proffit', and he found the activities of the French Revolutionary armies abhorrent: 'that under the mark of friendship to Mankind, wou'd subject them to the most degrading slavery that ever the human species groaned under'. General Calvert told his sister in 1794 that 'I would strain every nerve, and drain Great Britain both of men and money rather than permit the French to re-establish themselves in Flanders. A barrier must somewhere be opposed to their principles, their vices, and their arms'. More humble officers also demonstrated loyalty—the officers of HMS Clyde

---

23 Holland, *Memoirs*, i, 9; *P.H.*, xxxiii, 641, Sheridan, May 1797.

24 *Caledonian Mercury*, 17 November 1796, 10 December 1796, 7 January 1797, 8 October 1801.

25 Aspinall, *LCGIII*, ii, 543, the Duke of York to George III, 25 February 1797; ibid., iii, 580, George III to Lord Hobart, 22 July 1801.

26 For instance, 'Invitation to Repel Invasion' ([1796]) and 'The Patriot-Briton; or, England's Invasion, 1796' (1796), in the Madden Collection, Cambridge University Library, 1796.15.60, 64; BMC 9187, Rowlandson, 'England Invaded, or Frenchmen Naturalized' (16 March 1798).

contributed the equivalent of a full month's pay each to the Voluntary Contribution of 1798.[27]

Popular behaviour indicated some support for this particular conflict, although it was often a variation on the theme of a natural war-time cooperation with the government due to instinctive patriotism and self-defence—a traditional 'jingoism' with counter-revolutionary clothes on, particularly among the lower orders. Loyal addresses sent in the wake of the failed peace negotiations of 1796 and 1797 which expressed disappointment also declared resignation to the hardships of war and support for the government against an unreasonable enemy.[28] Pro-war songs frequently extolled the benefits of the British constitution and reviled French attempts to destroy it, seeing it as a chief stake in the war, but it seems likely that much popular pro-war usage of terms referring to Jacobinism was superficial—the current language of abuse towards radicals, putative grain-hoarders and all causes, French and British, of the war-time troubles of the ordinary people. One handbill called for 'Success to our Army and Navy. No Exportation of Grain. No Jacobins. No Assignhatts.'[29] Loyalist behaviour, moreover, even among most of the middle classes, fluctuated with the success of the war and the prosperity of the economy, and was unreliable.

II Popular Opposition to the War

However popular pro-war sentiment may have been, therefore, it was nevertheless neither unanimous nor constant. 'Deference', as Roger Wells has remarked 'was an all pervasive and powerful force, but it was not indissoluble.'[30] In Sheffield, Nottingham and Surrey, opposition was voiced to the loyal addresses to be sent in response to the May 1792 Royal Proclamation, and ten counties and eighty-one cities and towns appear not to have responded formally at all. A majority of those present at the meeting in Durham to discuss resolutions in response to the December proclamation, rejected them, and the loyalist minority had to convene separately in order to issue their declaration.[31] There was domestic unrest in the autumn of 1792 over a poor harvest and high

27 NMM, COL/14, f.10, Collingwood to the Rev. Alexander Carlyle, 21 January 1795; ibid., f.18, same to same, 25 February 1799; Sir Harry Verney (ed.), *The Journals and Correspondence of General Sir Harry Calvert*, p.273. On the officers of the Clyde, see NMM, CUN/1.

28 See, for instance, the addresses printed in the *London Gazette* from Bath (10–14 January 1797), the City of London (7–11 February 1797), Nairn (12–16 December 1797), Lanark (26–30 December 1797) and Bradford (13–17 February 1798). Cf. Dickinson, *Politics of the People*, pp.284–5; Cookson, *The British Armed Nation*, pp.233ff., 244.

29 'Britons are Happy, if They will Think So'.

30 Wells, *Insurrection*, p.258.

31 Dozier, *For King, Constitution and Country*, pp.21, 82.

prices, as well as that possibly stimulated by radicals. If these did not necessarily produce anti-war activism, it is unlikely that those already in such straits over matters of subsistence would have been happy at the prospect of war with all its concomitant burdens and distresses. Popular anti-war sentiment was produced mainly by the hardships of the wartime experience for ordinary people and partly, especially for the literate classes, by a simple desire, for whatever reason, to criticize the government, and it resulted in verbal and physical protests of various kinds. As with loyalism and pro-war sentiment, it is difficult to distinguish wholly between non-organized radicalism or pacifism and sporadic popular anti-war behaviour.[32]

Historians disagree on how the 1790s fit into a broadly improving trend in the economic situation—whether their relative difficulty was eclipsed by the general upward trend or whether it was a significant departure from it.[33] Whatever the case, it seems clear that in this decade population increase and repeatedly poor harvests forced food prices up: the cost of living rose by thirty per cent between 1790 and 1795, and its rate of increase doubled after the outbreak of the war in early 1793. Wages also rose, but not sufficiently to swallow the gap, and underemployment and rising taxation aggravated the difficulties. Economic trends were of little interest to those who struggled to make ends meet and, whether or not the war was genuinely to blame, it was an easy target. Petitions containing demands for peace began to arrive in Westminster in 1795, which also saw one of the worst harvests of the decade.[34] From that year on, bread and an end to the war were two demands regularly made by rioting crowds.

The middle and commercial classes also felt the financial burden of the British war effort. The *Sun* was already reporting on 7 March 1793 that the departure of the Foot Guards for Holland had deprived the coal wharfs of London of a substantial number of labourers, encouraging demands for a rise in wages by those who remained and found their labour a scarce resource. The caricaturists' frequent depiction of John Bull as a character overloaded, ground down, bleeding, or in some other way suffering from government taxation reflected public preoccupation with wartime stringency.[35] Often these prints questioned the validity of the government's claim of necessity for high taxes, suggesting that the French threat was not so menacing as it was declared to be.

---

32 Cf. Philp, 'The Fragmented Ideology of Reform', esp. pp.51–6.

33 Compare Christie, *Stress and Stability* and Wells, *Wretched Faces*.

34 Ehrman, *The Reluctant Transition*, pp.443, 451–2, 475–6. On popular antipathy to wartime taxes, see 'A New Song, To Spend All Our Cash in the Wars' ([1793]), British Library, 648.c.26, f.74.

35 Cf. also Philip Harling, *The Waning of 'Old Corruption': The Politics of Economical Reform in Britain, 1779–1846* (Oxford, 1996).

Some prints criticized the hypocrisy of wealthy statesmen and bishops appointing general fasts and the bitter irony of requiring the poor to fast.[36]

After the first months of the conflict, a simple weariness with war and its effects and a natural desire for peace grew widespread:

> I am a brave fellow, I love my country and king,
> And wish to do right to both country and him;
> But I still love the poor, that I always will do,
> And them that won't join me they're not true blue.
>
> Then fill up a bumper,
> Let's drink to the men that strive to make peace.[37]

It was, indeed, largely due to the impression that a majority in the country was impatient for peace that the ministry attempted to treat with France in 1796 and 1797. 'Lysons hears', wrote Farington in August 1796, 'that if Pitt does not make peace before November He must go out.'[38]

Public anti-war sentiment may have been provoked more than anything else by the actual exigencies of war for ordinary people, but anti-war propaganda may have played some part in suggesting further reasons for discontent. This need not have been printed literature; radicals addressing customers in taverns, street demonstrations and graffiti may have encouraged some who were beginning to grow impatient with the continuation of the war and its burdens to verbalize their dissatisfaction and perhaps even disaffection. A crowd pulled the carriage of the prominent radical Maurice Margarot to and from his trial for sedition in Edinburgh in January 1794.[39] Seditious language berating the King and the Duke of York for failing to appreciate the hardships of war for the generality of their people began to appear as early as 1793. A handbill condemned George III for missing a theatre performance to show his sorrow at the death of Louis XVI but enjoying the show as usual after fifteen Londoners were killed (crushed?) at the Haymarket Theatre. 'Who would not Die for such a Gracious King!!!' it ended sarcastically. One London tailor told a discontented crowd that the Duke of York's father was 'a Fool unless it is at Burthening the People and you like Fools to put up with it nay all the Family are Fools and Rogues'. It is more likely, however, that ordinary people who voiced

---

36 See BMC 8629, Gillray, 'Leaving Off Powder,—or—A Frugal Family saving the Guinea' (10 March 1795); ibid., 8323, Newton, 'Fast Day!' (19 April 1793).

37 'A Good Wish for Old England', Madden Collection, Cambridge University Library, 1785.4.698. See also the addresses printed in the *London Gazette* which expressed the hope for a swift, honourable and lasting peace, e.g. in November and December 1798.

38 Greig (ed.), *The Farington Diary*, i, 158, 3 August 1796.

39 *Caledonian Mercury*, 9 and 11 January 1794.

such sentiments wanted food and peace rather than political change as the radicals did.[40]

The caricaturists satirized the failings of Britain's allies, representing them as greedy, cruelly rapacious and unreliable, preying on the long-suffering John Bull, but this did not necessarily entail blame for the British government. There was, however, as the corollary of popular joy at British victories, deep disappointment and frustration with military or naval failure. The campaign of 1793, while hardly an unmitigated triumph, could still be argued to hold out hopes of future success; but the disappointments of 1794 and 1795 in the Low Countries provoked much public criticism. By 1796, the continental situation was going from bad to worse, while the British army was largely removed from the scene of action, leaving the British war effort in the hands of the navy, so that the public could only look on in helpless frustration. The prints captured these sentiments, mixing contempt with anger.[41]

Popular protests against the war were made in various forms and against various intermediary targets. The most common targets were, unsurprisingly, the government—especially Pitt—and the King. Local government officials were also attacked: an anonymous letter to George Phelps, chief magistrate of Tewkesbury, was printed in August 1795 in the *London Gazette*, demanding that he convene a meeting without delay to consider organizing a petition for peace to the King, and threatening 'a leaden bullit through your brains' if he did not comply. An indiscriminately anti-establishment paper found at Hammersmith in 1794 commanded

> Deal Destruction to the Foe
> Lay the *Haughty Monarch* Low
> *Pitt Dundas & Hood* shall fall
> Damn the *King* & Damn them all
> Arise & Destroy the Tyrant.[42]

Soldiers and sailors, as the agents of war, were also butts of criticism and sour ridicule. As the handbill quoted above shows, military and naval commanders were singled out for attack as names associated with the conflict. Lord Howe apparently talked of resigning his command of the Channel Fleet before his triumph on the 'Glorious First of June', 1794, because of the regular

---

40 British Library, 648.c.26, f.35; Morris, 'The Monarchy as an Issue', p.115; Emsley, 'The Impact of the French Revolution', p.53; idem, 'Revolution, war and the nation state', p.112.

41 BMC 8659, Gillray, 'A Keen-Sighted Politician Warming his Imagination' (13 June 1795); ibid., 8676, Will Hanlon, 'The State Caterpillar' (1 September 1795)—a reference to the Quiberon disaster.

42 *London Gazette*, 8–11 August 1795; PRO HO 50/385, f.524, Sir George Yonge to Nepean, 3 June 1794, encl.

attacks made on him in the newspapers and prints.[43] Ordinary members of the armed forces, however, were also assailed. Volunteers, militiamen and regular soldiers stationed locally in barracks could be very unpopular, being associated with disorder and brawling, unjust recruiting strategies and military government. Officers walking around Norwich after dark risked being attacked.[44] The prints reflected this unpopularity, usually ridiculing the Volunteers for their lack of horsemanship and general military skills (John Kay was particularly scathing about the Edinburgh Volunteers), or the regular soldiers in their training camps in the south of England. Sometimes they displayed a greater bitterness concerning military enforcement of law and order.[45] Despite the wide popularity of the navy, the residents of Sheerness, reported to have fled their homes during the mutiny of 1797 from fear and in order to make room for the soldiers called in to resist the mutineers, may have found their enthusiasm waning somewhat; and various addresses were sent to Westminster that year severely criticizing the revolt.[46]

The practices of crimping and impressment to recruit for the army and navy, and balloting to recruit for the militia, were deeply unpopular, and there were consequently many riots in specific protest against instances of these throughout the 1790s.

> Come rouse my good fellows to arms,
> And follow the sound of the drum,
> If you'd cut a fine figure in story;
> Inlist in my regiment, come:
> For wonderful sums we will promise,
> Which we possibly never will pay;
> But of this my brave comrades be certain,
> You'll be shot at for sixpence a day.[47]

As early as February 1793 crowds engaged violently with press-gangs in Whitby and in South Shields, and a group of colliers disembarked from their coal-ship near Patrington, some way up the River Humber from their usual port of Hull, in order to avoid the press-gang that was thought to be operating from a warship docked there; in Uig, Lewis, military recruiting parties were forcefully resisted. In March a large crowd at Norwich tried to persuade army recruits to

---

43 Greig (ed.), *The Farington Diary*, i, 63, 18 July 1794.

44 Harvey, *English Literature*, p.11; *Caledonian Mercury*, 29 April 1793; PRO HO 42/27, f.223, petitions on the cost of barracks for troops.

45 BMC 8513, John Kay, 'Edinburgh Royal Volunteers' (1794); ibid., 8733, Kay, 'Leith Volunteer' (1795); ibid., 8734, Kay, 'To the Right About-Face' (1797).

46 *The Times*, 3 June 1797; for addresses, see the *London Gazette*, June–July 1797.

47 'Serjeant Kite's Invitation to the Swinish Multitude To Be Shot at for Sixpence a Day', Madden Collection, Cambridge University Library, 1796.15.45.

desert.[48] Crowds of Londoners rioted in August 1794 against crimps and balloting for the militia. The press-gang was driven away by the people of Campbeltown, Argyll, in February 1795. Four or five hundred people were involved in the disturbance at Denbigh in March 1795 caused by opposition both to balloting for service in the navy and the militia and to the exportation of grain. A few days later there was trouble in Halifax when magistrates, overseers of the poor and churchwardens tried to persuade the poor to volunteer for the navy, because those authorities insisted on keeping two-thirds of each man's bounty in trust for him until he returned—the men naturally wanted the whole sum immediately.[49] In 1796 the Supplementary Militia Act increasing the size of the English force, caused riots in Lincolnshire, Buckinghamshire, Northamptonshire, Norfolk, Cambridgeshire, Cumberland, Merionethshire, Shropshire, Gloucestershire and Derbyshire. Sir Gilbert Elliot told Lady Palmerston in August 1797 that Scotland was 'in a flame from one end to the other' over the Bill introducing a system of militia into Scotland for the first time.[50]

Furthermore, soldiers and sailors themselves sometimes appeared to show a marked disloyalty instead of support for the war. The naval mutinies of April to June 1797 at Sheerness and the Nore were only the largest and most famous examples of this (although the sailors themselves claimed continuing and exemplary loyalty to the British state against the French).[51] Lord St Vincent complained to Evan Nepean at the Home Office in February 1800 of the lack of discipline still lingering in his fleet: 'The state of the Navy is so bad, that I begin

---

48 Emsley, *British Society and the French Wars*, pp.27-8; Logue, *Popular Disturbances in Scotland, 1780–1815* (Edinburgh, 1979), pp. 117–20; PRO HO 42/24, ff.549–50, Joseph Balmer to Robert Burdon, MP, 18 February 1793; the *Sun*, 28 February 1793; PRO HO 42/25, f.110, printed notice offering a reward for information leading to the conviction of rioters. See also PRO HO 42/24, f.356, for a handbill from Newcastle trying to dissuade potential sailors from being lured into the navy by the bounty a few days before the French declaration of war was known in Britain.

49 Stevenson, 'The London "Crimp" Riots', 40–58; Logue, *Popular Disturbances in Scotland*, pp.121–3; PRO HO 42/34, ff.277–9, John Lloyd to Portland, 1 April 1795; ibid., f.302-v, G. Armytage and others to Portland, 6 April 1796.

50 Bohstedt, *Riots and Community Politics*, p.173; Minto (ed.), *Life and Letters*, ii, 415–17, Elliot to Lady Palmerston, 28 August 1797; Logue, *Popular Disturbances in Scotland*, pp.75–115. On the Tranent anti-militia riot, see Kenneth J. Logue, 'The Tranent Militia Riot of 1797', *Transactions of the East Lothian Antiquarian and Field Naturalists' Society*, 14 (1974), 37–61; Sandy Mullay, *Scotland's Forgotten Massacre* (Edinburgh, 1979). See also Buddle Atkinson and Jackson (eds), *Letters to James Loch*, i, 21, Andrew Clephane to James Loch, 15 May 1798.

51 For the sailors' requests concerning wages, supplies, provisions and medical care, see *P.H.*, xxxiii, 493–501 n.; see also Wells, *Insurrection*, pp.81–3, 95–6, 100–2. See Dozier, *For King, Constitution, and Country*, p.44, on sailors' riots in November 1792 at Great Yarmouth, South Shields, King's Lynn and Ipswich. On army disaffection, see Wells, *Insurrection*, pp.104–6.

to despair of setting it to rights, for the moment any Ship of the old Leaven is out of my sight, both officers and Crews are as bad as ever, & no-one attempts to correct them ... In short my dear Nepean, it is high time to make peace.'[52] Some militiamen who had previously volunteered their services for Ireland fought shy when the time of departure arrived.[53] Eight regiments of Scottish fencibles mutinied between 1793 and 1804, in protest against the perceived abuse of their conditions of service.[54] Instead of restoring order, Volunteers in Dingwall and Peterhead in 1796, in Macduff and Devonshire in 1800 and in the south-west of England in 1800–1801 joined in local food riots, as did militiamen in Oxfordshire in 1795; in Honiton and Cullompton in 1795 and in Teignmouth in 1797 Volunteers refused to act against food rioters. Regular troops had joined in food riots in the south of England in 1794–95, but generally these soldiers did not refuse to suppress riots, perhaps because they themselves were not local to their areas of action, as were Volunteers.[55]

Soldiers and sailors might of course simply dislike the loneliness and hardships of war. Samuel Grant, ship's clerk, wrote in his diary in December 1793, 'This has not been one of the happiest years of my life—having been nearly 9 Months of it absent f[ro]m My Dear Wife & Children ... & 4 Months in a very ill state of health.' The following year was not a great deal better: 'had various alterations and disappointments with regard to the situation of my ship—*but, most particularly*, disappointed in going home when reduced almost to a certainty.'[56] For soldiers, this particular conflict could prove frustrating, since it involved British military campaigns relatively little in the 1790s and regular soldiers were often based at home: 'I feel that no possible advantage could arise from my being placed here if the enemy were actually at sea & on their passage', wrote Lieutenant General Lord Mulgrave to his brother from Bridlington in 1797, '(as this is the last point that their military knowledge would induce them

52 NMM, NEP/6, f.3–v., St Vincent to Nepean, 7 February 1800.

53 Aspinall, *LCGIII*, iii, 123, Portland to George III, 12 September 1798.

54 W. Hamish Fraser, 'Patterns of Protest', in T.M. Devine and Rosalind Mitchison (eds), *People and Society in Scotland*, vol. 1, 1760–1830 (Edinburgh, 1988), p.271; John Prebble, *Mutiny: Highland Regiments in Revolt, 1743–1804* (London, 1975); Brims, 'Scottish Democratic Movement', pp.554-5.

55 Logue, *Popular Disturbances in Scotland*, pp.43–4; Bohstedt, *Riots and Community Politics*, pp.29, 49–50; Emsley, *British Society and the French Wars*, pp.42–3; Wells, *Insurrection*, p.80; idem, 'The revolt of the south-west, 1800-1801: a study in English popular protest', *Social History*, 6 (1977), 713–44; Jupp (ed.), *Letter-Journal of George Canning*, p.259; see also PRO HO 42/34, f.348, Archdeacon John Turner of Wells to Portland, 28 April 1795.

56 NMM, GRT/1–2. See also Clive Emsley, *North Riding Naval Recruits: The Quota Acts and the Quota Men 1795–1797* (North Yorkshire CRO Publications no.18, 1978), pp.12–13.

to approach)'.[57] Criticisms of the government and the military administration for insufficient equipment, provisions or numbers of recruits were frequent.

As with the loyal addresses, it seems likely that the peace petitions of 1795, 1797 and 1801 were signed by non-partisans, simply because of the numbers of local people involved—the Yorkshire petition of 1801 bore 30,000 signatures.[58] Moreover, petitions for peace were not sent only at times of mass campaigns: the merchants, manufacturers and traders of Paisley, for instance, petitioned the King against the 'present unhappy & ruinous war' which was 'the source of all [their] unsupportable miseries' in January 1794. Hopes for peace were also expressed in loyal addresses. The caricaturists sometimes reflected literate opinion that the government's handling of the 1796-97 negotiations might have been more skilful.[59]

Similarly, on the news of peace being settled at Amiens, there was both widespread joy at the end of the war and criticism of its terms. Even at the signing of the preliminaries in October 1801, illuminations, the firing of guns and the ringing of bells were ubiquitous; the French diplomats Otto and General Lauriston were towed in their carriage from Downing Street to St James's Square and back; and the price of wheat fell by ten shillings a quarter. David Erdman notes that 'A publican at Lambeth, who had vowed that whenever peace was made he would give away all the beer in his cellar, opened his barrels on the thirteenth [of October]'.[60] The prospect of the end of the tax on incomes, of lower prices and of the reduction of the armed forces was very popular. Richard Westall wrote to his friend Matthew Flinders, a sailor: 'I remember when I had the pleasure of seeing you at Spithead, you lamented that in your profession, distinction was scarce ever to be obtained but by the destruction of our fellow creatures: you will therefore have rejoiced that long harassed Europe is at length at Peace.'[61] Approval was not unanimous, however. 'I am told', Thomas Grenville told his brother, the former Foreign Secretary, 'that though the word peace be popular amongst the lowest classes, yet amongst persons of all descriptions who affect to reason upon the articles, they are considered as a confession of our defeat.' Mr. Custance, the most influential property-owner in Parson Woodforde's area in Norfolk, refused to allow public celebrations of the

---

57 Quoted in M.Y. Ashcroft, *To Escape the Monster's Clutches. Notes and Documents illustrating the preparations in North Yorkshire to repel the invasion threatened by the French from 1793* (North Yorkshire CRO Publications no.15, November 1977), p.40.

58 Cookson, *Friends of Peace*, pp.19, 152, 161, 190.

59 PRO HO 42/28, ff.115–18; BMC 8829, [Cruikshank], 'The Messenger of Peace' (29 October 1796); ibid., 8832, Cruikshank, 'Lord Mum Sucking his Thumb!!' (10 November 1796); ibid., 9031, [Ansell], 'The Diplomatic Squad, or Harmony Interrupted' (21 August 1797).

60 Erdman, *Blake*, p.358.

61 NMM, FLI/1, Richard Westall to Matthew Flinders, 13 March 1802.

settlement in June 1802.[62] Napoleon became the hero of the hour, while Pitt, though now out of office, was unpopular and regarded as having been the stubborn obstacle to peace throughout the decade. This was reflected in the prints. In 'John Bull's Prayer to Peace, or the Flight of Discord', Roberts showed Napoleon exalted to the clouds and glorified together with Peace, while Pitt, the demon of discord, fled in terror and disarray.[63]

Popular antipathy to the war against revolutionary France is perhaps easier to detect than popular support for it, but it probably took still less account of the reasons for the conflict. The war was opposed by public opinion largely because of the strains and stresses it imposed on the population in common with all wars. It was perhaps particularly odious to the people because it affected such a wide cross-section of them, because it was so long and because it demanded so much in terms of human and material resources, but these were differences of degree and not of kind from other eighteenth-century conflicts, and a distinction was not often made between these in popular opposition to this war.

III Popular Volatility in Response to the War

Public opinion was, then, not entirely committed to one cause or the other over the whole period of the 1790s. It was not gripped by any ideological position on the conflict, and it therefore neither actively promoted the war nor actively campaigned against it on a consistent basis. Its acquiescence throughout allowed the government to pursue the policy of war, but at certain times it appeared to be more favourable than at others. The outbreak of war was quite widely popular, after the alarmism of late 1792 and the execution of Louis XVI; as the war wore on and the economic pressures of the decade squeezed more tightly, popular hostility increased; when French intransigence was revealed in 1796 and 1797, and when British troops or fleets were victorious in 1798, public patience with the war was restored; but peace in 1802 was almost universally welcomed. It would, however, be an oversimplification to imagine that everyone had an opinion or strong feelings about the struggle all of the time, and it seems much more likely that most British people were open to persuasion one way or the other for much of the time.

The work of the graphic satirists in the 1790s reflected the volatile nature of public opinion. There were no government engravers to give a falsely optimistic view of the British military situation for public consumption, as there were in France. The graphic prints produced by Gillray and other satirical artists

---

62 *Dropmore*, vii, 64, Thomas Grenville to Grenville, 22 October 1801; Beresford (ed.), *Diary of a Country Parson*, v, 391, 1 June 1802.

63 BMC 9737, Roberts, 'John Bull's Prayer to Peace, or the Flight of Discord' ([1801]).

were highly ambiguous, sometimes portraying Fox as a bumbling and oafish fool, conniving with the French enemy, yet sometimes attacking Pitt and the King and Queen as threatening and even demonic figures. These depictions of the British elite were so powerful that Jacques-Louis David used them as models for his own propaganda campaign against the British government.[64] This ambiguity not only reflected the market for prints, and thus changes in public opinion on the war through the decade, but also perhaps, in the case of Gillray at least, the artist's own political thinking. He did work for a while from December 1797 for the *Anti-Jacobin Magazine and Review*, under Canning, for an annual pension of £200. This seems to have been in line with his ideological standpoint, because of his disillusionment with the French Revolution especially after the rise of Napoleon, in common with many; yet he retained a mind of his own and could not be relied upon to ply the government with constant support—indeed, the savagery of his satire was feared by government and radicals alike, even when he was employed by the government.[65] Many prints, therefore, were double-edged, such as his 'Opening the Budget;—or—John Bull giving his Breeches to save his Bacon' (1796), which showed Pitt scaring John Bull into paying extra taxes to defend the country against a rumoured invasion, but also Fox beckoning the French over.[66] Other graphic prints appeared to show neither approval nor disapproval of the war—they were not satirical, but simply portrayed British soldiers in their uniforms, or conveyed news of continental events.

Moreover, apart from the swings of floating opinion, popular opinion cannot always be read simply from appearances. Earlier in the century Dr Johnson had warned in *The False Alarm* (1770) of taking 'public opinion' at face value, citing various reasons why one might sign a petition other than conviction of its importance, such as to annoy the authorities or to prove one's literacy. Mark Philp issues a similar caution concerning the efficacy of the *Cheap Repository Tracts*, suggesting that it is more likely that they were 'taken as entertainment than as gospel'[67]—though it should be remembered that entertainment can often be influential. Apparently pro-war activities engaged in by ordinary people, then, were not necessarily motivated by pro-war sentiment. Certainly, even some who were loyalist in sympathy thought that the government's alarmism in late 1792, for example, was unnecessary or

---

64 Kate Watson, 'Popular Loyalists: Subjects or Citizens? Case Study: Hannah More and James Gillray', unpublished paper given at the Colloquium on British Eighteenth-Century History, 1688–1832 in London (January 1993), p.4.

65 Dickinson, *Caricatures and the Constitution*, p.16; George (ed.), *Political and Personal Satires*, vii, p.xiii; Robert L. Patten, *George Cruikshank's Life, Times and Art, vol. 1: 1792--1835* (London, 1992), p.71; Donald, *Age of Caricature*, pp.42–3.

66 BMC 8836 (17 November 1796).

67 Gunn, *Beyond Liberty and Property*, p.278; Philp, 'The Fragmented Ideology of Reform', p.70.

exaggerated. 'A great alarm is gone abroad in this country of danger to the State, more than there is I think sufficient ground for', wrote Edward Law to his brother, the Bishop of Elphin. Dr John Symonds told Arthur Young that Sir Henry Moncrieff-Wellwood and Dr Thomas Hardy, luminaries of the Church of Scotland, had 'laughed at Dundas's account of the political riots in Scotland. They absolutely denied the existence of them—considered them as political; and when you read Hardy's pamphlet [*The Patriot*, (1793)], you will see that he would not have failed setting them forth if they had deserved any consideration.'[68] Donald Ginter concluded that the Loyal Associations of 1792–93 'were so effective', that is, attracted such a heterogeneous membership, 'as to be a most unreliable gauge of public opinion'.[69]

Recruitment to the army or navy cannot necessarily be taken as a sign of sympathy with the war. Unemployed men were attracted by the offer of a paid job, prisoners by the chance of a life outside jail, poor men by the bounty, and some, like Parson Woodforde's boy, by the glamour they imagined to distinguish the military or naval life.[70] Although sailors might occasionally receive a small share of prize-money, there was little else to offer rank-and-file military and naval recruits much hope of reward: ordinary soldiers were not awarded government medals for bravery until Waterloo. One wonders if some joined the army simply because it licensed violence—some of the worst domestic violence involved soldiers in theatres attacking members of audiences who refused to remove their hats when the national anthem was played.[71] Some also offered their services to the Volunteers because they were unemployed, or because of pressure from landlords or employers.[72] Another powerful attraction of Volunteer service, which was limited to action within one's home locality, was its privilege of exemption from the militia ballot. Others were unwilling to volunteer, but claimed that should a real invasion occur, they would be active in helping to resist it.[73]

Professional officers might care only about the war as a stage in their careers, or for its impact on the army or navy as a whole. Sir Ralph Abercromby, according to Piers Mackesy, although he cared deeply for the reputation of the British army, was not ideologically committed to the struggle,

---

68 PRO 30/12/17/2, f.106, Edward Law to John Law, 12 November 1792; M. Bentham-Edwards, *The Autobiography of Arthur Young with Selections from his Correspondence* (London, 1898), p.238, Dr John Symonds to Young, 8 April 1793.

69 Ginter, 'The Loyalist Association Movement', p.187.

70 Beresford (ed.), *Diary of a Country Parson*, iv, 276, 10 May 1796.

71 Morris, 'The Monarchy as an Issue', pp.267–8.

72 See, for instance, *Caledonian Mercury*, 13 February 1797, for a likely example of this; also Andrew Mackillop, *'More Fruitful Than The Soil': Army, Empire and the Scottish Highlands* (forthcoming), chapter 7.

73 Emsley, *British Society and the French Wars*, p.74.

believing that opinions could not be controlled by force.[74] Military memoirs often betray no recognition of the ideological issues at stake, focusing simply on the movements and battles in which their authors were involved, leavened by occasional anecdotes concerning friends and commanding officers. Patriotic expressions of pride in all things British, with no particular element of ideological conflict, were common in both sailors and soldiers:

> St Vincent drubb'd the Dons, Earl Howe he drubb'd
> Mounseer,
> And Gallant Duncan now has soundly drubb'd Mynheer,
> Thus Spaniards, French and Dutch, tho' all united be,
> Fear not, Britannia cries, My Tars can beat all three.[75]

Many ordinary people may have participated in popular celebrations of British victories more for the fun and excitement of the occasion than from any real sentiments of support for the war. Effigies of Pitt were burned on twenty of the London bonfires set ablaze in honour of Duncan's victory at Camperdown in 1797. On the other hand, attacks on Dissenters or radicals who failed to illuminate their windows during victory celebrations were less motivated by political loyalty than by a desire to punish nonconformity.[76] Some gentlemen in North Yorkshire found themselves in a quandary in 1794, when they were faced with the question of voluntary subscriptions. They eventually chose to pay in order to lessen the burden of taxation on the poor and to support the preservation of domestic order, but they resented the implication that they therefore approved of the war.[77] Cruikshank's graphic print 'The Victorious Procession to St Paul's' (1797), highlighted the burden of taxation imposed on ordinary people and the difficulty they would find in celebrating naval victories in their straitened circumstances.

Material self-interest could also motivate pro-war behaviour. Linda Colley has suggested that Volunteering represented for some an opportunity to improve business: many who joined the local corps were shopkeepers or tradesmen who were aware that their fellow-Volunteers were potential customers.[78] Other tradesmen advertised their wares as being particularly useful to Volunteers and other military men, from shoe-blacking to sheet music and luggage. War-time mementoes produced for the fashionably patriotic were many and varied—

---

74 Mackesy, *Statesmen at War*, p.138.

75 NMM, DUN/19, f.1.

76 Emsley, *British Society and the French Wars*, p.27; Wells, 'English Society and Revolutionary Politics', p.209; BMC 9046, Cruikshank, 'The Victorious Procession to St Paul's, or Billy's Grand Triumphal Entry a Prelude' (11 December 1797); Bohstedt, *Riots and Community Politics*, p.24.

77 Ashcroft, *To Escape the Monster's Clutches*, pp.19–20.

78 Colley, *Britons*, pp.300-2.

Nelson bonnets and silk sashes, crocodile bonnets, Nile plumes, music composed in commemoration of British victories, and so on.

Local politics has recently been shown to be another powerful influence which often stimulated apparently loyalist and pro-war behaviour. Local urban elites had much to gain from creating the appearance of a town united in its loyalty and patriotism, whether or not they were necessarily genuinely convinced of the merits of the government's case. Such a presentation of united civic loyalty and patriotism could act as an indirect but significant form of pressure on radical or liberal members of the local populace, who were inclined to oppose the war or other government policies and to undermine the urban social and political order. It might also stir up the apathetic to add their mites to the public effort. It could enhance the provincial importance of the members of the local propertied ranks by providing public positions and tasks for them, for instance in the Volunteers or in the organization of subscriptions, and by stressing the popularity of their activities and the patriotic value of their contributions. Finally, it might also enhance their national reputation as the governors of such a loyal and patriotic town.[79] Patriotic or loyal activities were often, indeed, evidently designed to exclude the poor, such as charity sermons attracting such fashionable attendance that there was no room for the poor to be admitted; charity balls; printed subscription lists which rarely acknowledged donations of less than five shillings; or the exemption of Volunteers from the tax on hair powder, which clearly supposed that many Volunteers would benefit from such a concession.

Similarly, however, activities which might have given the appearance of hostility to the war were not always influenced by anti-war sentiment. William Chaytor, chairman of the Quarter Sessions of the North Riding of Yorkshire, regretted the paucity of Volunteers in the district, but he thought that this was caused by 'the people in general being of opinion there is no prospect of an attack upon this country by the French rather than want of inclination to stand forward in its defence'.[80] Anxieties concerning trade and the scarcity of food at affordable prices were not necessarily vented in anger at the war, either. The Marquess of Lansdowne wrote to Admiral John Duckworth in December 1800:

> Our own interior is sadly clouded, not by any apprehension from abroad, for the people seem still insensible to the state of foreign politics, but are dreadfully alive to apprehensions of scarcity and fear of Famine.[81]

---

79 79 Paul Langford, *Public Life and the Propertied Englishman 1689--1798* (Oxford, 1991); Cookson, *The British Armed Nation*, e.g. pp.1, 5, 225ff., 236ff.

80 Ashcroft, *To Escape the Monster's Clutches*, p.54. See also Philp, 'Thompson, Godwin and the French Revolution', p.98.

81 NMM, DUC/6, Lansdowne to Duckworth, 4 December 1800.

Likewise, the sale of insurance against the militia ballot was clearly a demonstration of opportunism rather than a statement of anti-war sentiment.

Graphic prints in the 1790s usually demonstrated the views of the literate classes of British society, but their general reflection of the mercurial nature of public opinion on the wars against revolutionary France provides an accurate picture of popular views throughout society below the governing elite. Serving officers were no more united in their views on the war than were the general public. In the 1800s, when the threat of invasion was still more imminent, the grounds of war were much more clear-cut and comprehensible, and the figure of Napoleon was successfully made into an easy target for popular antipathy, British public opinion became much more united and inflexible in support of the government and in virulent hostility towards France.

The 1790s, however, saw constant variations in the public mood. Most people tended to respond to events as they happened, and particularly as they impinged upon their own lives, rather than to hold to one particular standpoint throughout the decade. The loud enthusiasm of February 1793 soon became subdued into resignation and fatalism in the face of economic hardship at home and military failure abroad. Victories temporarily rekindled morale in June 1794, October 1797 and August 1798, but while the government was given general public aquiescence in its conduct of the war, the public mood seems to have been one of resignation rather than of inspired and eager cooperation. The obscurity of the government's case against France in the 1790s made it much more difficult for them to carry public opinion with them than it would be in the 1800s, which was precisely Burke's charge against them. As John Ehrman notes, public loyalty and disaffection co-existed uneasily throughout the decade—order with unrest, subversion with counter-propaganda, discipline and patriotism with desertion and mutiny, attacks on the King with thousands of loyal addresses addressing him with reverent affection. Loyalist and radical activity were simply two ends of the spectrum along which public opinion—including, perhaps, most loyalists and most radicals—shifted back and forth depending on external and private circumstances. John Dinwiddy has argued that circumstances were more important in the success obtained by conservative propagandists in the British debate over the French Revolution than the superiority of their arguments and ideology over the radical case.[82] Circumstances were probably very important in determining public opinion on the war at any given time in the decade, but they did not allow a clear judgement on the general pro-war/anti-war competition in the 1790s to the same extent as that on the Revolution debate, which was more clearly won by the conservatives.

82 Ehrman, *The Reluctant Transition*, pp.155–6; Dinwiddy, 'Interpretations of anti-Jacobinism', p.48.

Conclusion

The wars against revolutionary France provoked many very practical responses from the British people. Economic, political or personal gain or loss (or their prospect) naturally determined the views of probably the majority of the population. Pittites, Portland Whigs and loyalists, by and large, did well politically out of the war. Pitt himself resigned in 1801, taking with him a substantial part of his Cabinet; but he did not go because of unpopularity caused by the war. Rather, he resigned over the substantially unrelated issue of Roman Catholic emancipation, on which he disagreed with the King, and probably also because his health was suffering badly from the long and heavy strain of conducting the British war effort. He was back in power in 1804, and he remained there until his death in 1806. The Foxites and the radicals tried hard to make political capital from the conflict, but they usually failed dismally. Instead of heaping opprobrium on the government, they more often succeeded in bringing it on themselves by making themselves vulnerable to the charge of support for the French armies and disloyalty to their own country. Most people probably made up their minds on the war according to how it personally affected them, economically or otherwise. Businesses flourished or withered; commerce prospered or was stunted; employment in individual trades expanded or contracted; prices rose or fell. Many were wounded or bereaved; some made their careers and some found fame. Most of those who lived on the south coast favoured the strengthening of the British defences against a French invasion attempt; many throughout the country were outraged by the activities of crimps and press-gangs.

Nevertheless, there was also a lively debate on many more ideological issues raised by the war throughout the 1790s, and this determined the attitudes of a minority to the conflict, notably Edmund Burke and the war crusaders, the radicals at the start of the war and churchmen. So much is uncontroversial. But ideas were also important in moulding the views of many others, including the government, Fox and his supporters, the radicals after 1793 and the loyalists, for all of whom the war was secondary to their first ambition or loyalty. Ideology was important to their opinions on the conflict partly because it was impossible to separate the war from the Revolution, and partly because Burke, as the earliest writer to express a forceful and cogent view of war against the French Revolutionary regime, was enormously influential.

Thus, the legitimacy of the war was debated heatedly throughout the decade, on moral, religious and political grounds. Was war ever to be justified? Could military hostility to a set of opinions be morally permissible? Was an armed conflict against the French Revolution desirable, and had it been provoked or not? The necessity of the war was argued as vigorously, in terms of politics, the economy, commerce, religion, and military and strategic interests. The aims of the war were also discussed. Should Britain be fighting to obtain territory in Europe, or rather new colonies elsewhere? Was the defeat of the French Revolution necessary, or would a change of the French government prove sufficient? Was it morally justifiable to pursue either of these latter objectives? Was the government really waging war abroad at least partly in order to suppress British civil liberty at home? Opinion also varied, therefore, on the nature of the conflict, whether it was purely territorial or partially or fully ideological, and whether it was defensive or aggressive. In a war on such a large scale, materially, geographically and temporally, it was inevitable that many opinions would be held concerning its conduct. Many views were aired on whether it would best be fought mainly by the navy or also by the army in conjunction with the allied armies, and on whether Britain should concentrate its efforts in the colonies, in the Mediterranean, on the continent or within France itself. The desirability of the involvement of women and of the lower classes in the British war effort was also discussed and, where favourably, to what extent and in what roles. Finally, peace was a constant topic of controversy. When could it be safe to treat with the revolutionary rulers of France, if ever? What, indeed, would constitute peace? What conditions ought Britain to demand, and what concessions, if any, should it yield?

British battle-lines over the French Revolution had largely been drawn before the outbreak of war in February 1793 and they remained little altered by it in the 1790s. While it seems that most ordinary people were less influenced by the ideological issues surrounding the conflict than by its practical impact on them, the nature of the printed controversy over the war and its close relation to the debate on the French Revolution suggests that, in the 1790s, politically literate British opinion perceived the role of ideology in the wars against revolutionary France to be significant.

Edmund Burke's views on the conflict were clearly born of his analysis of the French Revolution: having determined that the Revolution was a menace to the British constitution and to the political, social, religious and moral order of all Europe, he was convinced that it must be destroyed militarily by defeating its armies and restoring the pre-revolutionary government and social order of France as well as by exposing its doctrines as deceptive, false and wicked. This, to Burke, was the whole purpose of the war, and any diversification of British aims was a boost to the enemy cause. The British government, by the nature of its role, had to pay more attention to strategic and economic realities than did

Burke, and it was less preoccupied by the truth or falsehood of revolutionary principles in the abstract. Only a few ministers pressed for the objective of overthrowing the French revolutionary government to be accepted, let alone that of replacing it with a restored Bourbon monarchy. Nevertheless, all ministers were very aware of the danger of these principles becoming popular in Britain and they made strenuous efforts to help ensure that they did not; moreover, they recognized that the French foreign policy, and its conduct, which antagonized them to the point of warfare and which prevented them from negotiating before 1796 and between 1798–1801, emanated from the revolutionary administration of French affairs. Crusading commentators and pamphleteers sympathized with Burke's views and placed a corresponding importance on ideological hostility, though they were less rigid in their insistence upon it than was Burke. Loyalists' views were highly coloured by similar thinking, but they were more concerned to defend the government and its actions than were the crusaders and they were therefore less tied to ideological warfare and more ready to contemplate and even to support traditional colonial, maritime and continental objectives and strategies. They were also considerably more willing to accept the necessity of peace negotiations, for the sake of a war-weary nation, before the Revolution in France could be said to have been overthrown.

The attitudes of radical politicians to the conflict were, like Burke's, clearly determined by their opinion of the French Revolution. Their sympathy for the Revolution and their disgust with the British constitution caused them to oppose vigorously a war which appeared to be waged for the purpose of crushing the republican government they so admired. As the war wore on, however, they increasingly also tried to enlist discontent with war-time conditions to their own cause of opposition to the government and, more fundamentally, hostility to the current political system in Britain. Thus, the war became more important to them as a means of stirring up discontent than as a primary object of contention. Fox and his supporters also opposed the war because they sympathized with the French Revolutionary cause, but they, perhaps even more than the radicals, were also concerned to make use of the war to criticize the government, and ultimately that was more important to them than support for the French. The Friends of Peace were more anxious to attack the conflict because it was a war at all than because it was a war fought against the French Revolution; nevertheless, in expressing their disapproval of military opposition to political or religious opinions, they entered the British war of ideas. Churchmen articulated their support for or opposition to the war in highly ideological forms. Politically literate and interested women aligned themselves with one or other of these stances, recognizing the significance of ideas on the conflict as well as engaging in the separate debate over the proper roles of women.

This view, that politically literate opinion in Britain understood the role of ideology in the wars against revolutionary France to be at least significant, if not crucial, is reinforced by contrasting the 1790s with a projection into the following decade of Napoleonic warfare. The Peace of Amiens collapsed in May 1803 after it had become clear that Napoleon had no intention of halting his pursuit of continental hegemony. Britain demanded control of Malta to balance growing French influence in Switzerland and northern Italy, and eventually replied to continued French refusals with a declaration of war. From this time until the end of the war in 1815, British society displayed a much greater degree of unity in support of the conflict than had been the case in the 1790s.[1]

Some British radicals continued to admire Napoleon as a 'son of the Revolution', but the majority of the population associated him with military despotism and aggression. France no longer defended 'French principles' of democracy or republicanism, nor hid behind such a claim, but seemed to lust shamelessly after territorial power and control, eyeing greedily even Britain. Some liberal opponents of the war had already renounced their support of the French in the late 1790s in favour of the British war effort; with the advent of the threat of Napoleon's 'Army of England', many more who had been hostile to the war, or who had been uncommitted to supporting or opposing it, came to favour the war effort against France. After the failure of his invasion attempt had been sealed at Trafalgar, Napoleon's attempts to paralyze Britain economically by a blockade of continental Europe against British commerce hardened many others against him. The case for a defensive war appeared to be much more persuasive, and even those who continued to oppose Britain's involvement in the conflict, such as the Friends of Peace, might be persuaded to participate in defensive measures in such crises as the invasion scare of 1803–5. The war against Napoleon was thus much more popular than the conflict against the French Revolution had been. Resistance to recruiting diminished, as did radical criticism of the government.

On the other hand, opposition to the war in the 1800s was rarely caused by ideological sympathy for the French government or cause. The Friends of Peace continued to oppose it on grounds of religion and morality, but they were also much more successful than they had been in the 1790s in harnessing the economic discontent of industrial and manufacturing interests, in the north and Midlands of England particularly.[2] General public opinion in the 1790s was

---

1 See, for instance, Peter Spence, *The Birth of Romantic Radicalism. War, Popular Politics and English Radical Reformism, 1800–1815* (Aldershot, 1996).

2 See Cookson, *Friends of Peace*, pp.215–29; B.H. Tolley, 'The Liverpool Campaign Against the Orders in Council and the War of 1812', in J.R. Harris (ed.), *Liverpool and Merseyside* (London, 1969), pp.98–146; D.J. Moss, 'Birmingham and the Campaigns Against the Orders in Council and East India Company Charter, 1812–1813', *Canadian Journal of History*, xiv (1976), 173–88.

moved by similar considerations of defensive or economic interests, but there is also substantial evidence of a debate for and against the war in that decade which was motivated by political opposition to and sympathy for the revolutionary regime in France.

To the extent that comment on the war had any influence on its contemporary readers or hearers, it may have helped to strengthen British consciousness of national identity.[3] The debate on the war did not divide chiefly along regional borders, but rather over opinion on the French Revolution. Supporters and opponents of the war could be found throughout Great Britain. Most loyalist pamphlets on the conflict emphasized the threat posed by Revolutionary France to the components of what they portrayed as 'traditional' British identity: its laws, religion, constitution, liberty and property. Cruder loyalist propaganda also employed the notion of 'Britishness' in opposition to that of 'Frenchness', whether of ideas or of way of life. Pamphlets and propaganda which denounced the war did not do so on the basis of its adverse effects on any particular part of the country. Those who engaged in the debate may therefore have had their awareness of Britain as a national entity reinforced. However, it is highly questionable what material influence the polemic on the war had in this respect for the wider community. As we have seen, most ordinary people seem to have been affected by the ideological debate on the war only marginally, and its effectiveness in strengthening British national identity must have been further diminished by the vitality of localism as a factor in shaping many activists' attitudes to the war.[4]

To recognize this, and yet to focus on the ideological component of the conflict may be to run the risk of tunnel vision. Ideological warfare was clearly not the only aspect of Britain's struggle against France in the 1790s. Yet to downplay or reject the role of ideas is to neglect a very common contemporary perspective on the war. Since the majority of British commentators clearly accepted this perspective or remarked upon it, noting it as a distinctive characteristic, a grasp of the war of ideas is necessary to a proper understanding of the British war against revolutionary France. If ideas were not the sole component of British hostility to France, neither were strategic interests. As Lord Stair told the House of Lords in January 1794,

> If France were to depart from her recently avowed principles, if she would disavow her declared design of meddling with the constitution and government of other nations, every friend to his country would wish to make peace with her and leave her to herself; but in the present situation of affairs, he was convinced

---

3 Cf. Colley, *Britons*.

4 Cf. Langford, *Public Life and the Propertied Englishman*; Cookson, *The British Armed Nation*.

that nothing but the most vigorous perseverance would secure permanent tranquility.[5]

5 *P.H.*, xxx, 1064, Lord Stair, 21 January 1794.

Bibliography

The place of publication is London, unless otherwise stated.

Primary Sources

Manuscript Sources

British Library, London

Auckland Papers	Additional Manuscripts 36814, 38229, 38230, 42774, 45728, 45729.
	Egmont Manuscripts 3504.
Dundas Papers	Additional Manuscripts 34448, 34454, 34907, 35670, 35671, 37274, 38192, 38310, 38734–6, 38759, 40100, 40102.
Fox Papers	Additional Manuscripts 47565, 47569, 47571.
Grenville Papers	Additional Manuscripts 34442–34455, 34933, 35544, 36808–36810, 37077, 37846, 37850, 38228–38232, 38310, 38734, 40101, 41199, 41852, 42058.
Pitt Papers	Additional Manuscripts 27916, 33964, 34450–6, 38192, 38310, 40102, 40862, 42772, 46519.
Windham Papers	Additional Manuscripts 37843–4.

National Maritime Museum, Greenwich

Bridport Papers	MKH/510
Collingwood Papers	COL/14
Cornwallis Papers	COR/60
Cunningham Papers	CUN/1
Duckworth Papers	DUC/2–7
Duncan Papers	DUN/19–20
Flinders Papers	FLI/1, FLI/4
Grant Papers	GRA/1–10
Graves Papers	GRV/110
Howe Papers	HOW/2
Keats Papers	KEA/1
Melville Papers	MEL/2, MEL/6, MEL/9
Nepean Papers	NEP/4–8
Parker Papers	PAR/165 (1–4), PAR/188 (1–2)
Pole Papers	WYN/101–108

Public Record Office, Kew

Chatham Papers	PRO 30/8/101, 30/8/102, 30/8/197, 30/8/334, 30/8/335(3), 30/12/17/2.
Foreign Office Papers	PRO FO 7/59, 60.

War Office Papers PRO WO 1/344.
Home Office Papers PRO HO 42/ 20-37, HO 50/40, 385.

Cambridgeshire County Record Office, Cambridge
Correspondence of the Huddlestons of Sawston 488/C2, 488/C3

Published Primary Sources

Newspapers and Periodicals
Annals of Agriculture, xvii (1792), xxvi–xxviii (1796–97).
The Anti-Jacobin Review and Magazine, i (1798)–v (1800).
Caledonian Mercury, 1792–1802.
Critical Review, 12 (1794), 39 (1803).
Gentleman's Magazine, 65 (1795), 67 (1797).
Lady's Magazine, 26 (1795), 29 (1798), 30 (1799), 33 (1802).
London Gazette, 1792–1802.
Morning Chronicle, 1793–1800.
Sun, 1793–96, 1799–1800.
The Times, 1792–1802.

British Library, London
Miscellaneous anonymous songs, handbills and broadsheets, catalogue reference 648.c.26.
Banks, Sophia Sarah, Collection of broadsides, newspaper cuttings and engravings, held in the British Library, catalogue reference LR 301.h.6.

Cambridge University Library
Miscellaneous anonymous songs in the Madden Collection.

Pamphlets and Books
Account of the Proceedings at a General Meeting of the L.C.S. convened by public advertisement, and held in an inclosed field, behind the Long Room, Borough Road, St. George's Fields, on Monday, the 29th of June, 1795 (1795).
The Address of the British Convention, assembled at Edinburgh, November 19, 1793, to the People of Great Britain (1793).
An Address to the English Nation: with a Slight Sketch of the Existing Grievances, and a Recommendation to Petition with Vigour, as a Means of Obtaining a Repeal of Pitt and Grenville's Bills (1796).
Advice to the People, on the Prospect of a Peace. By a freeholder of the County of Surry (Edinburgh, 1796).
An Alarm to the Public, and a Bounty Promised to Every Loyal Subject, who will come forward to repel the enemy (Yarmouth, 1798).
The Anti-Gallican Songster (1793).
The Anti-Levelling Songster (1793).
An Appeal to the Head and Heart of Every Man and Woman in Great Britain, respecting the Threatened French Invasion, and the Importance of Immediately Coming Forward with Voluntary Contributions (1798).

An Appeal to the Moral Feelings of Samuel Thornton, Rowland Burdon, Hawkins Brown, Esq.rs, and to Every Member of the House of Commons who conscientiously supports the Present Administration. In a Letter to William Wilberforce, Esq. (1797).

Ask, and you shall have, or, the source of public grievances displayed, and their remedies pointed out. (n.p., n.d.).

The Blessings of War ([1795]).

Brief Reflexions, on the Correspondence between Lord Grenville and M. Otto, in August and September, 1800 (1800).

Britannia's Address to Her People (1793).

Comments on the Proposed War with France (1793).

Considerations on the French War (1794).

Considerations on the Principal Objections Against Overtures for Peace with France (1795).

The Contrast, or Two Portraits of the Right Honourable Charles James Fox (Edinburgh, [1793]).

'A Country Curate's Advice to Manufacturers', in *Liberty and Property Preserved Against Republicans and Levellers. A Collection of Tracts*, i ([1792]), pp.9–14.

The Crisis Stated; or serious and seasonable hints upon war in general, and upon the consequences of a war with France (Edinburgh, 1793).

DECLARATION. His Majesty's benevolent Endeavours to restore to His People the Blessings of Secure and honorable Peace, again repeated without success (Westminster, 1797).

A Defence of the Political and Parliamentary Conduct of the Right Honourable Edmund Burke (1794).

Desultory Thoughts on the Atrocious Cruelties of the French Nation (Bath, 1794).

The Dog and Bitch, and the Bees and Drones: Fables. With Applications, Moral and Political, adapted to the Times (Leeds, [1795]).

The Dutch Expedition Vindicated; with brief observations on the emigrants (1799).

'The Englishman and the Frenchman', in *Liberty and Property Preserved Against Republicans and Levellers. A Collection of Tracts*, iii ([1792]), pp.4–7.

The Evidence Summed Up; or a statement of the apparent causes and objects of the war (1794).

Facts, Reflections, and Queries, submitted to the consideration of the Associated Friends of the People (Edinburgh, [1792]).

Fast Day as Observed at Sheffield (1794).

A Few Plain Questions to the Working People of Scotland (Edinburgh, 1792).

A Few Words But No Lies; From Roger Bull to his Brother Thomas (1792).

The First Fruits of the French Revolution (Edinburgh, 1793).

Five Minutes Advice to the People of Great Britain (1792).

A Form of Prayer (1793), for the fast-day of 19 April 1793.

A Form of Prayer (1797), for the fast-day of 8 March 1797.

A Form of Prayer and Thanksgiving (1797), for 12 March 1797.

A Form of Prayer and Thanksgiving (1797), for 29 October 1797.

A Form of Prayer and Thanksgiving (1797), for 19 December 1797.

A Form of Prayer (1801), for the fast-day of 13 February 1801.

A Form of Prayer and Thanksgiving (1802).

French Famine (1795).

A Full, True, and Particular Account of the Birth, parentage and Education, Life, Character and Behaviour of that most notoriously notified malefactor WILLY PITTO (n.p., n.d.).

Further Authentic Proofs of French Perfidy and Cruelty ([1798]).

A general address to the representatives of Great Britain, on important national subjects, agitating at the present period. By an elector, M.A. (1797).

The History of a Good Bramin. To Which is Annexed, an Essay on the Reciprocal Contempt of Nations, Proceeding from their Vanity (1795).

An Impartial History of the War, from the Commencement of the Revolution in France (Manchester, 1799).

Inquiry into the Causes and Remedies of the Late and Present Scarcity and High Price of Provisions (1800).

A Letter from a Chancellor, out of office, to a King in Power (1795).

A Letter from an Independent Elector of Westminster to the Rt Hon. Charles James Fox (1793).

A Letter to the Greatest Hypocrite in His Majesty's Dominions ([1794]).

A Letter to the Right Hon. Charles James Fox; in which is proved the absolute necessity of an immediate declaration of war against France (1793).

Letters from Simkin the Second to his brother Simon (1796).

Mast and Acorns: Collected by Old Hubert ([1793]).

Observations Upon the Present War with France (Glasgow, 1793).

Our Good Old Castle on the Rock: or Union the One Thing Needful. Addressed to the People of England (1798).

Pax in Bello; or a Few Reflexions on the Prospect of Peace, arising out of Present Circumstances of the War (1796).

Peace. Reasons Why Terms of Peace Should Be Offered to the French Nation (1795).

'A Picture of True and False Liberty', in *Liberty and Property Preserved from Republicans and Levellers. A Collection of Tracts*, v (1792), pp.11-14.

'The Plot found out', in *Liberty and Property Preserved Against Republicans and Levellers. A Collection of Tracts*, iii ([1792]), pp.1–4.

The Poetical Works of S.T. Coleridge, Chandos edition (London and New York, n.d.).

A Political Dictionary for the Guinea-Less Pigs (n.p., n.d.).

The Principal Acts of the General Assembly of the Church of Scotland (Edinburgh, 1788–1803).

Proclamation for a General Fast (1795).

Reasons Against National Despondency (1797).

Reasons Against Refusing to Negotiate with France. By an Approver of the Measures of Administration, During the Former Periods of the War (1800).

Reply to the Sermon preached before the Lords Spiritual and Temporal, on Wednesday, January 30th, 1793, by Samuel, Lord Bishop of St. David's (1793).

The Retort Politic on Master Burke; or, a Few Words en Passant: Occasioned by His Two Letters on a Regicide Peace. From a Tyro of his own school, but of another class (1796).

A Retrospect; illustrating the necessity of an immediate peace with the Republic of France (Margate, 1796).

Revolutions without Bloodshed; or, Reformation Preferable to Revolt (1794).

The Rights of Man (n.p., n.d.).

The Rights of Princes (n.p., n.d.).

To the Right Honourable Edmund Burke by a Member of the Revolution Society (1790).

Rule Britannia! (Ipswich, 1793).

A Sermon, Composed for the Late General Fast, Observed on the Eighth of March, 1797. By a Minister of the Church of England (1797).

A Sketch of the Campaign of 1793 (1795).

The Soldier's Friend (1793).

Some Account of a Very Seditious Book, lately found upon Wimbledon Common (1794).

A Speech, in which the Question of a War with France is Stated and Examined. By a Lover of his Country (Birmingham, 1793).

Strictures on the Overtures of Peace, made by the chief executive magistrate of France, to His Majesty the King of Great Britain, and on the answer, transmitted by Lord Grenville (1800).

Thoughts on a Peace with France; With Some Observations on Mr. Burke's Two Letters, on Proposals for Peace with the Regicide Directory (1796).

Thoughts on the Defence of these Kingdoms (1796).

Thoughts on the New and Old Principles of Political Obedience (1793).

Three Words on the War (Edinburgh, 1793).

The Voice of the People, &c. (n.p., n.d.).

The Voice of Truth to the People of England, of all ranks and descriptions, on occasion of Lord Malmesbury's return from Lisle (1797).

War With France! or, Who Pays the Reckoning? (1793).

Warning to Tyrants (n.p., n.d.).

The Wrongs of Man. Consisting of Extracts from PIGOTT'S Political Dictionary, and others (1795).

Agutter, William, *Observations on the General Fast of the Year 1796* (1796).

____, *An Address to Every British Subject on the Late Important Victories* (1798).

____, *Deliverance from Enemies a ground for Thanksgiving. A Sermon, preached on the Day of General Thanksgiving, Dec. 19, 1797* (1798).

____, *The Faithful Soldier and True Christian; and the miseries of rebellion, considered in two sermons* (Northampton, 1798).

Annesley, Alexander, *Strictures on the True Cause of the Present Alarming Scarcity of Grain and other Provisions: and a Plan for Permanent Relief* ([1800]).

Ashcroft, M.Y. (ed.), *To Escape the Monster's Clutches. Notes and Documents illustrating the preparations in North Yorkshire to repel the invasion threatened by the French from 1793* (North Yorkshire County Record Office Publications no.15, November 1977).

Aspinall, A. (ed.), *The Later Correspondence of George III*, 5 vol.s (Cambridge University Press, 1962–68), i–iv.

Buddle Atkinson, R.H.M. and Jackson, G.A. (eds), *Brougham and His Early Friends. Letters to James Loch 1798–1809*, 3 vol.s (1908), i.

B., A., *Letters on the Character and Writings of Mr. Burke, by A. B. Published in the Scots Chronicle* ([Edinburgh, 1797]).

Balderston, Katharine C. (ed.), *Thraliana. The Diary of Mrs. Hester Lynch Thrale (later Mrs. Piozzi) 1776–1809*, 2nd edition, 2 vol.s (Oxford, 1951), ii.

[Barbauld, Mrs.], *Sins of Government, Sins of the Nation; or, a Discourse for the Fast, Appointed on April 19, 1793. By a Volunteer*, 2nd edition (1793).

[____], *Reasons for National Penitence, recommended for the Fast, appointed February XXVIII, 1794* (1794).

[Barrington, Shute], *A Fast Sermon for February the 27th, 1799, from Isaiah x.5* (1799).

Belsham, William, *Remarks on a Late Publication, styled The History of the Politics of Great Britain & France, &c. &c.* (1800).

____, *Reply to the Rev. Herbert Marsh's Vindication* (1801).

____, *Remarks on the Late Definitive Treaty of Peace, signed at Amiens, March 25, 1802* (1802).

Bennett, Betty T. (ed.), *British War Poetry in the Age of Romanticism, 1793–1815* (New York and London, 1976).

Bentham-Edwards, M. (ed.), *The Autobiography of Arthur Young, with Selections from his Correspondence* (1898).

Bentley, Thomas, *The Poor Man's Answer to the Rich Associators* (1793).

____, *Seasonable Advice to all People of Power, or wealth. Rulers of Britain, Civil and Ecclesiastic, Look upon France and Tremble!* (1793).

____, *A Warning to Britons of all Ranks; especially the King, the Parliament, and the Clergy* (1794).

[Bentley], *A Letter to the Rt Hon. Charles James Fox, upon the Dangerous and Inflammatory Tendency of his Late Conduct in Parliament* (1793).

[Bentley, Thomas Richard], *Considerations upon the State of Public Affairs at the Beginning of the Year 1796* (1796).

[____], *Considerations upon the State of Public Affairs, at the beginning of the year MDCCXCVIII—in three parts* (1798).

Beresford, John (ed.), *The Diary of a Country Parson: the Reverend James Woodforde, 1758–1802*, 5 vol.s (Oxford University Press, 1924–31), iii–v.

Bessborough, Earl of (ed.), *Georgiana. Extracts from the Correspondence of Georgiana, Duchess of Devonshire* (Murray, 1955).

Bicheno, James, *The signs of the times: or, The overthrow of the papal tyranny in France, the prelude of destruction to popery and despotism; but of peace to mankind*, 4th edition (1794).

____, *A Word in Season: or, a Call to the Inhabitants of Great Britain to Stand Prepared for the Consequences of the Present War. Written on the Fast-Day, Feb.25, 1795* (London and Edinburgh, 1795).

Bigge, Thomas, *Considerations on the State of Parties, and the Means of Effecting a Reconciliation Between Them*, 2nd edition (n.p., n.d.).

Black, Alexander, *National Blessings Considered and Improved, in a Sermon, preached on Thursday, November 29, 1798* (Edinburgh, 1798).

Black, William, *Reasons for Preventing the French, Under the Mask of Liberty, from Trampling Upon Europe* (1792).

Blair, Hugh, 'On the Love of Our Country' (Edinburgh, 1793), in *Sermons*, 5 vol.s (1818), v, 124–50.

Boothby, Sir Brooke, *Observations on the Appeal from the New to the Old Whigs, and on Mr. Paine's Rights of Man* (1792).

Bowdler, John, *Reform or Ruin: Take Your Choice!* 5th edition (1798).

Bowles, John, *Considerations on the Respective Rights of Judge and Jury: Particularly upon Trials for Libel* (1791).

____, *A Letter to the Right Hon. Charles James Fox; occasioned by his late Motion in the House of Commons respecting Libels* (1791).

____, *A Protest Against Thomas Paine's Rights of Man* (1792).

____, *A Second Letter to the Right Hon. Charles James Fox, upon the Matter of Libel* (1792).

____, *Dialogues on the Rights of Britons, between a Farmer, a Sailor, and a Manufacturer —in three parts* (1792–93).

____, *The Real Grounds of the Present War with France* (1793).

____, *A Short Answer to the Declaration of the Persons Calling Themselves the Friends of the Liberty of the Press* (1793).

____, *Farther Reflections Submitted to the Consideration of the Combined Powers* (1794).

____, *Objections to the Continuance of the War Examined and Refuted*, 2nd edition (1794).

____, *Reflections Submitted to the Consideration of the Combined Powers* (1794).

____, *The Dangers of Premature Peace* (1795).

____, *Thoughts on the Origin and Formation of Political Constitutions. Suggested by the recent attempt to frame another new constitution for France* (1795).

____, *Two Letters Addressed to a British Merchant, a short time before the meeting of the new Parliament in 1796* (1795).

____, *French aggression, proved from Mr Erskine's 'View of the causes of the war'; with reflections on the original character of the French revolution, and on the supposed durability of the French republic* (1797).

____, *A Third Letter to a British Merchant: containing reflections on the foreign and domestic politics of this country, together with strictures on the conduct of opposition* (1797).

____, *Postscript to 'The Real Grounds'* (1798).

____, *The Retrospect; or, A Collection of Tracts, Published at various periods of the war* (1798).

____, *Reflections on the Political State of Society at the Commencement of the Year 1800* (1800).

____, *Reflections at the Conclusion of the War*, 2nd edition (1801).

____, *Reflections on the Political and Moral State of Society, at the close of the eighteenth century* (1801).

____, *Remarks on Modern Female Manners, as Distinguished by Indifference to Character, and Indecency of Dress* (1802).

____, *Thoughts on the late General Election, as demonstrative of the Progress of Jacobinism, etc.* (1802).

____, *A View of the Moral State of Society at the Close of the Eighteenth Century* (1804).

____, *A Dispassionate Inquiry into the Best Means of National Safety* (1806).

[____], *Letters of the Ghost of Alfred, Addressed to the Hon. Thomas Erskine, and the Hon. Charles James Fox, on the Occasion of the State Trials at the Close of the Year 1794, and the Beginning of the Year 1795* (1798).

Broadley, A.M. (ed.), *The Journal of a British Chaplain in Paris during the peace negotiations of 1801–2; from the unpublished manuscript of the Rev. Dawson Warren, unofficially attached to the Diplomatic Mission of Mr. Francis James Jackson* (1913).

[Broome, Ralph], *Strictures on Mr. Burke's Two Letters, addressed to a Member of the Present Parliament* (1796).

Brown, Polemophilus, *A Sermon, Preached on the Day of General Fast, February 27, 1799* (1799).

Brown, William Laurence, *The Spirit of the Times Considered. A Sermon, preached in the English Church at Utrecht, February 13, 1793, the day appointed by the States for the General Thanksgiving, Fasting and Prayer* (1793).

____, *The Influence of Religion on National Prosperity. A sermon (Ps. xxxiii.12), etc.* (Aberdeen, 1796).

____, *The Proper Method of Defending Religious Truth in Times of Prevailing Infidelity. A sermon, preached before the synod of Aberdeen, October 11th, 1796, etc.* (Aberdeen, 1796).

____, *An examination of the causes and conduct of the present war with France; and of the most effectual means of obtaining peace; together with some observations on the late negotiations at Lisle* (1798).

____, 'A View of the Present Times, with regard to religion and morals, and other important subjects' in John Leland (ed.), *A View of the Present Times, with regard to religion and morals, and other important subjects* (1798).

Bruce, Archibald, *A Peaceable Declaration of the Sentiments of a Number of Presbyterians in Scotland, relative to the War between France and Great-Britain* (Edinburgh, 1797).

____, *A Penitential Epistle and Humble Supplication to His Holiness the Pope, in the name of the people of Great-Britain, for a perfect reconciliation and perpetual alliance with Rome* (Edinburgh, 1797).

____, *A Brief Statement and Declaration of the Genuine Principles of Seceders, respecting Civil Government; the Duty of Subjects; and National Reformation: and a Vindication of their Conduct in Reference to some late plans and societies for Political Reform; and the Public Dissentions of our Time. Proposed and Read in a Meeting of the General Associate Synod in Scotland* (Edinburgh, 1799).

[____], *A Serious View of the Remarkable Providences of the Times* (Glasgow, 1795).

Bunbury, Sir Henry, *Narratives of Some Passages in the Great War with France, 1799–1810* (1927).

Burges, Sir James Bland (ed.), *Alfred's Letters; or, a Review of the Political State of Europe, to the End of the Summer 1792. As Originally Published in the Sun* (1793).

Burke, Edmund, 'An Appeal from the New to the Old Whigs', in *The Works of the Right Honourable Edmund Burke*, Bohn edition, 6 vol.s (1883–86), iii, 1–115.

____, *The Writings and Speeches of Edmund Burke*, eds Paul Langford et al., 10 vol.s (Oxford: Clarendon Press, 1981ff.), viii and ix.

Burney (D'Arblay), Fanny, *Brief Reflections Relative to the Emigrant French Clergy: Earnestly Submitted to the Humane Consideration of the Ladies of Great Britain* (1793).

Burton, J. Hill (ed.), *Autobiography of Rev. Dr Carlyle* (Edinburgh and London, 1860).

Butler, Weeden, *Philanthropy, Religion, and Loyalty, the Best Characteristics of a Christian Soldier. A Sermon, Addressed to the Armed Association of the Parish of Saint Luke, Chelsea, and to the Inhabitants at Large, on Sunday, 8th July, 1798* (1798).

Canning, George, *The Poetical Works of the Right Hon. George Canning, M.P.* (Glasgow, 1825).

Carlyle, Alexander, *National Depravity the Cause of National Calamities* (Edinburgh, 1794).

____, *The Love of Our Country, explained and enforced in a sermon from Ps.137:5,6* (Edinburgh, 1797).

Chapman, R.W. (ed.), *Jane Austen's Letters to Her Sister Cassandra and Others* (Oxford University Press, 1932).

Cheetham, Robert Farron, *Odes and Miscellanies* (1796).

Clapham, Samuel, *A Sermon, Preached at Great Ouseborne, on Tuesday, the 19th of December, 1797, being the day appointed by His Majesty for a General Thanksgiving, to Almighty God, for our naval victories* (Leeds, 1798).

Clowes, J., *The Protection-Mark, or a View of the Principles Most Conducive to National and Individual Security, at this Most Important Crisis, Considered in a Sermon Preached at St. John's Church, Manchester, on Wednesday the 27th of February, Being the Day Appointed for a Public Fast* (Manchester, 1799).

Cobbett, William (ed.), *The Parliamentary History of England, from the Earliest Period to the Year 1803* (1806–20).

Copeland, Thomas W. et al. (eds), *The Correspondence of Edmund Burke*, 10 vol.s (Cambridge University Press, 1958–70), vi–ix.

Courtenay, Henry-Reginald, *A Sermon, Preached Before the Lords Spiritual and Temporal, in the Abbey-Church, Westminster, on Wednesday, February 25, 1795, being the day appointed by His Majesty's Proclamation for a general fast* (1795).

Dallas, Sir George, *Thoughts upon our present situation, with remarks upon the policy of a war with France* (1793).

Dalrymple, Alexander, *The Poor Man's Friend: an Address to the Industrious and Manufacturing Part of Great Britain* (Edinburgh, 1793).

Douglas, Niel, *Thoughts on Modern Politics* (1793).

[Eaton, Daniel Isaac], *Extermination, or an Appeal to the People of England on the Present War with France* ([1793]).

Eden, William (Lord Auckland), *Some Remarks on the Apparent Circumstances of the War in the Fourth Week of October 1795* (1795).

Edgeworth, Richard Lovell, *A Letter to the Right Hon. the Earl of Charlemont on the Tellograph, and on the defence of Ireland* (Dublin, 1797).

Emsley, Clive (ed.), *North Riding Naval Recruits: The Quota Acts and the Quota Men 1795–1797* (North Yorkshire County Record Office Publications no.18, 1978).

Erskine, John, *The Fatal Consequences and the General Sources of Anarchy: a Discourse on Isaiah 24:1–5* (Edinburgh, 1793).
Erskine, Thomas, *A View of the Causes and Consequences of the Present War with France*, 3rd edition (1797).
Fox, Charles James, *The Speech of the Right Hon. Charles James Fox: containing the Declaration of his Principles, respecting the Present Crisis of Public Affairs, and a Reform in the Representation of the People, spoken at the Whig Club of England, Dec. 4, 1792* (1792).
____, *A Letter from the Rt. Hon. Charles James Fox, to the Worthy and Independent Electors of the City and Liberty of Westminster* (1793).
____, *Mr. Fox's celebrated speech with the proceedings at the Shakespeare Tavern, on Friday, October 10, 1800, etc.* (1800).
Fox, William, *A Discourse on National Fasts, particularly in reference to that of April 19, 1793, on the Occasion of the War against France* (1793).
____, *The Interest of Great Britain, respecting the French Wars* (1793).
____, *Thoughts on the Death of the King of France* (1793).
____, *A Defence of the War Against France* (1794).
____, *A Discourse, occasioned by the National Fast, February 28, 1794* (1794).
____, *On Jacobinism* (1794).
____, *On Peace* (1794).
____, *Thoughts on the Impending Invasion of England* (1794).
____, *A Defence of the Decree of the National Convention of France, for Emancipating the Slaves in the West Indies* ([1794]).
Francis, Sir Philip, *The Question as it stood in March 1798* (1798).
Frend, William, *Peace and Union Recommended to the Associated Bodies of Republicans and Anti-Republicans* (Cambridge, 1793).
____, *Scarcity of Bread. A Plan for reducing the high price of this article, in a letter addressed by William Frend to William Devaynes, Esq.* (1793).
Gabell, Henry, *A Discourse Delivered on the Fast-Day in February 1799, in the Church of St. Lawrence, Winchester*, 2nd edition (1799).
Gardiner, J., *A Sermon Delivered at the Octagon Chapel, Bath, on Thursday, Nov. 29, 1798, Being the Day Appointed for a General Thanksgiving* (Bath, 1798).
Gerrald, Joseph, *A Convention the Only Means of Saving Us From Ruin* (1793).
Gifford, John [John Richards Green], *A Letter to the Earl of Lauderdale, containing Strictures on His Lordship's Letters to the Peers of Scotland* (1795).
____, *A Letter to the Hon. Thomas Erskine; containing some strictures on his View of the causes and consequences of the present war with France* (1797).
____, *A Second Letter to the Honourable Thomas Erskine, containing farther strictures on his View of the Causes and Consequences of the War, etc.* (1797).
____, *A Short Address, to the Members of the Loyal Associations on the present state of public affairs; containing a brief exposition of the designs of the French upon this country, and of their proposed division of Great Britain and Ireland into three distinct and independent republics; with a List of the Directories and Ministers of the same, as prepared by the directory at Paris* (1798).
Gisborne, Thomas, *An Enquiry into the Duties of the Female Sex*, 8th edition (1810).
Greig, James (ed.), *The Farington Diary by Joseph Farington, R.A.*, 8 vol.s, (1922–28), i.
Lord Grenville, *The Letters of Sulpicius* (1801).
Hall, Robert, *An Apology for the Freedom of the Press, and for General Liberty. To which are prefixed remarks on Bishop Horsley's Sermon preached the thirtieth of January last* (1793).
Hamilton, James Edward, *A Letter to the People of England Upon the Present Crisis* (1793).

Hampson, John, *A Sermon Preached in St. John's Chapel, Sunderland, on Friday, April 19, 1793, being the day appointed for a General Fast* (Sunderland, 1793).

____, *Observations on the Present War, the projected invasion, and a Decree of the National Convention for the Emancipation of the Slaves in the West Indies* (Sunderland, [1793]).

____, *A Sermon Delivered on Thursday the 1st of January, 1801, before the Sunderland Loyal Volunteer Infantry* (Sunderland, 1801).

Hardy, Thomas, *The Patriot, addressed to the People of Great Britain on the Present State of Affairs in Britain and in France, with Observations on Republican Government, and discussions of the Principles advanced in the writings of Thomas Paine* (Edinburgh, 1793).

____, *Fidelity to the British Constitution, the duty and interest of the people* (Edinburgh, 1794).

____, *The Importance of Religion to National Prosperity* (Edinburgh, 1794).

____, *The Progress of the Christian Religion* (Edinburgh, 1794).

Hartley, David, *Argument on the French Revolution* (Bath, 1794).

[Lord Hawkesbury], *Reflections on the Present State of the Resources of the Country* (1796).

Hawkins, Laetitia Matilda, *Letters on the Female Mind, its Powers and Pursuits. Addressed to Miss H.M. Williams, With particular reference to Her Letters From France*, 2 vol.s (1793).

Hay, Thomas, *A Sermon preached before the Hon. House of Commons on January 30, 1793* (1793).

____, *A Sermon preached before the House of Commons on Jan. 30, 1794* (1794).

____, *A Sermon preached before the House of Commons, on Jany. 30, 1795* (1795).

Hemlow, Joyce (ed.), *The Journals and Letters of Fanny Burney*, 12 vol.s (Oxford: Clarendon Press, 1972–84), i–v.

Hill, George, *The Present Happiness of Great Britain: a Sermon, Preached at St. Andrews, October 7th, 1792, and in the High Church of Edinburgh, November 18th, 1792* (Edinburgh, 1792).

____, *Instructions Afforded by the Present War, to the People of Great Britain* (Edinburgh, 1793).

Historical Manuscripts Commission, *Report on the Manuscripts of J.B. Fortesque, Esq., Preserved at Dropmore*, 10 vol.s (1892–1927), ii–vii.

Holcroft, Thomas, *A Letter to the Right Honourable William Windham, on the Intemperance and Dangerous Tendency of his Public Conduct* (1795).

Lord Holland, *Memoirs of the Whig Party During My Time*, 2 vol.s (1852), i.

Horne, Thomas, *A Sermon, Preached Before the Chiswick Military Association, on Sunday, Sept. 2, 1798* (1798).

Horne Tooke, John, *Address and Declaration, of the Friends of Universal Peace and Liberty* (1792).

Horsley, Samuel, *A Sermon preached before the Lords Spiritual and Temporal on Wednesday, January 30, 1793, etc.* (1793).

[Hubbard, J.C.], *Jacobinism; a poem* (1801).

Hunter, Andrew, *A Due Attention to the Public Institutions of Religion Recommended* (Edinburgh, 1793).

____, *The Duties of Subjects* (Edinburgh, 1793).

Hutchinson, Thomas (ed.), *The Poetical Works of Wordsworth* (1932).

Jackson, William, *A Sermon, preached before the Honourable Society of Lincoln's Inn, on Wednesday, Feb. 25, 1795; Being the Day appointed by His Majesty's Proclamation for a General Fast* (Oxford, 1795).

[Jebb, Ann], *Two Penny-Worth of Truth for a Penny; or a True State of Facts: with an Apology for Tom Bull in a Letter to Brother John* (1793).

Jefferey, Reginald W. (ed.), *Dyott's Diary 1781–1845: A Selection from the Diary of William Dyott, Sometime General in the British Army and Aide-de-Camp to His Majesty George III*, 2 vol.s (1907).

Johnson, R. Brimley (ed.), *The Letters of Hannah More* (1925).

Johnson, W. Branch (ed.), *'Memorandums For...' The Diary between 1798 and 1810 of John Carrington, Farmer, Chief Constable, Tax Assessor, Surveyor of Highways and Overseer of the Poor, of Bramfield in Hertfordshire* (London and Chichester, 1973).

Jones, John, *The Reason of Man: Part Second. Containing Strictures on Rights of Man, with Observations on Mr. Erskine's Defence of Mr Pain, and Thoughts on the War with France* (Canterbury, 1793).

[____], *Remarks on a Pamphlet published as Mr. Fox's Speech, at the opening of the Parliament, Including Some Observations on the Nature and Causes of the Present War* (1793).

[____], *Sentiments on a War with France* (1793).

[Jones, William], *Answer from John Bull to Thomas Bull* (1792).

[____], *One Penny-Worth More, or a Second Letter from Thomas Bull to his Brother John* (1792).

[____], *A Letter to John Bull, Esq. From his Second Cousin Thomas Bull, Author of the First and Second Letters to his Brother John* (1793).

Jupp, Peter (ed.), *The Letter-Journal of George Canning, 1793–1795*, Camden IVth series, vol. 41 (Royal Historical Society and University College, London, 1991).

Keynes, Geoffrey (ed.), *Blake. Complete Writings with Variant Readings* (Oxford University Press, 1969).

Knapp, Oswald G. (ed.), *The Intimate Letters of Hester Piozzi and Penelope Pennington 1788–1821* (1914).

Knox, Vicesimus, 'The Prospect of Perpetual and Universal Peace to be Established on the Principles of Christian Philanthropy' (1793), in *Works*, 7 vol.s (1824), vi, pp.351–70.

____, Preface to 'Antipolemus; or, the Plea of Reason, Religion, and Humanity, Against War. A Fragment; translated from the Latin of Erasmus', (1795), in *Works*, 7 vol.s (1824), v, pp.405–30.

____, 'The Spirit of Despotism' (1795), in *Works*, 7 vol.s (1824), v, 137–403.

Knox, William, *A Sermon, Preached Before His Excellency the Lord Lieutenant, on Thursday the 29th November, 1798, Being the Day Appointed For a General Thanksgiving* (Dublin, 1798).

Koops, Mathias, *A Development of the Views and Designs of the French Nation* (1796).

Landon, James, *A Sermon preached before the University of Oxford, at St. Mary's, Jan. 30, 1800* (Oxford, 1800).

[Lee, Richard], *The Rights of Swine. An Address to the Poor* ([1795]).

Lewis, Lady Theresa (ed.), *Extracts of the Journals and Correspondence of Miss Berry from the Year 1783 to 1852*, 3 vol.s (1865), i—ii.

Lister, Thomas, *Opposition Dangerous* (1798).

Lloyd, Christopher (ed.), *Above and Under Hatches, Being Naval Recollections in Shreds and Patches with Strange Reflections, By James Anthony Gardner, RN* (1955).

Long, Charles (Lord Farnborough), *The New Era of the French Revolution; or, Observations upon the Constitution Proposed in the Convention, on the twenty-third of June, 1795* (1795).

[____], *A View of the Relative State of Great Britain and France, at the Commencement of the Year 1796* (1796).

[____], *A Temperate Discussion of the Causes which have led to the Present High Price of Bread* (1800).

Lovett, John, *The Citizen of the World* (1793).

MacLeod, Col. Norman, *Considerations on False and Real Alarms* (1794).

Madan, Spencer, *A Sermon preached before the Lords Spiritual and Temporal on January the 30th, 1795* (1795).

Magee, William, *A Sermon, Preached in the Chapel of Trinity College, Dublin, on Thursday, the 16th Day of February, 1797, Being the Day Appointed for a National Thanksgiving* (Dublin, 1797).

Maitland, James, *Letters to the Peers of Scotland* (1794).

Mallet du Pan, Jacques Francois, *Considerations on the Nature of the French Revolution; and on the Causes which Prolong its Duration. Translated from the French* (Dublin, 1794).

____, *Dangers which threaten Europe* (1794).

Malmesbury, third Earl (ed.), *Diaries and Correspondence of James Harris, First Earl of Malmesbury*, 4 vol.s (1844), ii–iv.

Marsh, Herbert, *The History of the Politicks of Great Britain and France, from the time of the conference at Pillnitz, to the declaration of war against Great Britain*, 2nd edition, 2 vol.s (1800).

____, *The History of the Politics of Great Britain and France, Vindicated from a late attack of Mr. William Belsham* (1801).

Mathias, Thomas James, *The Imperial Epistle from Kien Long, Emperor of China, to George the Third*, 4th edition (1798).

[____], *A Letter to the Lord Marquis of Buckingham* (1796).

Maurice, Thomas, *The Crisis of Britain* (1803).

Memes, John S. (ed.), *The Miscellaneous Works of William Cowper, Esq. of the Inner Temple. With a Life and Notes* (Edinburgh, 1834).

Miles, William, *A Letter to Henry Duncombe, Esq. Member for the County of York, on the Subject of the very Extraordinary Pamphlet, lately addressed by Mr. Burke, to a noble Lord* (1796).

Miln, Robert, *The Rise and Fatal Effects of War: A Discourse Delivered on March 28, 1794; being the day appointed for a General Fast* (Carlisle, 1794).

Countess of Minto (ed.), *Life and Letters of Sir Gilbert Elliot, First Earl of Minto, from 1751 to 1806*, 3 vol.s (1874), ii–iii.

Moir, John, *Irreligion the Stigma of our Public Profession, and the Source of our National Calamities* (1799).

Moody, Christopher Lake (ed.), *A Sketch of Modern France. In a Series of Letters to a Lady of Fashion. Written in the Years 1796 and 1797, During a Tour through France. By a Lady* (1798).

More, Hannah, 'Remarks on the Speech of M. Dupont, with a Prefatory Address in Behalf of the French Emigrant Clergy' (1793), in *Works*, 3 vol.s (1847), ii, 377–408.

____, 'Strictures on the Modern System of Female Education' (1799), in *Works*, 3 vol.s (1847), iii.

____, 'Cheap Repository Tracts' (1795-98), in *Works*, 11 vol.s (1853), i–ii.

Morgan, J., *A Sermon Preached in the Parish Church of Towcester, on Thursday, 29th November, 1798, the Day Appointed by His Majesty, to return thanks to Almighty God, for our Recent and Important Successes in Distant Seas and Elsewhere* (Towcester, 1798).

[Morgan, Maurice], *Considerations on the present Internal and External Condition of France* (1794).

Morgan, William, *Facts Addressed to the Serious Attention of the People of Great Britain Respecting the Expence of the War, and the State of the National Debt* (1796).

Morres, Hervey Redmond, *The Crisis* (1794).

Moss, Charles, *A Sermon, preached before the honourable House of Commons, at the church of St. Margaret, Westminster, on Wednesday, March 7, 1798, Being the Day appointed by His Majesty's Proclamation, to be observed as a Day of Solemn Fasting and Humiliation* (1798).

Moylan, Dr. Francis, *To his beloved flock, the Roman Catholics of the Diocess of Cork* (Cork, 1796).

Munkhouse, Richard, *A Sermon, preached in the Church of St. John Baptist, Wakefield, December 19th, 1797. On occasion of a General Thanksgiving* (1798).

____, *A Sermon, Preached in the Church of St. John Baptist, Wakefield, on Thursday, November 29th, 1798; Being the Day Appointed for a General Thanksgiving* (1799).

Nares, Robert, *Man's Best Right; A Solemn Appeal in the Name of Religion* (1793).

____, *A Thanksgiving for Plenty, and a Warning against avarice, a sermon, preached in the Cathedral at Lichfield, on Sunday, September 20, 1801* (1801).

[____], *A Short Account of the Character and Reign of Louis XVI, showing how little he deserved, from his ungrateful people, the name of tyrant.*(1793).

Newton, John, *Motives to Humiliation and Praise. A Sermon, Preached in the Parish Church of St. Mary Woolnoth, Lombard-Street, on December 19, 1797, the Day of General Thanksgiving to Almighty God, for our late naval victories* (1798).

Nickolls, Robert Boucher, *The Duty of Supporting and Defending our Country and Constitution* (York, 1793).

O'Bryen, Dennis, *Utrum Horum? The Government; or, the Country?* 5th edition (1796).

Owen, John, *Righteous Judgement. A Sermon Preached in the University Church of Great St. Mary's, before the Hon. Sir. W. Ashurst, Knt., on the 11th of March, 1794, Being the Day of Assize* (Cambridge, 1794).

Partridge, Samuel, 'Observations upon a Militia of Property', *The Annals of Agriculture*, xxi (1793), pp.513–16.

Patton, Lewis and Mann, Peter et al. (eds), *The Collected Works of S.T. Coleridge*, 16 vol.s (Princeton University Press and Routledge, London, 1970ff.).

Piozzi, Hester Lynch, *British Synonymy*, 2 vol.s (Menston, UK: Scolar Press Ltd, 1968).

____, *Retrospection: or a Review of the Most Striking and Important Events, Characters, Situations, and their Consequences, which the last eighteen hundred years have presented to mankind* (1801).

Playfair, William, *Better Prospects to the Merchants and Manufacturers of Great Britain* (1793).

____, *A General View of the Actual Force and Resources of France, in January 1793* (1793).

____, *Thoughts on the Present State of French Politics, and the Necessity and Policy of Diminishing France, for her internal peace and to secure the tranquillity of Europe* (1793).

____, *The History of Jacobinism, its crimes, cruelties and perfidies* (1795).

Plowden, Francis, *A Friendly and Constitutional Address to the People of Great Britain* (1794).

Polwhele, Richard, *The Unsex'd Females; A Poem, Addressed to the Author of the Pursuits of Literature* (New York, 1800).

Price, Cecil (ed.), *The Letters of Richard Brinsley Sheridan* (Oxford, 1966).

Price, Richard, *A Discourse on the Love of Our Country* (1789).

[Price, Theodore], *Brother Fustian's Advice to the Inhabitants of Manchester and Salford* (Manchester, 1792).

[____] *Advice to sundry sorts of people, by Job Nott, Framework-knitter, first cousin to John Nott, the Sinker-maker* (Nottingham, 1793).

[____], *More Advice from Job Nott, the Birmingham Buckle-maker, first cousin to John Nott, the celebrated Button Burnisher* (Birmingham, 1795).

[____], *A Continuation of my last book, or, a Back Front View of the Five Headed Monster* (Birmingham, 1798).

[____], *A Front View of the Five Headed Monster* (Birmingham, 1798).
[____], *The life and adventures of Job Nott, as written by himself* (Birmingham, 1798).
[____], *Birmingham in Danger! of which Job Nott gives fair warning* (Birmingham, 1799).
[____], *Further Humble Advice from Job Nott* (Birmingham, 1800).
Publicola, Horatius, *The Prospect Before Us!!! Or the state of France in the month of August, 1794; in reply to Montgaillard's state of France: to which are added, reflections on the expedience and necessity of an immediate peace with the French Republic* (1794).
Raithby, John, *Peace. Reasons why Terms of Peace should be offered to the French Nation.* (1795).
Rees, Abraham, *The Privileges of Britain. A Sermon, preached at the Meeting-House in the old Jewry on Thursday the 29th of November 1798, being the day appointed for a General Thanksgiving* (1798).
Rennell, James, *War with France the Only Security of Britain, at the present momentous crisis* (1794).
Rennell, Thomas, *The Connexion of the Duties of Loving the Brotherhood, Fearing God, and Honoring the King, considered and explained, in a sermon, preached in the Parish Church of St. Magnus the Martyr, London Bridge, on Sunday, the 30th of December, 1792* (1792).
____, *Principles of French Republicanism essentially founded on Violence and Blood-Guiltiness, a sermon, preached on Sunday, the 26th of October, 1793, in the Cathedral Church of Winchester, occasioned by the murder of Her Most Christian Majesty* (Winton, 1793).
Reynell, W.H., *Two Sermons Preached to a Respectable Congregation at Hornchurch, in the County of Essex* (1798).
Rhys, Ernest (ed.), *Orations on the French War, to the Peace of Amiens, by William Pitt* (New York and London: Dent & Co., n.d.).
Ridgway, James (ed.), *The Speeches of the Hon. Thomas Erskine (now Lord Erskine), when at the Bar, on subjects connected with the liberty of the press, and against constructive treasons*, 5 vol.s (1810).
Rivers, David, *Thoughts on the necessity of prosecuting the war with France with vigour and energy: with remarks on the present scarcity of provisions, and particularly bread. In a letter to a friend* (1800).
Robinson, Thomas, *A Serious Exhortation to the inhabitants of Great Britain with Reference to the Approaching Fast* (Edinburgh, 1797; also published in Leicester, 1795).
Robison, John, *Proofs of a Conspiracy against all the Religions and Governments of Europe, Carried on in the Secret Meetings of Free Masons, Illuminati, and Reading Societies. Collected from good authorities* (Edinburgh, 1797).
Roscoe, Henry, *The Life of William Roscoe* (1833).
[Roscoe, William], *On a Late Declaration, guaranteeing against Revolutions, etc.* (1794).
[____], *Thoughts on the Causes of the Present Failures* (1793).
Rose, J. Holland (ed.), *Pitt and Napoleon. Essays and Letters* (C. Belland, 1912).
Russell, Lord John (ed.), *Memorials and Correspondence of Charles James Fox*, 4 vol.s (1853–7), ii–iii.
'Rusticus, Junicus' (pseud.), *Enumeration of the contributions, confiscations, and requisitions of the French nation; with an account of the countries revolutionized since the commencement of the present war. Extracted from official documents. Translated from the German* (1798).
Shanks, Alexander, *Peace and Order Recommended to Society, in an Address to the Associate Congregation of Jedburgh from Jeremiah 29:7* (Edinburgh, 1793).
Somerville, John, *A Short Address to the Yeomanry of England, and Others* (Bath, 1795).

Somerville, Thomas, *The Effects of the French Revolution with respect to the interests of humanity, liberty, religion and morality* (Edinburgh, 1793).

____, *Observations on the Constitution and Present State of Britain* (Edinburgh, 1793).

____, *My Own Life and Times, 1741–1814* (Edinburgh, 1861).

Earl Stanhope, *Life of the Right Honourable William Pitt with extracts from his Ms. papers* (1879).

Steevens, Lt.-Col. Charles, *Reminiscences of My Military Life from 1795 to 1818* (Winchester, 1818).

Stephens, F.G. and George, Mary Dorothy (eds), *Catalogue of Political and Personal Satires Preserved in the Department of Prints and Drawings in the British Museum*, 11 vol.s (1870–1954), vi–viii.

Stewart, Alexander, *Account of a Late Revival of Religion in a part of the Highlands of Scotland* (Edinburgh, 1800).

[Still, John], *Fraternity, Humanity, Peace* (1795).

Stuart, Daniel, *Peace and Reform, against War and Corruption. In answer to a pamphlet, written by Arthur Young, Esq., entitled, 'The Example of France, a Warning to Britain'*, 2nd edition (1794).

Sullivan, William Francis, *The Test of Union & Loyalty: a new piece, on the present war with France. To which is added, three new songs* (Margate, 1795).

Surtees, William, *Twenty-Five Years in the Rifle Brigade* (Edinburgh and London, 1833).

'Sydney' (pseud.), *War!* (Nottingham, 1792).

Thelwall, John, *An Appeal to Popular Opinion, Against Kidnapping and Murder; Including a Narrative of the Late Atrocious Proceedings, at Yarmouth. Second edition: with A Postscript; containing a particular account of the Outrages at Lynn and Wisbeach* (1796).

____, *The Rights of Nature*, 2 vol.s (1796).

____, *Sober Reflections on the seditious and inflammatory letter of the Rt. Hon. Edmund Burke, to a noble Lord, addressed to the serious consideration of his fellow citizens* (1796).

Thomas, Robert, *The Cause of Truth* (Dundee, 1797).

Thomson, James, *The Rise, Progress, and Consequences of the new Opinions and Principles lately introduced into France, with Observations* (Edinburgh, 1799).

Towers, Joseph, *Remarks on the Conduct, Principles, and Publications, of the Association at the Crown and Anchor, in the Strand, for Preserving Liberty and Property Against Republicans and Levellers* (1793).

[____], *A Dialogue Between an Associator and a Well-Informed Englishman, on the Grounds of the Late Associations and the Commencement of a War with France* (1793).

Valpy, Richard, *A Sermon, Preached August 13, 1798, Before the Reading and Henley Association, the Woodley Cavalry, and the Reading Volunteers, at the Consecration of the Colors of the Reading Association* (Reading, 1798).

Vansittart, Nicholas, *Reflections on the Propriety of an Immediate Conclusion of Peace*, 2nd edition (1794).

Vaughan, Benjamin, *Letters, on the Subject of the Concert of Princes, and the Dismemberment of Poland and France*, 2nd edition (1793).

____, *Two Papers by the Calm Observer, not printed in the collection of his letters extracted from the Morning Chronicle* (1795).

Verney, Sir Harry (ed.), *The Journals and Correspondence of General Sir Harry Calvert* (1853).

Vernon, Hon. Edward, *A Sermon preached before the Lords Spiritual and Temporal on Thursday, January 30, 1794, etc.* (1794).

Vincent, William, 'A Sermon delivered in the Church of St. Magnus, London Bridge, November 25; and in the Church of Allhallows the great and the less, Thames Street, December 16, 1798; before the Associated Volunteer Companies, in the Wards of Bridge, Candlewick, and Dowgate' (1799), in *Sermons on Faith, Doctrines, and Public Duties*, 2 vol.s (1817), i, pp.259–92.

____, 'A Sermon preached before the Honourable House of Commons, at the Church of St. Margaret, Westminster, on Tuesday, June 1, 1802, being the day appointed for a General Thanksgiving' (1802), in *Sermons on Faith, Doctrines, and Public Duties*, 2 vol.s (1817), i, pp.322–54.

Waddington, Samuel, *Remarks on Mr. Burke's Two Letters* (1796).

Wakefield, Gilbert, *Remarks on the General Orders of the Duke of York to his Army, on June 7, 1794* (1794).

Walker, George, *The Vagabond, A Novel* , 3rd edition, 2 vol.s (1799).

Walker, James, *A Sermon, Preached in an Episcopal Chapel, Edinburgh, on Thursday, 20th October, 1803. Being the Day of a National Fast, on Account of the War with France* (Edinburgh, 1804).

Wallace, Lady Eglantine, *The Conduct of the King of Prussia and General Dumourier Investigated by Lady Wallace* (1793).

____, *A Sermon addressed to the People, pointing out the only sure method to obtain a speedy peace and reform* ([1794]).

Wardle, Ralph M. (ed.), *The Collected Letters of Mary Wollstonecraft* (New York and London: Cornell University Press, 1979).

[Watson, Alexander], *The Anti-Jacobin, a Hudibrastic poem in twenty-one cantos* (Edinburgh, 1794).

Watson, Richard, *An Address to the People of Great Britain*, 2nd edition (1798).

____, 'A Charge Delivered to the Clergy of the Diocese of Landaff in June 1798' (1798), in *Miscellaneous Tracts on Religious, Political,and Agricultural Subjects*, 2 vol.s (1815), i, pp.121–54.

____, *Anecdotes of the Life of Dr Watson, Bishop of Landaff*, 2nd edition, 2 vol.s (1818).

Webb, Mrs. Jane, *A Letter to His Grace the Duke of Portland, on the Late Alarming Parties in this Country* (Plymouth, 1795).

Wilberforce, R.I. and S. (eds.), *The Correspondence of William Wilberforce*, 2 vol.s (1840), i.

Williams, Helen Maria, *Letters from France: Containing Many New Anecdotes Relative to the French Revolution, and the Present State of French Manners*, 2nd edition (1792).

____, *Letters Written in France, in the Summer of 1790, to a Friend in England: Containing Various Anecdotes Relative to the French Revolution; and Memoirs of Mons. and Madame du F__*, 3rd edition (1792).

____, *Letters from France: Containing a Great Variety of Interesting and Original Information Concerning the Most Important Events that have Lately Occurred in that Country, and Particularly Respecting the Campaign of 1792* (1793).

____, *Letters Containing a Sketch of the Politics of France, From the Thirty-first of May 1793, till the Twenty-eighth of July 1794, and of the Scenes which have passed in the Prisons of Paris* (1795).

____, *Sketches of the State of Manners and Opinions in the French Republic, Towards the Close of the Eighteenth Century. In a Series of Letters* (1801).

Williams, J.H., *Two Sermons Preached on the Public Fasts of April 1793, and February 1794* (1794).

Williams, William, *A Reply to Mr. Burke's Two Letters on the Proposals for Peace with the Regicide Directory of France* (1796).

____, *Rights of the People; or, Reasons for a Regicide Peace* (1796).

Willis, Irene Cooper (ed.), *Speeches During the French Revolution: Charles James Fox* (New York and London: Dent, 1924).

'Wilson, Jasper' (pseud., Dr. James Currie), *A Letter, Commercial and Political, addressed to the Rt. Hon.ble William Pitt: in which the Real Interests of Britain, in the Present Crisis, are considered, and some obsevations are offered on the General State of Europe*, 2nd edition (1793).

'Wilson, William' (pseud.), *A Dialogue Upon the Two Bills Now Depending in Parliament, Relative to the Rights of the People. Transcribed by William Wilson, Jasper's brother* (1795).

Wollstonecraft, Mary, 'Letter: Introductory to a Series of Letters on the Present Character of the French Nation' in Janet Todd and Marilyn Butler (eds), *The Works of Mary Wollstonecraft*, 7 vol.s (Pickering, 1989), vi, pp.443–6.

____, 'An Historical and Moral View of the Origin and Progress of the French Revolution; and the Effect it has Produced on Europe' in Janet Todd and Marilyn Butler (eds), *The Works of Mary Wollstonecraft*, 7 vol.s (Pickering, 1989), vi, pp.1–235.

Wordsworth, William, 'A Letter to the Bishop of Llandaff on the Extraordinary Avowal of his Political Principles Contained in the Appendix to his late Sermon By a Republican' in W.J.B. Owen and Jane Worthington Smyser (eds), *The Prose Works of William Wordsworth*, 3 vol.s (Oxford, 1974), i, pp.19–69.

Workman, James, *An Argument Against Continuing the War* (1795).

____, *A Letter to His Grace the Duke of Portland, being a defence of the Conduct of His Majesty's Ministers in sending an ambassador to treat for peace with the French Directory, against the attack made upon that measure by the Right Hon. Edmund Burke; and an endeavour to prove that the permanent establishment of the French Republic is compatible with the Safety of the Religious and Political Systems of Europe*, 3rd edition (1797).

____, 'A Memorial, Proposing a Plan, for the Conquest and Emancipation of Spanish America, by means, which would Contribute to the Tranquillity of Ireland' (1801), in *Political Essays, relative to the War of the French Revolution* (Alexandria, 1810), 142–74.

Wraxall, Sir Nathaniel William, *The Correspondence between a traveller and a Minister of State, in October and November 1792* (1796).

Young, Arthur, *Travels, during the years 1787, 1788, and 1789. Undertaken more particularly with a View of ascertaining the Cultivation, Wealth, Resources, and National Prosperity, of the Kingdom of France* (Bury St. Edmunds and London, 1792).

____, *The Example of France, a Warning to Britain*, 4th edition (1794, first published 1793).

____, *An Idea of the Present State of France, and of the consequences of the events passing in that kingdom* (1795).

[____], *National Danger, and the Means of Safety* (1797).

Young, John, *Essays on the Following Interesting Subjects* (Edinburgh, 1794).

____, *A History of the Commencement, Progress and Termination of the Late War between Great Britain and France* (Edinburgh, 1802).

Count Zenobio, *An address to the people of England, on the part their government ought to act, in the present war between the combined armies of Austria and Prussia, and the armed mob of France* (Sheffield, 1792).

Secondary Sources

Alger, J.G., 'The British Colony in Paris, 1792–3', *English Historical Review*, 13 (1898), pp.672–94.

Atherton, Herbert M., 'The British Defend Their Constitution in Political Cartoons and Literature', *Studies in Eighteenth-Century Culture*, 11 (1982), pp.3–31.

Ayling, Stanley, *George the Third* (Collins, 1972).

Barker, Hannah and Chalus, Elaine, *Gender in Eighteenth-Century England* (Harlow: Longman, 1997).

Barnes, Donald G., *George III and William Pitt, 1783–1806* (California: Octagon Books, 1939).

Bellesheim, A., *History of the Catholic Church of Scotland*, 4 vol.s (Edinburgh and London, 1887).

Bindman, David et al., *The Shadow of the Guillotine: Britain and the French Revolution* (Trustees of the British Museum, 1989).

Black, Jeremy, 'The Coming of War Between Britain and France, 1792–1793', *Francia*, 20 (1993), pp.69–108.

____, *British Foreign Policy in an Age of Revolutions 1783–1793* (Cambridge University Press, 1994).

Blanning, T.C.W., *The Origins of the French Revolutionary Wars* (Longman, 1986).

Bohstedt, John, *Riots and Community Politics in England and Wales 1790–1810* (Cambridge, Mass. and London: Harvard University Press, 1983).

J.E. Bradley, *Religion, Revolution and English Radicalism* (Cambridge University Press, 1990).

Brewer, John, *The Common People and Politics 1750–1790s* (Cambridge: Chadwyck-Healey, 1986).

Brims, John, 'The Scottish Democratic Movement in the Age of the French Revolution', unpublished Ph.D. thesis, University of Edinburgh, 1983.

____, 'The Covenanting Tradition and Scottish Radicalism in the 1790s' in T. Brotherstone (ed.), *Covenant, Charter, and Party: Traditions of revolt and protest in modern Scottish History* (Aberdeen University Press, 1989), pp.50–62.

Brooke, John, *King George III* (Constable, 1972).

Burne, Alfred H., *The Noble Duke of York* (Staples Press, 1949).

Butler, Marilyn, *Jane Austen and the War of Ideas* (Oxford: Clarendon Press, 1975).

Canavan, Francis P., *The Political Reason of Edmund Burke* (Durham, NC: Duke University Press, 1960).

Carnall, Geoffrey, *Robert Southey and His Age: The Development of a Conservative Mind* (Oxford: Clarendon Press, 1960).

Carretta, Vincent, *George III and the Satirists from Hogarth to Byron* (University of Georgia Press, 1990).

Chandler, James K., 'Poetical Liberties: Burke's France and the "Adequate Representation" of the English' in François Furet and Mona Ozouf (eds), *The French Revolution and the Creation of Modern Political Culture*, iii: *The Transformation of Political Culture* (Oxford: Pergamon, 1989), pp.45–58.

Chapman, Gerald W., *Edmund Burke: The Practical Imagination* (Cambridge, Mass.: Harvard University Press, 1967).

Christie, Ian R., *Wars and Revolutions: Britain 1760–1815* (Arnold, 1982).

Christie, Ian R., 'Conservatism and Stability in British society' in Mark Philp (ed.), *The French Revolution and British Popular Politics* (Cambridge University Press, 1991), pp.169–87.

Claeys, Gregory, 'The French Revolution Debate and British Political Thought', *History of Political Thought*, 11 (1990), pp.59–80.

Clifford, James L., *Hester Lynch Piozzi (Mrs. Thrale)*, 2nd edition (Oxford: Clarendon Press, 1952).

Cobban, Alfred, *Edmund Burke and the Revolt Against the Eighteenth Century* (Allen and Unwin, 1929).
____, 'British Secret Service in France, 1784–1792', *English Historical Review*, lxix (1954), pp.226–61.
Colley, Linda, 'Whose Nation? Class and National Consciousness in Britain 1750–1830', *Past and Present*, 113 (1986), pp.97–117.
____, *Britons: Forging the Nation 1707–1837* (London & New York: Yale University Press, 1992).
Cone, Carl B., *Burke and the Nature of Politics*, ii: *The Age of the French Revolution* (University of Kentucky Press, 1964).
Cookson, J.E., *The Friends of Peace: Anti-War Liberalism in England, 1793–1815* (Cambridge University Press, 1982).
____, 'The English Volunteer Movement of the French Wars, 1793–1815', *Historical Journal*, 32 (1989), pp.867–91.
____, *The British Armed Nation 1793–1815* (Oxford: Clarendon Press, 1997).
Cottrell, Stella M. Ní Ghallchóir, 'English Views of France and the French, 1789–1815', unpublished D.Phil. thesis, University of Oxford, 1991.
Crossley, Ceri and Small, Ian (eds), *The French Revolution and British Culture* (Oxford University Press, 1989).
Cunningham, Hugh, 'The language of patriotism', in Raphael Samuel (ed.), *Patriotism: The Making and Unmaking of British National Identity*, vol. i, *History and Politics* (Routledge, 1989), pp.57–89.
Davis, Richard W., *Dissent in Politics 1780–1830: The Political Life of William Smith, MP* (Epworth Press, 1971).
Derry, John W., *Charles James Fox* (Batsford, 1972).
Derry, John, 'Popular Radicalism and Popular Protest 1789–1815' in H.T. Dickinson (ed.), *Britain and the French Revolution 1789–1815* (Macmillan, 1989), pp.61–82.
Dickinson, H.T., *British Radicalism and the French Revolution 1789–1815* (Oxford: Blackwell, 1985).
____, *Caricatures and the Constitution, 1760–1832* (Cambridge: Chadwyck-Healey, 1986).
____ (ed.), *Britain and the French Revolution 1789–1815* (Macmillan, 1989).
____, 'Popular Conservatism and Militant Loyalism' in H.T. Dickinson (ed.), *Britain and the French Revolution 1789–1815* (Macmillan, 1989), pp.103–24.
____, 'Popular Loyalism in Britain in the 1790s' in Eckhart Hellmuth (ed.), *The Transformation of Political Culture. England and Germany in the Late Eighteenth Century* (The German Historical Institute, 1990), pp.503–33.
____, 'Britain and the Ideological Crusade Against the French Revolution' in L. Domergue and G. Lamoine (eds), *Actes du Colloque international* (Toulouse: Presses Universitaires du Mirail, 1992), pp.153–74.
____, 'The French Revolution and the Counter-Revolution in Britain' in Hans-Christoph Schröder and Hans-Dieter Metzger (eds), *Aspekte der Französischen Revolution* (Darmstadt: Technische Hochschule Darmstadt, 1992), pp.231–63.
____, *The Politics of the People in Eighteenth-Century Britain* (Basingstoke: Macmillan, 1995).
Dinwiddy, John R., 'Utility and Natural Law in Burke's Thought: A Reconsideration', *Studies in Burke and His Time*, 16 (1974–75), pp.105–28.
____, 'Burke and the Utilitarians: A Rejoinder', *Studies in Burke and His Time*, 19 (1978), pp.119–26.
____, 'English Radicals and the French Revolution, 1800–1850' in François Furet and Mora Ozouf (eds), *The French Revolution and the Creation of Modern Political Culture*, iii: *The Transformation of Political Culture* (Oxford: Pergamon, 1989), pp.447–66.

____, 'Interpretations of anti-Jacobinism' in Mark Philp, *The French Revolution and British Popular Politics* (Cambridge University Press, 1991), pp.38–49.

Donald, Diana, *The Age of Caricature: Satirical Prints in the Reign of George III* (Yale University Press, 1996).

Doody, Margaret Anne, *Frances Burney: The Life in the Works* (Cambridge University Press, 1988).

Dozier, Robert R., *For King, Constitution, and Country: the English Loyalists and the French Revolution* (Lexington: University Press of Kentucky, 1983).

Dreyer, Frederick, 'Edmund Burke: the Philosopher in Action', *Studies in Burke and His Time*, 15 (1973–74), pp.121–42.

____, 'Burke's Religion', *Studies in Burke and His Time*, 17 (1976), pp.199–212.

Duffy, Michael, 'British War Policy: the Austrian Alliance, 1793–1801', unpublished D.Phil. thesis, University of Oxford, 1971.

____, 'British Policy in the War Against Revolutionary France' in Colin Jones (ed.), *Britain and Revolutionary France: Conflict, Subversion and Propaganda* (University of Exeter, 1983), pp.11–26.

____, *The Englishman and the Foreigner* (Cambridge: Chadwyck-Healey, 1986).

____, *Soldiers, Sugar, and Sea Power: The British Expeditions to the West Indies and the War Against Revolutionary France* (Oxford: Clarendon Press, 1987).

____, 'British Diplomacy and the French Wars 1789–1815' in H.T. Dickinson (ed.), *Britain and the French Revolution 1789–1815* (Macmillan, 1989), pp.127–46.

____, 'Pitt, Grenville and the Control of British Foreign Policy in the 1790s' in Jeremy Black (ed.), *Knights Errant and True Englishmen: British Foreign Policy 1660–1800* (Edinburgh: John Donald, 1989), pp.151–72.

____, 'War, revolution and the crisis of the British empire' in Mark Philp (ed.), *The French Revolution and British Popular Politics* (Cambridge University Press, 1991), pp.118–45.

____, 'William Pitt and the Origins of the Loyalist Association Movement of 1792', *Historical Journal*, 39 (1996), pp.943–62.

Eastwood, David, 'Patriotism and the English state in the 1790s' in Mark Philp (ed.), *The French Revolution and British Popular Politics* (Cambridge University Press, 1991), pp.146–68.

____, 'E.P. Thompson, Britain, and the French Revolution', *History Workshop Journal*, 39 (1995), pp.79–88.

Ehrman, John, *The Younger Pitt*, ii: *The Reluctant Transition* (Constable, 1983).

____, *The Younger Pitt*, iii: *The Consuming Struggle* (Constable, 1996).

Elliott, Marianne, 'French Subversion in Britain in the French Revolution' in Colin Jones (ed.), *Britain and Revolutionary France: Conflict, Subversion and Propaganda* (University of Exeter, 1983), pp.40–52.

Emsley, Clive, *British Society and the French Wars 1793–1815* (Macmillan, 1979).

____, 'An Aspect of Pitt's Terror: prosecutions for sedition during the 1790s', *Social History*, 6 (1981), pp.155–84.

____, 'Repression, "terror" and the rule of law in England during the decade of the French Revolution', *English Historical Review*, 100 (1985), pp.801–25.

____, 'The Impact of the French Revolution on British Politics and Society' in Ceri Crossley and Ian Small (eds), *The French Revolution and British Culture* (Oxford University Press, 1989), pp.31–62.

____, 'The Social Impact of the French Wars' in H.T. Dickinson (ed.), *Britain and the French Revolution 1789–1815* (Macmillan, 1989), pp.211–28.

____, 'Revolution, war and the nation state: the British and French experiences 1789–1801' in Mark Philp (ed.), *The French Revolution and British Popular Politics* (Cambridge University Press, 1991), pp.99–117.

Erdman, David V., *Blake. Prophet Against Empire: A Poet's Interpretation of the History of His Own Times*, 3rd edition (New York: Dover, 1991).

Fennessy, R.R., *Burke, Paine, and the Rights of Man: A Difference of Political Opinion* (The Hague: Martinus Nijhoff, 1963).

Freeman, Michael, *Edmund Burke and the Critique of Political Radicalism* (Oxford: Blackwell, 1980).

Frey, Linda and Frey, Marsha, '"The Reign of the Charlatans is Over": The French Revolutionary Attack on Diplomatic Practice', *Journal of Modern History*, 55 (1993), pp.706–44.

Fry, Michael, *The Dundas Despotism* (Edinburgh University Press, 1992).

Fryer, W.R., *Republic or Restoration in France? 1794–97* (Manchester University Press, 1965).

Gascoigne, John, 'Anglican latitudinarianism, Rational Dissent and political radicalism in the late eighteenth century', in Knud Haakonssen (ed.), *Enlightenment and Religion: Rational Dissent in Eighteenth-Century Britain* (Cambridge University Press, 1996), pp.219–40.

Geggus, David, 'The Anglo-French Conflict in the Caribbean in the 1790s' in Colin Jones (ed.), *Britain and Revolutionary France: Conflict, Subversion and Propaganda* (University of Exeter, 1983), pp.27–39.

Ginter, Donald E., 'The Loyalist Association Movement of 1792–93 and British Public Opinion', *Historical Journal*, 9 (1966), pp.179–90.

Goodwin, Albert, *The Friends of Liberty: The English Democratic Movement in the Age of the French Revolution* (Hutchinson, 1979).

Gray, Denis, *Spencer Perceval, 1762–1812: The Evangelical Prime Minister* (Manchester University Press, 1963).

Gunn, J.A.W., *Beyond Liberty and Property: The Process of Self-Recognition in Eighteenth-Century Political Thought* (Kingston and Montreal: McGill-Queen's University Press, 1983).

Harvey, A.D., 'European Attitudes to Britain during the French Revolutionary and Napoleonic wars', *History*, 63 (1978), pp.356–65.

____, *English Literature and the Great War with France* (Nold Jonson, 1981).

Hempton, David, 'Evangelicals and Eschatology', *Journal of Ecclesiastical History*, 31 (1980), pp.179–94.

____, *Methodism and Politics in British Society, 1750–1850* (Hutchinson, 1984).

Hellstrom, Ward, 'Francophobia in *Emma*', *Studies in English Literature*, 5 (1965), pp.607–17.

Hole, Robert, 'British Counter-Revolutionary Popular Propaganda in the 1790s' in Colin Jones (ed.), *Britain and Revolutionary France: Conflict, Subversion and Propaganda* (University of Exeter, 1983), pp.53–69.

____, *Pulpits, Politics and Public Order in England, 1760–1832* (Cambridge University Press, 1989).

____, 'English Sermons and Tracts as media of debate on the French Revolution 1789–99' in Mark Philp (ed.), *The French Revolution and British Popular Politics* (Cambridge University Press, 1991), pp.18–37.

Hubback, J.H. and Edith C., *Jane Austen's Sailor Brothers. Being the Adventures of Sir Francis Austen, GCB, Admiral of the Fleet, and Rear-Admiral Charles Austen* (1906).

Hudson, Arthur Palmer and Virginia Mary, '"The Coast of France How Near!" French Invasion and English Literature, 1793–1805', *The South Atlantic Quarterly*, 40 (1941), pp.269–91.

Hutt, Maurice, *Chouannerie and Counter-Revolution: Puisaye, the Princes, and British Government in the 1790s*, 2 vol.s (Cambridge University Press, 1983).

Innes, Joanna, 'Politics and Morals. The Reformation of Manners Movement in Later Eighteenth-Century England' in Eckhart Hellmuth (ed.), *The Transformation of Political Culture. England and Germany in the Late Eighteenth Century* (The German Historical Institute, 1990), pp.57–118.

Jewson, C.B., *The Jacobin City: a portrait of Norwich in its reaction to the French Revolution, 1788-1802* (Glasgow and London: Blackie, 1975).

Jones, Colin (ed.), *Britain and Revolutionary France: Conflict, Subversion and Propaganda* (University of Exeter, 1983).

Jupp, Peter, *Lord Grenville 1759–1834* (Oxford: Clarendon Press, 1985).

Kelly, Gary, *Women, Writing, and Revolution 1790–1827* (Oxford: Clarendon Press, 1993).

Kelly, Paul, 'Strategy and Counter-Revolution: the Journal of Sir Gilbert Elliot, 1–22 September 1793', *English Historical Review*, 98 (1983), pp.328–48.

Kirkland, William, 'The Impact of the French Revolution on Scottish Religious Life and Thought, with special reference to Thomas Chalmers, Robert Haldane, and Niel Douglas', unpublished Ph.D. thesis, University of Edinburgh, 1951.

Kramnick, Isaac (ed.), *Edmund Burke* (Englewood Cliffs, New Jersey: Prentice-Hall, 1974).

____, *The Rage of Edmund Burke: Portrait of an Ambivalent Conservative* (New York: Basic Books, 1977).

Lewis, C.S., 'A Note on Jane Austen', *Essays in Criticism*, 4 (1954), pp.359–71.

Lewis, Michael, *A Social History of the Navy, 1793–1815* (Allen and Unwin, 1960).

Lipking, Lawrence, 'Analyzing Burke', *Studies in Burke and His Time*, 20 (1979), pp.65–81.

Logue, Kenneth J., *Popular Disturbances in Scotland, 1780–1815* (Edinburgh: John Donald, 1979).

Lovegrove, Deryck, 'English Evangelical Dissent and the European Conflict 1789–1815', *Studies in Church History*, 20 (1983), pp.263–76.

Lucas, Colin, 'Edmund Burke and the *Émigrés*' in François Furet and Mona Ozouf (eds), *The French Revolution and the Creation of Modern Political Culture*, iii: *The Transformation of Political Culture* (Oxford: Pergamon, 1989), pp.101–14.

McCalman, Iain, 'New Jerusalems: prophecy, Dissent and radical culture in England, 1786–1830', in Knud Haakonssen (ed.), *Enlightenment and Religion: Rational Dissent in Eighteenth-Century Britain* (Cambridge University Press, 1996), pp.312–35.

MacCunn, John, *The Political Philosophy of Burke* (Arnold, 1913).

Mackesy, Piers, *Statesmen at War: the Strategy of Overthrow, 1798–1799* (Longman, 1974).

____, *War Without Victory: The Downfall of Pitt, 1799–1802* (Oxford: Clarendon Press, 1984).

Macpherson, C.B., *Burke* (Oxford University Press, 1980).

McCarthy, William, *Hester Thrale Piozzi: Portrait of a Literary Woman* (Chapel Hill and London: University of North Carolina Press, 1985).

Matheson, Cyril, *The Life of Henry Dundas, First Viscount Melville* (Constable, 1933).

Masters, Brian, *Georgiana, Duchess of Devonshire* (Hamilton, 1981).

Mitchell, Austin, 'The Association Movement of 1792–3', *Historical Journal*, 4 (1961), pp.56–77.

Mitchell, Harvey, *The Underground War Against Revolutionary France: The Missions of William Wickham 1794–1800* (Oxford: Clarendon Press, 1965).

____, 'Presentation' in François Furet and Mona Ozouf (eds), *The French Revolution and the Creation of Modern Political Culture*, iii: *The Transformation of Political Culture* (Oxford: Pergamon, 1989), pp.3–18.

Mitchell, L.G., *Charles James Fox and the Disintegration of the Whig Party 1782–1794* (Oxford University Press, 1971).

____, *Charles James Fox* (Oxford University Press, 1992).

de Montluzin, Emily Lorraine, *The Anti-Jacobins 1798–1800: The Early Contributors to the 'Anti-Jacobin Review'* (Macmillan, 1988).

Moorman, Mary, *William Wordsworth: A Biography* (Oxford: Clarendon Press, 1957).

Mori, Jennifer, 'Responses to Revolution: The November Crisis of 1792', *Bulletin of the Institute of Historical Research*, 69 (1996), pp.284–305.

____, *William Pitt and the French Revolution, 1785–1795* (Edinburgh: Keele University Press, 1997).

Morris, Marilyn A., 'The Monarchy as an Issue in English Political Argument during the French Revolutionary Era', unpublished Ph.D. thesis, University of London, 1988.

Murley, J.T., 'The Origin and Outbreak of the Anglo-French War of 1793', unpublished D.Phil. thesis, University of Oxford, 1959.

Murray, Nancy U., 'The Influence of the French Revolution on the Church of England and its Rivals, 1789–1802', unpublished D.Phil. thesis, University of Oxford, 1975.

Newman, Gerald, 'Anti-French Propaganda and British Liberal Nationalism in the Early Nineteenth Century: Suggestions Toward a General Interpretation', *Victorian Studies*, XVIII (1975), pp.385–418.

____, *The Rise of English Nationalism: A Cultural History 1740–1830* (Weidenfeld and Nicolson, 1987).

O'Brien, Conor Cruise, *The Great Melody: A Thematic Biography and Commented Anthology of Edmund Burke* (Sinclair-Stevenson, 1992).

O'Gorman, Frank, *The Whig Party and the French Revolution* (Macmillan, 1967).

____, *Edmund Burke. His Political Philosophy* (Allen and Unwin, 1973).

Oddy, J.A., 'Bicheno and Tyso on the Prophecies', *Baptist Quarterly*, 35 (1993), pp.81–9.

Oliver, W.H., *Prophets and Millenialists: the uses of biblical prophecy in England from the 1790s to the 1840s* (Auckland University Press, 1978).

Olson, Alison Gilbert, *The Radical Duke: Career and Correspondence of Charles Lennox, third Duke of Richmond* (Oxford University Press, 1961).

Parkin, Charles, *The Moral Basis of Burke's Political Thought* (Cambridge University Press, 1956).

Pendleton, Gayle Trusdel, 'English Conservative Propaganda During the French Revolution, 1789–1802', unpublished Ph.D. thesis, Emory University, 1976.

Philp, Mark (ed.), *The French Revolution and British Popular Politics* (Cambridge University Press, 1991).

____, 'The Fragmented Ideology of Reform', in Mark Philp (ed.), *The French Revolution and British Popular Politics* (Cambridge University Press, 1991), pp.50–77.

____, 'Vulgar Conservatism, 1792–3', *English Historical Review*, 110 (1995), pp.42–69.

____, 'Thompson, Godwin, and the French Revolution', *History Workshop Journal*, 39 (1995), pp.89–101.

Pocock, J.G.A., 'Burke and the Ancient Constitution—A Problem in the History of Ideas', *Historical Journal*, 3 (1960), pp.125–43.

____, *Politics, Language and Time. Essays on Political Thought and History* (Atheneum, 1971).

____, 'The Political Economy of Burke's Analysis of the French Revolution', *Historical Journal*, 25 (1982), pp.331–49.

____, *Virtue, Commerce and History* (Cambridge University Press, 1985).

____, 'Edmund Burke and the Redefinition of Enthusiasm: the Context as Counter-Revolution' in François Furet and Mona Ozouf (eds), *The French Revolution and the Creation of Modern Political Culture*, iii: *The Transformation of Political Culture* (Oxford: Pergamon, 1989), pp.19–43.

Poovey, Mary, *The Proper Lady and the Woman Writer: Ideology as Style in the Works of Mary Wollstonecraft, Mary Shelley, and Jane Austen* (University of Chicago Press, 1984).

Radcliffe, Evan, 'Revolutionary Writing, Moral Philosophy, and Universal Benevolence in the Eighteenth Century', *Journal of the History of Ideas*, 54 (1993), pp.221–40.

Reid, Loren, *Charles James Fox, A Man For The People* (Longman, 1969).

Richards, Norman Frank, 'British Policy and the Problem of Monarchy in France, 1789–1802', unpublished Ph.D. thesis, University of London, 1955.

Rigby, Brian, 'Radical Spectators of the Revolution: the Case of the *Analytical Review*' in Ceri Crossley and Ian Small (eds), *The French Revolution and British Culture* (Oxford University Press, 1989), pp.63–83.

Roberts, Warren, *Jane Austen and the French Revolution* (Macmillan, 1979).

Rodger, N.A.M., *The Wooden World: An Anatomy of the Georgian Navy* (Fontana, 1986).

Rogers, Katharine M., *Frances Burney: The World of 'Female Difficulties'* (New York and London: Harvester Wheatsheaf, 1990).

Rose, J. Holland, 'The Struggle with Revolutionary France, 1792–1802' in A.W. Ward and G.P. Gooch (eds), *The Cambridge History of British Foreign Policy* (Cambridge University Press, 1922), pp.216–308.

Sapiro, Virginia, *A Vindication of Political Virtue: The Political Theory of Mary Wollstonecraft* (University of Chicago Press, 1992).

Schmidt, H.D., 'The Idea and Slogan of Perfidious Albion', *Journal of the History of Ideas*, 14 (1953), 604–16.

Schofield, Thomas Philip, 'English Conservative Thought and Opinion in Response to the French Revolution', unpublished Ph.D thesis, University of London, 1984.

____, 'Conservative Political Thought in Britain in Response to the French Revolution', *Historical Journal*, 29 (1986), pp.601–22.

____, 'British Politicians and French Arms: the Ideological War of 1793–5', *History*, 77 (1992), 183–201.

Scott, Iain Robertson, '"Things As They Are": the Literary Response to the French Revolution 1789–1815' in H.T. Dickinson (ed.), *Britain and the French Revolution 1789–1815* (Macmillan, 1989), pp.229–49.

Scruton, Roger, 'Man's Second Disobedience: A Vindication of Burke' in Ceri Crossley and Ian Small (eds), *The French Revolution and British Culture* (Oxford University Press, 1989), pp.187–222.

Sherwig, John M., *Guineas and Gunpowder: British Foreign Aid in the Wars with France 1793–1815* (Cambridge, Mass.: Harvard University Press, 1969).

Shoemaker, Robert B., *Gender in English Society, 1650-1850* (Harlow: Longman, 1998).

Soloway, Richard A., 'Reform or Ruin: English Moral Thought During the First French Republic', *Journal of Politics*, 25 (1963), pp.110–28.

Sparrow, Elizabeth, 'The Alien Office, 1792–1806', *Historical Journal*, 33 (1990), pp.361–84.

____, 'The Swiss and Swabian Agencies, 1795–1801', *Historical Journal*, 35 (1992), pp.861–84.

Spence, Peter, *The Birth of Romantic Radicalism. War, Popular Politics and English Radical Reformism, 1800–1815* (Aldershot: Scolar Press, 1996).

Stafford, William, 'Religion and the Doctrine of Nationalism in England at the Time of the French Revolution and Napoleonic Wars', *Studies in Church History*, 18 (1982), pp.381–95.

____, 'Narratives of Women: English Feminists of the 1790s', *History*, 82 (1997), pp.24–43.

Stanlis, Peter J., 'A Preposterous Way of Reasoning: Frederick Dreyer's Edmund Burke: the Philosopher in Action', *Studies in Burke and His Time*, 15 (1974), pp.265–75.

____, 'Reflections on Dinwiddy on Mill on Burke on Prescription', *Studies in Burke and His Time*, 18 (1977), pp.191–8.

Stevenson, J., 'The London "Crimp" Riots of 1794', *International Review of Social History*, 16 (1971), pp.40–58.

Struthers, G., *History of the Rise, Progress, and Principles of the Relief Church* (Glasgow, 1843).

Thompson, E.P., 'Hunting the Jacobin Fox', *Past and Present*, 142 (1994), pp.94–140.

Vaisey, D.G., 'The Pledge of Patriotism: Staffordshire and the Voluntary Contribution, 1798' in M.W. Greenslade (ed.), *Essays in Staffordshire History* (Staffordshire Record Society, 1970), pp.209–23.

Veitch, G.S., *The Genesis of Parliamentary Reform* (Constable, 1965).

Vincent, Emma, '"The Real Grounds of the Present War": John Bowles and the French Revolutionary Wars, 1792–1802', *History*, 78 (1993), pp.393–420.

____, 'The Responses of Scottish Churchmen to the French Revolution, 1789–1802', *Scottish Historical Review*, 73 (1994), pp.191–215.

Virgin, Peter, *The Church in an Age of Negligence: ecclesiastical structure and problems of church reform, 1700–1840* (Cambridge University Press, 1989).

Wahrman, Dror, 'Virtual Representation: Parliamentary Reporting and Languages of Class in the 1790s', *Past and Present*, 136 (1992), pp.83–113.

____, *Imagining the Middle Class. The Political Representation of Class in Britain, c.1780–1840* (Cambridge University Press, 1995).

Walsh, John, 'Methodism at the End of the Eighteenth Century', in R. Davies and G. Rupp (eds), *A History of the Methodist Church in Great Britain*, vol. i (Epworth Press, 1966), pp.278–308.

Ward, W.R., *Religion and Society in England, 1790–1850* (Batsford, 1972).

Warner, Marina, *Monuments and Maidens: The Allegory of the Female Form* (Vintage, 1985).

Watts, M.R., *The Dissenters*, vol. 2 (Oxford University Press, 1995).

Wells, Roger, 'The revolt of the south-west, 1800–1801: a study in English popular protest', *Social History*, 6 (1977), pp.713–44.

____, *Insurrection: The British Experience, 1795–1803* (Gloucester: Alan Sutton, 1986).

____, *Wretched Faces: Famine in Wartime England, 1793–1801* (Gloucester: Alan Sutton, 1988).

____, 'English Society and revolutionary politics in the 1790s: the case for insurrection' in Mark Philp (ed.), *The French Revolution and British Popular Politics* (Cambridge University Press, 1991), pp.188–226.

Welsh, Jennifer M., *Edmund Burke and International Relations* (Basingstoke: Macmillan, 1995).

Western, J.R., 'The Volunteer Movement as an Anti-Revolutionary Force, 1793–1801', *English Historical Review*, 71 (1956), pp.603–14.

Woodcock, George, 'The Meaning of Revolution in Britain, 1770–1800' in Ceri Crossley and Ian Small (eds), *The French Revolution and British Culture* (Oxford University Press, 1989), pp.1–30.

Yang, Su Hsien, 'The British Debate on the French Revolution: Edmund Burke and His Critics', unpublished Ph.D. thesis, University of Edinburgh, 1989.

Ziegler, Philip, *Addington: A Life of Henry Addington, first Viscount Sidmouth* (Collins, 1965).

Index